HOWARD BARKER: POLITICS AND DESIRE

Also By David Ian Rabey

Criticism:

BRITISH AND IRISH POLITICAL DRAMA IN THE
TWENTIETH CENTURY

DAVID RUDKIN: Sacred Disobedience

ENGLISH DRAMA SINCE 1940

THEATRE OF CATASTROPHE: New Essays on
Howard Barker (*co-edited with Karoline Gritzner*)

HOWARD BARKER: ECSTASY AND DEATH: An Expository
Study of his Drama, Theory and Direction, 1988–2008

Drama:

THE WYE PLAYS

LOVEFURIES

Howard Barker: Politics and Desire

An Expository Study of his Drama and Poetry, 1969–87

David Ian Rabey

palgrave
macmillan

First published 1989 by Macmillan Press Ltd
This paperback edition first published 2009 by
PALGRAVE MACMILLAN

Palgrave Macmillan in the UK is an imprint of Macmillan Publishers Limited,
registered in England, company number 785998, of Houndmills, Basingstoke,
Hampshire RG21 6XS.

Palgrave Macmillan in the US is a division of St Martin's Press LLC,
175 Fifth Avenue, New York, NY 10010.

Palgrave Macmillan is the global academic imprint of the above companies
and has companies and representatives throughout the world.

Palgrave® and Macmillan® are registered trademarks in the United States,
the United Kingdom, Europe and other countries.

ISBN-13: 978–0–333–44340–8   hardback
ISBN-10: 0–333–44340–3   hardback
ISBN-13: 978–0–230–57740–4   paperback
ISBN-10: 0–230–57740–7   paperback

This book is printed on paper suitable for recycling and made from fully
managed and sustained forest sources. Logging, pulping and manufacturing
processes are expected to conform to the environmental regulations of the
country of origin.

A catalogue record for this book is available from the Library of Congress.

British Library Cataloguing in Publication Data
    Rabey, David Ian
    Howard Barker: politics and desire: an expository study of his
drama and poetry, 1969–87.
    1. English literature.   Barker, Howard, 1946–   I. Title
    828'.91409
    ISBN 0–333–44340–3 (cloth)   978–0–230–57740–4 (pbk)

10   9   8   7   6   5   4   3   2   1
18   17   16   15   14   13   12   11   10   09

Printed and bound in Great Britain by
CPI Antony Rowe, Chippenham and Eastbourne

Contents

Acknowledgements

The author and publishers wish to thank Howard Barker and Judy Daish Associates Ltd who have kindly given permission for the use of copyright material and made available copies of as yet unpublished Barker work.

How many breaths in a gale? This book would have been impoverished without the contributions of certain people. I wish to record my personal appreciation of them:

My editor at Macmillan, Frances A. Arnold, for her support of this project; Roger Gregory (BBC Pebble Mill) for finding me copies of the trio of early radio plays; John O'Brien and the Dublin Players cast of the 1984 stage production of *Pity in History*, particularly Roddy Gibson, John O'Donohue, Stephen Bradley, Eimer Walsh and Donald Clarke; my fellow Europeans Lars Burman and Carina Persson-Burman for their hospitality and understanding during a difficult period; Stephen Booth (from whom I have stolen the title INCONCLUSION) for the enduring value of his teaching; Marian Rooney for advice and support; Rosalind Reedman for permission to quote from her essay; Penny Downie, Paul Freeman, Gary Oldman, Maggie Steed, Robert Wilcher, Harriet Walter and Ian McDiarmid for their conversation, interest and encouragement, of which the printed words are only partial evidence; and my fellow members of the Lurking Truth Theatre Company/Cwmni'r Gwir Sy'n Llechu, particularly Jacqui Burgess, Ian Cooper, Debi Gilbert, Suzan Holding, George Jones, Alistair Kerr, Prys Lewis, Ian Lucas, Richard Lynch, Eddie Maddox, Gwenith Owen, Roger Owen, Charmian Savill and Eric Schneider, for their energy, faith, purpose, imagination and insistence.

In apparent contradiction of the general dedication, I wish to specify that Independence and the Family is dedicated to my parents Ken and Roma Rabey for their careful negotiation of the minefield; Pain and Breakthrough and Catastrophe is also Birth are dedicated to Charmian Savill; deepest gratitude to these and to O'Brien, Jones, Cooper, Lucas and Lynch (the man I blame for all this) for all they have proved and given.

Howard Barker: A Chronology of His Work

Dates are of first stagings, broadcasts or publications (not subsequent productions in the same medium). All places of publication London, unless otherwise noted. 'JC' = John Calder; 'OB' = Oberon Books.

All first stagings occur in Britain except where noted; 'HB' = production directed by Barker.

* Indicates that this unpublished text is summarised and considered in this volume

\# Indicates a non-professional university production

~ Indicates that this unpublished text is summarised and considered in Rabey (2009)

1970: *One Afternoon on the 63rd level of the North Face of the Pyramid of Cheops The Great*: broadcast BBC Radio 1970; unpublished*

Cheek: staged 1970; published in *New Short Plays: 3* (Eyre Methuen Playscripts 1972, volume credited to Barker, Grillo, Haworth and Simmons)

No One Was Saved: staged 1970; unpublished*

1971: *Henry V in Two Parts*: broadcast BBC Radio 1971; unpublished*

1972: *Herman, with Millie and Mick*: broadcast BBC Radio 1972; unpublished*

Edward – The Final Days: staged 1972; unpublished*

Alpha Alpha: staged 1972; unpublished*

Faceache: staged 1972; unpublished

1973: *Skipper*: staged 1973; unpublished*

My Sister and I: staged 1973; unpublished*

Rule Britannia: staged 1973; unpublished

Bang: staged 1973; unpublished

1975: *Claw*: staged 1975; *Stripwell*, staged 1975; published together (JC, 1977)

1976: *Wax*: staged 1976; unpublished*

Heroes of Labour: unproduced television play; published in *Gambit* 29 (JC, 1976)

1977: *Fair Slaughter*: staged and published (JC)
   That Good Between Us: staged; published 1980 with *Credentials of a Sympathiser*, unproduced television play (JC)
1978: *The Love of a Good Man*: staged; published 1980 with *All Bleeding*, unproduced television play (JC)
   The Hang of the Gaol: staged; published 1982 with *Heaven*, unproduced television play (JC)
1980: *The Loud Boy's Life*: staged; published 1982 in *Two Plays for the Right* (JC)
   Birth on a Hard Shoulder: staged (Stockholm, Sweden); published 1982 in *Two Plays for the Right* (JC)
1981: *No End of Blame*: staged and published (JC)
   The Poor Man's Friend staged*
1983: *Victory*: staged and published (JC)
   A Passion in Six Days: staged; published 1985 with *Downchild* (JC)
   Crimes in Hot Countries: staged#; published 1984 (JC)
1984: *Pity in History*: published in *Gambit* 41 (JC); staged 1984#, and broadcast BBCTV 1985
   The Power of the Dog: staged and published (JC)
   'Art Matters' (sketch) staged (published in *The Big One*, eds. Bill Bachle and Susannah York, Methuen, 1984)
   Don't Exaggerate (performance poem): staged, published with other poems 1985 (JC)
1985: *The Castle*: staged and published with *Scenes from an Execution* (JC)
   Scenes from an Execution: broadcast by BBC Radio
   Downchild staged
   The Blow: unproduced filmscript*
1986: *Women Beware Women*: staged and published (JC)
   The Breath of the Crowd (performance poem): staged and published with other poems (JC)
1987: *Gary the Thief/Gary Upright* (performance poems): published with other poems (JC)
1988: *The Possibilities*: staged and published (JC)
   The Last Supper: staged and published (JC)
   The Bite of the Night: (written 1985) staged and published (JC)
   Lullabies for the Impatient: poems, published (JC)
   The Smile: published in *New Plays: 2*, ed. Peter Terson (Oxford University Press)
1989: *Seven Lears*: staged and published with *Golgo* (JC)
   Golgo: staged and published with *Seven Lears* (JC)

The Europeans (written 1987) staged (Toronto, Canada) and published with *Judith* (JC)
Arguments for a Theatre (essays): first edition (JC)
1990: *Scenes from an Execution*: stage production
The Early Hours of a Reviled Man: broadcast by BBC Radio; stage production#
Collected Plays Vol. 1 (*Claw, No End of Blame, Victory, The Castle, Scenes from an Execution*) published (JC)
1991: *The Europeans*: staged#
The Ascent of Monte Grappa (poems): published (JC)
1992: *A Hard Heart*: staged, broadcast by BBC Radio, and published with *The Early Hours of a Reviled Man* (JC)
Ego in Arcadia: staged (Sienna, Italy) (HB)
Terrible Mouth (opera libretto): staged and published (Universal Edition)
1993: *Collected Plays Vol. 2* (*The Love of a Good Man, The Possibilities, Brutopia, Rome, (Uncle) Vanya, Ten Dilemmas*) published (JC)
Arguments for a Theatre (essays): second edition, Manchester University Press
All He Fears (marionette play): staged and published (JC)
1994: *Hated Nightfall*: staged (HB) and published with *Wounds to the Face* (JC)
Minna: staged (Vienna, Austria) and published (Alumnus, Leeds)
1995: *Judith* staged (HB)
(Uncle) Vanya (written 1992) staged#
1996: *(Uncle) Vanya* staged (HB)
Collected Plays Vol. 3 (*The Power of the Dog, The Europeans, Women Beware Women, Minna, Judith, Ego in Arcadia*) published (JC)
The Tortmann Diaries (poems): published (JC)
Defilo (Failed Greeks) ~ written
1997: *Arguments for a Theatre* (essays): third edition, Manchester University Press
Wounds to the Face staged
An Eloquence (film) ~ written
The Blood of a Wife (film) ~ written
The Seduction of Almighty God written
1998: *Ursula* staged (HB)
Collected Plays Vol. 4 (*The Bite of the Night, Seven Lears, The Gaoler's Ache, He Stumbled, A House of Correction*) published (JC)
Ten Dilemmas staged#

1999: *Und* staged (HB)
    Scenes from an Execution staged (HB)
    A House of Correction broadcast, BBC Radio
    Albertina ~ broadcast, BBC Radio
    The Swing at Night (marionette play) written
    A Rich Woman's Poetry ~ written
2000: *The Ecstatic Bible* staged (Adelaide, Australia) (HB)
    He Stumbled staged (HB)
    Animals in Paradise staged (Malmo, Sweden)
    The Twelfth Battle of Isonzo staged (Saint-Brieuc, France, in French)
    The Swing at Night (marionette play) staged and published (JC)
    Stalingrad (opera libretto) ~ written
2001: *The Twelfth Battle of Isonzo* staged (Dublin, Ireland, in English) (HB)
    A House of Correction staged (HB)
    Collected Plays Vol. 5 (*Ursula, The Brilliance of the Servant, 12 Encounters with a Prodigy, Und, The Twelfth Battle of Isonzo, Found in the Ground*) published (JC)
    Two Skulls ~ written
2002: *Gertrude* staged (HB); *Knowledge and a Girl* broadcast (HB), BBC Radio; published together (JC)
    Stalingrad (opera libretto) staged (Denmark)
    Brutopia staged (Besançon, France, in French)
    N/A (Sad Kissing) ~ written
    Five Names ~ written
2003: *13 Objects* staged (HB)
    The Fence in its Thousandth Year written
    The Moving and the Still ~ written
2004: *Dead Hands* staged (HB) and published (OB)
    N/A (Sad Kissing) staged (Vienna, Austria)
    The Moving and the Still broadcast, BBC Radio
    Christ's Dog ~ written
    The Dying of Today written
    Acts Chapter 1 ~ written
2005: *Death, The One and The Art of Theatre* (essays) published (Routledge)
    Animals in Paradise staged (Rouen, France, in French) (HB)
    The Ecstatic Bible published (OB)
    The Fence in its Thousandth Year staged (HB) and published (OB)

Christ's Dog staged (Vienna, Austria)
Two Skulls broadcast (Danish Radio)
Dead, Dead and Very Dead (libretto) ~ written
Heroica (film) ~ written
Adorations Chapter 1 (film) ~ written
Let Me ~ written
Howard Barker/Eduardo Houth: *A Style and its Origins* written
2006: *The Seduction of Almighty God* staged and published (OB)
The Road, The House, The Road broadcast, BBC Radio
Let Me broadcast, BBC Radio
A Wounded Knife (formerly titled *A Living Dog*) ~ staged (Odense, Denmark)
Plays: One (Victory, Scenes from an Execution, The Possibilities, The Europeans) published (OB)
Plays: Two (The Castle, Gertrude – The Cry, 13 Objects, Animals in Paradise) published (OB)
The Forty (Few Words) written
I Saw Myself written
2007: *Lot and his God* ~ written
Howard Barker/Eduardo Houth: *A Style and its Origins* published (OB)
The Dying of Today staged (Caen, France)
Actress With an Unloved Child written
Deep Wives, Shallow Animals written
2008: *Twelve Encounters with a Prodigy* staged (Odense, Denmark)
I Saw Myself staged (HB)
Plays: Three (Claw, Ursula, He Stumbled, The Love of a Good Man) published (OB)
Plays: Four (I Saw Myself, Found in the Ground, The Dying of Today, The Road, The House, The Road) published (OB)
Hurts Given and Received written
Aceldama written
The Dying of Today staged (London)
Sheer Detachment published (Salt Publications)

Foreword to the Paperback Edition: *Politics and Desire* Twenty Years On

Howard Barker: Politics and Desire was written 1987–8 and first published in 1989. As you will discover from its first chapter, it is not only an exposition of dramatic literature and poetry. It is informed by personal theatrical practice (which in turn informs the detailed readings of *Pity in History, Victory, The Castle* and *Don't Exaggerate* in particular). It is also an existentialist manifesto championing what it calls 'personal reformulation for one's own needs', rather than for those of an externally (and variously forcibly) imposed programme of social engineering.

Politics and Desire is relaunched as a companion volume to my more recent work, *Howard Barker: Ecstasy and Death* (Palgrave 2009), which offers an expository study of Barker's drama, theory and direction from 1988 to 2008. We hope to present a third volume *circa* 2028 if circumstances permit. The terms of analysis in *Politics and Desire* are somewhat different from its companion, as the period of this book's review, 1969–87, pre-dates Barker's emergence as a confident and startlingly original director of his own stage work, and as a speculative philosophical theorist on aesthetic purpose and the theatricality of human specificity. These aspects of his achievements are broached in *Ecstasy and Death*, which incorporates critical accounts of some theatrical productions of the work, by Barker and others. My identification in *Politics and Desire* of how Barker's theatre is built on 'drastic action pushed to the limit' holds up, but my proposition, that his principal means of pursuit of this Artaudian objective is linguistic, now requires qualification. *Ecstasy and Death* aims to give at least some sense of how Barker's orchestration of scenography – sound, light, set, costume, movement, space and stagecraft – develops to provide unique, and uniquely haunting, visual counterpoints to his mesmeric language. Similarly, my statement in the first chapter of *Politics and Desire* that Barker's grounds of enquiry are political and existential rather than metaphysical now seems a false, or facile, distinction; Barker's work has gone on to identify the interpenetration of these terms, particularly where religious edicts are invoked and institutionalized in order to support or challenge social power, in projects which I term, in *Ecstasy and Death*, 'Wrestling with God'.

Politics: It is salutary to reread accounts of Barker's 1970s satires on the compromises and failures of Edward Heath's and Harold Wilson's governments and ethos, with their resonances for subsequent forms of authoritarian myopia and strained bids to 'make stupor rhyme with socialism' (in the words of *Downchild*). In the last twenty years, we have lived through further examples of how the perpetuation of violence to language issues in the perpetration of violence to people, to foreground an observation from *That Good Between Us* (1977), and the implementation of the recommendations of the 1997 Dearing Report, which has increasingly recharacterized tertiary education as a form of social control (of both staff and students) predicated on debt; and some dark nights I find it hard to maintain faith with John O'Brien's brave assertion that 'possibility and power reside in language, not in theories'. If British theatres had the courage to undertake reassessments of *That Good, Downchild* and *A Passion in Six Days* (and, for that matter, of Howard Brenton's *Thirteenth Night*) we might rediscover some prescient and prophetic indictments of how careerist politicians of various hues opportunistically debased noble values, and diminished reductively and systematically the terms of British culture, whilst instituting a 'neo-liberal' society of surveillance in ostensible self-justification. Note also how *The Bite of the Night* dramatizes the forcibly imposed paradigm of the mythic family unit (and its attendant polarizations of hygiene and sexual criminality), *The Europeans* depicts populist masquerade and state coercion in the wake of threats posed by Islamic cultural fundamentalism. It couldn't happen (again) here, could it? We won't get fooled again . . .

By way of refinement, John adds in an e-mail (August 2008, responding to a draft of this Foreword), 'I don't think I've changed or lost faith in the principle' that possibility and power reside in language, but I think I may have been shocked to realise that like all principles it is amoral and will work as well for one purpose as for another. A brief look at the way language has been inverted in the last decade illustrates this thought (revolution, liberal, structural adjustment programme (SAP), democracy, collateral damage, ministry of defence, buy this and save money). But it is important to keep the concepts of theory and hypothesis separate. Theories are often overarching and final, in order to confine and explain the universe; hypotheses however can be formulated on the hoof and dispensed with when the job is done, they are fleeting, infinite, and replaceable. Any one of us, in any situation can formulate and test an infinite range of hypotheses – a fact that renders theory almost impossible when you think about it. This faith, in the infinite necessity of renewal, seems to lie at the heart of all Barker's work: like one of his characters, he has pursued this philosophical/historical principle to its extreme ends, played it out through a vast pantheon of characters'.

Weaknesses: Sometimes *Politics and Desire* seems over-reliant on quotation of Barker's work – particularly where, at the time of writing, I felt my powers of summary and paraphrase inadequate to capture the exhilaration, thrill, wit and sensuality of Barker's lines. Now that many of the texts considered here are more difficult to find, this flaw may prove more forgivable and encourage an appetite to seek them out, lobby for and ideally prompt their wider availability. My exposition of *The Possibilities* is very brief (indeed, to several A-level students and teachers who contacted me, disappointingly scant), not out of a lack of admiration for Barker's first compendium of short plays, but because I have little to say about them beyond that recorded here; I feel inclined to respect their intrinsic thematic refusal of explication, rational and otherwise; and I admire even more the succinctness and power of many of the propositions in *Gary Upright* (including 'to accept the power of the obvious/Is only sometime the mark of the wise'), so that work receives more space. I admit I am no longer sure what 'essence' refers to on the otherwise satisfactory p. 100; here, and when I invoke the (crucially unprescribed) 'essence of the self' on p. 1, it might be best to take this as referring to individual 'innate knowledge of other life', by which Barker characterizes 'soul' ('not an immortal thing' nor 'immune from damage', *Arguments for a Theatre*, third edition, Manchester University Press, 1997, p. 70). The same applies to the references to 'hope' on the last two pages of Chapter 11.

Strengths/Desire: This was written, and may read, with the (somewhat desperate) energetic momentum of someone who had discovered his native society's promises to be empty, well aware of how 'responsibility' and 'maturity' were invoked to cauterize dissent and ardour, and who was actively engaged in breaking himself (and others) apart; so that by the time the first copy of the book appeared, I was rebuilding my life, in the most profound senses, from new laid foundations. I count myself very fortunate to have the opportunities to express and profess my enthusiasm for the works considered here.

Reception: Those who want a critical work to collate and pre-digest a *range* of secondary opinion were, and will be, disappointed by both *Politics and Desire* and *Ecstasy and Death*, in which I have more ambitious and exciting things to do than document (even to identify critically) the timidity of much British cultural discourse; though contextualizing (and, I hope, surprising) references to international artists and philosophers increase steadily through the volumes. John Bull, reviewing *Politics and Desire* for *Theatre Research International*, concluded by calling it 'a book for disciples written by an acolyte'. I decided to accept as a profound compliment that which might have been intended as a rebuke. Significantly, the most subtly appreciative observations of my style and objectives were expressed in a review by another dramatist-director, James D. Balestrieri (in *Theatre Three* no. 9, Fall 1990, Carnegie Mellon Drama, Pittsburgh, pp. 129–33, abridged with his permission), in whose hands I leave you (for the moment):

In any reading of *Politics and Desire*, it is crucial to know that Rabey has acted in and directed a number of Barker's works, because Rabey casts the reader in the role of audience, witnessing his shifting personae as one would witness an actor's onstage transformations. In *Politics and Desire*, Rabey is variously a literary critic, an aphorist, and an interviewer. But like a Barker character becoming aware of the alienations that accompany the predominance of any labeled self, Rabey subverts each of the roles he plays in his book, insisting on the right to make, unmake, and remake himself at will and with will. *Howard Barker: Politics and Desire* emerges as nothing so much as a demonstration of Barker's principles operating in the sphere of literary criticism, a series of performing presences that, taken together, constitute an unsanded edge, like a tongue sere from talking itself to death – and again into life. Like Barker, or a Barker character, Rabey presses language into service as a tool of self-excavation . . . It is as if Barker has transformed the Aeschylean maxim that there can be no law without crime into a postulate that reads: because there is law, there must be crime for the self to exist. Thus every Barker character is potentially a *pharmakos*, receiving lacerations, suffering Dionysian dismemberments, but in the service of the self rather than the community. In the most fully-realized Barker characters, these lacerations are self-inflicted, rendering them into what I would call *autopharmakoi*. Barker's term for this transformation of the self through pain is the Theatre of Catastrophe, his response to Aristotle's pity and fear, to Brecht's alienation, and to Artaud's cruelty . . . [where the syllable] 'But' signals the moment (often darkly comic) of anagnorisis, beyond which lies a veritable minefield of choices and consequences: the wanting to exceed, but provisionally, leaving the question 'How?' to the audience. Rabey structures *Politics and Desire* in a similar way, treating the reader as an active participant in the critical process. [He] satirizes and subverts traditional British literary criticism, with its emphasis on summaries, by thrusting Barker's characters onto the critical stage at a vertiginous pace, as though they were already and instantly familiar to the reader. The effect – like a Dickens novel gone desperately and perversely wrong – unsettles the reader (left wondering whether a joke has been played by a clown masquerading as an intellectual tyrant) and forces him to turn to Barker's plays themselves, thus engaging in a dialectic with Rabey's interpretations [as] explication of character quickly heightens, first into the discourse of the revolutionary manifesto, then into the kind of philosophical poetry worthy of Artaud, as he mobilizes powerful metaphors, almost as responses in kind to Barker's lines, in sentences that have the quality of muscular poetry, and Rabey seems to have become the Exaggerator he played on stage. Rabey – or this persona, at any rate – seems to have discovered that the page is a stage that he must make the most of, [until the last page where] Rabey the actor plays Gary Upright, uttering Barker's line, addressing it to Rabey the critic, and thus undermining even Barker's dialectic of self-making to the point where the process of making, unmaking and remaking are simultaneous and indistinguishable. It is perhaps no wonder that [he] leaps into the role of interviewer to conclude the book. At the border between criticism and theatre, Rabey's book stands opposite Brecht's *Messingkauf Dialogues*, challenging critical boundaries of theatre, and inviting us to experience the catastrophic throes of tragic transformation.

DIR, Machynlleth, August 2008

Notes on the Texts: Quotations from Howard Barker's published plays are reprinted with kind permission of the publisher, Oberon Books (James Hogan); quotations from unpublished work are reprinted by kind permission of Judy Daish Associates Ltd. Page references to Barker works herein are based on their first publications in John Calder's editions; however, the editions of Barker's plays, formerly published by John Calder and Calder Publications, are no longer available for order and purchase from this source (but may be available for consultation though library holdings). The plays formerly published by John Calder and Calder Publications are being republished by Oberon Books as part of their ongoing programme of making Barker's complete dramatic *oeuvre* available in book form. The updated chronology of this book details publication as well as production history up to the time of going to press, and alerts the reader to the new collections where they can currently find *Claw, Scenes from an Execution, The Love of a Good Man, Victory, The Castle, The Europeans* and *The Possibilities*. Chapter Ten analyzes draft scripts of *The Bite of the Night* and *The Europeans* which pre-dated production or performance, hence some anomalous references. The subsequently published and staged version of *Bite* added a further twist to Savage's journey through existential murder, and finally positioned him as a mute relic in the classical ruins of a civilisation. In the subsequent staged and published versions of *The Europeans*, the character Hrkaly was omitted, and some of his lines (principally the speech on 'the art that will be') transferred to Starhemberg; moreover, the timescale of the second half of the play was condensed, so that the child Concilia remained a babe in arms rather than a walking, talking infant; and now Katrin (not Susannah) undresses for Starhemberg (and he for her); Katrin does not provide the word 'birth', but assists, speaking *'with infinite calculation'*, in the explanation to Leopold. I hope many other texts considered here will soon enjoy new reaches of availability (including *Crimes in Hot Countries* with its superior but never published ending).

1

Lubricating Progress Through the Forbidden

I'll take you
I'll hold your throat
I will
And vomit I will tolerate
Over my shirt
Over my wrists
Your bile
Your juices
I'll be your guide
And whistler in the dark
Cougher over filthy words
And all known sentiments recycled for this house

.   .   .

I honour you too much
To paste you with what you already know so

from the 1st Prologue to The Bite of the Night

This book does not prescribe, it *offers* a structure for perceptions, centred on the plays and poems of Howard Barker (born in London, 1946). This book, and Barker's plays and poems, are defiant of prescriptive ideologies, which depend upon the suspension of experience in the face of ideas. It rejoices in the dismantling of prescriptive and conventional structures from the inside, until reaching the essence of the self.

Individuals internalise prescriptions amid a retrenchment of curiosity, in a climate which impels them to accept *other people's* formulations of experience. This is, literally, discouragement. It seeks to bind individuals with fear, to use a phrase from Barker's *The Loud Boy's Life*. It attempts to convince people that the only possibilities that are operational alternatives to the here and now are *negative* possibilities, as opposed to the status quo. Theories provide governments with symbolic worlds which they find manageable;

individual experience eludes them. Legislation cannot cope with pain except through making it symbolic. What keeps people 'in their place', and defines that place, is the power of symbols. When the symbol becomes an end in itself, the self is dissipated into discouraged, timid, diffused non-being which denies even its own rights to experiences and opinions. Language and articulation are impoverished.

However, the barrier between the dissipation of self and the self-determination of the self is as thin as a plate-glass window. The individual is capable of his/her own terms of definition, his/her own language and symbols. The individual can resist policy through articulation. In a populist society isolation may be a key to imagination, the wellspring of liberating formulation, whereby the individual articulates perceptions to self and others. Through articulation, we instinctively stumble on liberating formulations.

Theatre can offer liberating formulations, make *wanting* a habit, encourage seekers not happy with the here and now, or with deferral of self-realisation. It can encourage people to discover and confront their personal and common pain. Individuals can rediscover a hope and joy in *saying* and in *a way of saying*: developing a personal definition, as opposed to absorbing, talking and thinking in stock phrases. Actor and audience can embrace the experience of retelling and listening, developing a contemporary history of individual collision, experience and perception which can stand as anti-history against the state's endorsed definitions.

Prescriptive ideologies attempt to instil *not wanting* power or expression, to develop a preferential longing to be subservient to another's vision. The individual surrenders his/her responsibility of definition and action to the centralised prescriptive corporation.

Howard Barker's protagonists achieve splendour when they INSIST. Faced with the theoretical prescription to wait, suspend feeling while the social experiment works itself out at their expense, they say 'NO. I may or may not accept your theory is sound and possibly works, is true even, *in its own terms*, BUT it is not anything approaching my experience of material reality and it denies my ability to make and remake myself'. The central 'BUT' is a hinge on which the character swings into an entirely different *personal* set of references, experiences and definitions, on which theory has no bearing. They re-tell and re-experience pain, in historical ages when the acknowledgement and infliction of pain are two of the few methods of self-definition left. Their central activity is that of talking about themselves, expanding, redefining and altering themselves with the words they utter. They deny incorporation. They are self-consciously performing characters who overshoot and under-cut themselves, and therefore expose themselves, often quite vul-nerably, to the interceptions of other characters. Barker's work is frequently a performance of the self, the presentation of a self-making which is then continually subverted by the pain involved.

Art can attempt to create situations in which people discover the personal challenge to change for themselves; the artist can offer experience to an audience and then ask *them* what *they* will do with it. The artist's imaginative power is the power of formulation.

As John O'Brien says:

> Barker's plays stay in the mouth long after conventional involve-ment with a production has ended. His words, phrases and images have a uniquely liberating effect on the speaker.
>
> There is an approach to acting that starts with the play as text (not the play as interaction) from which a picture of the character and its function is derived (based on subtext, emotional memory and other such tools). This picture is then used as a backdrop to inform the speaking of the lines — the working out of inten-tions on the basis of this backdrop. This approach makes perfect sense in that school of drama concerned with problems of private readjustment. For example: a character is behaving strangely; he may in the course of the evening effect a compromise with those affected by his strange behaviour; or he may commit sui-cide; or he may leave his context in search of another context in which his behaviour is not seen as strange (this context may not be defined by the play, but remains a possibility). This formula has many possible permutations and has produced many plays successful on these terms. The problem is that the contexts of behaviour remain external to the protagonists and are ultimately unchangeable; the characters are never responsible for their contexts.
>
> Barker's characters know what they want, even though what they want may change from one moment to the next (in the words of *Don't Exaggerate*, 'Truth is not stable/Any more than passion'). In an important sense, they talk reality into exist-ence. In Part Two of *Women Beware Women*, the Ward describes an idyllic erotic encounter with a strange woman by a river. The

story introduces a hush of possibility into the auditorium. He concludes 'True story . . . *(Pause)* . . . TRUE LIKE FUCK IT IS'. Reality or context in a Barker play is what the characters say it is. Definitions and possibilities shift and collide, lasting only as long as those who are speaking can keep them in the air (like Toplis juggling with his balls in *Crimes in Hot Countries*). In Barker's worlds, there are no winners — nor can there be. A situation persists only insofar as those responsible for it can assert its — and their — existence.

This tension carries over into a relationship between actor and audience. We are not privileged observers allowed to witness semi-coherent characters trying to cope with their frustrated or diverted desires. Our preconceptions are questioned from the outset, as in the first scene of *Victory*: the vocabulary used by the actors/characters demands that we "take sides", place our sympathies; yet to our dismay we find that the poetic and rational may be dangerous, and the coarse and abusive may have justification. The actor who plays with Barker's language knows that s/he walks a tightrope between holding and losing an audience. S/He also knows the power of that tightrope — the thin line between the alienation of the word and the attraction of its image. Possibility and power reside in language, not in theories.

Barker's characters introduce and talk about themselves compulsively, challenging interruption but implying that their eloquence has to be matched before anyone else has the right to interrupt; this is taken to the extreme in *Don't Exaggerate*, which actually confronts the theatre audience with the quizzical challenges of a character. Barker describes his approach to, and exploration of, characterisation thus:

> I depict the self as wholly articulated. Whereas most drama relies on the unexpressed moment — the loss of speech — my characters excoriate language for emotional exposition, it is a need and hunger in them. In a sense, this is itself a performance, within the performance of the actor, a self-consciousness and a self-making, for others as well as for self. So that the insistence on knowing, which characterizes so many of my inventions, is only subverted by the impossible pain of the effort. They rack themselves, falter, insist again, on the public nature of their experience.[1]

Barker's drama fulfils Artaud's personally-unrealised call for a theatre rebuilt on a concept of drastic action pushed to the limit, where 'One cannot separate body and mind, nor the senses from the intellect, particularly in a field where the unendingly repeated jading of our organs calls for sudden shocks to revive our understanding'.[2] But whereas Artaud urged the pursuit of metaphysical principles and trance-like states through combinations of sound, light, movement and general stagecraft, Barker achieves Artaud's less indulgent or mystical desired effects through language which is impassioned and convulsive, drastically strict, extremely concentrated in severe purities and discords; no syllable is wasted, all move to create an engaging and compelling rhythm. Barker's characters express themselves in a ferocity of ruthlessness and eroticism, beautiful in its emblazoned explicitness (the beautiful and the explicit are not opposed to each other as is conventionally suggested — on the contrary, beauty is shameless). The actor is not required to 'build a character'; Barker creates the character through language. The character effectively leaps off the page shouting 'This is what I am', proclaiming understandable if disturbing wants. The actor's problem is locating those wants in him/herself and coping with them; as in vocal and physical exercise, this may involve some painful stretching, but recognition unleashes energy. The compulsive process of self-discovery extends from dramatist to performer, who offers it to audience.

Barker's characters move in a world of warfare, cultural or personal. They attempt to negotiate a terrain where man-made laws have broken down, and may attempt to reassert divine or moral law in the aftermath of catastrophe. Barker's drama shares some qualities with what Kenneth Steele White has identified as Savage Comedy, where humour springs from slashing verbal confrontations, linguistic whiplash and split faiths. Bettina L. Knapp further characterises this genre: 'logic must be disrupted by the onslaught of improbable situations . . . terminating in a crescendo of virulence'; humour is savage in its use 'to provoke a dissociation between thought and expression' and 'vanity, egotism and cruelty are brought forth in all of their disquieting grandeur'.[3] Kenneth Steele White also notes the 'Ultimate Metaphorical Aims' which he claims to be the distinguishing marks of Savage Comedy: 'To intimate that Cosmos, science and society are flawed, degrading mechanisms . . . To convey belief that new types of fierce riposte against these adversaries are imperatives': 'The savage comedy hero does not see his environment and its ravages as fixed. Nor does he deem them philosophically absurd or inconsequential ... metamorphosis is their law. They are not predictable. Nor is he. Form changes, mutations are rife'.[4]

Knapp and Steele White's examples of Savage Comedy are generally concerned to scourge cosmic and metaphysical ideals, whereas Barker's drama grounds itself in political and existential enquiry. But their identifications of uneasy laughter, fragmented form and ruthless exposure are pertinent to Barker's work, and these factors extend further into the even more severe fractured expectations and persistent dislocations of his fully developed tragic work.

Contradiction is a crucial concept here. This is not the same as contradictoriness of character, a trait which many Barker characters exhibit. Contradiction in character, writes Roger Howard, 'is the meeting point of opposites ... but while the opposites may collide inside the person, their fission is triggered by a conjunction of that person with a social force'.[5] This generates an impression of the fluidity of the dramatic personality, in its abilities to reverse expectations derived from conventional images of drama and experience, so that the action hurtles into areas normally identified as incomprehensible or impossible, where ostensible opposites struggle together: a character's kernel instinctive self wrestles with the image of the self generally adopted for accepted social interaction: his/her inner possibilities wage war against his/her social self (the self as cast within the terms of conventional social definition, as an image perpetuated by the self and accepted by others). Thus, characters attempt to realise both intransigent sides of the Janus-mask of the personality, where every expression is conscious of its antithesis, and of the illusory nature of the exclusiveness which each side is nevertheless driven to insist upon. The complete realisation and expression of the divided self is both desirable and traumatic — perhaps impossible. The dual instinct is to reach out and to withdraw: the dual sensation is of attraction and repulsion.

Maro Germanou's comments on a Roger Howard play are also pertinent to Barker's drama, particularly his recent tragedies:

> The play refuses to satisfy the spectator's basic expectation, that of identifying with a central character. Several consequences follow from this, in relation to the production and consumption of

the play itself. The lack of a dominant discourse allows the play to be traversed by a variety of different discourses of equal status that indicate contradictory ways of conceiving and articulating reality never to be resolved in the action. Since the action as a whole does not progress on the basis of an evolutionary inevitability the play rejects what conventional naturalism glorifies: the overall aggregation of ideas towards a final meaning. By the end of the play the spectator who would try to find its "message" will probably conclude that the play does not make any sense. The characters refuse to be categorised; everyone criticises each other; the political discussions at the table do not end anywhere. The multiplicity of positions and the dialectical treatment of the dramatic material work against any sort of self-containment in the structure. This establishes an intimate relationship between the performance and the spectator and helps the latter to be engaged in the argument.

The changes in naturalism here, as well as in characterisation and structure, derive from a different conception of reality. The erasure of a dominant discourse and the lack of resolution in the play indicate that "truth" is not a pre-given essence nor can it be embedded in a single individual but, on the contrary, is produced within and by social and individual contradictions under a specific historical conjuncture. The play is an unconcluded dialogue; it is important for what it does not say, for positioning the spectator within the unresolved contradictions and by asking him to carry the dialogue further, appropriating critically the multiperspective provided by the play. The spectator, engaged in the practice of reading, avoids the position of the consumer provided by the "finished" text of conventional naturalism.[6]

Barker is similarly conscious of the work's effect on an audience:

The play for an age of fracture is itself fractured, and hard to hold, as a broken bottle is hard to hold. It is without a message. (Who trusts the message-giver any more?). But not without meaning. It is the audience who constructs the meaning. The audience experiences the play individually and not collectively. It is not led, but makes its way through a play whose effects are cumulative. The restoration of dignity to the audience begins when the text and production accept ambiguity. If it is prepared, the audience will not struggle for permanent coherence, which is associated with the narrative of naturalism, but experience the play moment by moment, truth by truth, contradiction by contradiction. The breaking of false dramatic disciplines frees people into imagination.[7]

In John Osborne's *Look Back in Anger*, the protagonist presents and proclaims himself to an apparently exhaustive point – but other characters act as foils or wallow in sentimentality; this is also true of Howard Brenton's *Magnificence*. In Barker's plays, every character expresses him/herself fully (according to the line in *The Breath of the Crowd*, 'Every man's evil expresses me'). When writing the character Staveley in *Fair Slaughter*, Barker locates the essence of Staveley and lets the character speak that essence, writing himself from within by continually advancing his own definitions of himself and others. *Victory* is a striking example of the way that so many Barker characters make cases for themselves. Truth does not reside in any one character, as authorial mouthpiece; as Maggie Steed comments in the Appendix, there is no single 'voice of the play', its vision is split up through characters and events, demonstrating the fallacy of depending on interpreters and leaders.

Correspondingly, vital theatre is not the product of a single unified vision or located aspect (such as 'director's truth', 'playwright's truth', 'actor's truth' or 'critic's truth'). The actor approaching Barker's work should not aim for anyone else's truth, but decide 'I want to discover my truth, and by extension we want to discover ours', with each company member using every other company member en route to self-discovery, 'and if we have the good fortune to all discover a similar thing, therein lies our power'. For the play to work as completely as possible, the production should be a process of personal self-excavation for each person involved. This involves a recognition of the element of using each other in all human relations, and how we prefer the company of those who facilitate or enable us to realise our ends and truths on the more regular basis, until the possibilities of self-discovery are exhausted in any given configuration (at which point, discard). This is not exploitative because in using others, we change ourselves, no one is constant. Correspondingly, Barker's characters need and want different things at different times because involved in creating and re-creating themselves, and cannot afford to stop on a single want; each statement is a building block to the next, whatever that may be, but all involved are changed in a semi-conscious way. The compulsive power as actors of Ian McDiarmid and Jonathan Pryce lies in their ability to be continually surprising, and to seem (if not be) continually surprised by their own reactions to events. Barker's characters, situations, verbal rhythms — and ideally his actors — are similarly compelling in their power to be surprising and imaginative, as they testify to submerged or marginalised human experience in an age and society ravaged by decay, even where decay masquerades as rebirth. Barker's plays and poems assert the individual's right to re-examine values, and INSIST that progression is impossible on the basis of received 'wisdom' as a substitute for personal experience and imagination, which are the only means to acquiring knowledge. Text and performance push the audience to pursue lines of enquiry and insight beyond convention, beyond surprise, beyond habitual limits of concentration and sympathy, chasing possibilities wherever they may go, with their consciousness glued by text and actor's power of formulation. Thus the discouraging effects of theory and the dissipation of the self are overturned, in a triumphant joint venture into self-determination, through the complete exploration, expression and redefinition of the self.

You know what I mean
What wouldn't you give for one bit of
Not debating heroes of the universities
Or thirty volumes of intentions
Giggling celebrities clutching one another's
Parts beneath the desk
BUT ONE BIT IN YOUR FIST OF
WAIT
I'LL GIVE IT TO YOU
WAIT

(*Don't Exaggerate*)

2

Innocence and Authority

*ONE AFTERNOON ON THE 63rd LEVEL OF THE NORTH FACE
OF THE PYRAMID OF CHEOPS THE GREAT, HENRY V IN TWO
PARTS, HERMAN, WITH MILLIE AND MICK*

The essence of government is the establishment of rules which the
governor himself has no intention of keeping. Universal approba-
tion of principles like justice, law, democracy . . . suffuse the mass
consciousness, enabling the governors to practise duplicity to
their heart's content

Crimes in Hot Countries

John Berger and others write in conclusion to their book *Ways
of Seeing*: 'Capitalism survives by forcing the majority, whom it
exploits, to define their own interests as narrowly as possible. This
was once achieved by extensive deprivation. Today in the developed countries it is being achieved by imposing a false standard
of what is and what is not desirable'.[1] In this social system, social
and sexual identity is constituted by financial power and capacity
for monetary income, the psychological reflection of which is the
work ethic; and a person's definition in relation to self and others is largely determined by one's response, degree and means of
submission to the priorities of capital, which influences possibilities of interaction, influence and integration into an ideal of community.[2] Barker's early trio of radio plays examine ways in which
the majority are forced to define their interests, with an increasing
sense of individual isolation which moves from the splendid to the
deadening.

*One Afternoon on the 63rd Level of the North Face of the Pyramid of
Cheops the Great* (broadcast 1970) recounts an episode in the pyramid's construction. The slave workers are relatively reconciled
to their narrow degree of afforded choices, though one fondly
recollects the 'luxury' of the galley. They are introduced to a new
member of the workforce, a delicate slave named Cerebes, whose
innocence prompts him to question the purpose of the pyramid and

why the men co-operate in building it. The workers outline the enormity of their conditions with amused patience at his naive outrage; he protests to the officers that he is not prepared to participate in the hardships of constructing 'this absurd geometrical farce'. Cerebes is taken away by gloating officers to experience what they term a lesson in 'productivity consciousness' and 'corporal incentive', and the audience's concern for his fate is encouraged and gently mocked by the speed with which another slave, Caries, develops an affection for him ('I could have been a . . . a father to that lad'). Cerebes is eventually returned, racked and apologetic ('They only spared me because I was so . . . innocent'), but the men's affection overrides his sense of fault ('We felt bigger, stronger . . . we felt we had a spokesman'). Cerebes remains modest about his function and pessimistic about their capabilities of united revolt, but evolves the notion of doubling their output, subverting the symbolism of the pyramid: 'they'll think of us, the hopeless ones, the poor devils who spent their lives putting it up!' Cerebes is again arrested but calls out in *'a Christlike voice of renunciation'* for them not to resist or care about his salvation but to keep working, 'This is the supreme protest, the ultimate resistance!' The men work even faster in a blend of inspiration and defiance. Only the audience are party to a subsequent interview between a servile official and Cerebes, alias Cheops, who greets with pleasure the news that the slaves are working at an unprecedented rate. Cheops/Cerebes concludes: 'I've always believed that you only achieve real satisfaction through exerting oneself to the full . . . I can't help feeling I'll be blessed in the Underworld. I've done so much good'. A veil is drawn across the tale with an ambiguous testimony from The Voice of History to the Pyramid, 'an imperishable monument to the greatness of Egyptian culture' and 'a glorious era in the gradually unfolding story of man and his never ending quest for grandeur and glory'.

One Afternoon is a simple but ingenious exposure of the confidence trick as social edifice and means of integration. Viewed in hindsight it anticipates some themes which Barker's later work incorporates with sophistication that is, admittedly, not predictable from the basis of *One Afternoon* alone: nevertheless, in comic miniature form, we encounter an absurd geometrical edifice which confirms and consumes those building it, like the more wilfully malign horror of *The Castle*; the unseen torture and martyrdom of a self-proclaimed dissenter who is in fact shocked by the extent of malice concealed in the bowel of the state, like Skinner in *The Castle*

and Galactia in *Scenes from an Execution*; and the beginning of speculation as to whom extravagant masonry reflects, commissioner or
creator, as in *Pity in History*. Barker's choice of the comic realisation
of a distant historical period for *One Afternoon* affords a heightened
image of restricted definition of workers' interests. In case deprivation alone is insufficient spur, Cheops 'sells' his slaves the perfectly
formed placatory myth of Cerebes, an image of selflessness used to
give the slaves an illusory sense of their own function and importance. Cheops justifies himself by reference to results: the growth
of the pyramid and the men's appetite for subordination to a comforting lie, a false image of revolt which serves to absorb their
efforts all the more gracefully. The sting of the paradigm is that it
may trick the audience into the selfsame trap of sympathising with
Cerebes before the consequences are revealed.

Henry V in Two Parts (broadcast 1971) introduces us to another
innocent abroad, Dick Oldham, who likewise acts as an audience
guide through an initially unfamiliar, self-perpetuating and watertight social system answerable only to itself and its favoured. Oldham is a genial, easily gulled Yorkshire businessman meandering
through France in 1415 until accosted by English soldiers at Har-
fleur and conscripted into the army. The naïve recruit receives an
appallingly cheerful account of the horrors of warfare from his fellow men, but derives solace from Henry V's Agincourt address,
with its promises of historical remembrance, the feting and camaraderie of veterans and lasting brotherhood between monarch and
fighting subject. Flushed with success at the battle, Oldham promises a glorious return in a letter to his wife, but the supposed con-
quering hero is robbed on his return to London, ignored or jeered
at by his fellow villagers. Oldham travels to London, only to be
confronted by bland civil servants who are patronising about his
accent and attitude, until he finally achieves an audience with the
King, who laments Oldham's reiteration of his St Crispin's Day
speech with 'I do wish people wouldn't take things literally. It's a
sign of immaturity'. Henry upbraids Oldham for time-wasting and
insolence and adds 'since it's your day of disillusions, I'll do you
the favour of dispelling a few more. I wasn't even at the Battle of
Agincourt'. Henry admits to writing the speech, as is his forte, but
explains he has developed a corporate monarchy which allows his
counterpart, Henry V Part Two, to take his place in battle — Part
Two being a berserker thug who can just about muster a few stock
phrases like 'For England, Harry and St George' after a three-week

study period. Moreover it emerges that the battle was fixed with the King of France as a way of relieving him of a troublesome surplus of upper-class knights. Henry lets Oldham go, secure that his revelations will provoke only disbelief.

Ruminating on the happy gullibility of the misled, Oldham realises 'the bigger the lie, the more people'll believe you' and promptly takes advantage of the civil servant's new-found deference to order a carriage home on the strength of his position as valued adviser to the King. Oldham and his discontent are absorbed into a new mood of admiration for the effective dispensation of power in itself ('Understand human nature and you're half way there. Oh, it's a gift all right, people aren't in high positions for nothing').

Thus, as in *One Afternoon*, a central character's viewpoint unites all sections of society's rigid hierarchy. Although Oldham loses his dream of English postwar egalitarianism, he finds the fraternity of power sufficiently flattering to seek identification by upholding it and reconciles himself to the private enjoyment of privilege. The mind-boggling scale of the pyramid work in *One Afternoon* makes the subject admirably suited to the radio medium, where the audience are challenged to imagine the size and extent of the operation and manpower. *Henry V* is also well suited to radio in its emphasis on the power and effect of language, with Oldham's prosaic Yorkshire interjections proving a bathetic counterpoint to Henry's Agincourt oratory, without any distracting visual pageantry of massed soldiers and horses. Barker's play depends on mobilising contrary images of involvement in warfare, and the schizophrenic division of monarch into orator and warrior, like the distinct gradations between king, civil servant and subject, are deftly established by language and accent. The audience are witness to the manufacture of state history, and its promise to be visible, inclusive and ongoing. But Oldham is dispossessed of experience, frozen into a museum pageant for the protection of the privileged. Disturbingly, his happiness in subservience soon overcomes his outrage in perceiving the contradiction in authority.

After *Henry V in Two Parts*, Barker leaves earlier centuries of English history until *Victory* (1983) when the disillusioning return of an idealistic English soldier is given full-blown tragic expression in the experiences of Ball; Oldham is a necessarily more mechanical comic figure in a satirical anatomy of his society and the myths of community on which it depends. *Herman, with Millie and Mick* (broadcast 1972) has a contemporary and domestic setting. It opens with Herman being groomed for a job interview by Millie; he is notably childish in his self-centred apparent incapability, which turns out to be a delaying tactic until the arrival of his friend Mick, who ensures that Herman misses the bus to the job interview. Herman is thereby freed to spend his time playing snooker with Mick, who, he maintains, has brought him to the realisation that all life is meaningless or corrupt. Though Herman admits that sometimes 'It isn't a very happy prospect seeing one's life is an eternal circularity, a grinning stallion on a merrygoround', Mick assures him 'At least you know you're going nowhere, don't you? All happiness a farce, all pleasure transient'. Herman self-righteously admonishes Millie from leisure pursuits with a cruel fervour which compounds the teachings of his snooker-hall guru ('All pleasures are illusions. As for work, that's an organized system of self-deceit') in a way which is particularly hurtful to her doting concern for his welfare. He undertakes a life of monastic austerity, punctuated only by his own comically overblown expressions of nihilism.

Mick's pique at losing money (previously dismissed as 'a meaningless convention') in a snooker match is succeeded by Herman acting on Millie's suggestion to take a job. It involves him working from home, counting buttons, a task which rapidly dominates his life as completely as Mick's studied unemployment, and to similar exclusion of Millie. It transpires that Mick runs the button company and is only too pleased to give lost souls like Herman, 'not made to carry the burden of truth', a way of 'shaking off these mortal coils' to his own commercial advantage. Once having convinced his prospective employees of the futility of time, Mick offers his disciples the means of 'taking it off their hands'. Whereas Cheops in *One Afternoon* galvanised the slaves into enthusiastic labour with a hollow inclusive myth of future historical importance, like Henry V, Mick prospers by preaching an austere dismissal of worldly pomp and gain, while personally profiting from the time and labour which Herman comes to hold in such disregard, until the button-counting itself becomes an all-pervasive source of zeal, the work ethic displacing the effects of the work itself. Like Cheops and Henry, Mick is a persuasive speaker who prides himself on being sufficiently 'mature' not to take his own teachings too literally, or else excuses them on the grounds of the fulfilment they provide for innocents who crave a prescriptive ideology or inclusive sense of community to bolster their sense of purpose. In *Herman, with Millie and Mick*, the pivotal battle for Herman's soul gives the play a morality structure, with Millie representing the pole of worldly involvement, but Mick representing the apparently inevitably triumphant capitalist who can trick Herman into defining his own needs as narrowly as possible, by means of his clinging to a gospel of personal futility.

The innocents of these three plays demonstrate an openness and vulnerability which generates its own perilous charm, usually according to an outdated ideal of decency of behaviour: Cerebes (the 'decoy innocent'), the slaves who warm to him, and Oldham, are deferential, romantic and optimistic; Millie centres her share of these qualities on Herman, who in turn focuses his worldly considerations on inordinate sympathy for Mick. We are not prepared for Barker's subsequent grotesque, prickly protagonists by the wide-eyed childishness of these figures. But in each case, Barker demonstrates that there is no virtue in meekness or innocence, as these prove weaknesses by which the characters are ensnared into submissive roles in power structures whose overall designs they fall short of perceiving. Their fates provide warnings against the hazards of pledging one's sympathies — dramatic or otherwise — with the recklessness which convention precipitates.

3

Independence and the Family

CHEEK, NO ONE WAS SAVED, EDWARD — THE FINAL DAYS,
ALPHA ALPHA, CLAW, STRIPWELL, SKIPPER, MY SISTER AND I

I hate maturity. Mature notions, mature writers, it's a con to rub
the edge off a decent blade.

Downchild

The old know nothing. Fling them down. They made the world
and they need punishing.

The Castle

Forgive me. The young are vile.

The Possibilities

Allied but opposed considerations of social independence and the
supportive family unit are natural dramatic means to exposing
the essential link between public and private, political and personal facets of conduct and identity. Henrik Ibsen's *Pillars of the
Community* (1877) is a notable formulation of the theme, depicting a supposedly exemplary member of the community, Karsten
Bernick, who precipitates a dilemma by acting in accord with his
interpretation of society's prescriptions: Bernick permits the dangerous voyages of an unseaworthy vessel, kept afloat through persistent but perilously frail patchwork, in order to build an empire
of profit for his family, particularly his son — then discovers that
his son is aboard the vessel. With tragic irony, capitalism endan-
gers even those who are ostensibly successful through maintaining
its existence, and also the innocents, like Bernick's son, on whose
behalf Bernick claims to be labouring. Social distortions wreak their
effects on future generations and competition for power informs
private life; in the words of Leo Lowenthal, 'Life becomes a game
that one hopes to win by achieving success, only to find that the

specialization and exertion required for this success add up, after all, to failure'.[1]

Pillars of the Community demonstrates how the 'bait' of personal financial independence, on which many conservative forces and edicts rely in order to flatter their agents into identification and obedience, is ultimately and tellingly limited; in fact, the possible benefits of supposed personal independence and advancement are a partial, fleeting and circumscribed aspect of a much wider social drift towards isolation and disaster; any possible brief personal benefit is only available to those at the apex of the social hierarchy who define its terms and permit the promise of a degree of middle-class affluence and 'independence' to serve their own interests, secure in the knowledge that they have the power to check any more radical developments. The family, and the incentive to its members to ensure familial security in opposition to those outside its limits, is a crucial means to fostering capitalist competition by offering power through — apparently shared but ultimately vulnerably limited — ideals of independence. Many models of social maturity, especially male ones, demand that individual identity be established by carving out a personal territory, beyond or even in defiance of the family, beyond a given age. Barker's early plays explore this minefield of entangled social pressures and psychological instincts by dramatising their costs and consequences, with particular attention to the problematic transitions of parent-child relationships — problems of independence, obligations towards both supportive duty and personal autonomy (often expressed in terms of sexuality), which are in turn informed and defined by larger hierarchies of social power, and the promise of improving status in their terms.

Cheek (staged 1970) exposes the link between social power and sexual identity, namely the cash nexus. Laurie, an unemployed 20-year-old, is distinguished from his friend Bill in the first scene by his having 'a way with words'; but even Laurie's self-consciously and self-delightingly lurid imagination cannot intrinsically realise his salacious fantasies about local schoolgirls.

LAURIE: ... how do we achieve maximum profitability with minimum effort? How do we come into loads of loot without lifting more than a couple of fingers? ... There are a couple of ways open to you. One is crime ... But that's not for me. Not that there's any risk, it's just that criminals haven't got any class. Take the Krays. The only other thing is property ...

You see, the thing to do is to get hold of some bleeding great Victorian house and let it out to students and immigrants. They live anywhere, don't they? Don't bother to tell me it's not allowed under the mortgage, I know that, but who's going to know? You have to use your imagination, if everyone stuck to the rules there wouldn't be half the number of millionaires there are today. Rules are made to be broken.   (12–13)

Laurie's sense of initiative is founded on a sense of kinship between the ostensibly 'free' and the black market economies: 'It's like everything else, you have to go that bit further than everybody else. We have to be beyond the run of common men' (9). Laurie's hopes of attaining adult power, particularly sexual, but without the debilitating effects of supposed 'adult responsibilities', rest with his sense of nerve and eloquence, 'cheek', which mark him out from the moribund landscape; however sordid or reductive his preoccupations may initially appear, they are simply less decorously expressed than those of his mother and lack the parochial dimensions of her vanity; while his potential male role models are figuratively 'tubular steel spastic' like his sluggish friend Bill or literally vegetating like his dying father. He tries to entice nextdoor neighbour Shirley with wilful unconformity ('Nights round the tele, mowing the lawn on Sunday, that's not a life, is it? That's not living', 32) but, as with the local girls, his impatience drives her away and he falls back on male braggadocio to Bill, who still favours the standard route to success. But Laurie's tactics seem retrospectively vindicated when Shirley returns and makes a pass at him. However, her fundamental motive of gaining a Georgian house from Laurie's non-existent collection provokes mutual disappointment: hers in Laurie's lack of wealth; his in the bankruptcy of her professions of 'love' and clichéd terms of strategic endearment.

The final thwarted sexual offensive occurs when Bill suddenly acts on Laurie's advice and summons the 'cheek' to say he fancies Laurie's Mum, temporarily and enticingly collapsing the age barriers between them and positing a sexual potential which has been hinted at in the near-Oedipal compliments and compliment-seeking which has occurred between son and mother. The Ortonian elements of Laurie's calculatedly shocking verbal elegance find a counterpart in scenic indiscretion when Bill begins kissing and fondling Mum in front of comatose Dad, merely drawing the understated rebuke 'There's a time and a place!'

Laurie's counter-offensive involves an extrapolation of his initially amusing role-reversal conceit, identifying his Dad as the helpless family baby whom Laurie, man of the house and tantamount
'father', must not spoil through indulgent over-attentiveness. Son
uses father as a puppet infant to compound his mother's sense of
shame, 'Baba might have seen it! He might have seen his mumsa
being dirty with his dad's best friend! What will he grow up like!'
(53), and his sense of outrage and disgust has a partially self-ref-
erential double edge: 'In front of your own baby! You bloody bag!'
(54). By reminding Mum of her double-locked role status in relation
to father-child and child-father, Laurie stifles the sexual transcend-
ence of generations by embodying it in a particularly grotesque
form, practically claiming parodic conjugal rights from his depart-
ing mother, 'Here, we were going to have a good time, you and me!
Eat out for a change!' (54). But Laurie's strategic victory over his
mother leaves him alone with his father in a sexual and economic
no-man's-land. Nominally head of the household but nevertheless excluded from any chance of sexual reciprocity, Laurie ends up
with the responsibilities of adulthood without its compensations,
rather than vice versa as he wished. He takes refuge in parodying
the absurdities of sexual and generative processes, nomenclature
and their present pathetic interrelation, placing his mother's knickers on his father's head and speaking aloud to the unresponsive
figure:

You saw all that, did you? Out of the corner of your eye? Of
course, you wouldn't have known what it meant. I mean, you're
just a baba . . . You wouldn't think he had his fingers up her fanny,
would you? It's funny, but I came out of there. In the afternoon,
it was. Out I came, sliding onto the table — bump! Wheeeee —
bump! Funny that. Funny fanny. Fannies are funny! Fun in the
funny fanny!
(Pause)
I bet she had to squeeze though. She's got such little hips. I expect
those officers put their finger up her fanny. What a history her
fanny's got. Not that you care, eh? I can see you don't care. I'm
the only one who's actually lived in there, actually been in all the
way, head and shoulders. I expect you wish you could. But you're
too big.
(Pause)
She messed us about, didn't she, baba?   (54–55)

Laurie's sexual failure is further wryly acknowledged in his final baby talk to his father, where their inverted relationship effectively suggests that Laurie is landed with the responsibilities of caring for a virtual 'child' without the pleasures of sexual intercourse or the fulfilment of paternity *en route*. Laurie's attempts to step outside social convention have brought him to a particularly grotesque parody thereof, leaving him trapped in the forms of a mock masculinity and further than ever from any meaningful contact with women; rather than transcend his class status and sexual alienation, he is more literally bonded to the forms and results of his father's life. Having correctly deduced the analogue between monetary and sexual power, Laurie discovers, ironically and pathetically, that his withdrawal leads to impotence.

No One was Saved (staged 1970) sustains the theme of exploitation, characteristic of this period of his work, here focused in the story of a working-class unmarried mother, written as an act of double-edged criticism: of Edward Bond's play *Saved* (staged 1965) and of the Beatles song *Eleanor Rigby*. Barker:

> I'd gone to *Saved* on the strength of a review we'd read saying that this was life in South London epitomized. We just didn't think that this was so — we didn't understand much about what Bond was trying to do with the language of the play. That was why I wrote *Cheek*, and also why I took up the gang of youths from *Saved* and used them in *No One Was Saved* . . .
>
> The song had a rare concern with despair and defeat — very unlike a modern pop song — but I was always suspicious of the Beatles, and Lennon in particular: all the financial manipulation and posturing with maharishis struck me firmly then as an indictment of the Sixties. So I created a fantasy in which Lennon had actually known this girl Eleanor Rigby, who was not an old woman as I thought the song implied, and served her up as song material.[2]

In *No One Was Saved*, Eleanor Rigby is a young woman of about 20 who is first seen extricating herself from the graceless clutches of Ray; like all the other characters in the play, Ray has a set of appeals, arguments and slurs all ready to justify the primacy and fulfilment of his own interests and values. Eleanor's withdrawn nature seems only to excite further unwelcome interest from loud and vociferous appetites, making her self dissipated into a blankness onto which others hurry to impress their fantasies. A policeman becomes fascinated with her soon after she has escaped from Ray, then becomes angry and blames her for the response she unwillingly elicits; she then falls in turn into the arms of an Indian who stresses his own loneliness and romantic sensitivity, but this more decorous façade also collapses in a blackly comic acceleration of personal sexual interest and disappointment in the frustration of his self-justifying expectations. Eleanor's mother is also shown to be chronically joyless and selfish; the young priest Father MacKenzie shows a voyeuristic interest in her life as fuelling the essential self-righteousness behind his persona of progressive clergyman, and his ultimately condescending Olympian interest in 'the people' from whom he secretly enjoys his celibate separation; and Eleanor's 'friend' May pours out her own addiction to male attention, along with her denunciation of all men as 'rotten'. May's lack of real interest in Eleanor is demonstrated by her cursory and belated questions about her welfare, and Eleanor's non-committal answers ('I don't know what to suggest') suggest not only lack of communication but even the lack of need for it in predictable social conversation; the characters use Eleanor and apparently anything else as support for their own egocentrically-constructed definition of life which cannot be disrupted, only confirmed and deepened by events: nothing seems able to resist being requisitioned or force change.

John Lennon appears, with quasi-mystical joss-stick philosophising from his *Sergeant Pepper* phase, then briefly lapses into the 18-year-old Liverpudlian rocker who can proclaim he likes people as a whole, if no one in particular, in contrast to Eleanor's increasing distaste for mankind. His Christmas cracker motto 'love is all you need' is greeted by Eleanor's puzzlement; his aphorisms ('beauty is the recognition of our perpetual nothingness in the greater nothingness of the forever') sound increasingly like Herman's invocations of Mick's philosophies in *Herman, with Millie and Mick* and likewise depend on the coiner's ironic, profitable relationship with the supposedly meaningless world.

Eleanor's baby Scott is killed in his pram by a gang of young men (whom Barker mischievously calls 'Edward Bond's Gang'), who even lack the conscious malicious interest of the torturer; the baby is not deliberately stoned as in Bond's *Saved* but used as an object to thrust or duck behind in an internal squabble. Even Scott's death is used by the Indian as a pretext for ingratiating himself, and by

Lennon as an occasion for glib, vacuous metaphysical pronouncements.

At least Eleanor's hard-pressed streak of romantic idealism sets her apart from the prevalent ironic plastic egoists, but it also makes her fatally vulnerable when she hears herself used in the eponymous Beatles song: her very name is stolen for commercial use, driving her to complete the song's scenario and act on its suggestion of suicide. Even beyond death she is exploited: as a pretext for Father MacKenzie's smug assault on his congregation in his self-styled office as 'The Gestapo of God's Third Reich'; and as the object of curious fingering by the Edward Bond gang who enter the church, prise open her coffin and rifle the offertory box.

This conclusion is a good early example of Barker's characteristic relentlessness in pursuing his theme — in this case, the admittedly and necessarily simple one of the ubiquity of selfishness and exploitation — with wilfully shocking directness at the expense of characters' and audiences' demands for mitigation or redemption in any form. Its refusal, and inventively thorough demolition, of any grounds for false hope anticipates future cleansingly ruthless dramatic representations of cruel actions, events and conclusions in works like *Victory, The Power of the Dog, Don't Exaggerate* and *The Bite of the Night*. In *No One Was Saved*, Eleanor is too passive a victim to sustain interest; Laurie in *Cheek* had more power to surprise. The most startling movement in *No One Was Saved* occurs when Barker has ceased to gloss *Eleanor Rigby* and *Saved* and continues the events of Eleanor's *play* and *story* after her *life* is over, in the last two scenes. Thus the reach of catastrophe — in this case, the insistence of the human predatory drive — is extended past the reach of the character's life and suggests that there is no escape or peace in or beyond death, refusing to close our notional circuit of the world of the play, which must persist beyond her personal tragedy, and with a likely marked lack of deference towards it. I would expect the last two scenes to be the most effective in performance — above all, the last, which demonstrates the continuing imminence of the gang rather than permit them to be dismissed as a plot device limited to a single intervention.

Barker's ability to perceive and portray the interpenetration of political and psychological characteristics, to provide a distinctly related social context for the consequent effects of sublimated or explosive sexuality, is a principal hallmark and strength. *Edward — The Final Days* (staged 1972) is a broad slice of agitprop for a radical consensus audience, staged at the mid-term of Edward Heath's four-year Conservative government.

The play depicts Prime Minister Eddie Egdon, waited on by an absurdly deferential butler, Stanley, who parodies the humble, resourceful and eloquent servant familiar from Wilde and Wodehouse, proclaiming himself sub-human ordure with notable imaginative fluency. Mrs Egdon orders her son to 'get on' and not bother with girls ('Leave all that to the stupid types. Then when you're a famous big man with your picture in the paper every day, then you can have your pick'), an extravagant but accurate account of how the English version of the will to power is instilled on the basis of self-monitoring guilt, the work ethic and the national preference for the continual deferral of the fulfilment of desire. Mrs Egdon's prescriptions are reinforced by Mr Egdon's emphasis on self-regulation and disgust at the body. Hence Eddie's preference for the abstract delights of music and a restless appetite for short-term personal success over long-term general interests ('Ambition is the certain knowledge that you'd have a cancer grafted on your arse — if it would get you where you're going in a shorter time').

The only respite from this internalised careerism occurs among the hierarchic brutalities of the English grammar school, with a fellow schoolboy's offer of affection, but Eddie rejects him as a possible source of future embarrassment, comforting himself with the self-justifications of pre-emptive suspicion and heroic sacrifice. Eddie flatters television viewers into association with his platform of 'Honest greed in the cause of good taste', but his contempt for the electorate erupts through the ordered surface of a party political broadcast and drives him to order a nuclear attack ('There seems no valid point in permitting the continuation of this disgusting race').

This drastic action stirs even Mr Egdon into resistance, interrupting his berating of Eddie for association with a female with whom we have also seen the father coupling. This extremity of reaction confounds Egdon Sr, but he cannot answer the logical extrapolation of his own teaching. While Stanley rushes off, flushed with pride in his official government function of triggering multilateral annihilation, Eddie orders himself shot and Mr Egdon bursts in on his corpse with news of a landslide victory.

Though Barker's basic strategy of demolishing the public self by satiric exposure of the private one is not original, his account of the manufacture and appeal of a figure such as Eddie is more reverberative in relation to the national psychology than agitprop grotesquerie suggests or intrinsically demands. Though rejected by his parents as a 'monster', Eddie is a direct consequence of their influence, and their dissociation from him only deepens his alienation and vindictiveness, as in all his relationships. His electoral appeal and theatrical vividness depend on his being a recognisable product of his times and national attitudes, thereby illuminating distinctly English knots of shame, hypocrisy and resentment, sexual nausea and competitive sublimation, self-denial and suspicious vengefulness towards others, which finally leave even those who act upon and embody these social-psychological myths stranded and aloof on a plateau of terminal cynicism. Mr Egdon proudly proclaims: 'My son thrived on opposition, he grew strong on rivalry', but fails to foresee the distortion and despair his teachings produce.

The theme of unexpected manifestation of parental influence in shockingly literal acts of independence frequently occurs in Barker's drama, usually among characters who have assimilated edicts in a lurid or over-simplified way in order to re-write their own origins in a kind of immaculate self-begetting, which often leads to a position of isolation and despair. Even the innocents Oldham in *Henry V in Two Parts* and Herman in *Herman, with Millie and Mick* are to some extent embarrassments to their mentor figures by seeking to act on their prescriptions too baldly, cutting themselves off from their former fellows. Laurie in *Cheek*, Noel in *Claw*, Tim in *Stripwell*, Eddie in *Edward — The Final Days*, Rhoda in *That Good Between Us*, McConochie in *Victory*, Dementia and Supporta in *Scenes from an Execution* all demonstrate a wilful reaction against the elements of themselves they may perceive in their parents by developing idiosyncratic extrapolations of parental influence; Lalage in *The Love of a Good Man*, Cropper in *Victory* and Gay in *The Bite of the Night* react and act with more true individuality.

The East End setting of *Alpha Alpha* (staged 1972) provides an apt terrain for Barker's characteristic interests at this stage of his work, given the London district's associations of an ostensibly tightly-knit, fiercely protective and supportive working-class community which is also characterised by individual impulses towards material advancement and independent status, often acquired by illegal means. *Alpha Alpha's* central family unit of widow Nora Kersh and her twin gangster sons Morrie and Mickey is a semi-naturalistic microcosm of a society's patterns of indulgence and licence, and the introduction of the figure of Lord Gadsby adds the dimension of voyeuristic fascination and exploitation barely concealed beneath the moral disgust of Father MacKenzie in *No One Was Saved*. The stable triangular relationship between Mrs Kersh, Mickey and Morrie provides an emotional equilibrium of sorts; when the twins shoot or stab photographers or policemen, Mrs Kersh's anger quickly modulates into indulgent resignation towards what she characterises as the mischievous antics of roguish scamps. Thus the Kersh family bonds tighten in defence against social objections and even seek to legitimise deviant behaviour by grotesquely misplaced parental mercy, scaling down the twins' criminal activities to the level of naughty boys playing in neighbourhood backyards. Incarnating many popular associations of offsprings of the East End, the Kersh twins also demonstrate a correspondingly characteristic wish to grow beyond its immediate confines:

MICKEY: The people are disgusting in this area.
MORRIE: Among the very lowest of the low.
MICKEY: I personally have no compunction in exploiting them for my own ends. If I don't, someone else will —
MORRIE: Someone from a different part of town maybe.
MICKEY: I much prefer to keep things on a local basis. Ties in the East End are very strong.   (I.4.17.)

Significantly, the Teacher who complains about their conduct, and has plans for improving the area in his capacity as Labour Party candidate, shows his dislike for the district to be motivated fundamentally by his own ambition for social advancement. A different response to the twins is that of voyeuristic fascination and limited association, like that of Gadsby who interests himself in the twins' legal and penal welfare because personally excited by their 'urge to power, that ruthless, merciless, unbending, cruel, naked, erect thrusting to win! Win! Win!' (I.5.26.).[3] But the ultimate absorption of the twins' activities occurs at a national level, when 'certain members of the government' decide that the only way to face problems in Northern Ireland is by referring them to the twins, whose thuggery is now granted new respectability and licence.

The first evidence of their involvement is their capture and torture of a young Irish Member of Parliament, Bernadette, who is in turn rather eager and over-rehearsed in her bids for heroic martyrdom. But the Kersh familial support system is fatally unbalanced when Morrie and Mickey witness their mother responding to a suitor,

Cyril, and find this displacement of the revised nuclear family image irreconcilable with their ideal of their mother. The consequent feelings of betrayal, anger and sexual nausea often accompany children's and parents' greedily over-protective and impossibly abstract definitions of each other, most frequently shattered by the sudden awareness of possible independent sexual activity, which displaces the primacy of their own claims on parent or child. Correspondingly, Mickey and Morrie are disappointed that their clandestine imperialist activities cannot be sanctioned by a personal meeting with the individual and maternal representative of the nation, the Queen.

Their sense of familial and national betrayal compounding each other, the twins shoot Bernadette and then their mother, to the increasing excitement and gratification of the observing Gadsby. After their arrest, Gadby terminates their relationship because it no longer exists to 'mutual benefit', or, more precisely, his benefit, but that distinction is lost on the twins, who still pathetically hope to meet the Queen and be embraced and legitimised by the national family, to whom they threaten to 'report' Gadsby, failing to recognise that he is its essential agent in his programme of self-interest and exploitation.

Left in helpless isolation, the twins try to re-animate their mother, propping up her corpse and assuming the same relaxed positions around her with which the play began — an image of their desperate, doomed wish to regress to relative stability, a bid to deny the full consequences of their action, and a demonstration that, even beyond death, people can be used as puppets in the scenarios of the remaining, as the calculatedly indecorous conclusions of *No One Was Saved* and subsequently *My Sister and I* also show.

Alpha Alpha's webs of mutual dependence suggest the extent to which the lower-class characters' control over their lives is illusory and fatally limited; only Gadsby is permitted independence from the consequences of his involvement with, and exploitation of, the twins, and the play shows the spuriousness or vulnerability of other forms of interdependence. Ingenuity, however selfish, is thus identified as the feature of the perpetrators of the 'confidence-trick' of authority rather than of their victims, whose limited perspectives do not yet permit them a fully tragic articulacy or even developed sense of suffering.

Barker's genre is, as yet, satirical depiction of the mechanisms of society, rather than a reply to it or a tragic engagement with the full depths of its consequences; and his method is principally that of demonstrating that the familial or associative bonds which people attempt to perceive and act upon are frequently mistaken or fatally fragile before larger all-consuming social forces of exploitation, whose interests these smaller alliances can ultimately serve.

Claw (staged 1975) continues *Cheek's* quickfire technique of characters pinpointed in spotlights amid frozen action, or making conspiratorial asides to the audience, to expose the discrepancy between action and thought, or else, consolidating the breakthrough energy of *My Sister and I*, to provide an exposition of their fantastic dreams of defiant fulfilment and self-definition, usually through the satisfaction of thwarted appetite. Thus the audience has something of an X-ray view of the characters' impulses and witness to what extent these govern their actions; but the effect is not inevitably reductive, as the fantasies which Barker creates for his characters are so organically linked to their selves as to provide further illumination of them, and in some cases to evoke moments of unexpected sympathy as well as revulsion at moral degradation.

The first example in *Claw* is Mrs Biledew's presentation of her illegitimate child to her incapacitated soldier husband (ironically named Victor), when she says in aside to the audience: 'I could lie to him. I could say I found it in the ruins of a house, after a raid, clinging to its dead mother's tits' (127). Thus the audience is permitted a closeness to a character's motivation while also being encouraged to exercise continuous judgement, a characteristic Barker technique and one which accommodates more dramatic complexity than the literal dictates of Brecht's *Verfremdungseffekt*, where the spectator is urged to remain detached and pass judgement on the basis of social action. In the case of Barker's characters, the motivation or impulse which springs from inmost instinct, however lurid or fantastic, may stand in contradiction of the action, to either comic or pathetic effect, and demand an appropriate complexity of response through this deeper understanding of character.

This is not to say that the characters will be absolved from atrocious acts or even their compliance in an exploitative regime excused on the grounds of liberal humanist understanding (such as Stripwell invokes in self-defence), far from it; rather, the *individuality* rather than the *universality* of their motivation will be exposed, their instinctive drives which are likely to seem all the more vital, however idiosyncratic, eccentric or obsessive, if they are opposed to the dominant flow of a falsely and forcefully harmonising, constrictive atmosphere and landscape of moral exhaustion and self-surrender.

The mature figure of the boy Noel explodes into the spotlight describing his own origins, thus establishing his close association with the audience and his distinctive, confident verbal style which recalls something of the mischievous Morality Vice or Elizabethan Fool. But although Noel associates himself with challenging authority and lucrative corruption, he is more of an Everyman figure than his vanity would care to admit. The play's sub-title, '*An Odyssey*', suggests Noel's voyage of social discovery, but he also initially occupies a pivotal role in the demands of his individualistic mother and Communist father who struggle for his soul in Morality Play terms. But Noel develops distinct ideas of his own possible direction involving an uncertain mixture of both elements of parental influence, setting himself up as pimp to a female fellow member of the Young Communists League in ostensible escalation of capitalist decay, though this is comically short of the 'carrying anthrax' into the 'woolly nests' of the bourgeoisie that these would-be 'heroes of labour' would wish. The absurdity is heightened when the first prospective client is a policeman, who accepts the proposition and subsequently beats up Noel to retrieve the one pound fee. Rather than change Noel, this propels him quicker into infamy on a larger scale, as demonstrated in the next scene.

Mrs Biledew is stuffing herself with pastries in Fortnum and Mason's tearoom; she is annoyed by the indiscreet behaviour of her son when he visits the scene in person, and further pained by his lack of feeling for her. This discomfort is brought to a head when Noel begins recruiting waitresses to prostitution on inspection of their thighs and the disembodied conscience-voice of Biledew booms apocalyptically: 'This is where your cream horns come from!' Yet after brief misgivings, Mrs Biledew accommodates herself to the situation. In inevitable contrast, this triggers Biledew's rejection of his stepson, whom he attempts to chastise by appearing like a supernatural scourge and smashing the errant youth over the head with a framed portrait of Karl Marx.

Noel's dealing with his mother and employees fail to afford the understanding, emotional or carnal, which he craves ('Oh, the leadweight of their intellects . . . and me like lightning on the icecap') and lead him to daydreams of courting acceptance from the society of spectacle only to spurn it:

NOEL: I have a dream ... To be a sort of Cecil Beaton ... in big
hats ... and white suits ... with chiffon neckscarves blowing in
the wind ... on beaches in Jamaica ... with women and celebrities ... and flashbulbs popping at me ... and my memoirs in the
Sunday Times ...
MRS BILEDEW: That's nice ...
NOEL: And then, in front of everybody ... I would disembowel
myself ... and chuck my innards in Mick Jagger's gob ...   (159)

The ghost-like apparition of the imprisoned Biledew picks up
on Noel's potentially redemptive inability to take social success on
the same completely fulfilling face value as his mother, and chides
his adolescent fantasies of a frustrated rebel's motorcycle doom
('Thinks he's T. E. Lawrence. Wants to rub himself out with the
seedy panache of a hero of imperialism. No such luck'). Thus the
First Act concludes, with its comedy and tension springing from
the discrepancies between Mrs Biledew's materialism and self-
interest, Biledew's preaching the Communist gospel in extravagant
neo-Biblical utterances such as 'Revolutionaries are the tallow in
the candle of our dreams', and Noel's contrastingly emblazoned,
incessant melodramatic bastard self-characterisation as profitable
nemesis to the monied, donning his dazzling silver suit and alias
of 'Claw'.

However, Noel's escapade as bargain-basement Pandarus to
the constabulary has demonstrated a fatal discrepancy between
intention and effect, which dogs his subsequent actions. Tony
Dunn has noted how 'discerning that sex and power desire the
most intimate relations, he sets up a middleman between these
two forces'.[4] Dunn claims Noel maintains 'a rigorous distance
between image and reality',[5] but it is arguable how consciously
voluntary this is on Noel's own part. His name provides an ironic
counterpoint to Noel Coward in *In Which We Serve*, and his Cecil
Beaton speech shows an iconoclastic recognition of the cynicism
of a culture whose publicity prizes eventless isolation as enviable and glamorous. But his personae of Young Trotsky of the
YCL, Claw, and now 'court jester' to the powerful seem sincere
bids to close the circuit between self and role in order to influence the reality of others, though he has consistently wished to
achieve this self-definition and defiant self-begetting in a solitary,
unreciprocal way.

While speculating in sex, Noel has generalised commodity and consumer to make it unspecific, displacing and shortchanging desire into fantasy as capitalist consumerism demands it must be, in order to maintain control of its force. When Noel attempts to gain sex from power he finds the equation is not so easy for him to reverse. His prostitute Nora will not permit their association to stray onto a personal level (or even to let money render it quasi-professional) and she insists on calling him 'Claw' rather than 'Noel' despite his demands; image ('Claw') and self ('Noel') cannot coalesce, even seem inimical, despite Noel's wishes and the promise of successful independence and financial power which he took to be implicit in the successful assumption of his soubriquet. Like Laurie in *Cheek*, Noel has discovered that the promises of masculinity as defined on the terms of capitalist society do not deliver; they are fundamentally a confidence-trick, like all other forms of advertising, which sells the sense of the self short. As John Berger and others write: 'Being envied is a solitary form of reassurance. It depends precisely upon not sharing your experience with those who envy you. You are observed with interest but you do not observe with interest — if you do, you will become less enviable'.[6]

The glamour-image of 'Claw' and associations of power thus drive a wedge between Noel and others, precluding any relationship with women other than the commercial, on which its associations of power are founded. His first shared sexual experience with Angie Clapcott in Act Two 'dislocates him out of the agent role and onto the dangerous terrain of the mutuality of love', in the words of Tony Dunn.[7] Angie's husband, the Tory Home Secretary, ruminates on how the sentimental associations of scenes from her former career as a chorus line dancer in musicals ignited his longings, and even his wedding ceremony was memorable for its cultivation of anticipatory fantasy; however, Angie's incapability of remaining within musical theatre's kitsch images of womanhood disappoint Clapcott and damage his chances of the Treasury; 'I wished to Christ I'd never set eyes on *Showboat'*, he concludes ruefully. The sudden electric attraction between Angie and Noel is accordingly represented by, and enacted through, the banalities enshrined within the lyrics of *All Shook Up, Showboat* and *South Pacific*, though when the couple begin singing after their Kingston By-Pass roadside tryst it is less to suggest the bankruptcy of the vocabulary of desire than to demonstrate their mutual playfulness with received forms.

Unfortunately for them, their song alerts a Police Motorcyclist to overhear the drift of their next variations on a theme, where sexuality's explosion of all sense of potential leads them into speculations of violent defiance (which are also comically counterbalanced by the scenic form, specifying the policeman's comparatively unintoxicated presence):

NOEL: We'll murder him.
ANGIE: Pump him full of lead.
The POLICE MOTORCYCLIST *jots it down with renewed interest.*
NOEL: You beautiful angel . . .
ANGIE: Blow his brains out.
NOEL: You beautiful sinner . . .
ANGIE: Rape him with chrome handlebars.
NOEL: Dismember him.
ANGIE: Cut off his little true blue penis.
NOEL: I love you. I am raging with love for you!
ANGIE: No, not again . . .
NOEL: It hurts . . .   (191)

However, they elude police surveillance and Noel believes he is secure in the forging of this bond against Clapcott. But he has misinterpreted the bond between Clapcott and Angie, which thrives on the lure of cruelty and material security, as this intercut between their thoughts demonstrates:

ANGIE (ASIDE): Sitting there, like some boiled lobster, faintly blue around the ears . . . and in his belly, pasta and liqueurs . . . churning slowly . . . while he plots some mean revenge . . .
Pause
CLAPCOTT (ASIDE): One day, come in, burst in, kicking the door down like some Operation Motorman, catch them and throw acid on their writhing backs . . .
Pause
ANGIE (ASIDE): Static like beef . . . his podgy hands, made for fondling pens and the stems of glasses . . .
Pause
CLAPCOTT (ASIDE): Her bony fingers, the skin more mottled as she gets older, stained with endless fornication . . .
Pause
ANGIE (ASIDE): Little food stains on his tie . . . on his flies, grubby

marks . . .
        Pause
CLAPCOTT: Tired sometimes, has to stay in bed with tonics . . . and
her pubic hair is rather grey . . .
ANGIE: Short-breathed on staircases . . . forgets to change his
underwear . . .
        A Pause. They remain still. Cut in music of the old ragtime number,
'I'm Happy, If You're Happy'. *It is faded out.*
CLAPCOTT: Finish with him. *(Pause)* When I've cleared this. *(Pause)*
We can't have this. You know that.
        Pause
ANGIE: Yes . . .   (200)

This sequence demonstrates the resentful fascination between the
couple as their catalogue of details animates them to break from the
detachment of their asides and recognise, in the charge the details
still hold, a mutual knowledge and equilibrium which the ironically
jaunty ragtime song nevertheless suggests. Despite her taste for
moments of 'delirium', Angie likes, belongs to and cannot shift from
her social milieu; she subverts her socially conditioned role, but not
her society, except incidentally. In fact there is a suggestion that part
of the attraction of such 'delirium' involves goading her husband
to reaction, preferably to the ruthless exercise of power which she
finds exciting, as she proclaims 'after all the filth I've been with, no
one can twist my womb like you. You freeze my blood' (209), and
he makes arrangements for them to eat, presumably at an expen-
sive restaurant, his own sense of power and appetite galvanised in
turn. Noel has merely been the latest morsel of grist to their voracious partnership, his dismay continuing the play's sequence of disappointments which make it so apt a paradigm for the Wilson era
of its first performances.

Act Three affords a glimpse inside Clapcott's empire, where
an Irish bomber and a former hangman have been inveigled, by
the baits of privilege and professional specialisation, to take up
positions in the beehive of power, staffing a mental institution
in Hampshire where Noel is imprisoned. Lily and Lusby's confident senses of their own backgrounds give them an impervious,
monolithic quality which highlights the futility of Noel's appeals
to images of liberal English civilisation focused in the journalist Ludovic Kennedy. Biledew's teachings here assume their full
weight, however bombastic their sometime expression, and Noel

tries to enlist his wardens' sympathies by stressing their common situation, their absorption into national hierarchies, and the annexing of potentially deviant energy and definitions in the service of corporate organisations — but Lily and Lusby exemplify this process to an extent which Noel cannot suspect. Noel re-writes his previous declaration of ruthless individualism in recognition that the real destructive claw-like power is that of the ruling classes, against which the oppressed and exploited have only 'Our common nothingness. And our caring for each other'. But Lily and Lusby are cheerful automata, as safe and respectable as their superior, Clapcott, happy in the sense of power and belonging afforded even by their dungeon position in the system, even proud in their agency of executing its darker mandates.

The play's comic irony blackens towards pathos with Noel's lonely murder and the completeness with which Clapcott 'cements over' his passing in a statement to Parliament, a final challenging image of the extent of the power of governing institutions and their capacity to dwarf, absorb or crush the individual, whose dreams of control are, while defined in isolation, permitted and defined by such forces and their interests.

The title character of *Stripwell* (staged 1975) is a judge on the Southern Assize circuit whose sense of professional futility is focused by receiving a death threat from a sentenced offender, Cargill, and his liaison with a go-go dancer, Babs; he is also the butt of dismissive humour from his wife, Dodie, and his former Labour minister father-in-law, Jarrow. Graham Stripwell is himself also disarmingly aware of his lack of conviction. Dodie is, as Ruth Shade has noted, like several Barker mothers such as Laurie's Mum and Mrs Biledew: 'contemptuous of their husbands, pragmatic, mostly unfaithful, yet they are loyal to their children, often turning a blind eye to their misdemeanours. Their relationships with their children are articulate and honest in a sense because, although their mutual animosity is evident, it is expressed in such a way that it becomes a bond between them'.[8]

Stripwell's son Tim has, like Noel Biledew, incorrectly assimilated Marx to the point of identifying himself with the dominant climate of profiteering corruption, though Tim presents himself with the black-leather-and-wisecracks panache which Noel dreams of but falls comically and sympathetically short of achieving for any sustained period. Tim's chosen route to material success is smuggling packs of heroin concealed in the vaginas of two elephants. Ostensible voices for reform like Jarrow are also part of the atmosphere of genteel paralysis: Jarrow condoned Dodie's affair with a Conservative, and drifts through life as a semi-conscious vengeful anachronism subsisting on memories of the past (Clement Attlee supposedly said 'Jarrow, do we *really* want to turn over the apple cart? ... And I said ... it is in our power ... but I don't ... do you?', 38) and his collection of pornographic magazines ('Best in the Labour Party. Mediocre for the Tories'). Babs resembles Angie Clapcott in her decision to disappoint the title character of the play; but Babs is more sympathetic, trying to shape her future using what means and opportunities arise, for all the clanging platitudes which support her misguided canonisation of Samuel Beckett and her constant look-out for her projected autobiography's colourful raw material. Babs's attractions towards the superficial are comprehensible given the choices of her social context, and is merely naive compared to Angie's manipulations based on fundamental personal security. Babs severs herself from Stripwell with astringent honesty: 'The point is, I have met someone. And that someone has offered me, in terms of life-enhancing possibilities, more than you can' (97).

Part of the play's humour and interest has sprung from observing Stripwell's faintly ludicrous bids to embrace 'the guerilla aspect' of sex ('I always thought that if you met someone and you both felt — desire, then it happened, you came together like two pieces of a jigsaw. But it wasn't ever like that. There was always fisticuffs', 48), most amusingly in the face of a voyeuristic vigilante ice-cream vendor, Pennells, a vintage Barker comic invention. But Stripwell himself is perhaps less engaging than Barker gives him credit for, as the pathos of his hangdog self-characterisations (claiming his gradual absence will merely be noted in the household like that of some 'decomposing domestic pet') and the barbs from the sharper characters (Tim remarks 'You must admit, Graham, if you got a three-minute warning of an H-bomb going off, you'd start taking the library books back') tend to accumulate as overly meretricious bids to elicit sympathy in terms of drawing-room comedy banter.

Stripwell discovers a loss of moral detachment in the wake of his rejection by Babs and discovery of Tim's trade. He announces 'there is no public morality without a corresponding private one. And no change without indignation' (115), and betrays his son's drug trafficking to the police; but Cargill arrives to remind all concerned about the relative newness — and by implication excessive lateness — of Stripwell's acquisition of moral fibre. Just as Clapcott had a text prepared to unsettle potential assassins of whatever cause or nationality, Stripwell begins to dissuade Cargill from homicide, admittedly with more spontaneity than the character in *Claw*, mobilising standards of English decency and liberal humanism in their traditional functions of bolstering the already privileged. Cargill parries deftly, insisting on his own rights to a sense of injury and impulse to action:

STRIPWELL: You can't allow your personal compulsions to just — take control.
CARGILL: I have.
. . .
STRIPWELL: We have to live with one another in this life . . .
CARGILL: I don't have to live with you.
. . .
STRIPWELL: If everybody went around just following the ictates of his anger . . . and there wasn't any compromise . . . I think you'll see there wouldn't be much . . . of a world to live in. We're always having to cut down on our good intentions . . . make do with less . . .
Pause
CARGILL: Oh. Shall I just cut your leg off, then?   (120)

Stripwell invokes reasonableness ('That's how we do things in this country. We keep our grievances down to a manageable size') and a 'necessary' divorce between impulse and practical action. After seeming momentarily swayed, Cargill denies everything Stripwell has said by shooting him, and thus emerges as the first in a series of Barker heroes who refuse to have their 'obsessive' feelings (that is, feelings threatening to the dominant hegemony) apportioned and diffused in the interests of maintaining a superficial harmony. But his lengthy absence from the stage fails to provide any alternative image to Stripwell in terms of character and humanist sympathy, which are the main features which lodge in the minds of West End theatregoers, and so the indictment of the partiality of Stripwell's morality may not seem as clear as it might have done were Cargill a less elementally structural force; whether or not the drawing-room comedy vehicle could sustain this, is admittedly difficult to speculate upon.

Familial power structures also exert a strong influence in *Skipper* (staged 1973), a parable resembling a sort of inverted *Heartbreak House* with its set of disappointments and unlikely alliances across three generations. Sir Harry Winchester sails out to sea on his yacht, turning his back on an England he denounces as a stunted, rotten island with no use for men of courage and vision. Like an imperialistic version of Shaw's Captain Shotover, he feels particularly disappointed in his own offspring as an example of national frivolity and decadence, as shown when a broadcast appeal from his son comes over the radio:

OSWALD: Hello, Dad, it's me. Oswald.
SIR HARRY: You cringing scum!
OSWALD: Look, Dad, let bygones be bygones, shall we? This can't be the time for recriminations or reproaches —
SIR HARRY: There is always time for recrimination! There is always time for shouting your contempt to the whole world!
OSWALD: All right, I haven't lived up to your expectations, I don't mind admitting it —
SIR HARRY: I was betrayed!
OSWALD: Children always disappoint their parents, it's traditional —
SIR HARRY: I was betrayed! When I gazed down at you as you lay in your mother's arms, I thought I saw the image of a pioneer, a ground-breaker, a Cecil Rhodes! By God, it was there in the genes, you had no excuses, I've been undermined!

Even a direct appeal from the Queen, who understands his dilemma as a similar self-conscious anachronism, fails to avert his chosen course. However, once Sir Harry is in fitful slumber, two stowaways emerge from the lifeboat: Albert Osgood and his teenage grandson Kevin have stolen aboard hoping to pursue Kevin's mother to Illinois, where she has absconded with an American airman from RAF Mildenhall. Like Antonio and Sebastian in *The Tempest*, they consider murdering the sleeping old man, oblivious to the problems of their immediate whereabouts; but Kevin's respect for aristocracy makes him waver until Sir Harry awakes and explains that he is bound for oblivion, not America: 'You've hi-jacked a coffin, skippered by a living corpse'.

Once adjusted to these circumstances, Kevin becomes increasingly fascinated by Sir Harry's reminiscences of a bygone golden age of Empire, to the extent that he turns against his own mutineer grandfather (who killed officers in trenches) for unbalancing this mythical society's equilibrium with discontent: 'You wouldn't make the most of it, you had to spoil things, always criticising, never satisfied, you buggered up the whole system you selfish sods!' Kevin cuts across invocations of 'flesh and blood' to murder Albert, who bequeaths his grandson to Sir Harry even as they chant 'England!' over his prone body. But the teenager recovers from his moment of intoxication and realises his lack of control in direction or survival as tempestuous waves toss the ship; Sir Harry goes blithely towards death, picturing the relief of his merciful end, whereas Kevin becomes increasingly fearful and conscious of his own (self-)betrayal and foolishness in trusting to Winchester's consciously outdated yarns.

Skipper is a concise fantasia with recent parallels in the Thatcherite project to engage the déclassé in myth. Kevin rejects the submerged tradition of revolt his grandfather represents for the lure of tribal security and 'independence' which Winchester's nostalgic ideal offers. Significantly, Winchester cannot reciprocate or perceive any kinship between himself and Kevin, whom he dismisses as the product of a spineless age. Humour springs chiefly from Sir Harry's baroque imagery ('England, you bleed, your veins are emptied through great trenches hacked across your face') and Kevin's wide-eyed acceptance and mimicry of romantic imperialism. The struggle for Kevin's soul is conducted on a verbal level and Winchester wins because he has the more authoritative, because conventionally endorsed, rhetoric; the indomitable mutineer spirit of Albert will later be credited with more eloquence by Barker in Dockerill in *Heroes of Labour*, Gocher in *Fair Slaughter*, and Toplis in *Crimes in Hot Countries*.

The brief message by the consciously antiquated Queen in *Skipper* provides a possible starting point for My *Sister and I* (staged 1973), in which a queen, Liz, is all too conscious of the mechanical tokenism of her role and her own lack of inclination for it — 'If you asked me what I'd love to be, what I dream of, it's being the music teacher in an infants' school' — whereas her sister, Princess Marjorie, has been born with a sharp wit, tongue and sense of iconoclastic initiative, longing to shatter the prevailing miasma of polite jadedness by extravagant, ruthless exercise of power and appetite.

Our first sight of Marjorie is her rankled return from surveying orderly, submissive ranks of girl guides, who represent the cementing inertia of English life — of which Marjorie's husband, the sheepishly-grinning, self-confessed 'gutless nobody' Armstrong provides individual evidence, were any to be needed. Like all of Barker's most memorable creations, Marjorie is actively opposed to the notion of suffering in silence and provides a pointed contrast to Armstrong's vague woolliness of sensibility and phrase with her whiplash invective and impatience for some manifestation of passion equal to her own; but heredity relegates her to the sidelines of state life whereas Liz is by temperament the meek doll.

Marjorie's indignation is matched by her relish for danger and self-awareness:

MARJORIE: . . . I'm just born to be miserable. Some people are. And quite often we're the best people, the most exciting and imaginative, that's what makes it so unfair.

ARMSTRONG: I'm a dreadful failure, too.

MARJORIE *(turning on him):* Who said I was a failure!

Marjorie shows the fieriness of the Barker characters needled by a sense of existential pathos and in turn prepared to needle those around, the bland beaming human sandbags who tend to proclaim 'I like this life' rather than sense thwarted human potential and seek change. To draw another Shavian parallel, *My Sister and I* is sometimes redolent of *Misalliance* with its stifling hothouse atmosphere where the intellectual insults of a submissive routine are compounded by an unjust and disastrous distribution of familial and political power, until a farcical revolutionary crashes in to reinforce, with comic ineptitude, the critiques advanced by a woman with a taste for dangerous living.

Barker's Mick Girton is a modern counterpart to Shaw's Julius Baker, but like Kevin in *Skipper* he experiences a fluctuation in his murderous resolve ('No wonder you lot always win, we're too humane!'); though this is hardly surprising considering the personal pique and thwarted careerism which are subsequently proved to fuel his Marxist-jargon ardour, which is in his case an avoidance of basic human consequences compared to Marjorie's passionate insistence upon them. Marjorie has experienced the shortcomings of repressive desublimation — 'contrary to popular belief, sex is not a substitute for power!' — and she tries to infuse Mick's avowed passion for regicide with sexual passion. However, Mick's resolve characteristically falters and he and Marjorie are united in nothing but frustration; Marjorie for her 'dream of a sexual goddess' monarch, 'riding through seas of semen, vicious, spurred and merciless!'; Mick for the fact that, given the continuous postponement of proletarian insurrection, his mum will never see him in a suit:

MICK: ... The whole degree system's a farce! When I wrote off saying I'd passed my degree and would appreciate an interview at their earliest convenience, I got a letter from the tea-boy telling me to sign on down the dole. He had a Ph.D. himself. Naturally I was bitter. I realized this society is finished. I saw the need for total change!

MARJORIE: I blame the Queen.

MICK: She's just a symptom. It's the inbuilt contradictions of the final stage of capitalism —

MARJORIE: No, take my word for it. It's her.

The play thus initiates a characteristic Barker movement of the collusion of former enemies who perceive a point of common sympathy, suffering or in this case a comic frustration which is nonetheless grounded in recognisable pain. Marjorie attempts to focus Mick's blame on Liz and a slightly ludicrous notion of her autocratic political initiative; she also wins the support of a chauffeur who has previously expressed contempt for the modern 'farce of royalty' and yearns for the primeval grandeur of a savage Regina to whose interests he can submit. He readily agrees to crash the royal car to permit her usurpation (dreaming on 'England reborn ... through my supreme sacrifice'). Marjorie is also conscious of her actions' historical repercussions ('The little princes in the tower won't get a look in from now on') and Mick views it as a fillip to his dreams of status (to be published as 'My Glimpse Behind the Veil of History' by Mick Girton, BA). In something of a small-scale comic anticipation of Hogbin in *The Bite of the Night*, however, he draws back from the human cruelty their scheme involves to progress, drifting into horrified visions of 'limbless half-wits' with 'offensive stumps'. Marjorie is unrepentant, but once in power and forgiven by the typically saintly and boring ghost of Liz, she senses a lack of direction — 'The trouble with gestures is, they're so short-lived'. Her disgust seems in retrospect to have been more sensational than radical. She reinstates Liz as puppet ruler, with help from Mick in his new career of taxidermy. Marjorie is left in a trough of isolated ennui, begging Armstrong: 'I'm sorry I'm so clever ... will you forgive me ... ?'

Whereas in *Skipper* the characters tended to people an analysis and fulfil a paradigmatic structure, in *My Sister and I*, Barker expands his figures, imbuing Marjorie with a consciously surprising temperament and a linguistic power to be relished; even Mick is amusing and appealing in his copiously detailed fits of frustration and remorse. This new ease in permitting the characters to voice their idiosyncratic enthusiasms in jets of ingenious detail gives free rein to their individual imaginative worlds and their methods of constructing them, bringing them closer to the audience and liberating Barker's own verbal powers in their service, so that the writing flares with unapologetic energy which owes nothing to spurious, fettering concepts of naturalism which still dog the sporadic flatnesses of *No One Was Saved*.

Thus, with increasing confidence in surprising characterisation and distinctive verbal extravagance, Barker's early stage plays examine networks of social dependency in which the contrary individual impulse to independence is grounded. However, this independence has to be expressed in social terms, unless you wither into the position of solipsistic recluse like Herman in *Herman, with Millie and Mick*. To interact with others and to stand apart from them, we require a sense of self, initially furnished by the family and subsequently established through autonomy, which capitalist society recognises in terms of power, manifested in the inextricably linked spheres of money and sexuality. Many of the plays' protagonists fail to appreciate the extent or full ramifications of the link, or the partiality of their own models of associating with others, or the interests which these models serve and perpetuate. The working class are bemused and stricken by the skilful playing of ruling-class music and pageantry.

Stripwell is an anomaly: his social position is privileged from the outset, though he tries to demonstrate his independence from its ramifications, and from the limitations of his familial role, through new initiatives of sexual and moral response; but he is doomed to failure, like the other characters, because his revolt is insufficiently fundamental. The other exceptions to the trapped underdog characters are Eddie, victim and perpetrator of the repressive family who shapes the country in its image but with a significant lack of personal relief, and Marjorie, whose revolt against social and familial hierarchical networks is shown to be more rebellious than revolutionary.

The next series of Barker plays present more complex models of individual interaction, often centring on individuals struggling to reconcile their institutional settings or roles with an ideal which remains tantalisingly but agonisingly out of reach. The exploration of the relationship between power and desire, and the existential consequences of their disjunction, proceeds through social settings of a wider range, but remains mindful of the decisive influences of personal appetites.

4

Between Two Worlds

WAX, HEROES OF LABOUR, FAIR SLAUGHTER, THAT
GOOD BETWEEN US, CREDENTIALS OF A SYMPATHISER,
THE HANG OF THE GAOL, BIRTH ON A HARD SHOULDER,
THE LOUD BOY'S LIFE, DOWNCHILD

Wandering between two worlds, one dead,
The other powerless to be born

> Matthew Arnold; epigraph to *That*
> *Good Between Us*

But there is always this yawning gulf between what you know
and what you do about it.

> *Birth on a Hard Shoulder*

The Collins New National Dictionary (1959) defines 'institution' as
'an organised pattern of group behaviour established and generally
accepted as a fundamental part of a culture, such as slavery'; and
'ideal' as '*a*. existing in fancy only; satisfying desires; — *n*. an imaginary type or norm of perfection to be aimed at'. Barker's plays of
the late 1970s reflect the contemporary political climate in their fundamental sense of the disjunction between social institutions and
the ideals which they ostensibly embody, of the individual's alienation from the real and severance from the possibility of the ideal.
His principal characters are shown in conflict with the institutions
they encounter or represent, straining towards reformulations of
possibility, however inarticulated, dimly sensed or doomed to failure; or they are middlemen caught in a crossfire between largely
anonymous institutional forces, incapable of associating themselves
permanently with either side. This may provide fragile reassurance
of human resistance to theoretical rigour, but also bodes ill for their
chances of worldly success or survival in a climate which demands
this submission of self. In reply, the institutions bolster their own
insecurities with brutal demonstrations of power.

Wax (staged 1976) depicts an eponymous British general supposedly in charge of part of a NATO exercise in North Germany, whose concentration on military leadership is broken and refocused on his experience of a monstrous and uncharacteristic erection ('I'm sixty years old. The last time I had one of these was at a polo match at Guildford, Army v. Police, in 1924'), which he attributes to the presence of his niece Helen, whom he has not seen for 15 years. She is appalled by his fixation and solicitation for relief, but Wax can think of nothing else. Meanwhile, the other military personnel wait around for Wax's decisive commands in a parallel state of figurative impotence, particularly the shocked and ineffectual liberal lieutenant Truelove, who fears for the continuing viability of Operation Barrelscraper ('It was called Happy Family, but when the Norwegians and the Yanks dropped out they changed the name'), and Bannister, a strategist calculating implied civilian casualties ('He's got a little slide-rule which tells him how long the population will put up with it before they give up and join the Reds. At the moment it's eleven minutes twenty-seven seconds'). This triangular configuration of Wax, Helen and the military intelligence — raging personal appetite, shocked resistance and precise calculation rendered hopelessly askew and redundant by the local impingement of such factors — seems set for forcible resolution when Wax rapes Helen, but even after this eruption of personal violence amid the abstract calculation, and amid Helen's grief and Truelove's stunned transfixion, Wax remains tumescent, wracking him with fear for his personal physical health. An American General appears to declare the failure of the exercise, involving four fatalities, and tries to cover the central human factors in secrecy with sparse consolation for Helen:

A political rape is more or less the same as an ordinary rape, by which I mean, you couldn't be expected to appreciate the difference, but there is a qualitative distinction nevertheless, bestowed upon it by its context, and the context in this case is . . . It's NATO! For Christ's sake it's the freedom of the West! It's protecting our way of living, it's the free world and its credibility! And that credibility cannot will not shall not be undermined by the considerations of your prudery!

The straining logic whereby violation is equated with the protection and credibility of the free world, and a resistance and insistence on personal right is equated with prudery, is illustrated with agitprop or morality play simplicity, but Barker's portrayal of Wax's ludicrous fascination with his anthropomorphised, nodding erection and of Helen's pain are shock attempts to make the audience confront the specifically human basis and consequences of the exercise which, in their political reverberations, threaten to become almost unrecognisable under the official line of misinformation. But the characters and arguments in the play outstay their welcome, so persistently are their demands and reactions explored, and the audience may just shut off their responses. Also, in *Wax*, as in many plays considered in the last two chapters, our viewpoint tends to be that of Truelove — the transfixed stare of the humanist victim in the superior gaze of the miscreant, mute witness to his ravages.

The unproduced television play *Heroes of Labour* (published 1976) seeks to dramatise this problematic position with particular attention to the camera's ability to restrict and focus vision. Victor Shosterberg is a property dealer with a budding career in politics, Gloria his mistress with a budding tumour of breast cancer which Victor pays for her to have removed, but then he claims a loss of sexual interest in her following the mastectomy. Shosterberg trains his black rent collector Dawkins in applied intimidation, but his employee outstrips even his expectations and demands in terms of inspired viciousness, which meets its greatest test in expunging the clamours of an ageing Stalinist tenant, Dockerill, and prompts Gloria to attempt his enlistment to assist her revenge on Shosterberg.

The characters often address the camera directly to justify their positions: Shosterberg gives the audience the benefit of his personal philosophy, distinguishing between their lazy gawping and his competitive energy which marks them out as losers and winners respectively ('I happen to believe in enterprise. Which is another word for getting on. And that's not easy in this day and age. No one wants you to get on. Anyone who makes a fortune nowadays is a bloody hero'). He later practises his party political broadcast to camera, generalising his philosophy to 'the ordinary people of this country' whose interests he professes to serve as their humble agent.

Gloria rides the tide of the existing order with her vanity sated — 'I love this life. I love class' — reminiscing to camera about her first meeting with Shosterberg and her consciousness of her own allure. Dawkins is notable and unsettling in his marked absence of justification and tendency to describe himself with the distinctly and crucially external rhetoric of moral censure, insisting with imaginative lucidity on his own coldly mechanical malignity ('My Oxford honours were in spite, maliciousness and acts of utterly gratuitous violence'), possibly attributable to brain damage.

Dawkins's professions of cold-bloodedness expose unsettlingly the implicit condemnation in descriptions of amorality, to which he does not subscribe: he freely describes himself as 'abnormal', committing violent assaults for a consciously disproportionate 'vague feeling of discontent' to emphasise 'I have no idea what guilt is . . . I'd do almost anything. I really am beyond control'. These 'negative' definitions are rarely applied by a speaker to him- or herself; when this occurs, it becomes apparent that the ostensible volunteering of information expected from speech is denied, as Dawkins's self-descriptions demonstrate how a morality which cannot contain him, cannot explain him — he uses its discourse with no faith in its boundaries and so exposes its subjectivity and fragility. Correspondingly, the camera fastens onto close-ups of his face with unconventional insistence for us to attempt to reconcile voice with image — the televisual norm, but here again its rules of discourse are undermined by depriving the audience of the prevalent imagistic variety and its automatic reconciliation with the enactment of dramatised speech.

Thus the audience may come to feel themselves in the presence of characters with an inordinate control in terms of addressing them, and a lack of their own conventional understanding of characters and a lack of distance from the consequences of their actions; by implication, they are placed in the position of one of Shosterberg's intimidated tenants, such as Dockerill, whose self-consciously heroic marshalling of Stalinist rhetoric is undercut by the failure of his hoarded, faulty ammunition. Dawkins turns the old man's corroded armament cache against him by rolling rusty grenades towards him, with initially terrifying effect which gives way to boredom, even for Dockerill, as they successively refuse to explode, until an eventual latent possibility of combustion is suggested when Dockerill's *speech and expression freeze for several seconds. To the loud accompaniment of martial music, cut in a few seconds of Marshal Stalin reviewing the Red Army, then cut*.

After this, Dawkins seems cut adrift from his role as Shosterberg's agent — not because of remorse but on account of a new sense of destructive, anarchic possibilities — which Gloria attempts to harness for her own vengeance on Shosterberg, who is ironically outlining his belief in 'freedom' during intercuts to camera, but this freedom is 'freedom of enterprise . . . To earn yourself a fortune and be proud of it!', the illusory or limited independence offered on the terms of capitalist competition. Gloria and Dawkins imprison Shosterberg in a sack, and Dawkins makes a brief announcement to camera in close-up: 'I have had a traumatic experience. Consequently anything that I may do can be explained in terms of damage to my psyche. What I have a right to expect is sympathy. Thank you' (72). Sensing the prelude to personal danger, Shosterberg attempts to remain collected:

If this is some attempt to show that those who live by violence will die by it, all right, get it over with. I'll even make a goodbye speech. All right?
The camera closes on the hooded head
I have absolutely no regrets. I just had the bad luck to employ a crooked bloke. The fact remains that in this life, as long as human nature's what it is, the means will always justify the ends.
Pause.
Shall I go on?
Pause.
My mother died of cancer and my dad of galloping TB. We were so poor and terribly deprived that I was allowed to have two bottles of school milk a day. My arse was out of my trousers.
Pause.
And all this is irrelevant.
Long pause.   (74–5)

Cruelty is inimical to rationalisation, as Dawkins knows and proves throughout. Gloria begins to sense her lack of control over him, and Shosterberg realises the lack of any right of appeal in the presence of this wilfully amoral force; his surface calm splinters into terror as the play concludes:

Pause, then DAWKINS *turns to the camera.*
DAWKINS: The act of violence, removed from its social context, is an act of the unbalanced mind.
SHOSTERBERG: (*Fearful and out of vision, the camera staying on* DAWKINS) Gloria, ring the police!

DAWKINS: The rehabilitation of the mentally disturbed rests on their recognition of a social role.
SHOSTERBERG: (OOV) Ring 999!
DAWKINS: (To Camera, with an expression of joy) Dawkins is born! He raises a flick knife before his face and releases the blade. Cut to black.
(75–6)

Thus, in *Heroes of Labour,* we encounter for the first time in Barker's work an unassimilable challenge to the exploitative profiteer. Limitations are discovered in the apparently all-extensive powers of the privileged class, but the violent counter-response is not initiated by anything as pat or sentimental as Dockerill's ideology informing Dawkins's explosive potential, playing a successful Biledew to the black's Claw; rather, Dockerill and Dawkins remain destructively polarised (like Albert and Kevin in *Skipper*), as Dockerill's Red Army myths and ammunition have not survived into the present. Dawkins wanders between the worlds of Shosterberg and Dockerill, thesis and antithesis, until he perceives the possibility of his own existentially authentic action, in which he is answerable to no other person, institution or ideal — that includes those encoded in the dominant language of televisual discourse, which *Heroes of Labour* so deliberately and originally flouts. And Barker's world is no longer peopled only by privileged predators and hypnotised victims. Dawkins flies in the face of humanist assumptions and Stalinist neo-rationalism by inflicting conscious violence with a dark purity of intent, having discovered from killing Dockerill what he is, in fact, capable of. His final action might be described as evil or Jacobean in some circles, but Dawkins has been determined throughout to expose the insufficiency of morality's evaluative terminology if one does not happen to subscribe to its rules. The confidence trick is blown apart.

Fair Slaughter (staged 1977) boasts a surge of confidence and invention in the wake of *Heroes of Labour's* more local breakthroughs, expanding them into major themes. The Stalinist anachronism Dockerill provides the basis for the more developed figure of Old Gocher; an anomalous grotesque in the television play's landscape informs the evolution of a more poignant and pathetic figure permanently struggling to reconcile his life's experiences, through force and hope, with his commitment to the Communist ideal, symbolised by the startling talisman of the severed hand of Trotsky's engine driver.

The play's title implies its challenge to liberal humanism — Barker: 'the worst aspect of humanism is its rejection of blame, the idea we are all guilty. A wicked, paralysing posture'.[1] Rather, Barker and Gocher (and subsequently Bela and Galactia) are concerned to insist that certain people are demonstrably more to blame than others for the perpetuation of social injustices, and that the platitudes of the Christian-humanist tradition which define value, ethics and art also serve as a defence of existent hierarchies of social privilege. The civilisation and respect preached by arch-capitalist Staveley in *Fair Slaughter* are as partial in their ultimate manifestations as the limited independence permitted by capitalism as part of a divisive competition and repressive tolerance. The persistence of this situation depends upon crippling the confidence of the oppressed through internalised guilt and suggesting that it is hubristic or uncharitable on their part to assume the rights of judgement over their oppressors, who reserve the right to such powers.

Dramatically, *Fair Slaughter* establishes another Barker characteristic, the unconventional range and speed of movement in and between scenes, relying particularly on the rhythm and inventiveness of verbal exchanges to compel the audience's attention through a course of denied expectations and headlong charges at a conventionally inordinate number of 'large issues' with conceptual daring and nimbleness which demonstrate firm control beneath the surface of breathtaking speed. Rarely asked to work so hard, the audience may afterwards feel as if it has completed the theatrical equivalent of a switchback ride, charging through emotional and conceptual territory with an irregular high speed which is conventionally deemed impossible; but those prepared to suspend resistance (and Barker makes few concessions to those who are not) experience an exhilaration and challenge of unusual totality.

The play opens with Old Gocher, England's oldest living murderer, exciting the curiosity of his gaoler Leary by his bids to secrete the severed hand, and intercuts throughout with scenes of Gocher's youthful self, to which Gocher sees the hand as the symbolic link or key. Leary reductively assumes it is the relic of a sensational undiscovered murder ('in a prison, every little prejudice you have, it gets confirmed. And confirmed') but Gocher insists on trying to address Leary as a man, transcending their institutional positions, to awaken a recognition of a residue of idealism:

> For Christ's sake I am talking to you as a human being! Will you bring yourself down from there! Open yer fucking ears and listen to a man who's flesh and blood and chuck all this what you might do and might not because of your sodding uniform. I'm asking you to be a man and listen to me. Do you see that? It is never easy to be a man, but it is worth it, even for a minute. Try it. Open yer mind to me! (64)

Leary is duly intrigued and provides the chance for his and our introduction to the circumstances and driving forces of Gocher's life. We witness Young Gocher in the 1920s, a soldier with the British Expeditionary Force in post-revolution Russia, denounced by his complacent and self-righteous officer Staveley in the most demoniac terms because of his Communist beliefs; but pressure intensifies Gocher's commitment ('And in my bread and water I read GOCHER, IN THE FURNACE OF EXPERIENCE YOU HAVE FORGED AN IDEAL'). It is further compounded by a brief meeting with the Russian engine driver Tovarish, when the common idealism of the two 'opposing' soldiers allows them to transcend the national divisions and lurid moral cosmology which Staveley is seeking to establish. Staveley sanctions the murder of Tovarish, from whose body Gocher salvages the hand. Gocher discovers that Staveley is collecting his own icons, of looted property and artwork, while claiming for himself the status of an agent of civilisation, saving them for 'Man': 'They are Man in contemplation, in wisdom, serenity and repose, whereas you are Man in stinking sweat' (72).

Back in the present, Gocher has failed to pass on his politics to his daughter Moira, whose rebellion against an overbearing father has made her characterise independence and reasonableness as the province of the Right, convictions which she is defiantly handing down, as she tells:

> And then I was a teacher. All those rows of little heads. Not teenage fuck and scuffle, but big eyes you can shove ideas through. And I did. Jesus and Solzhenitsyn, the two big gentle people from the East. I had them screaming like a pack of Pavlov's dogs at strikers or trade unions. And why not? After what he'd

done to me with his whining at SOCIETY . . . I thought, you ignorant old sod, consumed with jealousy, you have no education, all
you've got is bitterness, you are sopping with it like an old incontinent.   (81)

Moira's reactionary views, cloaked in liberal humanist terms, lead
her to condemn her father as 'steaming with violence', but these
monochrome dissociations are given the lie through Old Gocher's
determination to strike a bond with Leary, relying on 'Pure truth.
A very fine oil, Leary, trickling down your earholes into your stiff
head, penetrating the clockwork of your indignation'. Gocher demonstrates how Leary's institutional role as gaoler exists at a debased
remove from his personal convictions; thus he exposes Leary's existential pathos, the lack of congruence between his ideal self and his
actual self: 'A man with a sense of Justice. Who thinks he finds it in
a gaol. A man who thunders at the raping of a kiddie, but has no
satisfaction from shoving the perpetrator down the stairs' (75).

In the intermittent flashbacks, Young Gocher is simultaneously
struggling to reconcile his desperate professional activities as a
street and music-hall entertainer, a popular singing tramp, with
the mute admonishments and pure resolve he associates with
Tovarish's bottled hand, ironically requisitioned to form an enigmatic central prop in his act. It is perhaps the exposure of this disjunction of inclinations which provides the climate for Leary to
throw in his lot with Old Gocher; in a turn of circumstances which
might have seemed fantastic or melodramatic in their most damning senses, Leary's striking a prison doctor with the bottled hand to
permit and join Gocher's escape occurs as relief. The leap from idealistic impulse to realistic action, from yearning to power, is made,
however comically — instead of being smothered, as is the norm.
Other circuits are closed, which had been painfully agape, by this
alliance: Old Gocher and Leary achieve reconciliation through hope
in human potential, in defiance of the divisive philosophy behind
the prison institution, echoing Young Gocher's sense of brotherhood with Tovarish; and Old Gocher has also transcended age barriers, finding in Leary a receptive pupil for his teachings, fulfilling
the hope which Moira disappointed.

The second half of the play, detailing Old Gocher and Leary's
flight, sets up a new opposition, as the first act's dynamic has been
resolved in their breakthrough to alliance. The second half locates a

new pathos in the disjuncture between the Southern English land-scape and Old Gocher's delusion that a mythic return to Russia is being completed, which Leary does not have the heart to disabuse him of. In parallel scenes from the 1930s, Young Gocher's self-loath-ing deepens at the contradictions between his anodyne clown act and his political impulses. He plans an outburst from the stage ('Stop smiling, it's not funny. It's a fucking tragedy. You and your wonderful good humour, your British talent for seeing it through, CHRIST! You would have your daughters in the brothel and still not lift a finger!', 84), but this self-expression is confined to the dressing-room, where his future wife Melanie questions his 'right' to such 'arrogance'. Young Gocher dismantles her liberal objections to show their implications:

> I have the right! Any man who has a vision has the right. Lenin had no right to kick the slob Kerensky, but he did it. There is too much chatter about rights. Always other people's rights. What about my rights? I claim the right, and balls to lawyers and pro-fessors and their sticky constitutions.   (84)

Staveley reappears as theatre manager, dictating terms to Young Gocher and objecting to his attitude towards his audience; Young Gocher physically quells him and pledges a new integrity, partially addressing the bottled hand and the youthful experiences from which he already perceives a shameful distance.

The parallel discrepancy for Old Gocher is between his heartfelt personal fantasia of a heroic odyssey back to Russia and the real-ity of suburban English railways on which he travels with Leary. This undercuts his fervent purpose, as in his ludicrous attempt at conversing with a bemused railway porter in pidgin German (though a tolerant sympathy is established if not an international understanding); but it shows the pathos of human hopes, in Old Gocher's occasionally tearful sense of personal futility and his mis-taken joy at finding what he takes to be the site of Tovarish's grave. The way Leary oversees, and even supports, such naked misin-terpretations of reality deliberately recalls *King Lear* and Edgar's conscious encouragement of blind Gloucester's clinging to a life-prolonging illusion of benign providence at 'Dover Cliffs': the effect is grotesque comedy shot through with a perception of deep human tragedy.

Young Gocher's struggles sound their own registers of pain, as in this attempted self-armouring against the tearings of loss when his wife leaves him:

> Finish with women! Finish with 'em! Easier said than done, of course, but possible. Has been done. Men have done it. Men with purpose. Men with work. *(Pause)* Had more than my share. More squirming tarts than I coud get my fingers up. As the Yodelling Tramp. Sliming up the dressing-room. Done everything. All that was possible. All that presented itself to the imagination of a normal man. *(Pause)* Just party work now. Like minds in the party. Not likely to damage you. The real intimacy of solidarity. *(Pause, then his face creases.)* MELANIE!   (92)

The way the final cry overturns the insistent effort of all its preceding speech makes for a cumulative force of pathos akin to the central effect of Beckett's *Krapp's Last Tape*, another dramatisation of sublimated energy and the final crushing realisation of its futility, where old and young selves confront each other, in a sudden illumination of lost ideals and forfeited love. In a subsequent monologue to his daughter, aged seven, Young Gocher likewise struggles for control over his indignation at their circumstances until his pain explodes in breakdown:

> LOOK WHAT THEY HAVE DONE TO ME BECAUSE I WOULD NOT PLAY THE BANJO TO THEIR BLOODY LIES! A FATHER AND A CHILD IN THIS DISGUSTING ROOM! LOOK AT THE FILTH THEY FLING US IN, THE BASTARDS, THE PARASITIC BASTARDS, THEY DRINK OUR BLOOD! I WILL KILL THEM, I WILL KILL THEIR BABIES, IT WILL BE A SLAUGHTER WHEN WE'VE FINISHED, A FAIR BLOODY SLAUGHTER, LET ME, GOD! *(He bursts into a fit of weeping, rocking back and forwards in his chair, hands to his face)* Daddy upset darling . . . sorry, darling, sorry, sorry, sorry, love . . .   (101)

In its full form, the build of this speech gives a range to the actor, and provides opportunities for sympathetic engagement for an audience, in advance of anything Barker has written before *Fair Slaughter*; new depths of emotion are being sounded in both.

The crosscutting movement of the play mobilises many reverberative ironies and juxtapositions of images, as when the sight of Old Gocher and Leary scrambling about on the South Downs looking for

Tovarish's grave dissolves into Young Gocher deciding to name his daughter 'in a fashion appropriate to the historic condition', rejecting Elizabeth after the queen in favour of a reflection of contemporary certainty that after World War Two 'there will be communism in these islands because our soldiers are not just going to hand their rifles back'; hence the choice of the Greek name for Fate, Moira. However, we know what politics the mature Moira favours, and the vulnerability of Young Gocher's hope cuts to an informs Old Gocher's continued self-delusion of a reunion with Tovarish's body.

Young Gocher's vehement bid to ensure there are 'No more Staveleys in the world' by striking at the capitalist when they are imperilled together in a blitz warehouse fire, seems an act of stark, heroic definiteness, until Staveley reappears to Old Gocher and Leary on the South Downs, the powerful arch-enemy now withered to a dribbling idiot who has become separated from a party of inmates from an Eastbourne hospital. Leary acts as prosecution in an improvised trial, arguing with all his newfound Communist zeal and eloquence for the extermination of the unchangeable social parasite; Old Gocher argues for pity, and the unlikely allies pit their differing invocations of Tovarish's hand, and definitions of what the ideal demands, against each other:

LEARY: You are not fit to have Tov.
GOCHER: Christ, do not lose sight of your humanity! You have so much good in you!
LEARY: To be licked up by that specimen. To be sucked on by his class.
GOCHER: Keep an open heart, son. Feed your heart. The angrier you feel, the more you have to feed the heart!
LEARY: I do what Tov says!
GOCHER: Fuck him! He was an ordinary bloke, that's all! Think for yourself. They stuck Lenin under glass, and look what they have done in his name. (104)

Gocher's injunction 'criticize, always criticize' is distrusted by Leary as being tantamount to 'revise', as two interpretations of Communism clash, until Old Gocher is spirited away by death to a spectral reunion with the handless Tovarish, a final synthesis of sorts; but Leary's suspicion of Staveley persists, and the latter's final slobbering acquisitive glee over a pocketed Picasso print suggests that, however entrenched in (or by) insanity, greed is inextricably rooted in some humans up the point of death itself: a possible qualification of the impulse to pity. *Fair Slaughter's* subtle and provocative orchestration of scenes of faith and delusion allows the audience a richness of levels of response, and a new depth of engagement emerges for dramatist and audience alike. Its entwined comprehension of historical, political and emotional reference points establish Barker's characteristic strengths and terrain of enquiry, and results in his first great play.

That Good Between Us (staged 1977) presents a more lugubrious landscape, unenlightened by *Fair Slaughter's* qualified hopes or even its invigorating delusions. Set in Britain under a Labour government, 'perhaps slightly in the future', *That Good* takes as its epigraph Arnold's lines, 'Wandering between two worlds, one dead,/The other powerless to be born'. Appropriately, the play dramatises existential pathos at an institutionalised and national level, where impulse and action have fractured apart, then been roughly clamped together for the sake of appearances, while secretly becoming fundamentally infected and creepingly parasitic. In this wintry, bleeding world, Billy McPhee's simple human attitudes and appetites mark him as an ignorantly disruptive figure amid the institutionalised entropy. Appropriately enough, the play begins with the attempted execution of this unlikely and incompetent secret agent (a flash-forward to the penultimate scene of the play, in terms of linear narrative). McPhee is concerned, like Brecht's Schweik and Galy Gay, to be 'no trouble' to those around, whom he is actually predisposed to trust and admire, with a misplaced sense of wonder. About to be ordered out of a rowing boat to drown off the Devon coast, he fails to realise the import of the trip and expounds in amazement on how the nearest lighthouse floats on a bed of mercury. The accompanying police agents, Knatchbull and Bleach, pay tribute to his co-operation in the trip; but when the purpose of the excursion dawns on McPhee, he condemns them with his incongruous innocence ('Yoo'll go to hell, the pair of yoo') and determines to try to swim to land ('I've done a mile. I've got the fuckin' certificate to prove it!'). Bleach smashes at him with an oar and Billy protests 'Tha's nae fair! . . . Gi' us a chance! . . . Yoo fuckin' cheat!' (6).

This beleaguered faith in fair rules and sporting conduct provides a blackly ironic, semi-comic prologue, as the play introduces a set of soldiers reluctantly policing British streets and breaking strikes in a state of national emergency. One protester appeals to their class loyalty ('You are workers and you're attacking us!') before he is seized and denounced by riot police as one of the 'communists' who 'are ruining Britain'. But once alone, the men admit to their personal disgust at their function and hopes of a countermovement which they are forced to disguise, with cruelty if necessary; as their fellow-dissenter Major Cadbury acknowledges, 'Only the best of you will keep faith' (8).

Meanwhile the Labour Home Secretary Orbison is attempting to bolster her sense and appearance of benevolence, on which she depends at a national level, and extend it into her personal sphere of familial relations. She tries to effect a reconciliation with her surly daughter Rhoda, who steadfastly refuses to observe any rules of decorum, describing bids to heal the rift between mother and daughter as 'abortive'. The sense of deadlocked stasis is interrupted by Godber, a prospective spy motivated towards political activism by the inherent sense of hierarchy and deflected sadism of the English grammar school, and protective of his capitalist right to acquire commodities, the gaining and holding of which he rightly sees as being threatened by Communism. Godber is both appalling and recognisable in his wish to serve the interests of his social superiors: having found his society's promises to be empty ('I had been misled. Although I had the A levels I was not invited to become a leader of society. I did not even have a job'), he blames the nominated enemies of that society ('I will not be nobbled by the communists') for impeding its agents and the realisation of the ideal they promise, which flatters his vanity and demand for consumer choice.

Orbison paves the way for Godber's recruitment, while recognising his poverty of intellect and meanness of imagination; she nominates him as an example of people's 'inalienable barbarity' which disappoints her missionary instincts 'With a terrible consistency'. Rhoda however sees Godber as the product, rather than the justification, of Orbison's luncheon-voucher socialism which breeds and requires egocentric hedonism: 'It is not a democracy. It is a slavish cacophony . . . Not that I love them, or anything. The PEOPLE, I mean. I don't come at the whiff of a donkey jacket. I just cannot stand their apeing the likes of you. And treading on each other's faces' (14).

This vision of the country seems borne out by the beginning of the next scene in a London disco pub, where McPhee is subjecting a stripper to a tirade of extravagant abuse intended to compound and surpass even the humiliations of her professional contorted postures of surrender. Rather than reply in kind, she dismisses him with 'You dirt. You nothing dirt'. However, scorn cannot wither Billy, nor custom stale his infinite resilience and misplaced optimism. He becomes fascinated by Godber, whose laconically selfish air he misconstrues as alluring depth and imaginative autonomy. Godber also attracts the attention of Knatchbull, who believes Godber's grammar school education ('Not too much and not too little'), patriotism and addiction to personal 'thrill' make him ideally equipped to serve his government's interests. Thus McPhee and Godber are joined, for all their difference of appetites and (fatally restricted) degrees of awareness, seduced into dancing to their society's tune and furthering its interests for the promises it extends, without asking by whom, to what extent and to whose ends these promises are bestowed — a lack of insight and imagination which links them to the innocents of Barker's early plays, who fail to suspect that the rules of approved conduct and legitimate success are being rewritten around them, as they operate on a radius of ignorance from the real power centre of their world.

Orbison and her minion Knatchbull may represent this central power but enjoy little sense of comfort; it is as if the society itself has assumed malign animation and runs them, in turn. Orbison is still unable to attain any equilibrium with Rhoda, who points out the limitations of private goodness: 'the creature who ran Auschwitz was a perfect family man' (22). As Orbison admits to Knatchbull: 'Our system relies entirely on consent. On confidence'; 'There is a danger we are making an obsession out of conspiracy' with the effect of breeding 'a race of agents provocateurs', 'monstrosities' who have mutated beyond control. When Knatchbull replies 'We are only acting in response', Orbison exposes the moral and ideological vacuity of the statement, which only serves to make action self-justifying and self-perpetuating. She attempts to stay personally mindful that a point must not occur when 'the scaffolding obliterates the edifice' (an image which foreshadows *The Castle*, the fortified stronghold's self-perpetuation and control of its denizens). Orbison maintains, 'Don't do violence to language or you will end up doing violence to people' (24) and objects to the last-ditch prospect of military dictatorship. Knatchbull telescopes the mutual justification of violence and language in one phrase: 'the army is the army, Mrs Orbison!' (25).

While Orbison strives to preserve faith in the referentiality of language as part of an essential chain of humanism, Knatchbull inhabits the practical world where words have broken loose from their moorings. Words become mere sounds, blank counters to be used in the strategies of power, as when Knatchbull makes McPhee repeat his 'Woof, Woof!' noises to indicate his complicity in a game where the rules are never specified. Even Knatchbull is driven to invoke the terms of popular myths, such as the innocence of children, when the consequences of the destabilised society spill over onto Wimbledon Common, where his paraplegic daughter discovers the corpse of a dissenting soldier. Knatchbull tries to maintain control of terms of reference, but the significantly named Verity demonstrates that her eyes and imagination have crucially avoided incapacitation; her constricted body provides a visual counter-image to her unconstricted mind:

VERITY: Shot through the head.
KNATCHBULL: Don't look.
VERITY: Through the back of the head.
KNATCHBULL: He's sleeping, that's all. You wait over there.
VERITY: Was he tortured?
KNATCHBULL: Pick some flowers. Make daddy a daisy chain.

      .   .   .

VERITY: Are those cuts made with razors, do you think? *(Pause)* Or
   bowie knives?
He looks at her a moment, then goes to her, takes her head in his hands and
   pulls her to him.
KNATCHBULL: No childhood. *(Pause)* No proper bloody childhood
   any more.   (31)

The Corpse refutes Knatchbull's professed ignorance of where he came from or how he died, and delivers Verity the injunction 'TELL SOMEBODY ABOUT MY PAIN!' (32) (foreshadowing the alarming and indignant revenant of *Don't Exaggerate*); but Verity is persuaded away, with the promise of an ice-cream.

Problems of formulation and referentiality also beset the counterforce to the government, the Democratic Movement of the Army, which is stumbling into existence in a pub run by an ex-prostitute friend of Major Cadbury, who won her affections and complicity with the proposition that 'nothing that is human is degrading, except we make it so' (33). However, Cadbury arrives in a different frame of mind:

CADBURY: I hate the body. The bloody thing is dying even in the
womb.
.   .   .
NADINE: You treat your body right, and It'll do the same by you.
CADBURY: Unfortunately, that is not the case. There is a terrible
injustice in constitutions. Not just political ones.   (34–5)

Use of the terms 'treason' and 'conspiracy' is debated by the soldiers, attempting to define their own activity and status, though Cadbury takes exception to 'conspiracy':

CADBURY: As soon as we think of ourselves as one, we will
become one. And then we will become a cell. Cells are private
and exclusive. I am not in favour of cells and I am not in favour
of exclusion.
TELLING: A subversive group must have a structure —
CADBURY: I hate this text-book phraseology! I am sick of the
Soviet example and the Algerian example. Let us do this our
way!   (35)

When Godber appears on a mission of infiltration, the audience will remember his introductory speech of self-justification from its previous deployment to Orbison. Its replay — with crucial adjustments — recalls Noel's eponymous speech in *Claw* and the telling shift of antagonism and personal potential it achieves in its second and final version. However, Godber is here using his personal grounding of discontent to inform a consciously deceptive difference of supposed response to thwarted appetites: 'I will not be nobbled by the capitalists'. The fact that the soldiers are convinced by this reflects badly on their own articulation of revolutionary motive: Godber's complaining that no one is in a position to own small estates and that moreover no one invited him to become a leader of society are dubious foundations for a belief in communism! McPhee plays his role even more cack-handedly, desperately nominating immigration policy as his basic grievance with the government. Cadbury attempts to dissociate freedom from privilege, or the personal license for which Billy takes it; at this time, 'Freedom is saying no', but McPhee is hopelessly confused.

Orbison and Knatchbull continue their self-justifying double act: Orbison maintains her increased police powers are exceptional, Knatchbull insists the situation is extraordinary. Knatchbull further comforts himself with his eradication of the questioning instinct: for him the end is all. When the intransigent Verity complains at the extent of their meagre garden compared to Orbison's, Knatchbull is driven to invoke a concept of natural injustice: 'Look, either you own things or you don't! It's like blue eyes. Either you have them or you don't. It's like spina bifida, either you get it or you don't!' (42). Thus, he claims to have found 'the quality of serenity. I bow to the inevitable. I am a man who is going to make old bones' (44), but has once more reckoned without the impingement of Verity's excited observation of the unexpected within this ostensibly placid world. She has witnessed Godber copulating with Rhoda on the tennis lawn, an event which seems to fortify the would-be special agent's sense of himself as ladykilling cynic with liberatingly laconic poise *à la* James Bond; even Knatchbull is impressed by his assumption and justification of the role ('I love your words. I think you string together lovely words . . .').

While Godber prides himself on cynicism, McPhee has swallowed the idealism of the Democratic Movement with alarming and somewhat ludicrous, if faintly touching, wholeheartedness; he now recognises himself as victim of a ruling class conspiracy: 'I wanna tell yoo what it means to look at mysel' in the mirror an' say, Billy, there are reasons yoo are the worm yoo are. To know tha'! It's like a puppet seein' it's got strings!' (47). This would verge on parody of Noel's political development in *Claw* were it not for the complete absence of vanity in McPhee which lends his simple professions surprising conviction; Godber, in contrast, is egocentric in his wish, like other dazzled characters in early Barker plays, to be a 'star' within the terms of the system, ideally sprinkled with the added glamour of rebel chic. He rejoices in social vertigo and the breakdown of verbal and moral referentiality for the opportunities of heroism and personal advancement afforded; as Eric Mottram points out, his thrilled anticipation is conducted in the language of science fiction and disaster movies:[2] 'The Big Dipper goes out of control. Monsters break loose. Monsters widely believed to be extinct' (48). Rhoda's similar taste for sliding categories harks back to her consciously 'corrupt' action in copulating with Godber, doing something just because your mother wouldn't' (43); her rebellion against Orbison is increasingly identified as simply that — less political critique than a family-oriented predilection for the short-lived, sensational gesture (like Marjorie in *My Sister and I*) which vindicates Orbison's early reading of her actions:

> You have to be so careful with disgust. It is so deceptive, it often tricks you into thinking it is radical. When all the time it is some strangled cry for feeling at any price. Which is not the same thing is it?   (22)

When the members of the Democratic Movement attend the funeral of their murdered colleague, their unity is splintered over the degree and manner of speech that is appropriate to mark his passing; while Cadbury maintains a circumspect attitude, Telling plans outraged oratory:

CADBURY: This is no time for heroics.
TELLING: It's not heroics, it's a speech!
CADBURY: You are after being a legend. You want to be a drunk's song. Show a little dignity.
TELLING: You and your dignity. You cannot run a revolution on your dignity!   (50)

Telling insists on shouting his outrage, despite the lack of any effect beyond incriminating the mourners, more 'feeling at any price'; Knatchbull, observing, finds this a damning reflection on the Democratic Movement's grasp of political realities ('And they want to run the country. They have aspirations to running England . . .'). He notes the sentimentality of Telling's bawled elegy as a failing of style: 'Have they never heard of Churchill? He could speak'. McPhee continues his personal odyssey of disappointment and awareness; political Pinocchio that he is, he storms with outrage at not being arrested with the other members of the Democratic Movement, as his 'cover' of sympathy has now shaped his true convictions. This plain congruity is embarrassing amid the duplicity and double-speak and prompts Knatchbull's decision to have him 'de-commissioned'.

ORBISON: You mean you want to kill him?
KNATCHBULL: ME? I don't.
ORBISON: Not personally, but you want him killed.
KNATCHBULL: I hate this 'killed'.

ORBISON: KNOCKED OFF! MURDERED! PUT TO DEATH! ...
There is so much abstraction in this business. We have to get
back to the personal pronoun. Stop hiding in the semantic
wood ...   (53)

Orbison laments the discrepancy between impulse and manifestation, deed and official word, but her wish for 'the personal pronoun' exposes the despair and dictatorship beneath her image of
consensus benevolence:

One gets this poisonous longing to just get on with it and RULE.
In a human manner, but in person. Cut through the shit. I firmly
believe that honesty and power are not compatible because the
people one is ruling are themselves not honest. That is not pessimism or manicheism, it is a fact.   (53)

But there is a forceful dramatic counter to the way she manoeu-
vres herself into a conviction of personal purity when a Council
Employee decries her social democratic 'stability': 'I was digging
when I first voted and I'm digging now. What has voting done for
me?' (54). This effectively demonstrates the extent to which Orbison
takes refuge in abstraction and hides in her own semantic wood of
self-justifying ideals: she cannot talk to the man, ignores him and
eventually walks away, compounding his anger.

With grim inevitability, McPhee's 'mate' Godber lures him into
a trap; while Bleach applauds Godber's efforts, even Knatchbull
is shocked by his ruthlessness, and senses a comparative sympathy for McPhee, expressed with characteristic circularity of logic:
'If you look at history there have been times when people seemed
to sink down very low. I think this must be one of them ... I'm
sorry, Billy, it must be the situation, you see. That's to blame for
your situation' (58). But it is Godber and Rhoda that perish, at the
hands of the Democratic Movement who erupt into the apparent
calm of a Devon village demanding retribution, like Cargill at the
end of *Stripwell*; moreover, the Movement seem to have learnt some
tricks from Knatchbull's self-serving fractures of formal terminology in justification of violent ends, when they shoot the couple
before asking in unison: 'The Sentence of the Court of the Democratic Movement is death. Have you anything to say?' McPhee
survives the drowning attempt witnessed in Scene One, to his own
astonishment, and as an improbable but theatrically gratifying,

limited redress to the play's intensifying climate of apparent pessimism, which seems to suggest 'Do not despair: one of the thieves was saved'.

This is not to suggest that Billy's survival is a melodramatic sop to the audience's sense of natural order, or, in itself, grounds for optimism. Barker has placed distinct barriers in the way of easy allocations of sympathy toward McPhee, notably his abuse of the stripper and his complicity in a re-enacted gang rape, so there is little room left for the idea of him as an 'angel, disguised as a tartan yob', to use Godber's mocking phrase. But his pitiful attempts to assert his homosexual love for Godber testifies to his apparent compulsion to place faith in something or someone now at least developed from thuggery to communist idealism, though we are not shown for how long or with what results.

That Good Between Us does not present a heroic world; the chill wind of ubiquitous disappointment that blows through it is doubtless testimony to its evolution in the debased 'social democracy' of the Wilson era. The strained logic and official misinformation of *Wax* finds a place of eminent national influence and control in the figure of Knatchbull, who is the reality of Orbison's political idealism. Though disaffected and dissociative, McPhee holds little of the danger of Dawkins in *Heroes of Labour* when he becomes similarly dislocated from sustaining his agent role; like Leary in *Fair Slaughter*, his conversion from being instrumental within the system to becoming its Communist critic is no matter for relief, as Knatchbull and his agents are likely to 'act in response' with all their available powers. The Democratic Movement themselves have little of the persuasiveness, integrity and celebratory openheartedness of Old Gocher. The prevalent mood of *That Good* is of dark irony, as only the audience are privy to all parts of the play's spheres and movements of events. The characters' awarenesses of their own part of the pattern, and its relation to the whole, is limited. They are fragments of the chaos, only capable of restricted knowledge and action. Even those like Godber who identify with the system fall victims to its ravages, as it outstrips even its darlings in predatoriness. The violence to people and to language in official interests — which Orbison perceives but ultimately depends on and is controlled by — seems part of an irrevocable slide into mayhem. Fragile consolation is that McPhee still looks for good deeds in naughty worlds, and that chance occasionally spills benefits.

McPhee and even Godber are characters caught in a crossfire, perhaps a model for much British social life, drifting between dead values and unborn ideals, where the fists holding institutional power grasp it so greedily that the very age is stagnant and sterile, or at worst an ideological miscarriage. Even operating within and against a system involves using its terminology, the dilemma debated by Telling and Cadbury; Godber plasters himself with images of James Bond and Keith Moon, McPhee takes recourse to Rolling Stones songs when events turn threatening.

'His style is all of him' — this is the intended withering pronouncement of an Irish Republican soldier on the British negotiator Gildersleeve in the unproduced television play *Credentials of a Sympathiser* (performed in a reading 1979). Gildersleeve in turn prides himself on the real tactical efficacy of style as a hallmark of unsettling self-assurance, unshakeable 'unstoppable maturity'; he reflects that the Republican 'has nothing but his exhibitionism to pit against our polish and stability' (82), and that the British government's annexing of sharply decorous dress implicitly drives the Republicans into a counter-uniform, 'The raggedness of phoney populism' (78). As the two sides meet for negotiations, contractor Alfred Hacker and assistant Clout try to weave between them, cleaning the meeting place and organising catering; outside of the negotiating room, the soldiers of both opposing sides tolerate each other uneasily, debarred from knowledge of higher-level debate while being the first to feel its consequences. The business opportunity which Hacker so relishes is a product of Gildersleeve's determination to have the hall 'spick' and impress a sense of order upon the Republican delegates; thus Hacker also deals in, and is constituted by, 'style', inhabiting what he believes to be a world of commercial opportunities rather than political sympathies: 'This has got to look good, Clout . . . These are our credentials. Seize the time, all right?' (64).

Gildersleeve securely believes that style denotes authority; just as he fondly recalls the efficiency of an immaculately groomed ticket inspector enforcing a no-smoking railway regulation, compared to a semi-apologetic 'slovenly' guard, he looks forward to attending negotiations 'Appearing like star actors from our dressing rooms. And them all creased and sweaty from their car'. But rather than Godber's power fantasies in *That Good,* this sense of 'star actor' capabilities is associated in *Credentials* with successful, distinctly English (self-)perception and stage-management of events in government interests. The precisely and distinctly English quality and interests of 'the English language' are identified as a further tool to this end, as used by the government representatives; the Republicans refute the labels 'terrorist' ('That is their word. They are the terrorists') and 'criminal'. Gildersleeve acknowledges 'The word is our word. For men who have been convicted by due process of law. You have your interpretation, we have ours' (89); but language mediates and implicitly colours the concepts with which senses of reality are constructed, shared or not (for example, the concept of a 'due process of law'). As the Republican negotiator Ducker recognises, 'Ever since we came here we have used their words . . . Their words are their secret weapons. We have to fight their language too';[3] the language itself reinforces a sense of reality and implicit authority — 'You English. You are all so English' (90). Even Gildersleeve's ostensibly 'helpful' re-labelling of prisoners and detainees with the nonsense word 'buzz' carries the tactical advantage of overlaying the men's principles with trivialising absurdity.

As the Democratic Movement of *That Good* discovered, even opposition to a system involves the use of its terminology, which carries implicit attitudes, yet has to be used for the sake of communication beyond the cell. Whereas Knatchbull operated in the deliberate moral vagueness of the semantic wood, and seemed something of a servant, if not victim, of his own processes, Gildersleeve uses language and boardroom tactics with forceful precision, counting the dials, levers, buttons and knobs of his discourse like a pilot in his cockpit, living out his fantasies and impulses of control. A fear of loss of control dominates Tully's private fantasies, across the other side of the negotiating tables: he imagines his imputed power to have permitted the seduction of a woman television journalist, a fatal lapse into a relish of personal style and sense of the figure he cuts, according to his former comrades, who appear to serve allegations ('You are so clean now . . . And your wardrobe, jammed with SUITS!'; 'After all the door panes he has shot through, the home is sacred suddenly!'). Charged in his nightmare with dissociating impulse from action, Tully shouts for the men to carry out his execution promptly — perhaps a last-ditch stab at the stoicism which he associates with male identity (as evidenced by his own memory of shooting British 'boy soldiers': '"Be good lads," I said, 'take it like men'. But they were not men, they were whimperers, which caused me to despise them', 75).

Outside the conference room, the British army and Republicans are attempting to lay the charge 'Mad dogs' to each other; the Brits describe the Republicans' sense of a cause as 'fanaticism', and the Republicans locate a madness in the dissociation of the British soldiers from their function: 'Tomorrow, they tell you — go and kill a Chinaman. On Friday, go and kill an African. On Saturday, a Jap. I call that mad. Mad dogs bite anyone' (91). But British Private Miller sees a 'purity' in the army's battle honours, the disinterest of a peace-keeping force of moral guardians, 'Against all your bleeding faith'. Correspondingly, Miller feels no guilt when he mistakenly shoots Hacker for a terrorist, maintaining that he shouted a challenge and followed proper procedures to the detail, 'So I've no cause to be ashamed' — thus highlighting the overriding function of a 'proper procedure' when observed by the person in full knowledge and command of it.

Hacker thought he could elude the two spheres of political reference by maintaining the 'omnipresent bottom line' of commercialism ('Terrorists may come and terrorists may go, but conferences will last forever. And the issuing of contracts to the likes of us', 81). Instead, he is forcibly defined by political forces as a 'sympathiser' where neutrality is seen as impossible. Hacker is, in effect, killed in a crossfire — as Miller and his companions, and the Republicans, may be later as a result in the breakdown in peace talks. Even Gildersleeve's assistant Amber operates from crucially limited knowledge and sacrifices his professional prospects by attempting to act upon it in order to call Gildersleeve's authority into question. Gildersleeve has characteristically dealt himself all the trumps: on the way home he reveals 'These talks were never taken seriously . . . Find out the compromisers. That's all we had to do'. And indeed, Tully has been earmarked as a weak link in the Republican chain, and Amber has exposed himself to 'irreparable harm' by this attempt at moral autonomy.

Credentials of a Sympathiser is a pithy companion piece to *That Good*, with a similar mood of dark irony in which the audience alone has access to all the characters' perspectives; though there is more of a sense of overriding control than in *That Good* because one character has control of all the threads of power, thus retaining mastery of events. The fact that this character is Gildersleeve is unsettling, as it implies the irrefutability of governmental control, especially when he holds the crucial knowledge of the nature of the talks, which the audience learn alongside Amber. In this respect, *Credentials* harks back to the 'confidence-trick' structures of early Barker plays, demonstrating the anatomical workings of repressive social authority and highlighting the element of 'confidence' — or, in this case, 'style' — which even a partially successful identification with its processes demands and accords. The limitations of *Credentials*, and of the early plays, are their comparative restriction of imaginative interest to engagement with those who pride themselves intellectually on running the game — or, more precisely, believe themselves to be running the game (Gildersleeve is comparatively rare, like Cheops in *One Afternoon*, in that he *really is* running the game of power as defined within the world of the play, making that world quite hermetically sealed). *Credentials* demonstrates how much of the action of the play and the society takes place over the head of Miller and his kind; it is not until Barker's portrayal of Ball in *Victory* that we encounter a full imaginative engagement with his position.

Jardine, the character at the fulcrum of *The Hang of the Gaol* (staged 1978), also drifts between dead values and unborn ideals as he investigates the self-justifying nature of social institutions. Jardine is a maverick, feisty ex-communist civil servant who does not believe in the surface manners of the system he serves and thus paradoxically seems one of its most effective agents; despite his institutional role he has a personal code, and the tension between the two naturally generates existential pathos. The modern malcontent's indignation extends to an element of self-hatred, a quality which marks characters of relative, if compromised integrity in Barker's plays (characters such as Bela, even Marjorie, compared to the self-satisfied hedonist leeches who proclaim they 'like this life' and their social position in it) When Jardine investigates arson at Middenhurst gaol, the governer Cooper recognises his iconoclastic potential and tries to impress it on his wife:

COOPER: Jardine is a Communist.
JANE: If we went back —
COOPER: Communist on opium.
JANE: Please, shall we just —
COOPER: Opium of hatred! *(Pause)*
JANE: Yes. All right.
COOPER: Listen. The man loathes himself.
JANE: Yes.

COOPER: Nothing worse. Nothing more likely to burst and scatter pain about. Never trust a man who hates himself.   (59)

The prison fire has prompted an inquiry, a phenomenon saliently glossed by the erudite screw, Udy:

> ... THE INQUIRY, Michael, protects you. Never was so much distance placed between a grievance and its object. Wrath dies from lack of nourishment, and revenge is withered by delay. Learn to love inquiries, Michael, for they love you. No one ever died from injuries received from two hundred pages of H.M. stationery.   (12)

The inquiry prompts the arrival at Middenhurst of Bloon and Dockerill, a camp symbiotic duo of the Fire Inspectorate who speak a restricted code so self-enclosed as to border on the telepathic; Stagg, fudging Wilsonian 'socialist' of a Home Secretary whose very appointment was a cynical compromise, who recognises with characteristic unruffled cheer that 'Inquiries are a sort of reflex aren't they? Something happens, bang, we have a load of geezers sipping gin and tonic while H.M. Government picks up the bill' (24); and the trio of investigators, Jardine of the battered, besieged but direct idealism ('I say shoot a man who abuses office'), the humanistic Guardian-reading tyro Ponting, and Matheson, who sees into Jardine's tensions ('Shit all over the job. And yet persist in doing it. It's a sort of grand machismo . . . He is one of those people psychiatrists describe as partially complete', 31) and consequently arouses his irritation and fascination.

The gaol officials close ranks against these interlopers, clinging to their own internal hierarchies for reassurance: as warder Whip explains to prisoner-dogsbody Turk, 'I have very little confidence. That is why, at odd times, I have to be so mean to you . . . There were geezers here who caught live mice and skinned 'em. Same thing' (40). This terse definition of the self-perpetuating social institution, streamlined systematic sadism in the service of bolstering insecurities of the vulnerably privileged, gains a further irony from its dramatic context, in that Turk is secretly an informer and 'plant' for Whip's social superior, Cooper. Thus Whip (like Amber in *Credentials*) exposes his own limited knowledge of, and power within, the game being played. Jardine is experienced in layers of misinformation deployed in such situations:

They think by giving a new name to an old complaint they will take the sting out of it. The Ministry of War is the Ministry of Defence. A rubber bullet is a Civil Authority Auxiliary. I hear they are planning to call cancer Libra. My belly won't be fooled by that.

. . . we are in England, and in England you may think a man is a liar but you are better not to call him one. That is called maturity. The more mature you are, the less you use the word you want. The purpose of wrapping meanings up in cotton wool is to stop them hurting. This is a very sick and bandaged race.   (45)

This disjunction of word from meaning, of impulse from action, is the national malaise and addiction of which the inquiry itself is a further example, placing 'distance between a grievance and its object' so that 'wrath dies' and 'revenge is withered by delay' while the culpable hide amongst the ubiquitous foliage of lies. Jardine is at least galvanised onward, if simultaneously tortured, by his flirtation with Matheson; his nagging obsession, which yearns to close the circuit of impulse and fruition, prevents him from subsiding into retirement and horticulture; but its failure also prevents him breaking his circular defeat. Jardine's moral limitations (to know but not to act, to satirise the system without absolving himself from involvement in it) is the same as his sexual incompletion — rather than desire he feels sexual curiosity, a sense of distant comfort, but by not breaching the barriers he allows to stand between himself and her, he cannot charge his own moral energy sufficiently to get off the wretched wagon he is on. Skinner in *The Castle* and Livia in *Women Beware Women* will later realise that desire has obligations and energies that affect all areas of life and force change. Jardine cannot love or change. Though relatively sympathetic, he is also an example of the burned-out sexual longing which drifts like smoke through all the characters, and centres on the death of love between Cooper and Jane.

Matheson admits to Jane an uneasy fascination for Jardine; she has applied for a transfer away from his presence, then torn it up: 'He has integrity, and that gives him pain, pain that is actually rather beautiful to watch. He is simply vile to women' (57). But there are limitations to the degree of sympathetic communication the women can attain, as defined by their political allegiances, despite their shared fascination with the sexuality of the gardener. When Cooper appears, berserk and distraught, Jane attempts to initiate supportive conversation which he denies as futile; Cooper can admit of no confirmatory or inspirational sense of sex, he sees it as distracting and perhaps draining in relation to his active social role; whereas Jane has found the denial of sexuality has alienated her from her social standing, short-changing her sense of identity on both fronts:

> JANE *(standing, furiously):* I HAVE STUCK BY YOU! Through all your shudderings. Through all your blanknesses and sheer arctic silences. I have gone dry because of you. And I do not think that it was love. Maybe it was honour. I only know I have had no nourishment from you.
> *(Pause.* COOPER *stares at her.)*
> COOPER: Jardine is here. How can I listen to you? I love you, but Jardine's here!
> *He hurries out.* JANE *collapses back into her armchair. Her hand goes to her crotch. Slowly, in the fade, she masturbates.* (60)

Turk announces that he is to blame for the blaze, perhaps hungry for a sliver of rebel chic, being mindful that prisoners elsewhere 'are desperate to know who did it, to carry his picture on their shirts like Chairman Mao' (62); he claims that the discrepancy between the approaches of a 'glad-handed Tory saint' of a governor and the uneasy over-defensiveness of the screws bred a 'painful tension for the inmates' overspilling into the maddening — Turk says to Jardine 'Tell 'em in Whitehall there is no reconciling E. M. Forster with a kicking in the testicles' (66), and smashes a chair as a climactic symbolic gesture. Jardine asks Dockerill to 'complete the metaphor and replace the chair', in what may be another latent critique by Barker of Edward Bond's *Saved:*

> MATHESON: Human nature won't just endure, will it? Thank God. Eventually, it chucks a brick. I am very glad of that. I am very glad of human dignity.
> JARDINE: Observe the new chair. I say no more on that one. There is a new chair.
> MATHESON: Yes, but —
> JARDINE: Let us have change. But change that matters. (70)

Turk's confession is a false trail, though his problem of reconciliation remains pertinent; the painful and maddening tension turns out to be located in Cooper, the governor whose humanitarianism goes unreturned and unsanctified until his frustration at the discrepancy between evangelical ideals and brutalising reality brings him to lethal flashpoint. But the truth about Cooper's arson, with all its implications of contradiction at the heart of society and disfigurement of its public face, is absorbed and contained by that society and its self-interested agent Stagg, who claims 'I mean a moral code is all very well but sometimes you have to scrub it! There's an election coming up ... Governors setting light to prisons isn't very good for confidence. It so happens I appointed him myself'. In a crucial debate, ex-Communist Jardine rejects Stagg's careerist expediency and revisionist pseudo-humanism, and recalls some nuns he killed in the war, 'Professional virgins who trusted the superstition of their habit to excuse them anything ... And now you come to me, chanting the Red Flag, and trusting in the superstitition of your parliamentary habit' (76). Stagg upholds the utilitarianism of deception at a national level, peddling the illusory placebo of 'freedom': 'We did not choose the system, but WE HAVE GOT TO GET THE HANG OF IT'. But Jardine's individual existentialism refutes collusion:

JARDINE: You ask me to be guilty. I have never been guilty before.
STAGG: Guilty, George? Guilty before whom?
JARDINE: BEFORE ME.   (77)

Stagg maintains this is impractical, superhuman idealism, and that, instead, 'ye 'ave to cling, ol' son ... CLING'. Though Stagg's definition of events is upheld and enshrined, his interminable 'clinging' is not, as he suffers a heart attack which makes even the defeated Jardine exclaim 'Oh, there is some justice lingering ... !' The coincidental reappearance of Ponting, previously traumatised into a latter-day Poor Tom figure by the discovery of his personal capacity for ruthlessness, adds a well-poised note to the play's concluding movements, as it is uncertain whether his new-found determination to 'come back and be dangerous', within the system's terms, will drive him to mimic Stagg's appetite for egoistic competition and advancement, or Jardine's characteristic insistence on the link between grievance and object; the timing of Stagg's advice to him suggests the former. Jardine's exhaustion finally seems complete, marked by his acceptance of a knighthood and submission to cancer, as well as his abandoning his chase after Matheson, telling her 'I am going home to study roses'; she adds with rueful affection 'England brings you down at last'.

As in many Barker works, the system's powers of self-defence and absorption have been demonstrated; Udy's epilogue 'They came, they saw, they whitewashed' would serve for all of Barker's plays up to and including *The Hang of the Gaol*, with the exceptions of *Heroes of Labour* and *Fair Slaughter*. And when Udy and Whip go through the motions of locking up the burnt-out gaol — 'Two hundred years of it. Oh, History! Oh, England!' — they effectively lock up the audience in the edifice of their complicity, just as Brendan Behan's *The Quare Fellow* confronts an audience with the prison setting their taxes support and admonishes them with a sign decreeing 'SILENCE'. The mixture of vivid grotesques and genuine sufferers that people the various layers of *The Hang of the Gaol* makes it one of Barker's most reverberative internal guides through what Shaw in *Heartbreak House* terms 'This soul's prison we call England', under the moral paralysis, palmed off as social democracy, characteristic of the 1970s. But the gruff vitality of Jardine, the stubbornly (self-) gnawing idealist, glances back to Gocher and forward to Bela Veracek. *The Hang of the Gaol* is not so sentimental as to permit Jardine unqualified victory, nor so pessimistic as to smother or preclude his voice entirely, perhaps testifying to Barker's increasing awareness that the depiction of paralysis, in whatever counter-entropic terms, is not enough, or that its seam might become as exhausted as the age itself. A truly critical spirit has to take the form of a character defiantly independent of social institutions, rejecting all professional or interventionist rationalisations, and it arrives in the extravagant form of Tom Downchild.

But before Downchild appears to place British social democracy on trial, Barker examines the emergence of right-wing ideals and practice in *Birth on a Hard Shoulder* (written 1977, staged 1980) and *The Loud Boy's Life* (staged 1980). The motif of arson, with motives of obfuscation and self-interest, recurs from *The Hang of the Gaol* in *Birth on a Hard Shoulder*. Security officer Rutkin burns down a hospital, shut as a social spending cut, out of superstitious fear that it is a source of blight and infection for the surrounding area; his social superior Nattress burns down a dockland warehouse which he owns, insisting that he is prompted to this action by a Labour government's return to power: 'If England has to be a desert, whose fault is that?' Nattress appears to have a sympathetic ally in Finney, a stockbroker who has killed his family rather than see them face personal retrenchment under socialism ('They are forcing you to acts which you are actually ashamed of'), but who finally shrinks from executing Nattress's plan out of reluctant affection he has discovered for two vagrants, Hilary and Erica, who are squatting in the warehouse. Finney meets this duo on an eerily deserted motorway, where the only response to Hilary's stillborn childbirth is an emergency phone's endless repetition of a dinner recipe involving 'home produced lamb'. The former stockbroker's interpretation of this dark irony mirrors his own Saturnine despair: 'Lucky not to see this. Decided not to, obviously ... First new baby under socialism kills itself' (75).

Despite his appalled observation of the 'aimlessness' of Hilary and Erica, or their persistent existence with their awareness of the bankruptcy of humanist ideals (which he also attributes to Labour governments), Finney impregnates Hilary a second time. Rosalind Reedman says of Hilary:

> She is a survivor who refuses to fight the battle of life. Her rule is 'at the first sign of struggle — quit'. Because of her animal reactions and the harmony she achieves with her own body and nature, she overwhelms the men in her life, whom she treats objectively, without compassion. She tells Finney, 'I am hyper-fertile. You were adequate. The rest is sentiment'. Her adaptability to her circumstances ('I could eat shit if I needed to') ensures her survival but there is a lack of responsibility bordering on the anarchic which diminishes the validity of her effortless freedom. It is won at the expense of others.[4]

Erica admires Hilary's pat formulae for absolution from commitment ('Language is the sledgehammer of social conformity') but insists she cannot tolerate Finney's views. Hilary maintains 'The world is hostile to preferences. It nullifies them ... The world is a constant image no matter how you shake the bits. It is kaleidoscopic. You shake it and the coloured bits move but the ingredients are the same. That is why we reject politics' (104). This concept of an essential conservatism within British social life also motivates Croydon and Brilliant, two policemen planning the revolutionary fascist 'Midnight Movement' in the face of Labour's return to office. Croydon argues for a coup, whereby 'a few good men' seize the machinery of power:

> How is it that some drunken homosexual of a minister can run the hospitals one day and the fucking air force the next? ... It's a

machine . . . It is a beautiful sight and could be commanded by a RABBIT . . . All that matters is that every little man who serves it, the bald-headed geezer with the mortgage and the shiny arse, turns up to the office. On that morning. That he persists. And he will, Brian, because not to do so is an effort and calls for thought, which he would rather not burden himself with. And the more days that pass the less likely he is to act, because it would cause chaos and HIS KIDS MIGHT BE HURT. History is the history of dedicated individuals. Do you see? (90)

The more ludicrous aspects of the initiative of Croydon and Brilliant do not prevent them from attracting the co-operation of Finney and Nattress; and their fundamental ideological brutality is demonstrated when their thug colleague blinds and kills an old tramp, who is another source of puzzlement to Finney's values of self-interest ('What makes an old tramp into a socialist . . . What did socialism do for him?' 108).

Erica tries to rouse Finney from his dazzled and unwelcomed sense of English heritage by suggesting that he is effectively worshipping the window-dressings of tourism rather than history: 'Is this it? Traitor's Gate and Horseguards? Houses of Parliament? . . . Looking for History? . . . History's on the telephone fixing a deal with Düsseldorf! They have chucked England, Finney, England's dead. England's a mothy uniform with Nelson's blood on it and Tudor clubs for financiers to dip their pricks' (113). He is in fact shaken from his programme of self-intoxication by the news that Hilary is pregnant by him and intends to let the child live, exposing his real despair with present-day England ('SHE CAN'T! NOT IN THIS — HOW CAN SHE!'); but the thought of the child burgeons into a sense of a future in Finney's mind, however recalcitrant. Hilary dismisses his involvement in the conception as one of biological formality to preclude his new-found passion making him 'sticky'; even Erica is repulsed by her untouchability ('I still think that you have style, but I don't think it matters any more . . . Blimey, DON'T YOU CARE!', 116). When Erica perishes in Nattress's successful bid to fire the warehouse, Finney believes Hilary and their child have died, impelling him to confront the Midnight Movement:

FINNEY: I'm sorry. I think we must be decent. First and foremost. Even before the ghosts. And you have killed somebody.

NATTRESS: You have to go steady with decency. It is inflammable,
you see. You have to know when to use it and —
FINNEY I don't see there is anything else, is there?   (121)

Finney appeals to the higher authority of the law as a supposed
enshrinement of this decency, naïvely failing to realise that its
agents are Croydon and Brilliant, who will not shirk from using it
to their own ends by gaoling him for murdering his family, maintaining that his idealistic purity is inconsistent madness. Hilary
meanwhile has found a brief idyll of sorts, reconciled with her
father, another disillusioned middleman idealist of the right and
ex-policeman colleague of Croydon and Brilliant, who has perceived 'I have stood between the shit and the sugar. I have seen the
ignorant carve the jawbones from the semi-educated and the savage kick the eyeballs from the sockets of the daft' (102). However,
the aptly-named Archie Flux is galvanised into missionary zeal of
the most utopian and abstract, as represented by his World Spiritual Regeneration Movement which bids to remove the obstacles
preventing people from recognising their intrinsic goodness, an
extreme swing away from the Right's sense of inalienable human
selfishness, into an idealism which is nevertheless so disengaged
from practical conduct as to be less threatening than Finney's
invocation of a vague, basic 'decency'. Finney, the unexpectedly
humanised 'Beast of Godalming', is consigned to Broadmoor,
where he labours in the garden whilst a Warder chants in a mood of
permanent wonder:

> The person dies. The person is cremated. The person's bits go
> up the chimney. The person's bits fall down. The bits are swept
> up. The sweeping are put on the dustcart. The dustcart empties
> on the fields. The fields grow cabbages. The cabbages are cut
> down. A person eats the cabbages. The cabbages turn into bits of
> person. The person dies. *(Pause)* The person is cremated . . .

The Sisyphean circulatory of this world-view, where life as a
sort of agricultural rondo is elevated to the level of benign pandeterminism, succinctly represents the essential reductivity of prison
life. When Finney tries to break its rhythm by throwing down his
hoe and insisting on his sanity, the more insistent and determinedly
unimaginative warder politely repeats the word 'hoe' until Finney
falls back into the oppressive rhythm of the working party. His

submission is politely received, and the litany continues as if the aberration had never occurred. This concluding scene is even more terrible and haunting than the end of *Claw*, where Noel's murder permits his absorption into state statistics; Finney's sentence is demonstrated to be death-in-life, with the systematic extirpation of all human intelligence, imagination, rights and dignity above the standard accorded to the vegetable.

The imposition of this punitive cosmology provides a critical echo of Hilary's creed, 'Acquiescence in Cosmic Inevitability'. If anything, the cosmic world seems to insist on a sense of purpose, if only through the comically inept materialisations of the Spectre, who tries to propel Finney into finding the strength to change England; like a fading and fitful descendant of Marley's Ghost, he proclaims 'there is nothing satisfactory in death', while acknowledging 'Got to be mad to live'. However shambling their nominated representative, the supernatural world itself seems to be labouring to spark a flash of existential resolve in the play's apathetic English wasteland, which otherwise recalls the entropic seediness and slide into fascist decadence which Stephen Poliakoff has subsequently made his characteristic terrain of observation.

The imperilled middlemen of *Birth on a Hard Shoulder* all sense that the country has moved away from their traditional values and try to subjugate it to their idiosyncratic versions of order; however, none of them is capable of realising their feverishly evolved reactionary ideals. Finney is perhaps the most engaging in his movement from homicidal despair to Quixotic action on behalf of an unborn child, all conducted at a consistent and fatal level of impracticality; nevertheless he remains unswervingly true to his chosen, outdated code, which at times imbues him with a romantic's vulnerability. Flux's evangelical resilience confers upon him the appeal and limitations of the essentially comic character. While Erica recognises the limits of Hilary's philosophy and 'style', it is a characteristic Barker black irony that the innocent dies in the crossfire of higher social forces and interests, whilst Hilary seems to attain a euphoria as superficial as her previous frosted neo-stoicism, sending out Archie's messages of salvation in bottles from Torquay beach. The play's major achievements are its sense of a nightmarishly unfeeling Southern English landscape of deserted motorways, blinking neon and suppurating, brutal grudges; and the hellish final scene, where the hypnotic suction into desensitisation verges on the complete for Finney and his zombie-like fellow prisoners.

Croydon and Brilliant may be grotesque in their obtuse hubris and imaginative meanness as they attempt to further the reactionary powers of the institution in which they are involved, the police force. Its official silence on the objectives they believe it should uphold and extend leads to their fumbling attempts to 'play midwife' to their ideal in the illegitimate form of the Midnight Movement, another nativity to which the play is witness. The contempt they may awaken in a theatre audience should be uneasy; as Crystal Backlawn says of Ezra Fricker in *The Loud Boy's Life,* 'Because he is funny does not mean we shouldn't be afraid of him. Fear the comic. Laugh, but hold the knife' (42).

Fricker, for all his eccentricities, is a character who has assembled from a historical rag-bag an ideal, and who is tortured by English life's discrepancy from this ideal, breeding the urge to force them to coalesce; such is his passion. As Barker notes:

> My plays have always been concerned with power, only rarely with conscience, and not yet with happiness ... The pursuit of power, like the pursuit of sexual love, is the mortal enemy of happiness. To be happy is to be without want, to be therefore in a state of intellectual and sensual suspension. And who will settle for happiness when he might have pain? Passion, the pain of wanting, is the only affirmation most of us can have.[5]

A precocious young man in 1942, Fricker observes the blitz of London and hears a remark on the basic impulse of conformity, be it homicidal or suicidal: 'War is all fear. When fear goes, fraternization rears its head. Stoke them with it, or they will roll in one another's arms' (26). Fricker realises that this has even wider implications for profitable divisions of human sympathies in peacetime, and exclaims 'BIND THEM WITH FEAR! ... I have the terms of my mission! I have the key which will unlock the stagnant passions of the English race!' (27). For a country in a state of expectation and shame, Fricker's appeal to unspoken impulses lies in his overt belief in a systematic balance of selfishness; he is The Man Who Is Not Ashamed, reading out of the national heritage a sanguinary mandate: 'we are an executing people, ruthless in authority and merciless in revenge' (28). However, his sense of this mandate becomes dazzlingly personalised to the point where he proclaims 'I am the spirit of the English race ... I HAVE TO KNOW WHAT HISTORY WILL SAY OF ME!' (37). His personal tragedy lies in his hubristic conviction of his own indispensability, when he convinces himself that he will be appointed the next Conservative Party leader: 'If they do not appoint me I will blow my lid, and half of London will be fizzing with me' (47).

In fact, a bloodthirsty interpretation of the English inheritance is of little use in the market of international capitalism, as Erica tried to tell Finney, and as Doggitt points out to his fellow cabinet members on blackballing Fricker: 'He will not do because money doesn't want him. Money has grown too big for England. You cannot dress her in a union jack. Her arse would hang out . . . Find what money wants, and want it' (52). Moreover, Fricker has become a champion for illegitimate right-wing voices who crave his association, such as the grotesquely misogynistic secret society, the Ancient Order of Savages, who reveal the tribal insecurities of the 'governing mob'; but this populist support brings no advantage and implicit damage to Fricker's legitimate prospects, as he himself adheres to the parliamentary means to power: 'I am not sure I see much glory in being carried shoulder high by lorry drivers. It is not, so to speak, an element of my world picture' (61). Unfortunately for Fricker, the British people's imaginative support for his initiatives depends upon the sense that they are extra-parliamentary, as when Croydon and Brilliant plan the Midnight Movement as a crucial adjunct to the police force in *Birth on a Hard Shoulder*. A focal moment occurs when Fricker visits a lunatic asylum on the day his parliamentary hopes are dashed, and an inmate impersonates him to his amused recognition; then the mimicry of public statements gives way to an intuition of private despair as the lunatic repeats 'Do not leave me on my own' — a characteristic Fricker is unwilling or, even worse, unable to acknowledge.

As a psychiatrist warns, 'Nothing is more likely to bring depression than adherence to a defunct idea', but Fricker and the idea of Right-wing heritage and history are inextricably bound together, accounting for his invocation as a popular hero or martyr even beyond death — a schoolboy worshipper eats his cremated ashes, and less distinctive governing opportunists donate a decorous nod of tribute. The man who answers a national sense of disinheritance can offer in return only heritage — his heroic hymns to London which punctuate the scenes — and both ideals are equally, crucially outdated; Fricker tries to raise the spirit of history, even sees himself as its genie, but is finally merely shackled to its corpse — which in itself maintains a fetishistic fascination for certain thuggish cliques.

Downchild (written 1977, but not staged until 1985) is deliberately intended as the concluding play in this series of descriptions of Britain in decline under Labour's 'social democracy'. Gossip columnist Tom Downchild stage-manages and stars in an outrageously vicious extravaganza designed to confront the age with its own image and consequences, scything through the lies of shifty Devon yokels and clergy who have sold themselves into complicity with the machinations of the former Labour Prime Minister, who 'made stupor rhyme with socialism and selfishness a passion', and his ambitious secretary. Downchild recalls Claw in his rare successful moments, a rude jester scourging the establishment from the inside, self-consciously 'the filth confronting the filth'.[6] His criminal lover Stoat, lying in a field, overhears an exchange between the ex-premier Roy Scadding and his mistress Ann Heyday, who bitterly senses an 'agony of freedom', being tired of sexuality, 'of wanting to be wanted', 'Enjoying my deadness. My coldness. Loving it'. But Scadding's ardour is undiminished, and he protests: 'Being out of office, is it, done this? Without the leadership, I look a seedy thing? . . . My resignation cost me dear, then . . . I would have staggered through if I'd known this' (61).

At the centre of this political thriller are two couples and two demonstrations of the 'ugly, chilling fact' of a Downchild epigram: 'No two lovers are ever thinking the same thing at the same moment' (70). Scadding realises that Heyday has grown apart from him sexually and politically: 'Ann isn't in my congregation any more. All her talk is absolutes' (73). Ann, of humble Catford origins, has used her sexuality to gain power, but has remained untouched by passion and consequently failed to sense purpose:

> I wanted power. Wanted it even more than Roy. And when it came, did not know what to do with it. The thing, I thought was getting my bum on the chair. Not true. The fish-eyed Tory never wonders why he's there. He knows. To serve the baying and the booming class. But me? For my pushy mother, was it? Why?
>
> (103)

Ann regrets that to triumph she had to maintain a superficial electrolysis-preened 'dolly' beauty and yet cultivate 'brute male sense, to spot an opportunity, to wring it out . . . Had to murder so much of myself'; Scadding adds 'We all do! It's called politics!' (102). Their uneasy alliance is attacked by Downchild, whose glee in iconoclasm and baroque verbal inventiveness is even turned against Stoat as a deflection of a fleetingly acknowledged self-loathing: 'The only person who could love me I could never love' (77). Downchild is excited by Stoat's proletarian background but also his lack of erudition in order to score points in compulsive wit, casting Stoat in the role of straight man, if not his personal dramatic creation ('Silence, Stoat. If I don't own you, you're not here. You have no existence. You are a figment of my brain', 88). Stoat bears the reduction of his rights, intelligence and existence to the genital with tautly strained tolerance. There is also a suggestion that Downchild prefers sexual memory to practice, through his fixation on Stoat's desperate life, which he uses to work himself up into a frenzy of imagining; 'Yer turning yerself on again' Stoat notes at one point.

'Was there ever such a spate of lying? It's endemic to the place' says Downchild of the landscape they have wandered into. Indeed, the Devon village seems self-consciously and ludicrously fictional in its hushed urgency to embody antiquated English idylls. The rustic Bevin family tug their forelocks and assume the roles of Mummerset peasants in thrall to the 'big 'ouse' on the cliffs in return for Chevrolets and quadrophonic stereos. The poet-vicar Moscrop proclaims God's licence of murder and closes ranks with Scadding and Heyday, even to the point of playing a demented apparition in a fluorescent gasmask, but Downchild realises that this is further distracting, picturesque gothicism; as he tells Scadding, 'The only ghost around here is you'. Roy and Ann's crooked business interests dictate that they protect and cover up for a demented aristocrat, Lucky Dicker. Even Lucky ruefully laments his own inbred lack of self-control and his ironic relation to the family motto, 'Do What You Will'. when his nocturnal excursions imperil the carefully-maintained myth of feudal equilibrium and lead to demands for his suicide.

The public role-playing exerts its private tensions, as characters become victims of the roles they have assumed, which impinge on and shape the reality of character. Heyday and Scadding find a lack of sexual reciprocity in the hollow shell of their apparent political success, Lucky becomes a maddened night-prowler like his ancestor; Downchild's trade is reviled by Scadding as 'sniffing laundry' and the journalist later finds himself literally engaged in this, inhaling sheets for a trace of the vanished Stoat and capitulating to sobs of loss before upbraiding himself 'GET A BIT OF DIGNITY!' (82). After years of playing the parliamentary democrat,

Scadding finds himself fatally incapable of murdering Downchild, confesses and surrenders; and Tom seizes the opportunity
for an antithetical drama, 'The Holy Inquisition of Lord Cocky',
over which he presides, draped in altar cloth and crowned with
newsprint, while Stoat ('Exhibit A. Dumb monster. British youth')
repaints the village church's murals ('Two tins of Woolworth's
vinyl silk. Saint Barry in the 'olocaust', a scene of disintegrating
cities, futile communication, riots, burning gaols, 'My English boy
in flames'; 'Front right, a sensitive policeman weeps, and prays —
vainly — for peace'). Downchild details the charges against Scadding on his behalf, with a vengeful flourish:

> I gave boots to the rotten to kick the healthy with.
> I helped old women bleed in gutters.
> I made young mothers take to drugs.
> I stuffed despair through letter-boxes of the flats.
> I made workmen in the factory ashamed of their beliefs.
> I made them kiss my picture in the city.
> I kicked hope out of the hearts of men I didn't know.
> I made a good thing fit for laughs.
> I could have flicked History but I dribbled in my pants.   (97)

Scadding counters that parliament moves by 'twitches' and
that his own actions were constricted like that of a 'baby' by the
guardians of the 'Real World' — 'civil servants, bankers, chiefs of
police' — and that Downchild's obloquy flung at the ex-premier
and secretary 'never touched the real dirt', but operated at one
remove from the source of actual power, as did they; thus, Scadding
presents the view of a world not unlike *That Good Between Us* where
the system is beyond the control of its ostensible governors, but also
claims to have acted as a buffer against the true savagery of the ruling class who would have countenanced civil war:

> Would have fired rockets in the flats. I saw that written in the
> marble teeth. Sir This, Sir That, and Sir the Other. Their silver
> partings whispered tanks. I never sat with bankers but their teeth
> clicked tanks. I was a very clever baby, Tom. Preferred delin-
> quents to dead boys. (100)

However, Downchild identifies a lack of shame in the speech, and
it is arguable to what extent the 'maturity' against which Scadding

was pitted, and with which he chose to act in accordance, was indeed, in Downchild's terms, 'a con to rub the edge off a fine blade' and the crippling of British socialism. Downchild insists their climb to power was 'out of hate', contempt for their former fellow members of the working classes, 'ALL BECAUSE YOU GOT NO LOVE' (103). But this is a crucial area for the journalist himself, who has been relishing extravagant self-descriptions and personal identifications with a corresponding nemesis of contempt: 'I am at one with my age, I am the Zeitgeist, fucking cold and dead within . . . Scadding, I find you guilty of humanity' (101). Even Downchild's revelation of his own real name, Ernest Broadbent, is used as an act of theatricality. But Stoat is unimpressed; the victim of the age, Scadding and Heyday's spiritual son according to Downchild, does not share Tom's self-foregrounding delight in the supposed revelations: 'So 'e's a ganster. So she's a tart. So the world's bent. 'Ow about that!' Downchild's extravaganza is an orgy of satiric poetry and drama, reinforcing his own authoritative control of words: 'LOOK, I'M GOD, AREN'T I? BECAUSE I'M LITERATE! . . . Teach you words, don't I?' But Tom's Caliban has achieved personal autonomy ('Fuck words. Picture's best') and prods a delicate wound, as Tom admits to doubts as to his own newsprint juxtapositions of luxury and squalor and their power to enrage readers: 'They read one, they read the other, wept in one, felt envy in the other. SAW NO DISCREPANCY' (104). He seizes the opportunity presented by Lucky's suicide and buys his child, in a second attempt to control a dramatic dynamic and thereby command the attentions of Scadding, Heyday and Stoat, as Lord Cocky's Inquisition has deflated through the redundancy of his satire and Tom's indulgent self-dramatising digressions on the importance of not being Ernest, which no one finds as riveting as he does himself.

Six months later, in a clifftop ceremony, Downchild christens the child 'in madness' and goes to drop it off the cliffs to the horror of the assembled village dwellers, in order to save it from 'our English mess', 'life of squalor on our barmy rock'; he confronts the representatives of collusion with the bankruptcy of hope, 'I'm tired of your old sin! Death's for the innocent . . . What baby with an ounce of sense would choose to struggle in Roy's desert?' (106). Stoat appears, having caught the baby, but not before Downchild has been battered by the outraged onlookers; but, though bloodied, Tom holds firm to his forcible stirring of pity: 'I made an English

politician cry! Have you no love of spectacle? Bevin, it's worth a box
of babies ... The dreamers, they are always crying, but this, who
never dreamed ...' (107). Even Stoat is horrified by the consequences
of Tom's Pyrrhic affirmation of the pain of wanting, though the prone
journalist retorts 'They call it passion, silly boy'. The homicidal youth
may be shocked at Downchild's willingness to face destruction in the
name of dramatising this passion, playing out the play and proving
it real by dying in it; thus Downchild finally establishes his licence to
be ruthless, in that, above all, he is ruthless on himself: 'No dignity.
No wisdom. Serenity. Or peace. Kick to the finish!' (107). His passion
play complete, Tom dies in earnest, not in jest.

The audience, if not Stoat, spend much of the play wandering in
the great big noisy fairground of Downchild's character, and that
character's control of events in the trial scene is so closely associated
with his creator's that the play is, for a moment, nearly swamped
by the thespian extravagance of Tom's personality. But its startling
set-pieces, artful use of the English village murder form and full
flourishing of Barker's elegantly scatological dialogue, imbue it
with immense theatrical force, vitality and resonance.

In a land and age of brutal facts and unreal dreams, passion, the
pain of wanting, becomes a limited form of affirmation. Gocher's
personal blend of faith and delusion, with its consequent effects of
pathos and bathos, at least make him burn brightly, if painfully and
self-consumingly, within a darkened landscape, where the prime
function of official institutions is to place distance between a grievance and its object so that revenge is withered by delay, as Udy recognises. Language may be used by the likes of Knatchbull as the
'sledgehammer of social conformity', but there is a sense in *That
Good* that its head is splintering and may even damage those who
wield it carelessly; style becomes another tactic of self-reassurance
in the war to bind dissenters with fear. Staveley, Orbison, Cooper
and Stagg, Nattress, Scadding are right to fear Gocher, McPhee,
Jardine, Finney and Downchild as they persist in believing in absolutes, tracing a grievance back to its object, rather than being com-
plicit in an age where politics involves murdering so much of one's
self, in order to preserve a relative personal privilege — though
Orbison, Cooper and Jane, Scadding and Heyday in particular can
testify to the limitations of this privilege.

For all his intentionally shocking self-identifications with the spirit
of the age, Downchild appears at the end of the group of plays like
a Socialist Antichrist, swaggering towards Devon to exact revenge,

threatening to smite innocent babes if necessary in his role of nemesis that brooks no object or delay. It is significant that Downchild has also developed an antithetical sense of personal style and language with which he flouts authority in a deliberate and fastidious way, reclaiming these attributes from associations of institutionalised power. He is the prime representative of, and spokesman for, the energising 'articulate heartlessness' Tony Dunn identifies within Barker's work, where 'the body, as an anarchic ensemble of drives and impulses, constantly defaces, via syntactically polished graffiti, the tables of rational calculation'.[7] However, Downchild has to realise that literacy does not bestow deity; rather than impress his superiority on Stoat, he finally asks his help and invokes the spirit of Guy Burgess as witness. On the clifftops, he forsakes the printed and spoken word for the outrageous power of the enacted theatrical event to suggest that, beyond the literal and metaphorical miscarriages which pervade the attempted births on the hard shoulder of 1970s Britain, for existence to proceed in the 'soul's prison called England', new justifications must be found and new terms invented.

The general impression of the plays is of a warring rodent world, mouths all blood and fur turned against each other in a caged era of soured hope and degradation, where the bizarre postures of political situations often have their origins in unlived sexuality. Fleeting illumination is provided by the antithetical self-invention and passion of those determined to trace the damaging effects of social institutions back to their cause: the vanity and attempted self-enclosure of the institutions' representatives. As *Downchild* shows, there is a price to be paid by existential mavericks who make stabs at unwelcome expositions, and by those close to them; and these drives and tensions are foregrounded in Barker's subsequent plays on the role of the artist of society.

5

New Manner for New Situation

*NO END OF BLAME, PITY IN HISTORY, SCENES FROM AN
EXECUTION*

I STIRRED THE POLICE, THEREFORE, I TOUCHED THE
TRUTH. You make my case for me . . .

No End of Blame

Barker explores the contradictions and tensions of the artist's relationship to society in the principal trajectories of three plays: *No End
of Blame, Pity in History* and *Scenes from an Execution*. The settings
are disparate, but all three are set during wars or in their aftermath,
when social upheaval suggests possibilities for re-evaluation.[1] The
role of the artist is crucial in this re-evaluation, but the reactionary
forces of society seek to limit the efforts he or she undertakes, and
displace any new sense of consequence in human events for which
this new age might permit opportunities. The power of the artist is
demonstrated in provocation of thought and sorrow issuing from
suffering. The power of the state depends on the unquestioned
acceptance of its hierarchical structure, and of the necessity — even
desirability — of suffering to affirm this structure. The climate of
upheaval prompts not only social but also artistic and personal
re-evaluation, and the artists have to adapt to circumstances, proving rather than compromising their integrity in the process. This
adaptation is particularly important when the state is hostile to full
recognition of the common bonds of sympathy linking its constitu-
ent members; it prefers to dazzle perception with images of isolated
privilege, and is prepared to revoke the rights of any fundamentally challenging critic. Though centring on the artist's dilemma,
the plays have wider reverberations in their scenes of opposition,
where the fetish of ownership pits its power against the reinvention
of forms of life.

In *Downchild*, Stoat demonstrates a disillusioned but not embittered autonomy in working on his mural painting of 'Saint Barry in the 'olocaust' rather than attend to Tom's verbal effusions, in which the journalist's supremacy safeguards his personal authority ('I'M GOD AREN'T I? BECAUSE I'M LITERATE!'). But Downchild failed to affect and move his readers fundamentally. Stoat proclaims bluntly, 'Fuck words. Picture's best'; and his unseen painting has dramatic resonance through its combination of verbally described detail and invisibility, challenging the audience to complete and embellish its images through the engagement of their own imaginations.

Each scene of *No End of Blame: Scenes of Overcoming* (staged 1981) incorporates Barker's cues for backdrop sketches by its two artist protagonists Bela and Grigor — realised for the original production by Gerald Scarfe and Clare Shenstone respectively. Two Hungarian soldiers on a First World War battlefield are rapidly distinguished by their response to the sight of a naked woman: Grigor admires the harmony of her form with gravity, her breasts 'CONCEDE' in a curve that 'eliminates all tension' and he attempts to prevent her movement in order to observe 'the essential female line'; Bela contrastingly experiences the tension of desire which drives him to act, grasp, particularise, engage, rather than observe — the totality of his impulses resists sub-categorisation, and his justification of the attempted rape rests on the recognition that, given the surrounding institutionally-ordained and systematic destruction of the body ('we have trod on babies' brains and caught our boots up in the entrails of an old woman, yesterday we ate our breakfast on a table made of half a man'), he does not understand 'a morality which says we have to draw the line at petty theft' (2).[2] The Officer commands that Bela justify his self-description as a poet through the use of rhyme and spurious associations of craftsmanship ('Poetry without rhyme is laying bricks without cement') over the recognition of explosive metaphorical insight. His humiliation over, Bela vows 'I shall never write a poem again'.

When the Red Soldiers appear and place Bela in a position of advantage over the Officer, Bela insists that the existence of authority does not excuse the individual's complicity in its ends and attitudes: Bela blames the Officer for hurting him, though he draws back from killing him at the last moment. He rejects the liberal humanist refusal to locate blame, as a socially institutionalised attitude placing distance between grievance and object so that wrath and revenge wither in deferral. Within the individual consciousness, there is a severance of impulse and action. The splintering of the self into internalised self-monitoring denounces specific impulses as being inimical to 'wider interests' than the individual's, engendering guilt, short-circuiting personal judgement, and ultimately opinion.

Grigor characteristically feels more at home than Bela in their subsequent art classes at the Budapest Institute of Fine Art, where the instruction centres on classical idealism and the image of the artist as one who 'looks for beauty everywhere' with the privilege of being ordained 'high priest in the temple art'. Such mystical conservatism is inimical to passion, the pain of wanting, as it restricts itself to wonder at inanimate, calm surfaces. But Bela is temperamentally attracted to the relation between impulse and action, cause and effect, as publicly demonstrated by the social range and purpose of the cartoon, rather than the 'metaphysical' rapture of the painting. The model's biography further destabilises the aesthetic of the studio. Whereas there was a gap in communication and understanding between Downchild's attempted demonstration of cause (the failure of social democracy under Scadding) and Stoat's image of effect (dispossessed British youth), Bela seeks to yoke cause and effect forcefully in a single image identifying both factors of contemporary social hypocrisy. This is in defiance of his instruction in 'art', identified as 'Perfect form. No grievance. No sin. No spit. No wit. No shit' (10). Bela rejects elitist invocations of divine or national genius, 'I hate oils, studios, manipulating colours inches thick. Give me ink, which dries quick, speaks quick, hurts', and his criterion of success is the fracture of tolerance, 'I STIRRED THE POLICE, THEREFORE, I TOUCHED THE TRUTH' (11).

When Bela and Grigor travel to Russia with fellow ex-student Ilona, Bela's cartoons bring him into conflict with 'the line Comrade Lenin is advancing' and a disciplinary tribunal of the Writers' and Artists' Union, Moscow. While the committee proclaims to be attacking 'existing cultural values' to evolve 'an art which is not bourgeois', they are in fact promoting a form of classical idealist values, as did the Budapest Institute, and allow no house-room to the grievance, sin, spit, wit and shit which constitutes individual imaginative insight. Like the tradition of liberal humanism, their enforced party-line consensus urges a disjunction between impulse and action so that individuals brake themselves before engaging in public judgement: 'there's a case for criticism, but it's not now'. One committee member refines the point:

FOURTH COMRADE: He is entitled to disagree with anyone he wants. That's freedom, isn't it? But he must be able to restrain his criticism in the wider interests of the people. That's responsibility, isn't it?

.   .   .

BELA: BUT I WANT TO PROTEST!
FIRST COMRADE: Tomorrow.

Thus, 'responsibility' is invoked, like 'maturity' in *Downchild*, to cauterise dissent and ardour. As Bela struggles with a manifestation of politics dependent upon the extirpation of grievance, Grigor is lured by the repressive tolerance of gratification and withdrawal into a pastoral idyll with Ilona, ideas which constitute what Bela terms 'The Woods Option as he pricks its pretensions:

> But I don't believe, in all honesty, given the complexity of the present social and industrial machine, the woods option is a wholly satisfactory response, since the deliberate rejection of experience contributes nothing to the alleviation of human pain, nor relieves you from its consequences, or to put it brutally . . . You don't miss the bullets by shutting your eyes!   (25)

Bela claims the real fight is 'against worship, it's against the surrender of your self!', though the personal insecurities of Grigor and Ilona make them attracted toward idylls, as the ideological insecurities and institutionalised defensiveness of the committee demand subservience to the myth of 'the great experiment'. Rosalind Reedman notes: 'Ilona is actually afraid of taking responsibility for herself. She offers herself as a fertility symbol to Grigor, distracting him from the real struggle, pulling him backwards with her fear of losing her own identity which she defines by the need others have of her'.[3] Bela's awareness of the fragility of idylls is informed by a sense of integrity and existential pathos, the compulsively disruptive discontent of the self-aware individual, self-consciously difficult. Grigor elevates Ilona, and implicitly himself, to semi-divine romantic status:

GRIGOR: I love you! Don't cry!

BELA (shakes his head): Oh, Grigor . . . as if that could make her stop!
Your little sticky thing of love! Your glue! Her head splits and he
offers his smelly little tube of glue.
GRIGOR: YOU DON'T KNOW HOW I HATE YOU SOMETIMES!
BELA: You don't know how I hate myself.   (26)

After defacing a floral tribute to Stalin as another form of secu-
lar idolatory, Bela escapes Russia through the benign intercession of
the Fourth Comrade. His infusion of political sympathy with desire,
when he describes the imaginary kissing of her breasts though their
bodies remain separate, demonstrates the delicate suggestive triumph of the sexual imagination over circumstances, as opposed
to Grigor and Ilona's refuge in idyllic suspension of possibilities
beyond those afforded by the vague pastoral-sensual. Bela's association with Ludmilla allows him a smudge of inspiration and the
chance to walk, independent, into Britain, even as the Hitlerine bat
of his cartoon casts a shadow over Europe; Grigor's association
with Ilona ends with the destruction of their mutually dependent
idyll, Ilona's death by machine-gunning during the Nazi invasion,
and Grigor's traumatisation.

In 1943 Bela visits RAF Basingbourne 'Brave New World Club' as
a guest speaker, and outlines his convictions:

I believe the cartoon to be the lowest form of art. I also believe
it to be the most important form of art. I decided in my twenty-
fourth year I would rather be important than great. I decided
this because I have always preferred shouting to whispering
and humanity more than myself. The cartoon is a weapon in the
struggle of peoples. It is a liberating instrument. It is brief like
life. It is not about me. It is about us. Important art is about us.
Great art is about me. I am not interested in me. I do not like me.
I am not sure if I like us either, but that is private and the cartoon
is not private . . .
   The cartoon changes the world. The painting changes the artist.
I long to change the world. I hate the world. Thank you.
Pause. He sits, blows his nose.   (32)

This speech triggers one airman's sense of his own existential
pathos ('I DON'T LIKE THIS FUCKING WORLD EITHER . . . WHY
ARE WE DROPPING PHOSPHORUS BOMBS ON KIDS?'). In
return, the RAF audience ask Bela to illustrate social contradiction,

the 'real war' of the English people beneath the war with Hitler; the outspoken airman reminds Bela 'I COULD BE KILLED TONIGHT . . . Don't want it to be for nothing, see? . . . Must have a little bit of truth to go with please . . .' (35). This stands as a rebuke to Bela's self-satisfaction, and an inspiration, driving him to overcome self, and change.

Just as Old Gocher put his faith in truth, a fine oil trickling into stiff heads 'penetrating the clockwork of your indignation', Bela tries to awaken thought with a cartoon of a profiteer strangling an English soldier who is struggling with Hitler. This arouses the ire of Churchill's representatives: Lowry, who upholds a notion of decorum (indicating that plurality of political opinion is possible 'within an accepted frame of reference'), and the harder Deeds, who is unconcerned with liberal opinion and the appearance of the state, denouncing the cartoon with the convenient moral indeterminacy and linguistic fascism of Knatchbull in *That Good:* 'It's you-know-what, isn't it? Pure you-know-what'. Bela objects:

BELA: My politics are to look for the truth, and when you find it, shout it. That's my politics.
LOWRY: Very good. But what are your politics? (38)

Again, Bela finds himself oppressed into association with a party line, that 'in a sense we are at war with the USSR, even though we are on the same side'; his editor consigns events to the judgement of the public, subjugating himself and the newspaper to keep it open, and suggesting Bela place his faith in the unusually perceptive member of the public, 'the ONE WHO THINKS. Who, by miracle, or accident, or because his brain is kinked WILL SEE THROUGH THE FLANNEL' (41). Bela duly questions himself, 'Supposing freedom's not the truth? . . . Supposing the truth is love?', but a conversation with a tolerant but oblivious tea-lady makes him realise that this path of thought leads to the Woods Option; he 'Can't keep the bombs off' with his 'little drop of love' any more than Grigor and Ilona could miss the bullets by shutting their eyes. For them, sexuality represented a relief, a clinging which Bela knows politics disrupts; Bela accepts that sexual attraction is temporary, will expire.

Grigor's withdrawal has in fact deepened to the point where he is housed, clothed and fed by the London County Council and passes his time passionately painting-by-numbers Windsor Castle and

Yankee Windjammers; and the *Daily Mirror* appoints a cartoon-ist whose zenith of insight is that 'life's a non-stop comedy show'. Surrounded by such instances of retrenchment and despair, Bela's cartoons reflect a sense of impotence and doom (the panorama of Europe in nuclear fire, *'They grew tired of thought'*) and he becomes self-consciously preoccupied with the image of himself as the sole sane guardian of the truth, fleeing from Grigor exclaiming 'Got to keep my lovely head! Last decent brain in Europe!', and telling the *Daily Mirror* manager, Diver, that the world is 'Like a great snake of blindmen tapping sticks, heading for the cliff edge . . . Rather fall off than hear the MAN WHO SEES!'; 'I GOT THE VISION AND YOU HATE ME!'. In the climate of entropy, there is an invigorat-ing quality to Bela's exaggerations (like Old Gocher's in *Fair Slaugh-ter*), especially in his rejection of words and newsprint 'streaming through the city, washing men away with lies . . . Where is the ark? I AM. I AM NOAH, GET ON BOARD!' (48).

This Downchild-like extravagant but futile self-characterisation gives way to recognition of the fact that Bela is struggling with the separation of impulse and action, as ever; Diver claims his insti-tutional role overrides personal inclinations just as the Hungarian officer begged, with his widowed mother, for clemency, depend-ing on a separation of person from social function. Bela argues that Diver's domain, 'soft mad places' replete with 'liquor and cunt' and the passive tense, permits him to suppress his totality of impulses and self for purposes of social expediency. But from glorying in his own shocking function, Bela wryly notes a secre-tary, who provokes a chastening realisation of non-communication: 'Oh, darling, all your sweet bits . . . I've not touched you so much with all my genius as one groove of a loud boy's disc'. Diver tries to lubricate and maintain his reluctant activities with alcohol, though Bela insists on first-person opposition: 'Not Johnny fucking Walker kicking Bela Veracek downstairs! You do it. Don't get Johnny in' (49). Even when lured towards suicide, last refuge of the impotent idealist, he encounters intervening policemen who seek to deny his autonomy and integrity, separating impulse and action with semantic blurs and platitudinous generalisations that pass for official psychology:

P.C. HOOGSTRATEN: You see — no one really wants to die.
BELA: I do.
P.C. HOOGSTRATEN: No. You only think you do.

BELA: Of course I think I do.
P.C. HOOGSTRATEN: That's it, you see.
BELA: What is?   (51)

Tony Dunn comments: 'Impasse, because for Hoogstraten thought means illusion compared with reality, while for Bela it means conceptual processes which issue in action'.[4] And there is further opposition to Bela's location of truth in conceptual energy and practical action: he finds himself sharing a hospital with Grigor, who has surrendered his self to metaphysics, and acts as a vessel for a spirit world of supposed higher forces which deem the material world itself to be an illusion. When this latest form of worship seems confirmed by Grigor demonstrating psychic powers, Bela's faith in himself seems at last overcome, and he is prepared to condemn himself, as well as the world, as mad. In Tony Dunn's words, 'Enclosure seems total';[5] and despair seems complete. But Nurse Glasson admonishes Bela, as did the Second Airwoman, for 'Artist Stuff', elitist subjectivism:

You build your little temple, somewhere in the bottom of your brain, put brass doors on it, and great big hinges, burn your little flame of truth and genius and worship it, WHAT ABOUT US? *(She points to the cartoon)* THAT DON'T 'ELP US! *(Pause)* Assign the blame. *(Pause)* It's madness if yer don't. Cos that's how we go on, blame this, blame that, get it wrong sometimes, of course, but never say we're barmy, or we will be . . .   (55)

Grigor's youthful instruction to become a 'high priest in the temple art' has become literalised into studied unworldliness. Glasson's speech suggests that even Bela's defiant self-identification with the truth has proved to be a suit of armour that has rusted upon him; he has forgotten that truth is not stable, any more than passion (anticipating two lines from *Don't Exaggerate*); she has to rekindle his wants, the appetite for struggle which constitutes a sense of dignity. Conceptual processes and practical action have to be endlessly renewed, else they ossify into committee room dogma. *No End of Blame*'s Scenes of Overcoming involve not only an overcoming of brutalised power and its representatives, but an overcoming of the self: a resistance to not only temptations of gratification but also to self-imposed rigour (in a more inspired moment, Bela says 'There, I contradict myself, but then I always

have') in order to guard against messianic self-righteousness —
another form of idyll leading ultimately to withdrawal (suicidal or
otherwise). Bela staggers out of his wheelchair, advances towards
the audience, demanding 'Give us a pencil', and the sense of enclosure is demolished, as is the 'fourth wall' of the proscenium arch
theatre.

In this stirring (in)conclusion, Bela acknowledges the audience as
sole witnesses to his struggle throughout the play and insists that
their role is not static, but as historically dynamic as his own. It is
a confrontation which denies the dominant sense of isolation for
character and audience members, and emphasises the essential
renewal and regeneration constituted by critical action, where the
conscious self-constructing histories of men and women mesh in
conflicting, confirmatory and occasionally inspirational ways: when
this ceases, life withers into routine. *No End of Blame* extends its
dynamic to the audience for protagonist and witnesses to engage in
mutual self-examination and possible co-operative self-definition;
the play's processes continue into the audience's lives. As Sartre
claims:

> If society sees itself and, in particular, sees itself as *seen*, there is,
> by virtue of this very fact, a contesting of the established values
> of the regime. The writer presents it with its image; he calls upon
> it to assume it or change itself. At any rate, it changes; it loses the
> equilibrium which its ignorance had given it.[6]

The theatrical performance of the play *No End of Blame*, along
with and beyond the events it enacts, offers an illustrative involvement with revolutionary self-consciousness: not the static, precious,
debilitating self-consciousness to which even Bela briefly falls prey;
but the self-consciousness that liberatingly identifies history as
a sequence of personal choices and mutual influences rather than
something beyond the individual's control. Bela is heroic but not
sentimentalised; even his resolve is sometimes deluded or overcome by the forces with which he engages, but the play asserts that
engagement is life's central dynamic necessity, and exemplifies this
assertion as forcefully as any dramatic fiction.

'When you're old you think of all the things that can't be done,
and when you're young you think of all the things that can'; Bela's
aphorism from *No End of Blame* (47) identifies a crux in Barker's
television play *Pity in History* (staged 1984, and transmitted in

1985), which, as its title suggests, is similarly concerned with supportive and destructive personal reactions involved in what are usually identified as larger, even impersonal, social forces such as war, religion, order and art. In an English cathedral in 1644, the moribund cook Murgatroyd anticipates his imminent status as 'War dead' while remaining indignantly garrulous, an unsettling displacement of official military terminology and philosophy. Like the Airman in *No End of Blame*, Murgatroyd is galvanised into a sense of absurdity in army instructions for participation, and accordingly asks 'bog questions', which are deliberately unanswerable in terms of the officially-recognised definitions: 'I ACCUSE THE ARMY OF FAILING TO INSTRUCT ITS SOLDIERS 'OW TO DIE! They teach you 'ow to kill, what about dying, I will raise this with my MP! REGULATIONS ON DYING GRACEFULLY!' (13).

Like Dawkins in *Heroes of Labour*, Murgatroyd is outside the established patterns of definition and motivation and thus beyond their command: 'you can't control me because you can't punish me! What are you going to do? Take my leave away? I'VE LOST MY LEAVE FOREVER YOU!' He also insists on locating blame: 'You want me to forgive you, 'ow nice if corpse forgives you, everything's smooth, everything's nice, lie down in yer 'ole and let us get on with it, I DON'T FORGIVE YOU, NOT THIS CORPSE, NOT CROMWELL NOR THE 'OUSE OF COMMONS NEITHER! NONE OF 'EM! YOU GOT MY BLOOD ON YER!' Even as he dislocates the symmetry of army definition, Murgatroyd is painfully aware of his exclusion from the promised ideals of warfare, and spits on placatory images of imminent freedom: 'Don't tell a dead man about the future, 'ave you got no tact?' (14).

Factor, the army captain, tries to instil a sense of class warfare in his dimly comprehending recruits; they are also instructed by Croop the chaplain who maintains 'Property is the basis of all order'. When the soldiers grope towards the realisation that property is also idolatry, and sense its relation to their own poverty rather than to a divine being, Croop steps up his measures to encourage a sense of divine inspiration in their destruction of a cathedral, and then uses religion again to brake and circumscribe their aggression ('now we learn patience, tolerance and self-control'). Thus the soldiers, like Grigor, feel themselves to be the agents of spiritual powers, while their captain insists on the materialist basis of their mission as a reclamation of self.

The only characters able to navigate these inclusive philosophies and self-justifying prescriptions are Murgatroyd and the
fatalistic mason Gaukroger, who sees death and destruction as historical inevitabilities. Both characters live for and in the moment —
Murgatroyd by physical necessity, Gaukroger by temperament —
which makes them resistant to the long-term objectives and
deferred fulfilments on which the authority of the officer and
chaplain class is grounded. But unlike Murgatroyd, Gaukroger
claims the word 'blame' is not in his dictionary: he sees no achievement as permanent and takes a basic pleasure in the means of survival, beer and sandwiches ('I have no pride. If you can't eat it,
chuck it, that's my motto'), and his trade represents his bartering
power to obtain these, however short-changed he may be in the
process. Indeed, he is paid in obsolete money by a landowner's
widow, Venables, who has commissioned a monument to her late
husband.

Like Gaukroger, Venables sees history as a disruptive, elemental
force, but believes that its vicissitudes can be weathered by conserv-
atives who can 'keep their feet, who say of all calamity, this is a set-
back, but I hold to my own truth' (28). However, any 'truth' which
remains unresponsive to any external event becomes malign in its
self-justifying rigour: Venables unhesitatingly kills Murgatroyd to
preserve her art from the soldiers. In this respect, Venables recalls
Staveley in *Fair Slaughter* in her maddened bourgeois sense of art
as property for obsessive hoarding, in order to define her identity
('We have to have art or we don't know who we are', 30). Thus art
is made prey to idolatry, combining capitalist associations of commodity and religious associations of superhuman icon, the keystone
of a false currency and value system which extends to the field of
morality. Gaukroger's jaded and personally utilitarian view of his
'product' is an ironic contrast to that of Venables, but he remains in
thrall to her economic power.

Another viewpoint in this densely layered short play is that of
Gaukroger's teenage apprentice, Pool. They work together with
comic inequality like other Barker double acts, Hacker and Clout,
Downchild and Stoat, Savage and Hogbin in *The Bite of the Night*,
as an initially secure, increasingly embattled self-centred philosopher and his rebellious pupil-servant, flattered with the status of
'*protégé*'. Whereas Gaukroger is the expedient spokesman for
impossibility and impermanence, Pool has a youthful sense of
possibility which leads to impatience with the limitations of his

tutor's skills but also to the lure of misguided idealism. Angered by Gaukroger's stoic response to Venables, he joins the army thinking 'the only skill worth having is skill with a rifle'. When the soldiers move to smash Gaukroger's masonry as vanity, hypocrisy, praise of greed and power, Pool insists that it is nevertheless a testament to Gaukroger's endeavour: 'Say what it is. It's YOU. Say it. SAY IT'. But Gaukroger knows that the completed object passes from his control and envisions it as an item of institutionalised reverence in a museum, where people spend lifetimes in service, maintenance and worship to valued objects, 'and a boy who tried to carve his initials on the tomb was beaten and called delinquent. And the Museum grew, until it covered England'. 'No pity in History' deduces Gaukroger, but Pool sees this as self-absolving laziness and reductivity: 'NO. ARGUE FOR IT'. He smashes the monument in anger at Gaukroger's self-engendered and self-protective cynicism. But as Gaukroger subsides into exhaustion at the spectacle of destruction, Pool returns to rouse him to a new dynamic of method and purpose:

GEDDUP, GAUKROGER! . . . Find the language. Find the style. New manner for new situation. When in doubt, invent. Copy. Cheat. Get by . . . Calamity, all right, bowled over, flat on yer back, looks bad, admitted, but not fatal, still got 'ands, still got eyes . . . STICK WITH IT, MICHAEL, EH?

The continued co-operation of the couple may involve working within commercial definitions to survive, as Gaukroger would emphasise; but it may also lead to possibilities of self-expression or influence beyond 'dead art', as Pool hopes. Their final embrace is beleaguered but resilient, and where Gaukroger is mindful of erosion, 'Too much imitation leaves you with nothing for the real', Pool sees a demonstration of integrity in action, whatever the cost: 'Was real . . . Was real' (31).

'Artists have no power and great imagination. The State has no imagination and great power'. The consequences of this tension are central to Barker's radio play *Scenes from an Execution* (broadcast 1984, Prix Italia 1986), in which the classical idealist Carpeta and the passionate social critic Galactia are joined by sexual attraction despite their divergent philosophies. Carpeta repeatedly paints Christ among the flocks out of 'a passion for perfection'; Galactia receives a state commission to paint the Battle of Lepanto in a presumed spirit of glorious celebration of imperial victory for the Venetian Republic and the Christian State, but she insists on locating responsibility for pain in the powerful. Carpeta accuses her of being incapable of feeling or depicting pity, but Galactia refutes his definition of the term: 'It's surrender, the surrender of passion, or the passion of surrender. It's capitulating to what is. Rather than pity the dead man I would say — there — there is the man who did it, blame him, identify. Locate responsibility . . . You paint pity very well, but you endure everything, and in the end you find Christ's wounds — enticing. You find suffering — erotic'.

Galactia's sense of pitiful eloquence is contrastingly focused in the image of the severed hand in battle (60). She bypasses metaphysical symbolism, and aims for the recognition of complicity in a savagery which is irresistible but unforgivable. Galactia wants her audience to experience the pain of the sea-battle rather than be oppressed into association with the institutionalised reverence of national sacrifice, its icons of celebration and monuments to majestic absorption. The Doge of Venice, Urgentino, believes a great artist must above all be 'responsible' to the cultivation of imperialist and humanist pride. But Galactia's work is inimical to the spirit of peaceful submission; her use of the maimed ex-soldier Prodo as a subject for painting detail demonstrates her preference for ruthless exposure: 'I have never been at peace with life, I would not be at peace with life, there is no such thing and those who claim they have it have drugged their consciences or numbed their pain with futile repetitions of old catechisms, catechisms like your patter, oh look at you. WHO DID IT TO YOU, PRODO, AND WHAT FOR?' (51).

Prodo is consequently dislocated from placidly identifying himself as a 'walking manifestation of organic solidarity and the resilience of the Christian state', to acknowledging the pain, anger and grief that are the dim truths and horror of his 'STUPID LIFE'. Galactia finds his grappling towards this 'wonderful' but her interest ends with their respective achievements and she dismisses the sobbing man.

The Admiral Suffici takes refuge in subjectivism: 'There is no such thing as what happened, surely? Only views of what happened. Just as there is no such thing as a man. Only images of him' (63). But this licenses the impersonality of the passive mood and passive tense. Galactia maintains her faith in precise identification — 'when I show meat sliced, it is meat sliced, it is not a pretext for elegance' (61) — which articulates and gives form to suppressed social responses: 'with one figure I transformed the enemy from beast to victim and made victory unclean' (58). Her daughter Supporta counsels restraint, claiming that offence eclipses brilliance (an issue in the general approach to Barker's work!), but Galactia sees this as a self-regulation like the Doge's invocations of responsibility and celebration, designed to preclude the totality of human response and impulses; she counters, 'It's an artist's job to be coarse. Preserving coarseness, that's the problem' (61).

Thus Galactia places her faith in the painting, the image of effects which begs questions of cause and cuts through algebraic sophistries of spoken and written word, weapons of the state. As with Stoat's painting in *Downchild*, the radio medium of *Scenes from an Execution* demands audience involvement in assembling a cumulative impression of Galactia's work and its force, stimulating imagination through suggestion, and demonstrating the pain and irony through which the assembling of imaginative detail progresses, for example the means by which Prodo comes to act as 'a barometer of human incomprehension, in contrast to the fixed and callous stare of the Admiral Suffici, a double-edged demonstration of the cost of knowledge. The critic Gina Rivera seeks to contain Galactia's explosive power, complaining of the consequences of embarrassment for the dominant regime. Like the committee in *No End of Blame*, Rivera promotes postponement and mitigation of grievance lest the discrediting of the Doge contribute to his fall and usher in a more brutal regime. Rivera's advancement of the 'party line' is testimony to her circumscribed, careerist interpretation of intellectual obligations:

GALACTIA: You're a critic, aren't you?
RIVERA: Yes, but I must have something to criticize. (67)

Rivera wishes to safeguard her own position within the system, accepting its terms. Galactia's power is her ability to highlight the cost of those terms, make a 'bawling pack of squaddies yelling male love' smell the lie beneath 'the catechisms of the state'. She tells Prodo 'there's no truth where men are being manly' and demonstrates to him and to the drunken sailors who invade the studio that their male martial idealism is a form of erotic capitulation, like Carpeta's suffering Christ.

Urgentino, in his luxurious palace, is nevertheless mindful of art's cumulative effect, but flatters himself through identification with it: 'Art is opinion, and opinion is the source of all authority' (71). In fact, his authority depends on the management of opinion and the suppression of the imagination, as shown by his judgement on Galactia's painting 'it is getting worse, not from the technical point of view but from the moral one' (72). He seeks an 'appropriate response' to 'this calculated and obscene affront to History' and attempts to intoxicate Galactia with a sense of her own martyrdom: 'Confirmation. Of our baseness. Is what she wants' (73). Indeed, as with Bela, Pool or Gaukroger, Barker resists audience inclinations to see Galactia in sentimental heroic terms. When she prides herself on 'shattering tolerance' and exults in her painting, her sense of herself becomes inflated and intoxicated, like Bela in his fears for his 'lovely head' full of truth:

> They are putting it on a barge, and the barge will sail up the canal, like some great bomb snuggled under tarpaulins, and they will unload it and carry it into the palaces of power, and it will tear their minds apart and explode the wind in their deep cavities, and I shall be punished for screaming truth where truth is not allowed. IT MADE CARPETA WEEP WITH ITS POWER!
>
> (75)

But Carpeta is weeping for himself, shamed by his guilty collusion with the state in seeking to supplant Galactia, and moreover by his not reciprocating her love. This irony at her expense is compounded when she admits to feeling 'Virtuous. And scared' before the Doge, who seizes the chance to fulfil his impulses of voyeurism and sadistic gratification implicit in institutionalised privilege, contrasting the cushions, carpets and windows on his side of the Bridge of Sighs to the straw, bare stone and darkness in the adjoining prison: 'I cannot tell you how it excites me to think of your bare breasts against the wall, and my buttocks on this brocade' (78). Indeed, Galactia's self-righteousness extends to fantasies of self-immolation, suggesting an unrecognised element of complicity in this lurid scenario, where the characters delight in personally-ordained melodrama. The Man In The Next Cell suggests that survival depends on restriction of ego and appetite, as opposed to the gestural flourish. Galactia describes her attachment to her surroundings in fetishistic terms when Carpeta visits the prison, but this displaced renewal of her pride and sexuality is fundamentally a wilful defiance of her enemies and an embarrassment of her lover; once released, she lapses into his arms.

Carpeta's anaemic attempt at painting the Battle of Lepanto drives Urgentino to acknowledging the despair beneath his liberal exterior, like that of Orbison in *That Good Between Us*:

I have been — through my own sensitivity — been drawn into needless conflicts with people who, crazed by self-indulgence, will not, and perhaps, God help them, cannot sympathize with the problems of governing a modern state! . . . I sometimes wish I was a brute . . . a brute with brute senses. Sending regiments to toss pianos out of windows. Really. You cannot imagine how I long to send pianos flying out of windows!   (83)

But Rivera prompts him towards repressive tolerance, absorbing the painting's effects rather than being scandalised by them. Galactia is appalled by this smothering comprehension which defines her effect as exhaustible, manageable and limited; the picture's position in the sanctity of the gallery precludes the effect of dockside mutiny. But the independence of the painting has ramifications beyond its function as tool of either repression or agitation. Urgentino congratulates himself and the State on showing victories 'not as parades of virility but as terrible cost', and predicts that wrath-withering time will accord the painting merely 'cold, dull respect'. Galactia falls short of single-handedly effecting the mass rising of the proletariat, but witnesses the instability of personal response to her work, and draws encouragement from one member of the public mutely clasping her hands: a personal arousal and experience of pity, on her own terms rather than Carpeta's. Her accord with the State, accepting Urgentino's invitation to dinner, is in contrast to Bela's persistent opposition but does not nullify the effectiveness of the canvas; the work of art lives its own subsequent life (demonstrated by its effect upon the Young Sailor and the weeping peasant) as a truthteller unreduced by the compromises — perhaps even personal corruption — of Galactia herself.

The pitiful eloquence of the hand is a crucial detail in these three plays. As Galactia says, 'hands are the points of contact between man and man, man and woman, the instruments of friendship, symbols of love and trust . . . in battles they drop from the sky, and men shake stumps in anger' (60). Bela practises his hand in drawing, Glasson points her finger in accusation at his despairing cartoon, he finally advances to the audience with an open palm, demanding the restitution of his instrument of expression.

Venables threatens the soldiers with the image of severed hands 'raised against God and King' nailed to a 'hand tree', and Pool signals his return to Gaukroger with a hand appearing from a tomb, holding a sandwich; he demands tuition in sculpting its nuances, 'the 'and recumbent, the 'and demonstrative', points out calamity is not fatal while 'still got 'ands. Still got eyes' and kisses Gaukroger's hand when it clenches back into action to bury Murgatroyd. Galactia perceives the truth of Suffici's nature and paints him with 'talons' and the man at the exhibition clasps her hands in mute expression of pity, the recognition of participation in unforgiveable, irresistible pain. The short play 'Kiss My Hands' in *The Possibilities* depicts its ultimate expression in the eponymous gesture at the separation of wife and doomed husband; in its companion play 'The Unforeseen Consequences of a Patriotic Act', Judith cuts off a hand which is offered in a gesture of love, as a symbolic rejection of her treason to Holofernes.

Barker's plays are exploratory strivings to locate truth beyond hypocrisy, blame behind idolatry, pity among dispossession; his characters are heroic when they keep faith with the 'cry of the blood' and shatter tolerance, rather than succumb to the surrender of passion and the passion of surrender, where wounds become enticing, suffering is erotic, and absorption stifles struggle. *No End of Blame* and *Scenes from an Execution* are further bids to locate and argue for 'Pity in History' through various historical and international settings; the characters experience collapse and concession, but persist in defiance of the fascination and threats of state power. Barker's plays proffer new values and invite contact and communion, like Bela's open palm; they accuse, like Glasson's finger; they rage, like the stumps of the maimed in battle. They call for ceaseless redefinition of the self and engagement in historical dynamics, seeking the truth which occurs when essence is illuminated by the renewal and regeneration of form: new manner for new situation.

6

Landscapes of Shame, Eruptions of Desire

THE LOVE OF A GOOD MAN, CRIMES IN HOT COUNTRIES, THE
POOR MAN'S FRIEND, THE BLOW

> The exercise of authority is contingent upon the longing for
> subordination that lies curled up in every human heart.
>
> .   .   .
>
> You can be governed, because you are ashamed.
>
> *The Blow*
>
> The ecstasy of the slap
> The longing in the blow
>
> *The Breath of the Crowd* 9

Governments are institutions that derive their power from the
submission of the governed. Their injustices are dependent upon
passive or active collaboration. Official definitions of tradition, religion and culture can inculcate an appetite for submission through
shame: the internalised feeling of humiliation excited by a consciousness of failure, guilt, shortcomings, offences against propriety,
modesty, decency or life itself. In wishing to avoid such humiliation,
the majority surrender powers of imposed restraint to a minority —
who can then increase their power by amplifying the majority's fear
of their own essential weakness and tendency to slide compulsively
into offence, disgrace or ignominy. Consequently, the majority
empower the minority with further strictures and generally abne-
gate the responsibility of self-monitoring and self-determination to
the quasi-parental forces they have called upon to 'save them from
themselves' (often formulated in terms of saving the mind from the
body). This relief at external regulation depends partially on a nostalgia for infancy, partially on a lack of faith in one's capacities for
adulthood or essential worth.

Desire restores or emphasises this faith, and ruptures shame.
Barker's drama demonstrates the collisions and collusions of these

contrary forces with unique exploratory insights and startling effects, across large and unlikely landscapes, rather than in the conventional domestic setting of most drama. His characteristic terrain of inquiry leads through large-scale manifestations of public absurdity, which depend on the orchestration of large groups; hence the frequent whiff of battlefields, corpses and money which blows through the events; and the unconventional flux of his characters, struggling to reconcile contradictory demands on their instincts, fighting an internalised war with surprising movements of collapse, restitution and development.

The Love of a Good Man (staged 1978) picks up on the talismanic definition of the flesh, first broached in the image of Tovarish's severed hand in *Fair Slaughter*, where fascination and authority persist beyond — even because of — death and dismemberment. Ronald Hacker's commission to erect a cemetery in Passchendaele, 1920, involves working a landscape 'not ground so much as flesh' into a suitable form to be consecrated as a monument to national investment, and to be ceremonially opened by the Prince of Wales. The Prince's naive simplicity nevertheless makes him personally favour a gauche gesture of redundant contrition: 100ft-high coloured lights spanning Flanders, spelling out the word 'SORRY'.

The Prince demonstrates that a sufficiently inept member of the monarchy can be contaminated by shame, as he rushes to prostrate himself before his own romanticised image of the commoner, but also revealing his dynastic predilection for the symbolically charged act, kissing a worker's hand in ostentatious self-abasement. He develops a fetish for suffering through his — mistaken and unrealistic — sense of his power to relieve it, so that his gaudy pity borders on the erotic: 'As soon as we've done the battlefields I intend to do the slums. I will go to them at their cottage doors, and pulling aside the rambling roses I will say tell me what is wrong. Do not be frightened. I am only a king . . . Give me the facts and I will act on them' (43).

Even the professional opportunist Hacker baulks at the impulse to wallow in annihilation ('I wonder if it isn't best forgotten? . . . A decent veil drawn over it?'), but Bride, the War Commissioner, holds fast to the sanctification of sacrifice, promising 'the people' an ascension from mean life and mean death by 'dazzling them with suffering' which Hacker must 'orchestrate' (7). Though Hacker maintains an ironic detachment from this ecstatic wonder, he perceives the chance for profit from this large-scale swing away from the 'whispering and decorum' of ordinary funerals to necrophilia on a massive scale. Other fetishes are evident through alliance: one soldier, Riddle, dissociates himself from wartime 'mania for bonhomie I could fight for twenty years if it were not for the singing'; and the bereaved tourists Mrs Toynbee and daughter Lalage sense the potential and quickening of their own magnetism and power. Mrs Toynbee finds a thrill in the speculation that 'No two women have ever been surrounded by so much male flesh', being addicted to images of enviable isolation; she wishes to rescue her son Billy's body from the uniformity of an official, standard grave, believing 'Every moving gesture, every beautiful thought, is hideous in proportion to its popularity', so that Passchendaele is reduced to a matter of choice 'between Billy and us' (12), and the instinctive promptings of her womb which assume a magical incontrovertibility.

Lalage also enjoys a sense of exclusiveness: her wilful scepticism makes her easy prey for the ironist Riddle, but he exposes the extent to which her thirst for experience betrays signs of exhaustive defiance of her mother's monolithic self-isolation, echoing the relationship between Rhoda and Orbison in *That Good*. Riddle perceives Lalage's sense of self-congratulation, 'I read what is engraved on every vertebra along her spine. It says I am clean, and I do good' (27), and envisions her search for knowledge degenerating into surreptitious sodomising, 'jellies, creams and second rate hotels'; he plans to turn away from Europe, 'dead continents and dead women', toward a place 'where there is desire in the hips of women and a slow look in their eyes, where flesh is flesh and as old as sex itself'. Lalage dismisses this as Dionysian romanticism, 'The lie of submissive, dark-skinned women', generating carnal mystery through biblical vocabulary (41); but her offer of help through marriage demonstrates her ultimate reversion to class type and existent social power structures.

Hacker provides an unlikely counterpoint in his experience of the upheavals of the body, as he is stricken to deifying Mrs Toynbee's physical essences with an extravagant abandon that is both comic and poignant: 'Oh God our 'elp in ages past . . . I could use 'er shit as toothpaste . . . I could crawl across three fields of broken glass just for a piss in 'er bathwater' (15). Mrs Toynbee is armoured in the secure consciousness of her own effect, such as her fainting which 'gave men the opportunity to fulfil a need. A need to be powerful' (19). The urgent, ubiquitous impulses to romanticisation are understandable partial rearguards against a predatory, reductive landscape: Flowers notes 'The human substance 'as a tendency to imitate the soil in which it's placed. In Palestine, our dead blokes are made of sand, while 'ere, unluckily, they absorb their weight in water and turn into mud' (19). Shared crisis can engender or precipitate desire, as the deadlocks of habitual superficiality dissolve; but it can also effect nostalgia for integration in reinforcements of allied imperialistic myths of national and sexual identity. Hacker berates Bass, a recalcitrant soldier, for his supposed lack of idealism:

HACKER: . . . Christ, what is England coming to? What did we fight the war for? Women, wasn't it? Women and their feelings?
BASS: I love the 'we'.
HACKER: Christ, appealing to Englishmen to 'ave an 'eart. I never thought I'd see the day.

Hacker is haunted by visions of himself withered into lonely, incontinent senility, and of Mrs Toynbee's son reduced to meat and dirt ('To think that — muck — down there came out between 'er lovely limbs'). It is a central irony in the promise of conservatism that Hacker's bids to elevate or immortalise his individual efforts both fuel and are fuelled by the dominant sense of human cheapness and squalor. Bride's professional elevation of ordered tabulation makes him a natural spokesman for a despairing distaste redolent of Eddie Egdon's father: 'The most repulsive aspect of humanity is the ease with which it reproduces. If conception were more difficult, we would be less contemptuous of our lives. Were we pandas, should we have fought the Battle of the Somme?' (22). England's recurring nightmare feeds on a sense of human multitude to sharpen a sense of territorial privilege by suggesting a threat of 'creeping socialism . . . lowering downwards . . . further evidence of the persistent erosion of individual choice' (25).

Colonel Hard intervenes as a missionary of hierarchical certainty over insurrections of the body, offering men and women an image of themselves as 'good' only in accordance with their service of a holy trinity of Sacrifice, Duty and Empire ('All men long to serve. Service to the Empire lifts us from our secret cess', 47). But the consolations of rigour lose ground amid these Scenes of Flesh and Calculation. Hacker searches for a dead son in order to win the live mother; Clout subverts Hacker's commercial equation 'I pay yer, so I own yer', suggesting their deadline can be met by burying four corpses to a grave and demanding half the profits for his inspiration. Hacker senses the vulnerability of his authority and invokes national idealism ('FUCK ME, WHERE IS YOUR LOYALTY! Not just to me. Not just to me who 'as provided you with work and wages when work and wages can't be 'ad, but to these dead Englishmen', 37). But Clout perceives that Hacker is himself in thrall to a larger conservative myth by seeking Royal Appointment. Even the Prince of Wales is systematically bound with fear and suspicion by the attendant Gentleman's assurances: 'Every flag-waver is an assassin in his darker blood. A proper king knows that. He never stops' (44).

Riddle can delve into situations as well as bodies, and query banal unison ('Singing is the slaves' consolation' he pronounces, like a wise escapee from *One Afternoon*), but rather than resist orders, he takes delight in the sensationalism of army life, killing Irishmen one day 'And making love to their widows the next'. Lalage can block her mother's plans to export Billy's remains, but her defiance is further self-congratulation, aspiring to the messianic. Hacker is driven to new depths of desperation, chasing receding promises of Mrs Toynbee's physical favours through Clout's increasingly labyrinthine and irreverent intrigues. Ian Lucas writes of their partnership.

> The attitude of existing in the face of overwhelming obstacles injects a gritty realism into Barker's comedy. Clout's knowledge is often used to show Hacker's flaws — he is continually correcting Hacker, quietly but confidently, and surprising Hacker with his acute knowledge of what is happening. Clout is the dependable, but continually mocked, member of the partnership, made fun of by his more boisterous counterpart until needed for something. His suggestion to ease the workload by burying the bodies four deep is treated with comic finesse in its construction, but is essentially not only poignant but harrowing. Barker's humour is frequently that of necessity and self-protection: the characters who seem the funniest are also the saddest and weakest. The comic elements within the plays are structured around high tension, acting as a displacement through which the audience and characters can assess the situations they are discovering.[1]

The forces of imperial order invoke mechanical structure and inclusive mythologies, from Hard's book *Cult of Empire* to the Royal

Visit to the religious sermon, but the unpredictability of human response continually defies rational calculation and produces explosions of appalling comedy which buckle the tramlines of imposed symmetry and send its agents careering wildly off the rails, crashing into each other. Mrs Toynbee blames *Cult of Empire* for her son's death, but, rather than rage against Hard, she demands a five-shilling refund, when Hard can only find three-and-ninepence; the Prince of Wales becomes incontinent though his attendant steadfastly refuses to countenance the very possibility; and the Bishop resolves to disrupt ceremonial decorum by voicing his personal chafing at professional and divine contradiction with an unrehearsed speech on 'Why God Likes Pain': 'we are situated in a sea of it. An Atlantic of stilled agony . . . Well, I will not apologize for Him. I am always apologizing for Him. It's getting a bit much . . . This mission — this so-called calling . . . which consists in making the vile palatable, and finding symmetry in the hideous, it is becoming an impertinence' (53–4). This is a supreme comic moment of wilful deviation from prearranged order (hence the Gentleman's attempted interruptions — an index to official distress) and valiant but incapable attempts to fit a Divine Being into the Procrustean bed of vicarage admonition, which terms cosmic injustice 'a bit much'.

The Bishop goes on to enquire 'I do not deny the existence of the person God. I merely ask what sort of character He has . . . I ask you, would you let Him near your child? Because, quite frankly, I would not!' The Prince's speech provides an opportunity to re-establish order, but he also diverges from arrangement and identifies himself as head of 'The g-g-great British Establishment that sends young soldiers to their deaths'; but his remedial programme is tellingly, ludicrously threadbare of realism and imagination: 'Finish with that. Altogether better establishment from now on. Promise' (54). He can only oppose national waste with the language of the school playground; like the Bishop's admonition, it is both comic and pathetic in its inadequacy. The crowning effect of the scene occurs when the ceremony of choosing the Unknown Warrior turns out to have been rigged by Clout, who copied out Billy Toynbee's ledger number 300 000 times for his financial gain and Hacker's sexual advantage.

However, Hacker is disappointed, and in disappointment gains dignity. Honesty has not been his staple characteristic until he realises Mrs Toynbee may succumb to the Prince's neurotic advances. He is driven to argue with the naked directness and desperate sincerity of desire: 'All right, I am, I'm married, but I'm lonelier than 'im. You can be lonely in a double bed. You can 'ave a body next to yer and it can be as 'ostile as lead ripped off a prison roof' (58). But she resists him, as she resists the Prince's offers of castles and begging for conventional verbal foreplay ('Say you wanted me from the day we met') until he is reduced to a position of shame before her:

> *She looks coolly at him.*
> MRS TOYNBEE: You are very childish and very weak . . . I don't think you will make much of a king.
> PRINCE: Poor old England. Rotten luck. *(Pause, then with desperation)* I WANT TO F-F-F- *(He shuts his eyes in despair)* FUCK YOUR CUNT!
> *He turns away, ashamed.* MRS TOYNBEE *goes to him, takes his hands.*
> MRS TOYNBEE: Don't be afraid, I desire you . . .
> *She releases them, just as* HACKER *appears from the darkness.* (67)

Witnessing this exchange stirs Hacker into new self-awareness and autonomy, as he ruefully wonders 'Why is it that the narky, dirty little corners of yer character are the places the truth chooses for its nest?' He is no longer subservient to the Prince or concerned for his contract, and acknowledges his collusion in a national confidence trick: 'England, what I would not 'ave done for it on condition I wasn't out of pocket. You people turn patriots into spivs'. In the wake of Bride's suicidal despair, Hacker feels doubly charged to 'be honest, 'ard as it is': while openly admitting his continuing fascination with Mrs Toynbee, he is incensed by the extent of her calculation in offering to fulfil the letter of the contract and let herself be made love to. Hacker recoils: 'I don't believe you 'ave a body. You 'ave a ready-reckoner bound in skin'. The Prince insists on his own culpability, despite the Gentleman's more worldly objections ('Nothing can be your fault. It says so in the constitution'); he seeks to absorb blame and abase himself in martyrdom: 'I don't think you should turn on England . . . because of me . . . it's the hereditary system . . . spewed up me . . .' (68).

But Hacker is determined to tear away the musty canvas and expose the machinery of the nation's self-deceit. Hoping to inflict a mortal wound, he tells Mrs Toynbee that the corpse is not Billy's, but she shelters in her mystical certainty of her womb's unanswerable promptings. As Tony Dunn has commented, 'Her alliance with the Prince of Wales unscrambles the class lines which have got danger-ously tangled up in the extraordinary battlefield situation'[2]; but Hacker sees the collusion in submission: 'I 'AVE MADE A BERK OF YOU! *(He shakes his head in amazement)* You people . . . yer gobs are clamped so tight on the tits of privilege, yer can't stop sucking even when the dugs are dry . . . ' (69).

Insight into complicity is the best that the characters of *The Love of a Good Man* can hope for. Riddle recognises Hacker's 'scuttling back to London with the profits', but is himself *en route* to Ireland to serve as a Black and Tan, instead of finding his non-European utopia of dusky sexuality. Hacker sees their folly but remains in sexual thrall to the memory of Mrs Toynbee, on whose vacant chair he places a valedictory kiss, not without shame. 'Fuck it', he says, 'I have the moral fibre of a rat', as he exits to a *'Slow fade'* of dawning realization.

The Unknown Soldier, elevated icon of pride in waste, is cen-tral to the play's activities as it offers alternative images of his-torical causality. A hapless German's remains will be interred and enshrined in Westminster Abbey for guilty adoration — perhaps recalling St Paul's Cathedral, where the ashes of Ezra Fricker ('for an ashamed people, The Man Who Is Not Ashamed') are licked up by a fascist schoolboy at the end of *The Loud Boy's Life*. The title *The Love of a Good Man* prompts associations of erotic redemption and correction of despair and deviancy: a characteristically reverberative black irony in a play in which sexuality bursts feverishly through symmetry and the human figures seem continually on the verge of a willed melting into the landscape of literal and metaphorical dead flesh; as Flowers says of Mrs Toynbee, 'She's over-ripe. Someone should pluck 'er or she's gonna drip' (23).

The problematic notion of sexual salvation is also crucial to *Crimes in Hot Countries* (written 1980, first full production 1983, revised for 1985), set in a sandy landscape which might be the terrain to which Flowers contrasted Passchendaele. Again, central characters are self-consciously 'women in a strange country' and Hacker is re-activated as Ronald's slightly more raffish elder brother Alfred, to suggest the universality of the type, advancing the spirit of free enterprise which combines patriot with spiv. Hacker announces his arrival with a fanfare of the determinedly plastic: 'I'm nothing if not an adaptor. I am going to like this place'. He is accompanied by a trio of prostitutes offering a form of commercial repressive tolerance for the seething troops stationed in a remote colonial garrison, and a sly

Puckish magician, Toplis, equipped with mutineer spirit, conjuring tricks and words.

Crimes in Hot Countries explores the psychology of imperialism, commercial degradation and sexual desire with particular elegance and poise of language; its aphorisms sparkle but cut with diamond hardness, in an inspired violation of comedy-of-manners trappings and form. Echoes of Wilde and Coward are instrumental in creating the dramatic atmosphere of the imperial outpost, wicker chairs and buzzing flies, frosted calm and yearning aches, in comic demonstration of the fragility of the line dividing mad dogs and Englishmen when man-made rigour is eroded by natural anarchy. Toplis is the agent of artful mischief, spending his sole currency of words in struggle with the local governor Tallboy for the hearts and minds of soldiers and prostitutes.

Lawrence of Arabia moves among the men under a cloak of anonymity and the pseudonym of Private Pain, like a latter-day Henry V on the eve of Agincourt, mindful of the delicacy of order: 'The common soldier is both the greatest object to efficiency and the ultimate condition of it. He has to be driven to take a bath. He reads comics. His vocabulary consists of stale abuse. Yet these are the very factors which enable him to lay down his life by numbers. An army is a fallacy sustained by contradiction' (5). He tries to educate the troops in classical strategy, struggling with his own contrary homosexual and abstemious impulses ('Oh, God, this is an awful place, and in their bronzed and burning beauty all my sin laps me with tongues of shame' (9).[3] One soldier, Eddie Music, sees through the tales of Caesar and the cult of kit to their essential slavishness: 'We are a mincing little race. The trilling and traipsing to some ninny's trumpet just to get your finger up some sad hint's slit'. Pain's cultivation of his ideal, 'symmetry of empire', is dependent on its separation from home truths and native realities, as Music senses: 'Rumour goes on to say England's so sad they are afraid to let us look at it' (12). Music, the sceptic, is joined by his ex-lover Toplis, the subversive (self-styled 'tickler of the imagination') who teases Music for failing to break ranks (like Riddle in *The Love of a Good Man*); Toplis insists Music cannot be happy in a place where he is not free, but Music ducks and weaves through his verbal slipknots. Hacker shares Toplis's sense of the outpost's potential as a challenge to personal power, pronouncing the country 'Beautiful with opportunity. Beautiful with nothingness waiting for somethingness to happen'.

All forces gather for a dinner party at the Governor's house, where his daughter Erica presides with aristocratic dog-in-a-manger imperiousness, acting as a goddess of fetishism for the salivating soldiers who compete to hook her dress and steal her laundry. She is wryly aware of her role and the 'bloody thoughts' which focus on her, which the arriving trio of women may relieve or deflect; but their spokeswoman, Mrs Struggle, insists they are 'Not PROSTI-TUTES', conscious as the Republicans in *Credentials of a Sympathizer* that 'We are in the hands of words' (17). *Crimes in Hot Countries* provides shining comic demonstration of this fact, especially in the incidents of literal misunderstanding or sarcasm contained within the dinner party scene: Erica orders 'Give the not prostitutes a drink, will you?'; Hacker sought chocolates but failed to make himself understood, 'Black Magic is something to do with toads and sheep's eyes, apparently' — instead he offers a chit, redeemable at his store, which Erica offers to put in water, the conventional response to a gift of flowers; the naïve hydrologist Porcelain fails to see the skill involved in Tallboy's demand that the magician 'cut a tart in half' until it is pointed out that he means a woman, not pastry; and Erica replies to Knotting's question 'have I seen Lawrence of Arabia?' with 'I find that rather hard to answer. What do people who have seen him look like?' (17).

Toplis proposes a relief from misunderstanding, shame and mood — a restoration of integrity, through magical truth that is opposed to the conventional associations of sleight-of-hand deception: 'My magic will spill continents, set pavements shaking and splash blood in the flower beds, but I will save you, spare you from the pain of painlessness, the half-fuck and the semi-anger, the endless rattle of your questions which are not questions, I will uncover you and you will say I never knew I was so beautiful, I will separate your clothes and set the tired flesh free' (19). Pain brands it 'Moscow magic', whereby 'Dr Marx has given soldiers a philosophical authority for doing what they only had an instinct for. Shooting their officers' (22). It provides Erica with an opportunity for fulfilling a sexual instinct, exposing her breasts and thereby placing her and Toplis in an equilibrium of witnessed nakedness, unbalancing her previous power through detailing his intrinsic physical banality on the beach. No longer guarding this power, she can admit to Trellis 'I could have licked him all over', and that her sexual curiosity has been stirred: 'Does he look ashamed or murderous? I prefer the look of murder, I do want to be murdered, do you?' She sublimates her frustrations in a staged boxing match with Pain (the other character 'so weak for flesh') in which she both dictates and flouts the rules in the established manner of government:

ERICA: YOU ARE NOT ALLOWED TO RUN AWAY!
PAIN: That is a rule!
ERICA (pursuing him); I WANT TO HIT YOU!
PAIN: Ah, yes.
ERICA: LET ME HIT YOU!
PAIN (trapped); DING!
ERICA: That wasn't three minutes!
PAIN: No rules!
ERICA (hitting him in the jaw); DING! Left hook!(21–2)

Pain performs submission and imbues it with idealised lyricism, as Erica performs ruthlessness, but she finds his predictability in 'death' a bore, especially as it terminates the game and exposes its lack of realism — and moreover its lack of risk, which she later identifies as the essence of passion (38), and passion refuses sublimation.

Meanwhile, Toplis's instruction in 'the joy of disobedience' has taken root. Three soldiers block Hacker's way and break his trade goods, coffins.

HACKER: ... What is the British army coming to? I 'ave been ambushed and my goods waylaid. You cannot rule the lesser breeds without superiority. WHERE IS YOUR FUCKING SUPE-RIORITY?
TOPLIS: Where are the lesser breeds?
HACKER: I begin to wonder. YOU 'AVE BUSTED THAT!
DITCH: We are the lesser breeds, ain't we?
HACKER: Many a true word —
ISTED: WE ARE VERY LESSER! VERY LESSER WE ARE! (24)

The soldiers dimly sense their class status and instrumentality in establishing imperial privilege, which often prefers to appeal to racial distinctions. Characteristically, Music was ahead of them in describing the country: 'I would not dignify this with the name abroad. Abroad is cold beer and wops with trays. We are completely wopless 'ere' (10). This recalls *The Love of a Good Man* and Flowers's plan for corpse retrieval, 'What is the Empire for if this degrading labour ain't given over to the chinks and wogs?'; but even this offends ingrained senses of privilege: 'The general opinion was that English soldiers' flesh would shrink from the touch of blacks' (*The Love of a Good Man*, 9). The soldiers in *Crimes in Hot Countries* become flush with poignantly reckless idealism like the Roundhead soldiers of *Pity in History*: one exclaims 'We are makin' a new England 'ere . . . From scratch. We are inventin' it'. But there is a sense that Toplis is dominating its invention, as suggested by his entice-ment to Music, 'This is my empire. Join my empire'. Music cuts the ground from beneath this ostensible emperor of resistance: he says 'I do resist. I resist you' (28).

Everywhere else, Toplis's new England gathers momentum and stages its first festival when the emperor sacrifices a Miss Havi-sham-like doll representing 'old England' and Porcelain's cult of motherhood; the prostitute Trellis steps forward to strike the first blow, like Pool with the statue in *Pity in History*, demonstrating the zeal of the newly converted. Toplis boasts how he has rescued the men from shame and servility, set free their dreams and made them, briefly, gods; but his new England contains limited allure for Erica, who still lacks someone to talk to, and only experiences cruelty in the presence of self-appointed 'saints'; and for Pain, who cultivates the power of abstention ('The authority of not . . . Because men will follow him who does not, out of respect for his will'), like a colonial Christ or Octavius Caesar. Erica's power is redolent of the Serpent of the Old Nile, as she comes to represent a fatal fascination for Top-lis, in political terms:

TOPLIS: I am running out of words. I am running out of magic.
ERICA: Yes.
TOPLIS: I find myself — in the midst of conjuring — I find myself — thinking of you.
ERICA: Me.
TOPLIS: Undressed.
ERICA: Yes.
TOPLIS: It breaks the spell you see. To think of women. Just as when you are with a woman it breaks the spell to think of anything else.   (38)

The relationship between Erica and Toplis demonstrates Barker's proposition: 'While passion may be the most certain form of liberation available to the human being, it carries also a certain rejection of society'.[4] Their story is the first full flourishing of the theme of desire, and its necessary opposition to politics, in Barker's drama, and sets the agenda for his subsequent explorations. I offer a definition of the experience and force of DESIRE: the willingness to acquiesce in the destruction of all previously held notions of one's self; in the demolition of all alternative notions of importance and worth for one's self; in order to pursue the unknown possibilities which may be generated by complete and explosive sexual engagement with the desired one.

Erica and Toplis seek affirmation in passion, the pain of wanting: Erica urges him to take her 'Rather roughly. Rather indelicately . . . As if you were mad. So that I know I exist? So that I know through all the chatter and the stale grey slime of this I am somebody's agony! Make me feel your pain' (38). *Crimes in Hot Countries* memorably conveys, through their encounters, the itch and thirst before the strip and grapple, and the atmosphere of heavy, prickling, trickling tropical heat. But Toplis is not Erica's equal in desire: her impulses compel the full headlong thrust which burns away all residual traces of former dead selves, toward a new state which shines in its previous impossibility. She asks 'Will you make me different? I am waiting to be different. Has it happened yet?' But Toplis feels an expense of spirit which returns him to former moulds of perception: 'Every time someone looks in our eyes, we wonder, could this be the man, the woman, who will make me different? But in the weary, yellow morning, the mirror tells us, no, if anything, you are more yourself . . .'. Erica persists, 'Will you touch me? Tell me I destroy you. Do I? Do I, a little bit' (43), and thrills to shatter laws of probability on his behalf: she says of the assassins come to shoot Toplis, 'I will kill them. Let me. Let me sin for you' (44). But the mutual, and self-, exploration of desire is exclusive and exhaustive of imagination. Pain squirms in his fearful preciousness of self, 'Nothing coarsens skin like skin, perishes it like passion'; Music knows that, even if true, this is irrelevant: 'No privacy in flesh. We own nothing, but we shall possess each other, charm or poach it' (46).

However, the eruption of desire is necessarily beset by forces of both radical and conservative rigour which would expunge all contradiction. Trellis preaches puritan collectivism with an 'unnatural capacity for understanding one another', which Erica finds self-righteous and simplistic; two public-school executioners, Slipper and Cashin, fly in fresh from Dublin to exterminate dissenters and enjoy 'The sheer perfection of being unmerciful'. Between them, Toplis and Erica stand as the waning Mephistophilis of words and the voracious egoist of desire: obsessions enliven, as opposites attract, and though Trellis objects to Erica 'You are ruinin' Toplis. With your sticky love', Erica insists 'I'll die for it. Or of it. Nothing else'. The central lovers become compellingly sympathetic with the effect of making the surrounding characters and concerns seem mean and partial; Toplis and Erica form the Barker equivalents to Shakespeare's Antony and Cleopatra. 'New England' still wants committees which conceal authoritarianism in their spurious dissidence, as did those in *No End of Blame*. In a community without supplies, Toplis's proud anarchy is not edible, so the New Englanders invite back Hacker and his profiteering expertise with provisions.

The final scene centres around a second dinner party, a bravura set-piece of comic tension in which Toplis baits Cashin with the implied seduction of his wife, so that the assassins' prearranged ploy goes as absurdly awry as the Bishop's sermon in *The Love of a Good Man*. In the 1984 Calder edition of *Crimes*, Erica shoots Slipper and Cashin, and Toplis leaves her in search of further intrigues, seduction and sedition; but Bill Alexander's 1985 RSC Pit production reinstated a superior ending, from an earlier version of the play entitled *Twice Dead*, in which Erica does not fire. Rather, Cashin runs off, but Toplis orders Slipper to shoot; Slipper's gun jams and he runs off; Hacker rejoices at his safety, Erica despairs at Toplis's readiness to die; Pain enters, and Slipper re-enters with Cashin's gun; Pain covers himself with a napkin as protection against spraying blood as Slipper prepares to shoot the laconic Toplis; lights snap out.

This alteration maintains a tragic weight of seriousness in the Erica-Toplis theme, and fits more comfortably with the mid-point development of the characters beyond their comedy-of-manners landscape. In both instances, Toplis refuses to confront what life with Erica in New England might entail. His return to philandering, in the published version, emphasises the briefness and triviality of his effect; his surrender to death, in the *Twice Dead* version, is a graver choice of escape from the consequences of his actions and adds to his dignity, while still testifying to a final lack of passion and risk on his part, compared to Erica, who would have died to save him or join him. Her desire, and pursuit of possibilities, outruns his. The development of her character from hysterical, soured patrician to tragic existential heroine is probably the most surprising and moving achievement of character development in Barker's drama up to *Crimes*, which stands as one of his most spectacularly inventive plays.

Barker's community play for Bridport, directed by Ann Jellicoe for the Colway Theatre, *The Poor Man's Friend* (staged 1981), lacks the density, ruthlessness and extremity of most of his work; rather, the play makes limited concessions to demands for celebration and solidarity, both of which, in the conventional sense, he regards as anathema.[5] Barker: 'in essence it was a parody of Thomas Hardy — fatalistic tragedy, with a mute victim. My real heroes are people who act, not suffer'.[6] Nevertheless, the play contains trenchant images of the spurious benevolence adopted by authority, and its acceptance.

'The Poor Man's Friend' of the title initially refers to the ointment panacea manufactured and sold by Roberts, an 18th-century tradesman-doctor who exists at a flirtatious remove from the women of the town. He participates in a seance which briefly raises the community's most feared spectre, Robespierre, who claims the real 'poor man's friend' and medicine for happiness is the guillotine: 'If you hate injustice, you must do injustice'. An apoplectic landowner Gurney proposes, with all the absurdity of the vulnerably privileged, to hang a fishing net around the town to prevent the influx of such inflammatory foreign ideas (which he imagines as slightly larger than English ones, measuring about four inches across), to which he attributes the burning of his hay-ricks.

The community itself is in decline, having been dependent on wars in France, Spain or Ireland to maintain demand for the locally-produced rope; in peacetime it languishes, like the ex-soldier Barefoot who demands a cure for righteous anger. Roberts prescribes patience, and the town liberals hold fast to committee regulations for protests against oppressive whims of governments that cause unemployment, maintaining 'We shall not tolerate illegality! We conduct ourselves in peace and dignity!' Barefoot counters 'I have neither peace nor dignity ... they would give you nothing if the likes of us did not make nuisance'. The community finds a sacrificial victim in Sylvester, a schoolboy arrested for burning Gurney's rick, separated from his playmates by his inability to conform to conventional signs of happiness; thus fated to be isolated, he exhibits some of the morose precocity of Father Time in *Jude the Obscure*.

Roberts eventually perceives the social contradiction, and objects: 'I cure an old woman of scrofula and down the road they hang a boy in perfect health. It is a nonsensical profession'. But the Magistrate is unmoved: 'What are you after, an ointment for politics?' Roberts's eminence and respectability do not translate into real power to change events, as he comes to realise. Vanstone the hangman emerges as a third claimant to the title of 'poor man's friend' for the care with which he selects and buys rope and calculates weights for use in Sylvester's execution:

> Because this is a world of pain, because the worse overcome the better, because boys suffer for old men, I do this, I do evil better than most. There is none brings more pity to his task than me, or has more skill in it . . .
> You with your medicines enable men to endure what no man properly should, like poverty and filth, cure them of sores they should not have. While I, if they should squeal, give royal medicine. I am — top physician.

The women of the town plan revolt, conceiving a flood of children all to be named Sylvester, but cannot prevent Vanstone dispatching the boy. Gurney, guilty and humiliated, engages the girl-witch Deirdre to afford him a glimpse of Sylvester, who is welcomed into the hereafter by the cacophony of hanged ghosts which she raised at the beginning of the play. Whereas their first materialisation had an atmosphere of 'raucous self-justification and comic argument', the ghosts' final appearance is marked by introspective, habitual mutterings which break into a song congratulating Sylvester on his enviably swift and smooth execution.

With a passive protagonist drifting into an inexorable fate to which he seems born, *The Poor Man's Friend* may sound as if it lingers on the enticements of submission as it assembles its detailed portrait of a town's (self-)crucifixion complex. Certainly the play recognises participation in unforgivable pain, but its cutting edge depends on balancing the question as to how irresistible the participation may be, even as the townsfolk of Bridport extend the enaction of their indigenous passion play into the present. The play's most memorable qualities are its carefully assembled sense of social structure, involving over a hundred characters; the irony of a community economically dependent upon the foreign slaughter of the nation's, and perhaps the town's, youth (compare the Elvis Costello and

Clive Langer song *Shipbuilding*); liberal paralysis in the face of draconian legality and imposed suffering (which acquired new contemporary parallels during the 1984-5 British Miners' Strike); and the babble of haggling ghosts, including shysters, desperate paupers, victims of empire, spivs, fops and the 1950s criminal of passion, Ruth Ellis.

Rather than flatter the community with its own humanism, *The Poor Man's Friend* is probably unique in the community play genre in that it identifies a tradition of passivity and submission that runs through Bridport and British history, inextricably bound up with that humanism and its sense of the ubiquity of blame, which prevents people breaking rank — even on the way to the gallows — and enables the governors to practise a duplicity of which only some are actually conscious. This inertia and sense of impotence on behalf of the governed — to select a suitably passive term — permits suffering, which when recognised compounds shame (rather than rouses righteous anger) and creates further fear of possibilities and appetite for abnegation of power, if not self-flagellation on a national psychological scale. Hence the nostalgia for 'traditional family values', surrender of power, and fear and attempted abolition of desire. Self-prostration before governors, forfeit of power and rights, and the reassertion of traditional sexual values (conjugality and fidelity) — all of which involve what Bela Veracek would denounce as 'idolatry' — are posited by governors and seen by governed as the answers to crisis.

Barker's filmscript *The Blow: Fragments of Spiritual Life During the Transformations* (written 1985) is his most ambitious, troubling and reverberative excavation of national psychological truths which permit co-operation in dispossession and the rise of authoritarianism. The script's production notes demand the de-naturalisation of costume and setting so that its scenes 'aspire towards the elimination of specificity and celebrate contradiction and incompatibility'; also, 'to break the documentary insistence of black and white, or the fictional banality of technicolour, the colour must be treated in such a way that it bleeds, like hand-tinted photographs of the 1940's, and states the deliberate refusal of historicity in the film'.

In a haunting series of uneasily garish and queasily artificial visuals, Senior Administrator Dickinson supervises 'The Transformations' of a remote rural area toward the imposition of centralised values. When her attached civil servant Gildersleeve is on the verge of resignation and disintegration, she excels in manipulating the reassurance of shame; she proclaims 'IT IS YOU WHO FORCES ME TO BE INHUMAN ... You think you are the only ones with pain ... And I am so depressed'; Gildersleeve concedes to her embrace. This crystallises Dickinson's ability to awaken the essential hope and secret passion to be annexed, which lies deep within the governed; where the right-wing delight in 'The sheer perfection of being unmerciful' is not identified; instead cruelty is assimilated and experienced as pain, and governors become recipients of pity; rather than blamed, they are eroticised, possibly through awakening cults of matriarchy or patriarchy (the prescription and celebration of the reassertion of traditional familial and sexual values is again paramount here). Dickinson's programme is watertight and self-generating in its sense of justification: 'We must not be deterred by resistance. Of course there will be resistance. It is the testimony to our truth. It is our medal'. Like Colonel Hard in *The Love of a Good Man*, she invokes and embodies Duty and Sacrifice, and the sense of their necessity to raise people from their 'secret cess': 'I prayed — even as a girl — as a child even — prayed for struggle, the struggle which would draw out of my depths some pure spinal fluid of my self, some essence of my truth and bring me to the rim of — saintliness. I longed to be a saint, beside a man who was also a saint. So pain was welcome to me'.

In a gesture of protest at the Tranformations, a local hangs himself in a barn, out of what Dickinson interprets as 'spite': 'That is no way to win an argument, is it? I am not persuaded by that. People think to dominate you by their deaths, my mother was the same ... Nigel, son of the local landowner Stucley, sees through the civil servants' avowed apoliticism and poisonous civility ('You trash the language with that deference', he exclaims) to the grip they have on the popular imagination, 'because they will not tolerate even the rebuke of silence. Acquiescence is not enough. You must approve'. Nigel churns in fiery, self-consuming sarcasm and scotch whisky; he combines the charming amorality of Edmund in *King Lear* with the frantic, determined hedonism of Charles in *Victory*, a similar self-conscious 'handsome and accomplished ... spewed up and diminishing stump of aristocracy'.

Nigel dwells in 'The Great Dead House Called Home' which dominates the landscape. His family, representing 'classes traditionally identified with feudal forms of tenure', are Dickinson's next targets for recruitment to acquiescence in the Transformations. Her conviction — 'I cannot be ashamed. And if I refuse shame, the shame becomes theirs' — works on the traditionally abased labourers, but Nigel's aristocratic refusal of shame renders him the erotic focus of Dickinson herself. However, the Stucley family are in, perhaps inevitable, disarray: Nigel's brother Hugo has subsided into sentimental peasant worship, idolatry of soil and bread, genuflection before the virtues of frugality, silence and subordination, and the sexual idealisation of the hanged man's wife; Stucley is fading, and seeks to extend Dickinson's invocation and offer of 'the ecstasy of irresponsibility' into love, but Nigel is withering of his senile nostalgia for 'genital oblivion'.

It is only Attila, illegitimate son of Widow Yaxley and Stucley, who represents a tauter knot of resistance to Dickinson. If Hugo recalls the ineffectual liberal intellectual Edgar of the early scenes of *King Lear*, Attila is a modern, unsettling holy fool-madman with echoes of 'Poor Tom', and a hint of the 'urban rodent' Sordido in *Women Beware Women*. Nigel reels and rails at the sky (like Stucley in *The Castle*) and proclaims the unmoved Attila the nearest local thing to divinity and beauty: 'YOU CANNOT WRECK HIM WHEN HE HAS NO HOPE! . . . His head is scarred from striking lintels, and his wrist from punching glass, and his nose from bursting mirrors'. Attila's imagination lends him the only source of resistance to Dickinson's webs of incentives, rationalisation and shame. Yaxley, Hugo's lover and Attila's mother, is courted by Dickinson to accede to the Transformations, but she remains silent: 'She has no vocabulary. She is immune to the disease of knowledge', explains Hugo in wonder. Dickinson offers money in public dumb-show, seeking to elicit the word 'Yes', but Attila disrupts the event and liquidises the coins.

But Dickinson is pathologically, religiously undeterred, chewing on her own maxims ('the craving for intimacy is a moment of panic in the race for pure selfhood . . . as the leading runner in a competition will feel clammy as her distance widens from the rest'), assuaging Gildersleeve's reservations that they are being too cruel: 'this word cruelty . . . I think it was invented to prevent the energetic moving through the mass . . . To suffocate the active with the blanket of conscience — oh, you have trod on a tadpole, stop! . . . Every tadpole potentially a frog and every frog potentially a prince ! Move not, therefore, lest you squash a prince!'

Stucley settles into resignation that 'You cannot stop the Transformations', though Nigel points out that the family held out against democracy for eight centuries, and goads Hugo for his self-congratulatory humanism: 'What separates the professorial from the ignorant is — only the — mode — of — violence'. Nigel locates shame in Hugo's sexual adoration of the Widow Yaxley, 'because she is — as near as he can find it in the age of speech — animal. Him who studied at greater institutes. All her brutality is virtue to him'; indeed, at their wedding ceremony Hugo asks Yaxley for assurance that she does not love him: 'We come together, there-fore, with no imagination, so we shall endure' — as if endurance were itself a virtue — 'To marry without love. To suffer without reason', the epitome of peasant life. Nigel is hunted for the murder of Gildersleeve, blowing power cables and burning customs posts, while Attila ransacks the Great Dead House after Stucley's death, burning his books and clothes on a pyre in a field.

An assistant administrator, Shardlow, attempts to strangle Dick-inson, but collapses weeping at her feet, clinging to her skirt; later, embracing her in her hotel room, marvelling at how 'You make everything all right. What we are not, what we fail in, doesn't mat-ter any more, because of you'. Nigel is reduced to playing dancing waiter at party to celebrate a childish delight in the first year of the Transformations. As its climax, in an ironic reversal of the dance of Salome before Herod, Dickinson produces Hugo's severed head to confound Nigel's sense of her political and erotic limitations.

A subsequent visit to Yaxley's cottage, where she sees her own framed picture hanging on the wall, awes even Dickinson to the point of vomiting and wonder at her own power. After a night with her ex-lover, who has come from the capital to restore order, she awakens to the sound of Attila's oration as he stands on a slope holding the body of his mother, Yaxley. His destruction of the library in the Great Dead House has liberated his power of language, and his sense of how it has been used to construct patterns of command and surrender, 'The doer and the done-to. The power of the done-to, and the lure of the doer'. He thunders 'GIVE US THE WORD BACK YER BASTARDS!', conscious of how Dickinson's attack on 'the great stiff basket of culture' has stolen language and sold him back 'words of such banality he could construct nothing but his own UGLINESS'. Dickinson attempts to leave in a car, but is frozen to the dashboard, immobile in the flow of Attila's words.

The Blow is a dense barrage of images and language: its feverish, hallucinatory vistas and surges of epigrammatic self-explication and poetic digression produce a deliberately thorough confound-ing of every naturalistic preconception; its structure initially seems fragmentary, as its sub-title suggests, but when the reader permits the script its own imaginative pace and flow, ceasing to expect traditional signposts of form and response, it wrenches into life a panoramic landscape of immense, gruelling scope and depth. Its uniqueness has provoked incomprehension on the part of filmmakers whose perceptions and purposes are still trapped by narrative and populist conventions, hence it remains unproduced at the time of writing; but its exploration of a society's 'spiritual life' has deep subterranean resonances and mythic force, akin to witnessing the sickening warp of nervous breakdown from the vantage point of a national collective unconscious. It progresses through visionary, psychological leaps and syntheses, achieving a poetry of collision in its images of social weakening, distortion and mutilation, which again identify conspiratorial passion in dispossession.

Dickinson is a particularly vivid portrait of the monstrosity of authority in recognisable human form and detail, calculating the dimensions of the human soul and swelling in the exhilaration of her mission: 'If life is agony, I must control others'. Her power is imaginative, she is not arid or conventional, but truly formidable. Her bid to paint her personality on the landscape itself provokes a significant polarisation of reactions among other characters, who are only able to identify the full force of her power through tragic experience. It is a compulsive and painful view of the imaginative blockage of a culture mesmerised by its own incessantly compounding servitude, probably Barker's most venturesome work to date.

Barker's landscapes are frequently overshadowed by a 'Big House', an edifice of authority in which dwellers or interlopers eventually release the confusion and upheaval which rages outside or below. The soldiers in *Pity in History* go 'barmy' in the big house and in the cathedral; the Devon yokels of *Downchild* can only speculate on the secrets of Scadding's mansion, which lead to Tom's trial and Stoat's redecoration in the church; the government house in *Crimes in Hot Countries* is an oasis of subterfuge which is invaded and finally reclaimed; *The Blow* shows the forces of Dickinson's 'Triumph Hut' taking over from the eight-century rule of the The Great Dead House Called Home. The pyramid in *One Afternoon* is the first kernel image of the domination of a landscape, which reaches its apotheosis in *The Castle*. *The Love of a Good Man* depends rather on an atmosphere of menacing agoraphobia as characters cross a quaking bog of mud and corpses, an almost tactile panorama which anticipates that of *The Power of the Dog*, and the emergence of the resurrected soldier in *Don't Exaggerate*.

In these settings of soured hope, the characters' desperation is often expressed through their turning to magic: the ouija games in *The Love of a Good Man* and *Birth on a Hard Shoulder*, Grigor's mental hospital mysticism in *No End of Blame*, Toplis's conjuring at the dinner party in *Crimes*, Dierdre's raising the ghosts in *The Poor Man's Friend*, and the cauldron ritual in *The Power of the Dog*. But magic yields no solutions. Toplis equates words with magic, but his verbal dexterity fades into desperate trickery. Pain realises that the soldiers' illiteracy and their vocabulary's limitation to 'stale abuse' enable them to collude in mass slaughter. Attila's book-burning ritual is an attempt to liberate the word, which has been annexed to impose patterns of submission and restrict the governed to terms of such banality they can construct nothing but their own ugliness and shame. Beyond the liberating force of unfettered language, the besieged but defiant flourishing of desire, such as experienced by Erica and Toplis, and even Hacker in *The Love of a Good Man*, is Barker's principal demonstration of the triumph of human spirit and dignity over banal unison and the spurious collectivism of shame. *The Blow* is his most detailed account of the encroachment and mechanics of shame; the counter-blast occurs in *Women Beware Women's* tumultuous explosions of desire.

7
Splintered Faith and Scar Tissue

> What's so precious about faith? Why can't it take a kicking like everything else?
>
> *Victory*

Victory: Choices in Reaction (staged 1983), as its double-barrelled title promises, offers new risks and openness for characters and audiences alike. Works as early as *Cheek* contain preoccupations with locating or creating identity; Noel in *Claw* cannot sense a personal essence, he wants comfort on society's own terms, but sexuality disrupts his ambitions. Bela in *No End of Blame* is Barker's most rationalist protagonist with a heroically iron sense of self in the face of 'idolatry'; but the note of sexuality is diminished in his characterisation and his risks involve uncovering things in other people rather than in himself. *Victory* continues the existential theme of individuals who are particularly engaged in creating *modi vivendi* for themselves, finding niches within a social structure which is hostile or alien; rather than accommodating themselves, like Jardine in *The Hang of the Gaol* or Diver in *No End of Blame*, with all the circumspection and self-contempt involved, characters are driven to invent themselves by pushing to the edge of experience and taking risks. *Victory: Choices in Reaction* dramatises images of life alternative to the familiar, and develops the tragic strain in Barker's writing. Play, characters and audience reactions are in a state of constant flux, and it is particularly crucial for the quality of the actors' performances to involve the audience in characters' experiences in order for new possibilities of life to be sensed, through a transitional stage of incomprehension and the demolition of conventional points of reference and sympathy. *Victory* is not without humour, but it shuns the comic laughter of integration, which seals perforations and indicates relief; it provokes tragic

laughter, unnatural, pitiful, to which an audience is audibly uneasy
as to its entitlement:

When did you last hear a laugh which was
Not a spasm of intoxication
Not a gesture of solidarity
Not a gurgle of vanity
The choral assent of intellectual poseurs but
The irresistible collapse of words
Before the spectacle of unbidden truth

(Don't Exaggerate)

Barker: 'Once that laugh occurs, the audience is open to a new
variety of experience, perceiving ambiguities and unorthodoxies
such as the simultaneous existence of cruelty and love, as when
two lovers fight or strike each other; there's a moment of bewil-
dering truth which encompasses cruelty and charity. I think real
social compatibility is only possible when we break limits rather
than keep imposing them'.[1] *Victory* testifies to Barker's increasingly
complex sense of character, where opposites exist within each figure, and there is no such thing as a stable character; also to Barker's insistence on exposing such contradictions onstage, whatever
confusion of the audience results. Correspondingly, his protagonists
push their selves as far as they will go, no matter what the opposition or awful discoveries entailed. The keynotes are risk and ruthless exposure — the ruthlessness of excavation and meaningful
discovery, rather than the ruthlessness of imposition and meaningless cruelty.

Victory picks up from *The Love of a Good Man* on the theme of the
body as talisman. Like Mrs Toynbee seeking her son's remains,
Susan Bradshaw has to collect her husband's remains from the shattered debris of a landscape that is Restoration England. The retrieval
of Richard Bradshaw's dismembered body, in all its scattered pieces,
becomes involved with a sense of Republican spirit, a broken form
to be retrieved before it, and the past, can be expelled, and those
close to it can be eradicated from too precious a sense of its power.
But in a wider sense, *Victory* depicts an experiential atmosphere of
rupture, where a vertiginous destruction of reference points has
occurred; characters stumble across a broken terrain, where only the
court of Charles II stands as a nauseously frantic, brusquely yoked
mosaic of traditional privilege and orgiastic excess.

The opening scene sets the tone with breathtaking economy and force. Richard Bradshaw's secretary, Scrope, enters and details his vow not to reveal his former master's burial site; then, with a gesture wrenched out by anxiety, breaks that vow. The royalist soldiers who proceed to dig up the body are deliberately casual and obscene, intensifying Scrope's sense of the desecration of ideals, political and sexual. Gaukroger, the captain, calculatedly violates the idyllic setting of field and church steeple with brutal linguistic power: 'How picturesque he was and diligent. Was he, Mr Scrope? Cunt picturesque, your master?' (2). Scrope bursts into tears on hearing these words.

The subsequent interrogation of Susan Bradshaw by Roast and Ball, two officers of the crown, sustains this force. Eric Mottram is right to note that 'Ball's Cavalier mix of bodily, religious and sexual abrasiveness' is directed as much to the audience as to Bradshaw: 'I WISH I COULD BE MORE OFFENSIVE I REALLY DO'; but as Mottram later comments, Bradshaw's insistence on the language of physicality in imagining her husband's corpse contributes to the prevalent verbal 'existential fleshiness which scorches the earth to prepare it for facts'.[2] This personal point of contact is crucial. Bradshaw is immediately distinguished from Scrope in her readiness to jettison picturesque idylls, and thereby the outrage of their desecration: she avers 'I do not wish to do things properly or keep them clean'. Ball's consciousness of personal exploitation gives him a sense of licence ('I will be rude because I have lost fifteen years!'), and he baits Bradshaw with relished threats to her body and implicit decorum: 'when you stand there icy in your purity I could really dagger you with my old cavalier dick, that or murder' (3). But Bradshaw is not scandalised; she defies Roast's pseudo-rationality ('people cannot swallow all the change you and your husband wanted') and perceives in Ball a common release from idylls: 'There is a sort of cleanliness in you. A sort of honour in your vileness I can understand'. It is Ball who is scandalised, rejecting any link between them which would negate his fascinated antagonism ('Ugh, she flatters me!'); rather he blames her for puritan restrictive annexing of the body, which he determines to contradict with his own sense of romantic offence: 'They say you killed old love in England. You never! . . . I shall come back. And give you a poem' (5).

Bradshaw's son McConochie cannot empathise with her situation, irritated by the way the interrogation has interrupted his studies, 'I am not a political person and it is most unjust!' He does not sense the power at stake in the spiking and exhibition of his father's body: 'when you love someone — I don't know this — I have not actually loved — but when you love — it is not the flesh, is it, that one loves? Am I being indelicate?' Bradshaw thunders back in contradiction, 'I LOVED HIS HEAD', even as she acknowledges that she has deliberately nurtured his protective numbed egocentricity:

> And you I created like this, to spare you pain. What more can a mother do for her child? No ardour to be bruised, no passion to be beaten for. A cold armouring of the eyes, the slowest of heart beats, and a tongue whose habit is to lie low in the mouth, dark as a bottom-fish, not red or roaring and at the end, ripped out. I think you will survive, my dear little blue-eyed boy . . .   (6–7)

The difference between Bradshaw and McConochie fuels their pride in each other. Bradshaw's daughter Cropper has more conventional attitudes, precluding insight: Cropper shrinks from and discourages Bradshaw's imaginative inventory of her husband's decomposition and thinks she has gone mad. Bradshaw in turn recoils from her 'sickening' piety, and determines to fly in the face of invocations of reason, decorum, sanity, to confront and collect her battered icons of faith and pain, her husband's 'chops and scrag', 'offal and lean cuts', 'I will bring your poor bald head away that hurt me so much with its arguments' (8).

Surprisingly, Charles II is another character who demonstrates considerable existential resources in *Victory*. His extravagant earthy humour springs from a recognition and flouting of the monarchist image, an ideal of himself he knows to be illusory; though his position is compromised, Charles himself is not — like Nigel in *The Blow* he pursues his wants and impulses. The 'peculiar and incomprehensible' personalities of his parents fuelled revolutionary stirrings, whereas Charles concentrates on the simplicities of appetite: 'I am a male bint pure and simple . . . there is no better stimulus to loyalty than for an apprentice to be molly shagging only minutes after I have left her off. He grasps your flesh, he shares your monarchy'. Charles has no time for the symbolic sophistries of Hambro the banker, who can dissuade resentment of regicides on the grounds that restoration honours monarchy and proves its indispensability. Charles sees the circuitous fallacy of such self-justification and rejects it for physical substance: 'Where is my duchess? I must grasp her arse' (10). At the centre of the court's hedonistic whirlpool, he realises its absurdity, though his drinking companion Nodd cajoles him like a precocious child, 'Now, now, this is the time of your life, silly' (11).

The pelting of Richard Bradshaw's spiked head acts as an unseen offstage counterpoint to Charles's masturbation by his mistress Devonshire; his post-orgasmic sobriety only highlights his (and the audience's) sense of the court's infantile frivolity. He uses his power to dismiss the revellers, invoking the mystique of the crown with antithetical irreverence: 'Oh listen, who is the monarch here? Who wears the ermine bum-fluff, me! I have been down, ain't I, in the sight of the tit of England, got the oil of Christ on me, out when I say it, Out!' Thus Charles dismantles the trappings of power while inside them, leaving at the centre his essential self, conscious of his absurdities and the insincerity of his sycophants. He is the diametric opposite of the Prince of Wales in *The Love of a Good Man*. Hambro's preference not to imagine the emergence of madness through royal inbreeding strikes Charles as piety, more sickening (because less sincere) than Cropper's to Bradshaw. Refusal to imagine is an index to fear of risk and passion, as Charles recognises; Hambro's support is calculatingly superficial, and Charles concludes 'I wish you fucked more'. He is a creature of insurrectionary appetite in a wasteland of bankrupt form.

Scrope confronts Bradshaw, flagellating himself with professions of abject shame, but she defuses his invocations of conventional courage: 'Let us chuck courage and hang on to our teeth'. She continues to jettison the conventional and extraneous forms of conduct, stripping herself down to pure essence: 'I am done with shame, and conscience, duty, guilt, and power, all of it! . . . standing up's for men with sin and dignity. No, got to be a dog now, and keep our teeth' (18). He insists on joining her out of 'duty' to her husband, whose book *Harmonia Britannia* he clings to for inspiration, and possibly also associations of heroic martyr status that it might accrue for him: 'It's gaol to have in your possession'. Ball thinks he has cornered Bradshaw in her house, but traps McConochie, who is required to perform in his assumed identity of Scottish surgeon more rapidly than anticipated, but his self-invention proves his salvation; Bradshaw's farewell note also emphasises willed self-transformation, 'Have gone to be an animal in time of animals', but her elusiveness fires Ball's sense of allure. Alongside his seething violence, his enthralled vision of Bradshaw drives him to a comically pathetic vulnerability, redolent of Hacker's upsurge of longing for Mrs Toynbee, together with a determination to pursue Bradshaw through whatever shapes, threats and unknown possibilities involved: 'Oh God and Christ, I do want a puritan woman! They know what they do with their eyes cast down and starchy collars! They do know it! "Gone to be an animal!" Well, mistress, I shall find you in your den!' (21).

Further patterns of conventional response are overcome, when Bradshaw and Scrope meet three republicans in a field, burying a gun that has done service in Scotland, Ireland, Flanders, Jamaica and the Republican cause. Just as they are consigning their emblem of idealism to the soil, Bradshaw's arrival rekindles their enthusiastic nostalgia for days when king's blood was proved the same 'red stuff' as any other, though Pyle remains mindful of the partiality of reform that kept them tethered to cultivating the same field of clay. Scrope attempts faltering intellectual apologia, then falls to gorging himself on the small parcel of food provided; when Bradshaw reveals he has stolen one of the rebels' wallets, he is appalled, and protests 'You must not injure people in their faith'. But Bradshaw has realised that, in certain social conditions, even the innocent are not your friends: 'What's so precious about faith? Why can't it take a kicking like anything else? I do them a favour, and I get a wallet. Cheap at the price, there is fuckall in it — Scrope holds fast to absolutist prescriptions, claiming that injury done by enemies can be overcome, but injury by friends encourages madness; but Bradshaw's victory is in overturning such prescriptions, overcoming her own instincts: 'I DO KNOW THAT. Do you think I found it easy? It wasn't easy. But that's my triumph. Any fool can rob his enemy. Where's the victory in that?' (27).

Victory's First Act ends with an Interlude of satirical comedy in the vaults of the Bank of England, where the subterranean impulses beneath a nation's management are exposed in all their parochial self-interest. The Bankers form another of Barker's committees, familiar from *No End of Blame* and *The Loud Boy's Life*, where authoritarianism is constituted by a crew of petty squabbling egoists and serves their purposes. Bonded by absurd rituals and oaths, the meeting still disintegrates into disorder through builder Mobberley's sensual delight in gold ingots and his distrust of his fellows; 'This is precisely why we have a bank' assures Hambro, secure in the knowledge that capital's power outstrips that of the monarchy: it is these profiteers and shysters who dictate the King's allowance.

The ludicrousness of the situation is consciously revealed when the meeting is circumscribed by the chief lawyer's social commitments to his wife; he is witheringly parodied by the toughest entrepreneur, Undy the exporter: 'We govern, and are governed in our turn, it seems, all our conference must hang on Stanley's wife. Does she know she governs the country, Stanley, may I ask? . . . I thought we had got rid of absolute monarchy, but no, there is Stanley's wife is more terrible than Louis le whatsname or the Tsar, kicking her heels in Putney, Christ help us —' (30).

Hambro's main item for the agenda is his personal decision to stop the terror, as the cavaliers' excesses are engulfing Undy's potential customers: he intends to enlist the cavaliers in a regiment, 'Give them a uniform with lots of tassel and gold facing. Call them The King's Own and send them on an expedition from which they won't come back' (32). Stockbroker Parry voices reservations and fears for personal security, but Hambro knows that governors' refusal of shame deflects the emotion onto the governed: 'I do think, when a man is governing England, he oughtn't to shudder so much' (33). Charles interrupts proceedings and senses conspiracy, but realises that, beneath their deference and his sarcasm, he is powerless before them: 'I can't bring charges, the chief lawyer's here himself'. Nodd's gangland belligerence is recognised by Charles as being a naïvely weak, outdated threat against the amassed economic power available to Undy or any one of the bankers.

The scene sharpens to a duel between Charles and Undy, with Charles producing Richard Bradshaw's head to embarrass and nauseate his former republican sympathisers and direct at them the full force of a passage from *Harmonia Britannia* seeking the abolition of private property: 'And there were some called rich, who gathered to themselves the labour and the inventiveness of others, and kept them brutally in place, but these were like a nightmare or bad memory' in a republic where capital has been made a redundant superstition. Undy seethes at Charles's humiliating little drama, but Hambro stays urbane, maintaining that the King realises his limitations of power in this new age; 'The rest is shrill and squealing. Never mind the squeal. I don't' (37).

The grotesque farce and satirical ironies of the Interlude give the audience a deliberate lack of preparation for *Victory's* second act, of which the opening Estuary scene acts as a hinge for the play — and Barker's writing in general — to swing from political satire into the passion and tragedy of desire. Even his first steps in this direction, the Toplis–Erica theme of *Crimes in Hot Countries*, give little warning for the imminent falling away of irony and the exploration of complexities of pain in the triangular configuration of energies between Bradshaw, Ball and Scrope. As a prelude, Devonshire's raptures establish a landscape of chill, windswept, pungent clarity, as she struggles with the counter-attractions of independent asceticism and Charles's yearning verses; her self-absorption is demonstrated by her exposition of 'pains of the mind' to beggars who scramble for her money before being beaten off by the Footman, who reassures her that she owns the beach 'Above the tidemark'. Bradshaw assents to all her statements as Devonshire reaches the resolution of compulsion: 'I go back tonight, I know all poems are dick but I go back, I will die of him, it is silly but he makes me feel alive' (40). When upbraided for threadbare repetition, Bradshaw details the knowledge involved in her self-prostration:

> Yes means no resistance. Yes means going with the current. Yes means lying down when it rains and standing up when it's sunny. Yes urge. Yes womb. Yes power. I lived with a man whose no was in the middle of his heart, whose no kept him thin as a bone and stole the juices from him. No is pain and yes is pleasure, no is man and yes is nature. Yes is old age and no is early death. Yes is laughter, no is torture. I hate no. No is misery and early nights. Do you follow or shall I say it again?   (41)

She formulates this experience into an almost ritualistic performance of ingratiating self-abasement akin to a Brechtian *gestus*, striking an attitude of wholly externalised meaning, cutting their relationship to essentials. Scrope perceives this as contradiction or betrayal of consistent faith rather than being able to see it as a part of a larger sequence of attitudes: he berates her and invokes the ghost of her husband as agonised witness, unable to reconcile his former sense of her near-saintliness with her hurried, doglike eating. However, Scrope's admiration of Richard Bradshaw incorporates the writer's ability to 'challenge every thought' and refusal to accept anything as fixed; ironically, Scrope has frozen him into a static icon (similar to Bela's sense of his 'flame of truth'), possibly arising from his own shame in thwarted literary and sexual ambition: 'it is my misfortune to have served him, who blew out my little candle with his great light . . . when I might have written . . . might have . . . LOST

MY CHANCE NOW!' Though Scrope denies Bradshaw's suggestion that he only cries to impress her, he may indeed be attempting
to stir her erotic pity; but then Ball bursts onto the scene and makes
her the focus of a second source of energy.

Ball glories at the opportunity to exercise his power as the agent
of authoritarian power, 'I AM ENTITLED TO PUNISH IN THE
NAME OF THE STUART', glimpsing the opportunity for licensed
fulfilment for which he has invested both suffering and suppression of personal feeling: 'I AM COME INTO MY RIGHTS . . . I AM
THE GOVERNOR NOW!' (42). However, the confusions implicit in
his 'Love Unexpected' stir an unwonted integrity of emotions; his
pride in being an efficient machine of violence is splintered in the
incomprehensible upheaval of desire: 'Be my darling, I have a thing
about you, you could be as rough as fifty hellbags, I still got a thing
for you, I don't know what my passion's coming to, to be honest
you are nothing to stare after, why am I fixed like this?' Bradshaw
says 'It happens'. Ball struggles with his contrary impulses: 'Fuck,
it does, and I shall love you on this shore or stab you, I am that
bewildered! Let me worship, God, your eyes are tired and yet full
of secrets, I wrote you a poem'.

Ball's kernel instinctive self, secret and protected, is tapped
here. In dedicating himself to a 'cause', Ball has adopted an image
of the self which suited the accepted definition of one dedicated
to that 'cause'; Bradshaw's attraction and attractiveness delved
beyond that image to the root of Ball's self. This attraction disturbs
but compels him to pursue and conclude his impulses; yet he is
trapped by the guise he has adopted in order to have an individual identity, an understanding of aims and meaning, with a course
to follow, under the terms of definition of 'royalist cavalier'. At the
stage of crisis and confrontation, like most people he lapses into
the imagery and actions of his adopted image — the social 'Ball',
a proven and secure image of his individuality up to this point —
rather than his inmost self. His imagery of sex in violence recalls
his earlier threat to 'dagger' Bradshaw with his 'old cavalier dick',
where dagger and dick are twin weapons of war, but permit no
embodiment of 'worship'. The formal sonnet style, 'twelve lines in
the Tuscan manner', has permitted him to abstract and formular-
ise courtly profession of 'old love' without impinging on his inmost
self. This romanticism has, in fact, supported and justified his imperial activities of murder, rape and pillage; but poetry disintegrates:
'I will fuck you or go mad. You have given me hell these last ten

nights'. Bradshaw's unexpected accordance of respect to him
in 1.2. ('There is a certain cleanliness in you') has activated semi-
conscious hopes of engagement with her as an unlikely but similar equal; Ball may be attracted by her essential purity — she has
removed all images and vowed to be herself, whatever the degra-
dations that this may incur. While under social terms of definition
they are poles apart, Ball finds her absolute dedication to selfhood magnetic, alluring and destructive. But she defers his offer of
his own inarticulate, struggling, inmost self, preferring the poem;
so he reverts to his accepted social image of violent rapist cavalier, where he is firmly identified as 'AN AGENT OF CHARLES
STUART, ALL I DO IS LEGAL, NAUGHT IS WRONG, SEE?',
even as his inmost self pleads 'I worship, I bring my poor love
to the altar'. This 'worship' can only be expressed in cavalier terms
of pushing her into a hut, to rape her out of the wind; but the rape
is a source of dissatisfaction to his inmost self. His inability to
express 'worship' and desire exposes the cracks in his hitherto crucial and exclusive sense of his institutional role, the communication
and control of his identity, and leaves him cut off in his self with a
sense of its shortcomings: 'I think love would be to come off and
be happy' (44). [This paragraph was written in collaboration with
George Jones.]

Scrope is riven by witnessing his own neo-Oedipal impulses
fulfilled, and by a royalist; he stares and quotes from *Harmonia
Britannia* in a traumatised whisper, contrasting the transaction to
his patron's ideal: '"And there will be love betwixt man and woman
of a sort not known yet, founded on freedom of will and desire,
so that she will not be hampered by false modesty nor him by his
cult manliness" . . . *(He shudders with a paroxysm of impotent anger)*
Oh, all you who come after, make your revolution right! *(He takes
the book from his pocket, flings it in the mud, weeps)*' (43–4). Scrope's
imagination is inflamed by Bradshaw recounting how she had
been untouched by her husband for seven years, and how Ball's
disappointment awoke the erotic force of her pity. Scrope's choked
anger explodes into his description as 'cowlike' in compliance, and
hints at his own denied impulses which might have been served
in such apparent indiscrimination. He misses the point: Bradshaw
doesn't 'wish it', though Scrope dismisses this as superficial subterfuge like his own crying: 'What are wishes, what are tears?' He
fluctuates between admitting adopting pitiable postures, appealing to a redundant sense of duty ('I have slept beside you on

trestles and on bales in barns and never once out of respect for him —') which might have entitled *him* to come into what he dreams of as his sexual rights with Bradshaw, and forsaking this high-handed sense of offence for a stab at what he sees as the innate banality of copulation: 'What of me, I have the same thing, don't I — Bradshaw maintains she saw him as a friend, not a sexual instrument, and Scrope's reply betrays his own essential 'cult man-liness' — 'No friend, never! I am a man, too!' — which he never-theless cannot execute convincingly. He makes another redundant protest against injustice, at his physical frailty, but drives on in des-perate, mistaken search for a release from self-loathing, grabbing Bradshaw roughly and urging 'Do it with me, now'; she rightly perceives the 'recrimination' that will accrue when his inflexible, absolutist social values once more hold sway, sensing that his aban-donment of them is momentary rather than fundamental; but she acquiesces to relieve his immediate desperation, conscious of subse-quent impending shame.

Unsurprisingly, I cannot agree with Ruth Shade's brief account of the scene: 'Scrope and Ball are degraded by their sexuality yet [Brad-shaw] discovers a sense of self'.[3] While an audience will not wish to condone the attitudes and actions of Scrope and Ball, the two char-acters' detailed expositions of their anguish show previously unsus-pected depths to their personalities and an agonised nakedness in their doomed attempts to conquer or express their passion; their unlived lives are partially broached, but their social selves prove decisive; they are failed men, pitiable in their pain, but more exis-tentially dignified by their (and the audience's) confrontation of it. Bradshaw discovers capacities for pity, rather than a sense of self, and the audience sympathises with her tragic treatment as the joint, unwitting focus of unforgivable but comprehensible cruelty which she cannot avoid. In the historical context of *Victory*, the characters are thwarted and distorted in expressing desire: even Bradshaw's husband is reported to have been forever shaming her, 'Getting his ugly reason out, his great moral purpose, showing it in public, and his wisdom!' (18). Ossified modes of being are shown to be inimi-cal to desire, and this clash leads to 'recrimination' — demonstrated in 11.2., when Scrope approaches Milton with the awed rever-ence of a priest consulting some omniscient oracle, but Bradshaw refutes the poet's idol status: 'I quailed before you once, couldn't bring myself to speak — not that Bradshaw wanted me to, did he — just cart the sandwiches this way and that — but really you made me tremble, and now you move me so little I could — *(with a sudden inspiration, she slaps his face)'*. This impulse scandalises Scrope, who denounces her as 'UGLY' in her shattering of self-imposed restriction; he sees her as anathema to his puritan rational idealism, but Bradshaw exults in her achievement. She proclaims 'I have broken myself into pieces to do this', exhilarated by shattering the fetters of an old, debilitating sense of self; but her action impels Scrope in the opposite direction, into a retrenched sense of desecrated ideals and personal shame. He shuns association or contact with Bradshaw and is particularly stung by her fondly terming him 'my little lover'; he encases himself in the armour of pride. But Milton finds her action 'comprehensible' and bursts into gnomic thunder:

> When the war is won, wage war on the victors. Every civil war must be the parent of another. Those given laurels praise then execute. And their executioners, when the time comes, execute them too. Any amount of war a man will take, will acquiesce in his own destruction even, provided that he knows the change takes place. That is the God in him. But if after the first war, you only heap praise on the victors, they will make themselves your masters, even ape the first oppressor and invite him back. Any amount of power a man will take, provided we permit it. That is the shit in him. Next time, should we start there must be no finish, or we shall slap one another's faces in the gardens of our enemies. (49)

This meditation on power and sacrifice reverberates through the rest of the play, with its keynotes of the literally revolutionary impulse and emphasis on constant demolition and self-overcoming, regeneration through destruction, renewal of essence through the breaking of all forms, as the only means by which to pursue, represent or experience briefly, the truth: such is the fleeting nature of existential victory. But the audience might do well to resist locating authority even in Milton's speech: it remains given wisdom, which invites the corporate body or party to be continually regenerating itself, not its individual members; he speaks of 'we' rather than 'you', and his vision of anarchy as social formation might degenerate into infantile vengeance on a previous generation, elevated to the systematic. The systematic might be opposed by the healthier use of anarchic instincts to encourage people to re-formulate themselves from within, for their own needs rather than those of an externally imposed programme of social engineering. II.3. opens with Bradshaw at a gate in Blackfriars, *'looking up at something black and shapeless on a spike. Long pause. She conquers herself'* (50), and pursues a digression of savage comedy based on the sight of her husband's corpse. This is a further demonstration of her maxim 'People will always go beyond the point they say stick at', which she next applies to her role as Devonshire's housekeeper, abandoning charity and self-esteem to ensure her own wages by cutting the servants'. The Footman's objection, 'I am a sodding Christmas tree, dangling with grandads and crippled kids', cuts no ice; her grasp of power is as brutally honest and realistic as the situation demands. Again, she cannot afford to regard the innocent as friends. Neither can Ball, who harangues Shade, a soldier, as a representative of army and country. The official withdrawal of Ball's certificate of royal commission is a further dislocation of his identity: 'I AM NO LONGER A KING'S MAN, WHAT OF THAT! No, it is a weird thing but I loved this fucking nation, and what is it . . . Is it hills? Is it rivers? Is it scenery?'. He sees Shade as visual evidence of the loss of an ideal: 'Because it can't be people, can it? It can't be YOU . . . Really you are a shambles of an English man, I say that — no offence intended — but to my mind you are not a man at all'. As Music sensed from afar in *Crimes in Hot Countries*, England has fallen embarrassingly short of its distant idyllic invocations, and stands as a disgrace to Ball's memories, 'I LOST SOME LOVELY COMRADES IN THE WAR YOU CUNT!' His severance from institutional role prompts him to dedicate himself directly to the nation's figurehead: 'Got to save the King, see? CUT THE GANGRENE OUT' (52). His romantic fascism recalls the misplaced idealism and fatally impractical integrity of Finney in *Birth on a Hard Shoulder*, as he extrapolates and realises ideals to the embarrassment of their institutional representatives.

At her wedding banquet, Devonshire claims she hates Charles, but he maintains 'No, it's only passion back to front' — an image of truth in opposites which, though casual, has many echoes for and in surrounding characters. Charles is scathingly buoyant, presiding over the marriage of Devonshire and Hambro, 'the RAW OLD UNION OF GAIN AND EXPEDIENCY'; he compulsively exposes the base reality beneath the romantic idealism of the occasion. A drunken Hambro takes the opportunity of his triumph to abuse the revellers in their indulgence, relishing his own sense of power and assurance in the new age of capital: 'YOU AREN'T IN YOUR TIME AND I AM, SEE? All that happens is as *I* want it, and everything suits me ... EVERY DAY I PICK UP THE PAPER I SHALL SAY "GOOD", SEE? The smoothness of my time. My life without rage, SEE?'

Charles appreciates that Hambro has come into his own, through fly-like stealth, rather than Ball with his outdated faith in monarchy and glory in war. But then occurs another of the play's characteristic unexpected transferrals of sympathy and dislocations of cruelty: Charles produces a large wrapped wedding gift which is revealed as Scrope, his lips cut off, a copy of *Harmonia Britannia* around his neck. The King delights in his sudden disruption of conventional response, claiming to have invented 'the sad present', and invites Scrope to communicate his knowledge of the 'filthy act of History'. But Scrope vehemently refutes any sense of human squalor. His actions leading to his arrest may have been prompted by his hearing and assimilating Milton's assertion 'Any amount of war a man will take, will acquiesce in his own destruction even, provided that he knows the change takes place'; his stand and martyrdom are his own interpretations of the edict, 'Next time, should we start, there must be no finish'. His courageous maimed struggles to shout Republican slogans are interrupted by Bradshaw, who rejects the very idea of acquiescence in destruction as vainglorious:

> What do you think you've got there, dignity? Really, I have seen some idiots, crashing about the doorposts of time and history, shouting out their old abuse, but you, what have you discovered, your MANHOOD or something? You absurd thing, you should be nailed to a board. SHUT UP. *(She looks around)* Excuse me. No. I'm perfectly all right. Well, I am, aren't I? Look, I have clean drawers on, courtesy of Madam, starched underthings. And lips. Not rose bud. Not what they were, of course, but lips. *(She curtsies, turns away)*　　　　　　　　　　　　　　　　　　(58–9)

Any residual audience abilities to locate heroism are diffused here: antithetical perspectives of courage and bathos play across the figures of Scrope and Bradshaw, and neither can be identified clearly or immediately as 'right'. The visual horror of Scrope's disfigurement and the unrelenting cruelty of Bradshaw's denunciation amplify the senses of confusion and depth of pain involved in choice. But Ball, the royalist idealist, remains; he picks this moment to act in his own faith, stabbing Hambro and exulting in his own simple heroism. But Charles is playing a game, by rules which Ball cannot comprehend. Ball tries to rouse him to infuse his figurehead status with faith and power; the terrible tension of delay in their locked stares may testify to Charles's temptation by the exhortation as well as Ball's dawning sense of isolation and disappointment, before Charles's resolution of the situation in courtly superficiality:

> BALL: . . . Charles Stuart, be a King! (CHARLES *doesn't move*) ENG-LAND CALLS YOU! BE A KING! *(Silence)* Come on, then. *(Pause)* Come on, I have liberated yer. *(Pause)* Oh, come on, be a FUCK-ING MONARCHIST.
> (*There is no response.* BALL *lets out a terrible wail.*)
> CHARLES: Drink my health and get off the table.   (59)

After Ball and Hambro are swept out, McConochie — now pox-doctor to the court — attempts to establish contact with Bradshaw, maintaining his assumed Scottish accent with great emotional strain; Bradshaw characteristically urges him to play out his role and fix his sights on survival, 'You must not weaken, you must not weaken', even as *'She weakens herself, kissing him'*. Charles's entry makes them recoil into control; he soliloquises, half to Bradshaw, subsiding into melancholia and humiliation at Ball's disappointment, mistaking her patience for sympathy. This patience, focused on retrieving the last part of her human jigsaw, Bradshaw's head, provokes a decisive severance on the part of her son: *'She is aware of* McCONOCHIE *looking at her. He seems to shudder, then turns away in disgust. There is a pause of ultimate tension before* McCONOCHIE *walks off'*. Lest the tying-up of plot-lines suggest the play is hastening to a conclusion of celebrating resilience, Barker reminds the audience of the cost and context of Bradshaw's actions, which prevents the simplicities of her possible elevation to heroic status: Devonshire's Footman, now a janitor, appears and blocks her way to tell her 'For six months I 'ave 'ad no work, you cow' (61). He beats her, as she forces her hand to her mouth to stifle her own cries.

The final scene shows Bradshaw with the tortured, muted figure of Ball, their baby (the product of rape), and the bag containing the remnants of her first husband, returned to Cropper's garden. Cropper bridles at this unexpected confluence of familial flotsam and the thought of her father's reappearance — 'In the bag. The dad' as Bradshaw puts it. Like McConochie, Cropper refuses to identify the body as essence and claims 'It is not him'; she overturns Bradshaw's withering sense of her restricted capabilities by proclaiming she is translating and printing *Harmonia Britannia*, her own repository of faith, which she is attempting to regenerate: here at least idealism has proved resilient. But Bradshaw does not share or perhaps even understand her enthusiasm. Cropper takes the baby, Bradshaw clasps Ball, as they move indoors out of the rain, leaving the bag of Richard Bradshaw's bones behind. The embrace of the battered, broken bodies is as eloquently, ultimately pitiful as Galactia's sense of the severed hand in *Scenes from an Execution*, though life is not extinguished in the shapes of Bradshaw and Ball. The embrace is also emblematic of an unlikely reconciliation of opposites, united in essence, the *leitmotif* of the play. If they resist shattering, shapes bend and twist into new and alarming configurations, wrenched into something disturbingly reminiscent of their ostensible opposites. Opposed formations are broken down into common components (Bradshaw says of Ball, 'He was a conspiracy, but a conspiracy of one'), and progression involves confronting, performing and embracing contraries, on the parts of characters, actors and audiences alike — all of whom become to some extent 'performers', *en route* to making their own choices in reaction, which will probably involve their surrendering preconceptions of limits, extremity and inconsistency.

Amid the shattered human, dramatic and philosophical forms are injunctions to reconstitution: Scrope's explosive cry to the theatre audience 'Oh, all you who come after, make your revolution right!', and Milton's appended warning 'Next time, should we start there must be no finish, or we shall slap one another's faces in the gardens of our enemies'. Thus the audience are invited to recognise and learn from historical moments of collapse, and Barker does not advance, impose or extract a simplistic formula for future success; the onus of 'choices in reaction', reformulation and regeneration, is located in the audience, should they rise to the challenge, extending the process into their own lives. Spectators accustomed to passivity may be confused and resentful, but Barker refuses conventional appetites for patronising drama of celebration or deterministic didacticism. His audiences are offered the chance to participate in, and extend, the processes depicted in the plays.

Nietzsche's reclamation of the term 'victory' and Barker's play stand in mutual illumination. Nietzsche:

> A sudden terror and suspicion of what it loved, a lightning-bolt of contempt for what it called 'duty', a rebellious, arbitrary, volcanically erupting desire for travel, strange places, estrangement, coldness, soberness, frost, a hatred for love, perhaps a desecrating blow and glance *backwards* to where it formerly loved and worshipped, perhaps a hot blush of shame at what it has just done and at the same time an exultation *that* it has done it, a drunken, inwardly exultant shudder which betrays that a victory has been won — a victory? over what? over whom? an enigmatic, question-packed, questionable victory, but the *first* victory nonetheless: such bad and painful things are part of the history of the great liberation. It is at the same time a sickness that can destroy the man who has it, this first outbreak of strength and will to self-determination, to evaluating on one's own account, this will to *free* will . . . [4]

The sense of active engagement in process is crucial to *A Passion in Six Days* (staged 1983), set at an early 1980s Labour Party conference by the sea, an elemental backdrop of both flux and constancy. As the party members struggle to reformulate policy and leadership, John Axt and his wife Annie attempt to establish new positions of personal imagination and mutual sympathy with regard to sexual freedom. Annie records her appreciation of Axt attempting to overcome familiar modes of thought, 'All the male possession stuff. Having and holding'. Her sense of her body is marked by her self-centred assurance:

ANNIE: My flesh. Lent, not sold.
AXT: Given . . .
ANNIE: Yes. Lent. (50)

She misses the distinction: 'lent' suggests a recall to essence and control in isolation; Axt's 'given' involves a surrender of definition exclusively by the self. She questions his compulsion to imagine another's hands and mouth on her body, as part of her clean and rational remedial programme for readjustment: 'The torture. Taking it out' (6). As they attempt a catechism, desire is opposed to freedom and possession is identified as poisonous in a concentration on the other's needs, pursuing Annie's conviction 'EXPRESS IT AND IT CAN BE DISCUSSED'. Their exchange is interrupted by prospective Party leader Brian Glint rescuing Wilsonian 'social-democrat' Harry Gaukroger from drowning: Gaukroger predicts their subsequent alliance in mutual self-interest, 'We shall be father and son'. Annie's attraction to Glint is physical, ostensibly precluding the ramifications of his background instigations of reactionary policies as a path to personal power: 'He was dark voiced in the dark night,/Altogether male stereotype,/But I liked it, is that so very wrong?'. Axt acknowledges the tangles of his own rationality and instincts as painfully resistant to separation:

> I can't make sense of my feelings
> But I would die if you had dealings
> With a traitor to the left like Brian Glint;
> I know the body, a contraption
> For finding satisfaction
> But anyone who touches him's a bint.   (9)

The songs in *A Passion in Six Days*, like those in *The Poor Man's Friend*, provide opportunities for characters' isolated self-presentations against large-scale raucous choruses. Whereas in *The Poor Man's Friend* Sylvester was defined in separation from the Bridport community, the Party members of *A Passion* reveal the hopes and fears of their personal stances against the lurching doggerel unison of the Absolutes; or, in the cases of Axt and Annie, characters are permitted self-explication, but frozen in position, with a poignant, aching gap in communication dividing them even in their integrity of soliloquy. Glint realises and embraces his essential isolation: 'Every leader from Jesus Christ to Fidel Castro/Knows the handshake is dishonest and the kiss is a disease,/It's the price the governor pays to be the governor' (17). His fantasies of enviable power are disturbingly reminiscent of Godber in *That Good*, and demonstrate a similar wish to be a 'star' on existing social terms, instead of testifying to any bid to encourage redefinition of society: his inspiration is gleaned from singer Tom Jones rather than Richard Bradshaw.

Boakes's sense of necessary expediency and calculated hypocrisy is demonstrated in political and sexual terms: she says 'I think I hate men more every year I come to conference . . . The groin. The power. The grab. The buttock. The whole fetid bullsmell of you lot';

nevertheless she resigns herself to circumscription by the male-dominated party as the laborious path to saving 'a scarred and scalded land . . . which stinks with rotting decencies and murdered hope'. The political correspondent and broadcaster Claxton is ironically dismissive:

> This is a party which suffers and suffers, is crucified and thinks to show its wounds will only win respect. But the public only say, look, it's being crucified again. Rather as they would laugh at Christ if he was up there not once, but time and time again climbed up to his calvary. (21)

Emily Drum identifies suffering as the price of regeneration: 'It is a real democracy, that is why it suffers. It's not a racket, or a front, it's a party . . . It's given me life'. Claxton wonders at her: 'You are a zealot, are you?' Another character, identified as an 'idealist' for his faith, is 90-year-old Lord Isted, unconcerned by the implicit rotting marginalisation of such titles. Isted has previously affirmed life through suffering in traditional Christian terms, when beaten as a wartime pacifist insisting on the Christ in every man; but now he rejects the dignity of passivity or debate: 'The arguments have all become redundant. The arguments and the counter-arguments'. Instead he expects disarmament in his own ironically frail and faltering lifetime, emphasising the urgency of his appeal to the assertion of the life-force: not 'the biscuit brains of strategists' but 'Women and moisture. Magic' (20). Thus he replaces passion in Christian and paternal suffering and faith in rational debate with passion for regenerative existence, rejecting the egocentric posturing of Glint's self-assertions and the careerist manoeuvrings of his peers through self-foregrounding and intimidation.

Thus, Isted has no time or patience with notions of rationalism and socialism that accord no central place to passion. However, the elevation of gratification in hedonist Gaukroger's 'Socialism à l'Anglais' is forming a link with Glint's calculated drive to personal reflected glory. Meanwhile, Axt proposes his motion on 'Socialist Love', rejecting 'the capitalism in our hearts' as enshrined in the property relations of marriage. Like Isted, Axt is attempting to work from a faith in fundamentals: 'Love, family, parenthood, marriage, are the primary experiences of the human animal, it is there that socialism must work its transformations if changes in our economic life are to have any meaning. What is the use of freedom on the factory floor if when you come home the woman hates you and you hate the woman?' (31).

While one woman, Boys, recognises the importance of his address and identifies marriage as a Tory stronghold of appeal, 'the stone on which property is built', the motion generally stirs uncomfortable Labour insecurities, a retrenched fear of passion's risk, both personal ('There's nothing wrong with my marriage and I'm not a Tory') and party-political ('a commitment to introduce legislation encouraging the development of alternative sexual and marital relations, come on, wake up, it's a gift to the Daily Fartbag!', 32). Debate is quashed by the patronising paternalism of Deasy, observing the letter of rules of order rather than the spirit of engagement and conviction. Gaukroger opines 'Yer cannot love the flesh and be a Tory', but his model of social-ism revolves around wallowing in gratification and indulgence — his vision of socialism as 'the biggest champagne party in the history of the world' recalls the court scenes in *Victory* — and banal unison, 'If yer can make people laugh yer'll have equality' (35).

Annie approaches Glint with a sudden directness which eclipses his opportunity to want; he objects, 'Darling, you try too hard. So hard you make desire feel redundant'. She acknowledges her own desire, 'Very basic, down-in-the-belly wants, tearing away and mak-ing me slightly sick', which impels her to an elevation of simplic-ity, 'simple rights' and 'absolute and simple wants', where pain and pleasure can be 'swapped' like stamps. Glint resists, as this occludes his vanity — 'What about me in all this!' — but then accepts her as further pluming of his will. Annie realises he wants to kiss her because she's weak, adding 'I hate your politics incidentally. Or is it incidentally?'; she may also find his sense of power alluring.

Fenton is a character spurred on, like Marjorie in *My Sister and I* and Ball in *Victory*, by the image of a monarchy disposing of real power in a constitutional coup rather than remaining contented with the trappings; but in Fenton's case, this is a nightmare situation whereby an elected socialist government might be forcibly dissolved. Gaukroger is appalled by Fenton's consequent drive to abolish the monarchy, as this threatens the country's nostalgia for secure stasis which Gaukroger identifies as self-evidently crucial, corresponding to his own affection for Harold Wilson's reassuring lies: 'Lies are very comforting. Yer can sleep with a lie. Yer can dine on one'.

Isted and Axt's faith in dynamics, and their direct powerful language in expressing this, are opposed both to Gaukroger's crackerbarrel philosophy and to the empty rhetoric of Toynbee's tortuous syntax, as Ian Cooper has noted: Toynbee's 'tired hyperbole and vacuous, devitalised sentiments characterise the uninspired reformist pose which seeks to plaster the cracks Axt cannot conceal; in its repetitive, meandering course, its staccato reiteration of worn faith and rhetorical over-emphasis, Toynbee's speech communicates its burbling intent to do nothing'.[5] Such compulsive self-qualification parallels Boakes's acceptance of England 'saved' though still populated with 'little twisted businessmen' and 'masons whooping it up in clubs' (18), and this arc of compromise extends to Gaukroger's vision of cosy stasis where revelry is a substitute for transition, as in Wilson's heyday. Glint has ensured Harry's vote by saving him from drowning. Cooper has also identified the pathetic irony of Gaukroger's mock-heroic eloquence when he rages at the sea, and draws a parallel with 'Falstaff, whose articulacy, hedonism and ambiguous conception of honour is contrasted to Hal's silence, acceptance and manipulation in embodying and commanding respect'. Glint rejoices in his Christ-like power in making the conference hang on his silence, 'The power of NOT. The honour of NOT. The great, eloquent, unforgettable NOT' (46). But his silence is not abstention from worldly temptation so much as Prince Hal's careful gauging of when and how to present himself to maximum effect and overall strategic influence.

Annie's news that she has copulated with Glint is couched in utopian pseudo-objectivity, countering 'Who was it?' with 'What's it matter?' and 'Oh, perfect husband, if you love me why don't you rejoice?' These qualities only intensify Axt's pain: he tells Drum 'I am sick, and dog tired with the strain of being me . . . my bones are breaking, little cracks inside my head, the strains, the splits, the hairline fractures' (48). Cooper again:

> The contradiction between subjective and objective political truth is embodied in Axt; commitment tears him apart because Annie's practise of policy and theory has wrought irrevocable change. The image of Axt fractured is powerful because the consciousness of self in the dialectical mess has been denied, not integrated, by theory. Annie has instigated the conference movement but Axt remains unreconciled to it. There is none of the intellectual playfulness of "bending the dialectic" of politics, because Axt is involved in it; he is bending and being bent, and the stress fractures show up as scars. Martin Glass, protagonist of David

Edgar's *Maydays* (1983), functions against a background of political events but has no entry-point into them; as a result identity is foreshadowed against ideology and not convincingly interrelated: we are left with bourgeois dilemmas, the fascination of the commercial stage. Barker's Axt is allowed no time for egocentric reflection because he is placed in a contradictory state of flux, where changing situations challenge conclusions arrived at in sedate seclusion. Barker disrupts the view of history as spectacle to place it messily, uncomfortably close to his audience . . . *A Passion in Six Days* uncovers the pain involved in belief, the anguish in assimilating knowledge. In essence it explores the suffering involved in making politics more than a pose, the inescapable reality that the regeneration of life involves the labour pains of birth. The individual endures the rigours of participating in history without becoming ossified into collective lies, and is warped by experience, but endurance lends dignity.

Isted's speech urging disarmament hinges on confronting the maddening facts of nuclear war and its threat to the generative impulse itself:

THERE HAS NEVER BEEN A SLAVERY LIKE IT. It mocks this democracy! It laughs in the face of your so-called choice! It hangs over you, and not over you alone, but over what you carry in your blood, and in your semen, and in your womb. What your parents gave you, and what links you to your ancestors, and what you hand on, your place in that endless chain which is the greatest comfort of mortality, THEY ROB YOU OF THAT!   (49)

Axt, despairing at his expulsion, pushed to breakdown by the thought of Annie with Glint, patronises Drum in her resilience: 'Oh, you good woman, laying your faith to be trod on, and your spirit to be whopped into dough' (48). But her faith and spirit are intact. She counters 'Don't be superior', and offers a more practical sympathy: 'I voted for your resolution. On Socialist relationships. I'm sorry that it failed'. Annie returns with the supposed reassurance that her liaison with Glint has left her fundamentally untouched and unchanged:

AXT: The delegates go — crack —
ANNIE: You see, I've come back and nothing's —

AXT: Pop go the delegates . . .
ANNIE: Not stained, not altered, just the same old —
AXT: Dry men, and dry women, like twigs —
ANNIE: What is it?
AXT: It must be moist. It must be passionate.
ANNIE: What? *(Pause. He looks at her.)*
AXT: Socialism.   (51)

Annie eagerly assumes the blame for his behaviour, 'I've driven
you a little bit mad', but Axt insists on the depth of change result-
ing from his chance meeting with Drum: 'I met a woman. And she's
stained me. And altered me. And I haven't touched her yet. And
may not'. The curse of debate is its arid abstraction of personal contact and instinct: Axt sees 'all this — can't save us because it isn't
passionate'. Annie maintains 'If it can't go into a resolution, it isn't
worth saying', though her earlier exchange with Glint would be difficult to formulate in these terms:

GLINT: Say I own you.
ANNIE: Nobody owns me.
GLINT: I do, I own your feelings, so I own you.
ANNIE: That turns me on but it's rubbish.   (47)

Nevertheless, she keeps up her prescriptive rationality in Axt's
presence, until he rejects such matrimonial compartmentalisation of
the self and dismissal of possibilities of insight:

AXT: I shan't lie with you again.
ANNIE: Lie with? What's this lie with? You'll be callin' spunk seed
   in a minute, and fuck a union.
AXT: IT IS A UNION. *(Pause)* Don't smash it, please. This feeling I
   have. Don't bash it up with sarcasm.
ANNIE: It's not sensible.
AXT: It comes that way because —
ANNIE: It's not rational —
AXT: Like poetry because —
ANNIE: It's codswallop in the bluebells —
AXT: DON'T HURT MY FEELINGS WITH YOUR BRAIN.   (51)

Gaukroger invokes heart over intellect, but in a reductive, sentimental way: 'buyin' drinks for workmen and their mates', the

vacuous promise of intoxication, integration and the bloated calm of consumerism which leaves Harry's own relative privilege undisturbed: 'I like my life, so please don't take it apart'. Gaukroger shies away from Axt, 'Yer thin and 'aunted, an' when I look at yer I see England burnin'. . .', but Axt has discovered through painful experience that wilful blindness and stunted imaginations cannot wish away self-consuming upheaval: 'It is burning. It's burning now'. Balanced against this vision of irresistible, indiscriminate vengefulness bursting Harry's champagne bubble, is the gradual, small-scale effect wrought by Drum, whose resolution is passed at the cost of 160 hours of her life; nevertheless, it is a form of personal intervention in the process of history, like Cropper persisting with the translation and dissemination of *Harmonia Britannia*, preparing groundwork for the future.

A Passion in Six Days dramatises the pertinence of Proud's aphorism in two spheres, party-political and sexual: 'the art of politics is to persuade others to accept you at your own valuation — the art of freedom is to persistently demolish that evaluation' (18). Annie's 'lending' of herself to Glint permits 'no fusion to confuse, to interfere with the unique experience', an attitude which Angela Carter identifies as 'a form of exacerbated auto-eroticism. Sexual pleasure is not experienced *as* experience; it does not modify the subject'. Annie's statement of being fundamentally unchanged by her fling with Glint suggests 'parlour game' sex, part social exploit, part infertility festival. Carter: 'When desire is a function of the act rather than the act a function of desire, desire loses its troubling otherness; it ceases to be a movement outwards from the self'.[6] Though Annie and Axt can rationally identify possession as 'poisonous' in its associations of retentive control over a less powerful being, there is another sense of the word: to be 'like one possessed' is to become host to a great inflammatory, almost demonic energy, of which Leantio and Livia achieve a sense in *Women Beware Women*, a mutual drive towards regeneration springing from total painstaking engagement. *A Passion in Six Days* suggests that a passionate socialism would parallel desire in this respect, and scorch away its egoistic parasites who cling to their essential securities of stategic seduction and sterile self-gratification, in fear of risking real change.

The Power of the Dog: Moments in History and Anti-History (written 1981, staged 1984) opens up into a larger, groaning, yawning, devouring landscape, spanning Moscow and the Polish plains and depicting the strain of survival — resisting the almost hypnotic temptation to relax and sink into the mud — with gruelling detail, as if stretching the form of *Victory* even further. Again, pockets of privileged security and feverish hyper-activity, 'soft mad places', are located above and away from the sucking squalor of the quaking, corpse-filled bog; for *The Power of the Dog* has a 'landscape of flesh', like that of *The Love of a Good Man*, as its voracious maw. But the play opens in what Scottish comedian Archie McGroot hopes will prove a safe house for him: he has been engaged to provide entertainment at the Kremlin, as what Russian officials hope will be a passable approximation to George Robey, thus amusing Churchill on his visit to Stalin, Yalta 1945. Archie fears for his survival, clinging to his flagging, unfunny act in a vacuum of response: 'A should ha' stayed in the clubs, but A'm an idealist'. The breakdown of the conventional entertainer— audience laughter contract provokes discomfort and embarrassment, but McGroot works on determinedly, the surrounding lack of vitality and sympathy driving him on to produce more frantic self-generated energy: 'It is a fact that the more resistance you encounter, the more effective yoo are bein'! A take a kick in the bollocks as a positive sign o' favour, it's all part o' bein' a radical comedian' (2).

This establishes a keynote of the play: feverous surface activity as a near-hysterical response to, and defence against, a general overwhelming sense of entropy; characters pursue idiosyncratic avenues of inventiveness without communication, spurring themselves on with nervous willed energy that is found beyond the conventional limits of exhaustion, or else twitching and flailing in a purely automatic sense as if decapitated. This is the atmosphere in which heads of state meet but are severed from possibilities of meaningful communication, and 'A Great Man Hallucinates'. The same grotesque displacement and approximation that served up McGroot instead of Robey dogs Stalin and Churchill's exchanges. Interpreters blur the essence of their words and characters, while drunkenly attempting to keep the conversation limping on rather than grinding to the dead stop of silence. Stalin laments the exclusion of accident from his life and Churchill launches into baroque, gargoyle-laden evocations of power, both lamenting loss of elementary human contact; but the meeting is barren, with banal paraphrase smothering the ignition of sympathy or passion, leaving these forces trapped and thwarted in the heads of state, who are more convinced of their isolation than ever. McGroot jabbers on, his sense of comedy snapped into desperate, awkward *non-sequiturs* cracked into the gulf of history's ironies and ravages ('In Manchester a geezer is lookin' at a woman in a train. In Manchuria they are cuttin' a woman's breasts off wi a bayonet, ye gotta laugh, noo, ye gotta laugh!', 5).

Photographer Victor and model Ilona meanwhile stumble across the war-pocked Polish plain with its threats of death and love, jettisoning ideals and stealing wallets like a latter-day Scrope and Bradshaw. Victor is correspondingly less adaptable than Ilona, who can assume shapes ('THIS IS MY HUMAN CONDITION FACE') and perform acts as *gestus-like* attitudes as part of a larger scheme of self-preservation and self-determination, staring out danger and resisting the pull toward annihilation. She deduces that her sister, whom she discovers hanged, relaxed into her fate rather than resist it with determined self-invention: 'I believe that every murder is an acquiescence, and every victim possessed the means of her escape. I believe in your eyes and in your mouth you own the means of your salvation, whether you want to be loved, or whether you want to be saved' (10). Sorge's kiln-fired willpower, demonstrated by his clasping the dead woman by the ankles and exulting in his ability to pronounce this 'a wonderful century', marks him out as more self-inventive: autonomous, dangerous and alluring.

Sorge characteristically wishes to impose form and ideology on film student Matrimova's attempts to create 'wholefilm', through which she hopes, in her naïve party-mindedness, to identify and freeze 'every political truth and every personal truth'. Sorge maintains 'The war film which merely dispenses pity does not help anyone'; he proposes she locate reasons for battles by reference to historical determinism and rationality, and thereby redefine courage in an anti-bourgeois sense, celebrating survival, endurance and cunning rather than sacrifice, heroics and bravery. But their debate is comically and touchingly counterpointed by Melankov's childish fantasies of wartime heroics and his sense of intoxicated vulnerability; and by Tremblayev's profession of desire for Sorge, which maintains his culpability, even intent, in heightening her sense of life and self: 'You deliberately set out to undermine my personality — you did — to demolish everything I was — for which I am entirely grateful' (15). But they are interrupted by Ilona, seeking her sister's body, to reclaim and inter this dead form from her past, like Bradshaw after her husband's 'bits'.

In the world of *The Power of the Dog*, such emphasis is placed on willed resolution as bulwark against encroaching death, that Victor's premonition 'I HAVE THIS FEELING I WILL END UP IN A DITCH!' is tantamount to inviting this fate; Ilona focuses her imagination on negotiating practicalities step by step, assimilating and evading history by fragmenting it through a prismatic perception of experience, of which her reiterated rhymes are a formally apt reminder: 'I say the answer lies in pain, what my mother went through I can again. Swallow the monster and don't strain, murders from the Bosphorus to the Hebrides render all complaints absurdities. Don't ask what makes the system, if it is a system, work, cover your indignation with your foot, don't think that black stuff is burned bodies, really it is only soot' (17). In contrast, her sister believed she could survive through enacting submission:

When the mad dog comes for you
Don't run, you'll only stumble.
Instead, lie down and show your throat,
Some dogs don't bite the humble . . .

But she was not a good enough actress: 'She had clear eyes, eyes which made lying impossible' (23).

Arkov berates Sorge for his performance of official duties, 'You are in terror of your sensitivity . . . One day your soul will burst out of its servitude' (20). But Sorge has chosen to live with the dark areas of his self rather than pursue them, conceding to necessity while preserving a detachment through ideology and wit, guarding him against the consequences of impulses, armouring him by dislocation: 'I hate simplicity. The intellectual laziness, the posturing of so-called simple men. They float through the world like icebergs, one tenth of sunlit ice . . . but what about the nine-tenths in the dark? . . . The contradictions? The counter-arguments? The necessary and the expedient?' (22). The desperate soldiers attempt a *Macbeth*-like cauldron ritual, hoping to 'release the power of the party' by stumbling magic, which, as in other Barker plays, precipitates a revelation of sorts, but not that invited or expected. Melankov's uncomfortably large questions — recalling the boyish bewilderment of Apps in *Pity in History* — are answered by the appearance of a female SS officer, who misinterprets Arkov's injunctions to throw away her uniform and escape, and resigns

herself to rape. Desperation and despair drive Arkov to cas-
trate himself, resisting the insurrections of the body with brutal
simplicity and impractical idealism, like Bloody Five in Brecht's
A Man's a Man; such are the demands of his clinging to a poetic
sensibility in times which render it not only redundant but
hazardous.

From Anti-History back again to History: in the Kremlin, Stalin
casts around for his reflection in an atmosphere of terminal piety,
like Charles in *Victory*, conscious that 'There are only two classes
of person able to be unreservedly themselves, to follow the absolute dictation of their personality. The supremely powerful and the
utterly insane'; he identifies Marxism-Leninism as the power that
prevents him sliding from one to the other, but is conscious of the
uniqueness of his human/superhuman dual vision:

> A building site, to the uninitiated, is the essence of chaos, but to
> the foreman, merely the first stage of the plan. I am the foreman,
> and Lenin made the plans. Of course, if you are sitting in a pud-
> dle with raw, bloody feet, it is hard to appreciate the beauty of the
> structure. I understand that! I am perfectly human.   (28)

Thus, social engineering is expressed as another form of poetry.
But Stalin has more power and faith in himself than Charles, as
shown when he decides to jolt an honest response from his sycophants: his sexual taunting of Poskrebyshev can go further than
Charles's of Hambro, where power was sliding from throne to
capital. Poskrebyshev's harmless attack on Stalin resolves itself
into a restatement of their relative positions of power which
Stalin finds amusing and reassuring; his outburst over, Poskrebyshev accepts the offered glass of water, and may also find reassurance in reconciliation, as Stalin replaces the gramophone
needle on his symphony of tribute. His view of artists is also free of
the self-conscious considerations of the liberal consensus shown
by the Doge in *Scenes from an Execution*, but he deals with them
comparably.

On the chaos of the plains, Matrimova strives to present a film
approximating Stalin's poetic pattern of perception: three screens,
dealing with Psychology, History and Possibility to 'maximalize
the audience's grasp of reality' — 'Until now, all film had been
warped by the single eye' (29). Expounding her theories absolves her
from the responsibility to talk to the self-conscious, isolated human

anomaly, Buber. Ilona and Victor weave their way through events, but Victor begins to crumble with guilty fatalism: 'I think we are going to die and we deserve it!' Ilona recognises his drift into exhaustion and disaster: 'you've got the sick dog's eyes . . . the eyes of old men who have sunk down and can't get up again . . . the eyes we've seen on every road in Europe . . . the eyes that beckon rifle butts' (31). He ignores the confessional outburst of the SS officer Gloria, wishing to be left alone to 'Just sit in a bar in New York'. Ilona sees this as a rejection of the pain involved in life; when Victor is accidentally killed, she deduces 'Victor is dead because he wanted to be dead. New York was just — a metaphor' for evasion. She becomes an object of idealised fascination for Matrimova and Sorge, who mistake her resilience for other-worldly purity. Ilona denounces their attention as sentimentality: 'Why do you want me to cry! To reassure you all the old emotions are still knocking around? To show you women are still women' (38). But Sorge is fascinated by the idea of thawing his ice-queen; while stirred by idealisation ('through all the clamour she walks untouched . . . She is unspoiled by History'), he also wishes to arouse and inflame her currently minimal wants: 'I want you to WANT to be my mistress . . . Not to acquiesce, but to will, and therefore — to suffer . . . For wanting'. But Ilona is mindful of where her sister's capacity for self-surrender led:

SORGE: YOU AGREE SO MUCH IT MAKES ME SUSPICIOUS.
ILONA: It's a habit, I — real feelings become — after so much — become impossible to —
SORGE: Perhaps you should resist me —
ILONA: Perhaps I should, yes —
SORGE: RESIST ME, THEN!
ILONA: Anything that has substance will be snapped, and anything that hasn't, can't be. She had substance, didn't she. So much substance I really hated her —
SORGE: I insist you are yourself —
ILONA: I am trying —
SORGE: No, you are hiding, you are hiding something, no one can be so —
ILONA: I am, I am myself —
SORGE: Let me make some mark on you, what are you, a saint! *(He kisses her violently, painfully. Pause.)*
ILONA: I think she killed herself. She did. She killed herself to get away from you. (39)

History intervenes: Sorge is arrested, on the promptings of the vengeful Tremblayev, and Ilona is summoned to photograph Stalin at the Kremlin, where, like McGroot at the start of the play, she previsions a meaningless death. Archie has now ensconced himself in the role of incomprehensible court jester, allowed a degree of irreverence because mainly ignored. But Ilona's self-control finally proves brittle; she nervously drops film plates and realises she is losing the ability to extirpate feelings. Stalin enjoys his ability to frighten her, a small and local index to his power, though Ilona tries to hang on to the idea of his ordinariness. His trump card is the revelation of Sorge's suppression of fraternisation evidence which carried the death penalty for Ilona: McGroot remarks on this merciful act, 'They do that, doon't they, it's called desire. How do ye knoo when a man loves you? He puts flowers on yer grave. 'AVE SEEN IT HAPPEN' (43). Hitherto safe in her chameleonic adaptability and restricted appetites, Ilona discovers a sense of 'substance' in herself which drives her to plead for Sorge's salvation, even as she realises it is irrational if not perilous. Stalin extends his arms: Ilona falls into them like an exhausted child seeking reassurance, 'Are we safe', surrendering herself to be subsumed by his power and determinism: she can avoid historical definition no longer. The light shrinks on McGroot, also finally exhausted in his 'radical comedian' idealism and invention. The dead stop of silence, so long fought off, finally occurs.

Barker is less pessimistic about the power of pity than Sorge, whose bids to maintain a clear sense of blame seem bedevilled, like Matrimova's film. Her mind is stretched to bursting when events cannot be tailored to her Procrustean beds of definition and analysis: 'I mean, if the impossible is true, where does that leave   how does an artist cope with that?' (40). *The Power of the Dog* explores pain and motivation through the medium of pity; as McGroot says of Ilona, 'She says yes . . . Ye canna blame her, maybe's hanging off a meathook and noo died of electric shocks' (41). The play has less impetus than *Victory* as the characters can afford less passion; when it does overcome Sorge and Ilona, they are engulfed by History. It is probably Barker's bleakest play in that it demonstrates there are times when the choice of passion over rationality proves fatal, even as it dignifies. *Victory, A Passion in Six Days* and *The Power of the Dog* dramatise the 'disturbing way that every argument has its counterargument, and one arrives at conviction not out of logic at all'.[7] Under pressure of experience, the characters are cleaved into numerous shards, exposing contrary forces, bursting faith in limits and definitions for all involved. Rationality is as redundant as an appeal to justice: Annie Axt's clinical programme to 'take out the torture' seems to deny, or break apart on, something essentially human. The essential stretching and tearing out of Axt's own shape, with all the mess and pain involved, becomes a process of discovery. As audiences watch Barker's characters flaying off their own dead skin, he unsentimentally maintains a clear impression of the cost involved for those characters; the knowledge of experience gained by recognition of the characters' instincts for truth, which can subsequently inform the audience's own individual choices in reaction, is therefore not cheap.

8

Power and the Body

THE CASTLE, WOMEN BEWARE WOMEN

No privacy in flesh. We own nothing, but we shall possess each
other, charm or poach it. Music's law.

> *Crimes in Hot Countries*

you are a rack also to stretch me on

> *Women Beware Women*

The Castle: A Triumph (staged 1985) springs from the epigraph 'What
is Politics but the absence/of Desire', the terms of which may be
illuminated by Proud's definitions in *A Passion in Six Days:* 'the art
of politics is to persuade others to accept you at your own evaluation — the art of freedom is to persistently demolish that evaluation'. Set in medieval England, *The Castle* depicts Crusading males
returning to their estates and discovering that a feminised community has flourished in their absence. The shock provokes a clash
between abstract rigour and natural impulses, the characteristic
nucleus of Barker's challenging and relentless examinations of politics and desire in their comic and tragic collisions and effects; *The
Castle's* themes provide perfect opportunities for the formulation of
such concepts, and for their demolitions of form. The knight Stucley orders the erection of the largest castle ever built, designed by
Arab mathematician and prisoner Krak, and the establishment of a
corresponding religion. The brooding menace of the Castle is briefly
alleviated by the outrageousness of the religion, but both testify to
Stucley's predatory wish to resolve contradictions (by intensifying
them, if necessary) — a wish enshrined at the core of many social
institutions or edifices which seek to reconstruct the instincts of the
people they contain. Characters like Stucley believe that resolving
contradictions will bring stability; they are the inevitable enemies of
'obsessive' characters like Skinner the witch — or Erica, Bradshaw,
Galactia, Livia and Sordido — who insist on complexities of vision
and instinct, and the sense that they are related. Bela's interview

with Diver is also pertinent here: characters like Diver invoke expediency and wit as a means to compartmentalisation of the self, preventing instinctive promptings from influencing behaviour, much less infusing the entire being.

The so-called 'obsessives' in Barker's canon resist others prescribing or imposing compartmentalisation of the self; they incur outrage and hostility through their rejection of wit and theory as used to fend off passion and commitment. Thus symmetry proves inimical to desire, 'stability' precludes change and breeds oppressive restrictions of freedom and integrity — forces which prove equally determined to burst through imposed form, rejecting divisions of the world and the self and refuting the circumscription of imaginative possibilities. Such is the clash of despairing irony with the essential hope of engagement. Barker's characters are inspired and inspirational when, rather than be forced to define their interests as narrowly and shallowly as possible, they insist on their autonomous senses of what is, and what is not, desirable — thus distinguishing between the painful dignity of exposure and striving, and the unnecessary pain of fearful insecurity and retrenchment, which enforces the restrictive definition of human potential and denies autonomy and integrity.

The Castle opens with Krak staring into the valley which was the crusaders' home. Stucley's disfigured retainer, Batter, sarcastically attempts to fill the tauntingly unfathomable cipher of Krak's silence for himself and for the audience, suggesting responses to immediate natural detail and a nostalgic sense of upheaval and imbalance. But the joke rebounds on Batter, who is outraged by the sight of his own unmown meadow; Stucley appears and amplifies the sense of nauseous offence in the landscape's lack of cultivation, identifying it as a spiteful demonstration of incontinence designed to mock the crusaders' idealism and suffering. His spiralling imagination characteristically recoils into the systematic: he elevates his injury and childlike sense of injustice into a personalised, universal cosmology of malice:

> ... I am so full of good, why does everything betray me? BECAUSE IT IS THE WAY OF THE WORLD! GOOD! All tenderness is doomed to ridicule, poetry is lies and mercy only fit for giggling over! IS MY WIFE DEAD? Must be, must be because I love her so, she's dead, it stands to reason, WHERE IS SHE

BURIED? What was it, fever? Fever, merciful fever? No, she was banged to death by bandits, CAN YOU FIND SOMEONE OR NOT? (4)

Thus he fills the void of response by careering into exultant pursuit of destined personal sleight, ridiculous and vulnerable in his boyish inability to deal with his thwarted ideals, 'injured in his faith'. The appearance of Cant and her immediate attraction to the crusaders' relative youth and virility, 'great stallion bits', makes Stucley recoil into sexual nausea ('I won't be fouled by you, mad bitch') and the sublimation of power through retentive imperial violence: he forces her down in the 'muck and nettle' to straddle and stab her, reclaiming the ground as 'MY TERRITORY'.[1] He immediately feels a shame of release, *'tosses the knife away, wipes his hand'*, assigning blame to Cant, 'LOOK WHAT YOU'VE MADE ME DO!'. After the reverberating ferocity of his outburst, the anticlimactic conclusion of his attempted rationale is uneasily comic and oddly pathetic: 'To come home and hear vile stuff of that sort is — when I am so clean for my lover is — no homecoming, is it?'

Krak finally speaks, with monolithically implacable rationality: 'Chaos is only apparent in my experience, like gravel shaken in water abhors the turbulence, and soon asserts itself in perfect order'. But Stucley's imagination is already pursuing the courtly-erotic opportunities of superficial chaos, with the eager anticipation of a child on Christmas morning: 'I run to my wife's bedroom. Catch her unprepared and all confusion. Oh, my lord, etcetera, half her plaits undone! Oh, my lord and all —'. He chases off; with horrible irony, his wife Ann appears from the opposite direction, riven by the sight of Krak: 'My belly's a fist. Went clench on seeing you, went rock. And womb a tumour. All my soft, rigid'. She claims the hill as hers: Krak turns, explaining he is 'Looking. In so far as the mist permits'. His training his gaze on her seems to enforce Ann's association of herself and the landscape, whether involuntarily or not, and perhaps makes her imbue it unconsciously with a coy allure: 'It always rains like this for strangers. Drapes itself in a fine drench, not liking to be spied on. A woman, this country, not arid like your place. Not brazen'. This blended sense of the enticing and the alien extends into her reflection on Stucley: 'My husband has turned skinny and beautiful. Was a fat puppy when he left'. Even as she dismisses Krak there is a sense of churning sensitisation, unexpected momentousness (and possibly prickling fur) issuing from their locked stares: 'THIS WAS AN ORDINARY AFTERNOON AND NOW YOU'RE HERE!' (5).

Skinner's impulse is defensive and violent: 'Stab him!' But Krak escapes, and Ann senses a looming fear that 'the fulcrum of disaster' has been set up; Skinner is also mindful of inexorability, 'Block the trickle before it's a stream, block the stream before it's a river'. Ann's attempts to reassure Skinner on the innocuousness of meeting Krak and of her description of Stucley are worse than useless; her remarks dress the vortex, which is tearing through the fabric of their imagined futures, with fascination. Cant is fascinated by the display of male power in Stucley's men 'In the big 'ouse, going barmy', and Ann sends for her husband, mindful of her own magnetic power through his anger: 'Tell him I'm here . . . He'll come'. Skinner recalls their overcomings in establishing the feminised community, breaking the trinity of bailiff, God and cock, 'Freed the ground, freed religion, freed the body', FOUND CUNT BEAUTIFUL that we had hidden and suffered shame for, its lovely shapelessness, its colour all miraculous, what they had made dirty out of ignorance, do we now . . . Just deliver it . . . Our bodies and our labour up to their groping fingers?' (6). Skinner creates an alienation between herself and Ann rather than simply exposing one: from recalling the previously unknown intimacy between herself and Ann, Skinner wryly recalls its matrimonial parody, and her deliverance from her husband ('suffocating thing in darkness') by his death; but her incredulity at the survivors' return provokes a laugh of solidarity, not bitterness, in Ann. Skinner thinks this testifies to relief and the flattered consciousness of a personal magnetism which Ann may feel, that she 'drew' Stucley back with her 'underneath'.

When Stucley arrives, it is his turn to conjecture and extrapolate on Ann's minimal or inscrutable outward shows, filling, interpreting and partly enforcing her silences with the flailing wildness of his invention and his unbottled self-expression and self-exploration. He tries numerous directions and angles of approach and attack, but his brittle attempts at self-control ('It is quite amusing coming back to this', 'it is not a desert, actually, it is full of fields and orchards the holy land') bring him to brinks of pleasurable memories in which his idealism has been rooted: 'everything changes and dreams are bollocks but you can't help dreaming even knowing a dream is —'; 'you said, do not feel you must do anything but may I kiss you, I have always loved your mouth'; 'I who jumped in every pond of murder kept this one thing pure in my head, pictured you half-naked on an English night, your skin which was translucent from one angle and deep-furrowed from another, your odour, even which I caught once in the middle of a scrap'. But he is no closer to fathoming the whirlpool of Ann's expression of 'trust' between Skinner and herself, until she claims not to have been equal to his fidelity. *'Pause. He is suspended between hysteria and disbelief'.*

Stucley's former circlings of enquiry, with penetration deflected, change to a reeling orbit, attempted pursuit and assimilation of the radical implications of Ann's core 'No'. Like the Bishop in *The Love of a Good Man*, he struggles with the hitherto impossible by shackling it to a malign cosmology where God is the supremely inventive sadist: each cumulative detail of what he sees as Ann's 'acquiescence in the riot of her cunt' makes him stretch his definition of indefinable resources of cruelty ('I know the source of our religion! It is that He in His savagery is both excessive and remorseless and to our shrieks both deaf and blind! I could be a bishop.') even as he feels himself stretched past recognisable grief on the rack of human contingency, the wrenchings of which defy description or response, whatever their residual compulsive temptations: 'You have to laugh, I do, I have great recourse to laughter, of the demonic variety, I could kill you and no one would bat an eyelid' (9). Her suggestion that he leave extends his outrage in injury, as he muffles explosions of anger: 'You see, you make me lose my temper, you make me abusive, why not stay, it is my home'. Ann replies 'not now', and urges him on to 'The horizon'. Stucley says 'I own the horizon'; Ann: 'Cross it, then'. She maintains, 'I'm cruel, but I do it to be simple. To cut off hopes cleanly. No tearing wounds, I'm sorry if your dreams are spoiled but — '. 'Perfectly kind and typically considerate of you', he says in pointed profession of detached sympathy. She detects the childlike thoroughness of his disappointment, and the immaturity which she may have found touching and attractive in their childless marriage: he recalls, 'I WAS YOUR CHILD, WASN'T I? *(Pause. He suddenly weeps. She watches him, then goes to him. He embraces her, then thrusts her away)* PENITENCE FOR ADULTERY!' (10).

Stucley is comic, pathetic and terrifying in his despair, like Scrope, Ball and Axt conflated and extended in their incredulous, anguished severance from a redundant ideal. Like Ann, the audience is probably attracted by pity at the nakedness of his suffering and appreciation of his imaginative expressiveness, while repelled by his consequent sense of license and uniqueness in response.

The subsequent exchange with Hush continues the scene's movement through incredibility but in a comic mode, as even Hush is amazed at the way he has fulfilled Stucley's fantastic allegations of mass insemination. This is an astonishing first scene in its demonstration of how every imaginable fear may be realised and then surpassed, to both tormenting and ludicrous effects, and the proximity with which we encounter Stucley's torment suggests the limited nature of the relief offered by Hush's appearance. Even as personal worlds apparently explode, there are suggestions of a cataclysmic force which will make them seem small bursting meteors in a chain reaction of apocalyptic catastrophe.

Scene Two establishes the characters operating at one remove from the molten centre of the play, and who are parasitical on the central monstrosity which they serve to create, in their own isolated spheres. Batter proudly extolls how Krak's genius 'will wring transformation out the dozing landscape. And he is mine, in all his rareness, mine, as if I'd birthed him'. Through his astonishing moment of 'kindness' in sparing Krak, Batter associates himself with the mathematician and with Stucley's project, while insisting on the limits of imagination to the old man: 'No one who was not there can imagine. Never say "I can imagine" again. It's a lie, nobody can'; and Sponge institutes this with comically prompt slavishness. Nailer the priest is embarrassed by his complicity in the feminised regime and his restoration by Stucley to church and authority; and Holiday the builder works on with cheerful simplicity and incomprehension, holding firm to the habit of craft and workplace relations in the face of the innovatory size and circularity of the Castle. Krak remains taciturn, believing 'To talk, what is that but the exchange of clumsy approximations, the false endeavour to disseminate truths arrived at in seclusion?' (16). Thus Krak sees truth as the product of isolation and calculation, and indeed not even Stucley can yet comprehend how the plan for the Castle 'makes war necessary' or is the best thing Krak has ever done.

The building site becomes a battleground for the opposed forces of Stucley and Skinner. Stucley believes he is saving those around him from themselves, the innate temptation of regression to primeval animal form: 'I do believe this, that human beings left without severity would roll back the ages and be hopping, croaking frogs, clustering thick on the female with the coming of the Spring, and sunk in mud for winter' (13); while alternatively seeking to assure himself and his followers of a briefly obscured pattern of conservative classical order: 'the world's here as we left it, just sunk a bit, like the Roman pavement'. Skinner contrastingly affirms the truth of nature, the 'superior geometry' of a flower's identical petals compared to Krak's arid computations. Holiday and Batter both draw scorn from Krak and Skinner; but Holiday addresses himself to familiar components, templets and quoins, while Batter takes refuge in a hooligan glory by associating his dagger and himself with tendencies to incomprehensible destruction and 'INERT BANALITY' (17). Thus Holiday and Batter maintain personal imaginative footholds on and in the burgeoning edifice: the audience remains mindful of the compulsion to establish such footholds, but the fragility of their partial, local efforts. Not even Stucley comprehends what he has unleashed and licensed, in all his tortured, fatalistic imaginings. Only Skinner seems to have a dawning sense of scale: 'I tell you, I know, I am the witch' (15). Her possible supernatural foreknowledge does not preclude her attachment to human forms and involvement in human issues, however: such is her personal pain and tension, generating impatience with those naturally or wilfully confined to short-term vision. Thus her position is analogous to *Macbeth's* title figure rather than to its Witches.

Scene Three depicts the disintegrating effect of events upon the women's personal resolve and collective unanimity. Skinner harangues Cant for fornication with a builder, characteristically evoking her sense of a causal chain or 'domino effect': 'You give her the truth, and she rejects the truth — And rejecting the truth she wrecks herself, and wrecking herself she wrecks others, and wrecking others — '. Cant attempts to assure her she is monitoring, if not regulating, her impulses: 'I gaze at their trousers, honestly I do, whilst thinking, enemy, enemy! I do gaze so, though hating myself obviously' (17). To Skinner, Cant's needs are the weakness by which she can be annexed; Skinner defines herself against male power, 'WE MADE OURSELVES WHEN WE DITCHED THAT!' Though Ann attempts to mitigate, Skinner argues for the need to limit humanist sympathy: 'to understand is not to condone, is it?' She senses her isolation in her radicalism — the radicalism which she had perceived as an inextricable part of herself, and therefore an inextricable part of Ann's love for her; she senses a tearing alteration, but attempts to remain dynamic in her determination,

'I love you and I wish we could just love, but no, this is the test, all love is tested, or else it cannot know its power'. As with Stucley, Ann is not forthcoming with declarations of feeling; Skinner attempts to characterise her sex's love as essential spiritual affection, but abstract generality is torn by her particular totality of engagement: 'We do not make a thing of flesh, do we, the love of women is more — they could eat flesh from off your body, we — no, actually I could eat yours, I could! Tell me why you love me!' (18). From this hinge of passion, Skinner argues wholeheartedly for desire's compulsive obligations and energies, and their ultimate priority over any action or moral absolutism: what does not change, is its will to change:

> They talk of a love-life, don't they? Do you know the phrase 'love-life', as if somehow this thing ran under or beside, as if you stepped from one life to the other, banality to love, love to banality, no, love is in the cooking and the washing and the milking, no matter what, the colour of the love stains everything, I say so anyway, being admittedly of a most peculiar disposition I WOULD RATHER YOU WERE DEAD THAN TOOK A STEP OR SHUFFLE BACK FROM ME. Dead, and I would do it.

This draws Ann's charge that Skinner is 'obsessive', which confirms Skinner's sense that Ann is not her equal in desire, and cannot accept Skinner in her totality. One phrase particularly resounds with the poignancy of Skinner's isolation: 'I am obsessive, why aren't you?' She extends her attitude to her opposition to Stucley, but grounds it on her love for Ann: 'I do think it's odd, so odd, that when you resist you are obsessive but when you succumb you are not WHOSE OBSESSION IS THIS THING or did you mean my love, they are the same thing actually' (19). She develops her sense of desire pre-empting contingency: 'I will not accept that everlasting love, even as you swear it, is a lie, a permissible lie, because you do not know the unforeseen condition . . . violence or pity threatening, it still takes precedence' (20). But Krak's appearance demonstrates Skinner's loss of control over Ann, who ignores her and addresses him. While Krak's knowing irony and poise has hitherto occasionally recalled Riddle in *The Love of a Good Man*, his entrance at this point echoes Sorge's first appearance in *The Power of the Dog*, closing a scene with a foreboding demonstration of alluring mystery, dangerous control and self-consciousness — which will likewise prove reversible, thereby taking others and himself to the edge of madness, annihilation and sacrifice.

Scene Four instigates another brief comic strain, as Nailer — permanently one step behind the rapid movements of events and comically off-balance — attempts to follow and record Stucley's latest attempts to define God's will in terms which will provide a systematic rationale for his own experiences. Having suffered in his deferral of desire for Ann and its sublimation into the so-called Holy War, Stucley cannot keep faith with the gospels' impressions of Christ's sexless character: 'There is one chastity and only one. The exclusiveness of desire, not willed, but forced by passion, that's chastity . . . The deity made manifest knows neither pain nor ecstasy, what use is he?'. Stucley rejects the image of 'this Christ who never suffered for the woman, who never felt the feeling which MAKES NO SENSE' (21); he tries to impose sense on this feeling by creating a Christ in his own image of suffering in passion, 'the Gospel of the Christ Erect' to whom the Magdalene becomes 'the possibility of shared oblivion, she sheds all sin, and He experiences the — IRRATIONAL MANIFESTATIONS OF PITY WHICH IS . . . Tumescence'. Stucley rejoices, 'Now we are closer to a man we understand, for at this moment of desire, Christ knows the common lot', and warms to the elaboration of his theme: the Magdalene proves sterile, 'Diseased beyond conception . . . So that they find in passion also tragedy', and Christ is killed by a lunatic God 'Because in the body of the Magdalene He found the single place in which the madness of his father's world might be subdued' (22).

Nailer joins in by proposing a trifocal communion of body, blood and semen for 'The Church of Christ the Lover', and Stucley's impulsive ordination of him — crowning him with a tool bag, the only suitable object at hand — demonstrates absurdity and idiosyncrasy in the wildfire enthusiasm of elevating his feverish inventions to the generalised system of religious authority. Idiosyncrasy of invention also incorporates and begets idiosyncrasy of interests, as immediately shown by Stucley's proposal to invoke the Church of Christ the Lover to increase the yield of the demesne to raise the necessary surplus profit for building costs. Ann berates Holiday and Batter for their limitations of imagination to the established, familiar courses of action, value and vision, but they are unbudged; she also tries to awaken Nailer to his ludicrousness, but his renewed sense of power crucially displaces his ability to envision alternative angles of perception — exposing the means by which authority lends itself to ridicule:

ANN: Reg, there is a tool bag on your head. *(Pause. He regards her with contempt)*
NAILER: Oh, you literal creature . . . It was a tool bag . . . it is no longer a tool bag, it is a badge . . . IF YOU KNEW HOW I YEARNED FOR GOD!
ANN: Which god? *(Pause, then patiently)*
NAILER: The God which puts a stop to argument. The God who says, 'Thus I ordain it!' The God who puts His finger on the sin.
(25)

This provides one of Barker's most triumphant comic moments, set among the rages of tragedy; it shows the absurd manifestations of the appetite for subjugation to simplistic authority and deliverance from contradictions — and demonstrates how the drift into disaster incorporates and is fuelled by the ridiculous detail.

Scene Five opens with Stucley and Krak, contending against the wind between the Castle towers. Flushed with a sense of Krak's power, Stucley orders his 'ice-cold shifter of old worlds' to make it snow; as some flakes duly flurry from the skies, Stucley gloats and characteristically tries to incite a snowball fight ('I did love boyhood more than anything!'), then a wrestling match, and Krak takes the opportunity to infuse the grapple with real strength and vehemence. Stucley wonders at this unexpected emotion, objects from its departure from unspoken 'rules' of conduct ('That hurt, that did'); Krak flees, demonstrating hitherto uncharacteristic anxiety at his own insurrection of feeling, which he thrusts into plans to compound the Castle's defences — 'Double the arches. Double the ditch' — as if in refuge from his own upheaval of emotions. In fact, the snowfall has been prompted by Skinner's magic, but she despairs of her apparently waning magical craft, as the snow is so thin; but the second elemental irony is that, after *'she kneels, her face covered'* in despondency, there is *'a heavy snowfall'*. However, Skinner is oblivious to its occurrence, in the grip of a nightmare vision; her supernatural foresight makes her witness a kaleidoscopic litany of authoritarian male bloodlust and carnage, scrambled across and uniting various historical periods, building to an orgasmic or fever pitch of intoxication. Skinner's experience of this vista of perpetuity in rage informs and directly inspires her decision to entice and kill Holiday, who is bewildered but gratified by her acceptance of his leering overture. Thus the First Act aptly concludes on an uneasily comic, ominous charging of sexuality with implicitly lethal polarisation.

Act Two opens with Krak, not taciturn but soliloquising on how the Castle has developed a self-generating power beyond even his control or intention, with all due consequences for positing and inflaming 'The unknown enemy, the enemy who does not exist yet but who cannot fail to materialise'; 'The castle is, by definition, not definitive' (29). Holiday's manner of death, 'Trousers down and head bashed', is identified as 'Woman murder', but Stucley is unswerving, if anything confirmed in his programme. He terms the killing an attempted hindrance of 'the inevitable' which provides him with the opportunity to appeal to more abstract but allied social institutions: 'the fifth wall' of the Castle 'is the wall of morals'. Adversity also impels him deeper into comi-tragic absurdity, suspicion and spite, describing a planning meeting in the terms 'Gang meets at sunset and no girls'. Left alone with Krak, Ann divulges her intuitive knowledge of his malice, grounded in injury and suffering which she finds attract her with sickening force: 'Success appals me but pain I love'. Stucley and Skinner have been former recipients of her erotic pity, which gratifies the donor in its confirmation of power to relieve suffering or raise the abject; its subsequent expression is in child-bearing, by which she idealistically and hubristically hopes to regenerate the entire world, at least partially in her own image. Krak bridles at her promises, 'you say, come under my skirt ... oblivion and compensation, shoot your anger in my bowel' and senses another form of entrapment in reconciliation, where Ann and surrounding edifice merge: 'CUNT ALSO IS A DUNGEON!' But his wariness of loss of self-control only excites Ann further: when Krak strikes her and makes her nose bleed, it is her victory, fracturing his control and giving her a badge of erotic pain which testifies to the depth of feeling she has tapped in him.

In Scene Two, a predisposed misogynist circuit judge presides over Skinner's trial for the murder of Holiday. Nailer accuses her of crimes against 'universal trust, that universally upheld convention lying at the heart of all sexual relations marital and illicit' and 'God-given' love and procreation. In ironic counterpoint, Skinner addresses Ann in her imagination, detailing the torture of her genitals while in custody — 'They have this way, you see, of relating the torture to the offence' — and her surprising gratification in martyrdom. Stucley is next to take the spotlight and expound his fears and feelings in a methodical scheme of suspicion that can be extended to the theatre audience, emphasising their invitation to judge the characters and sense themselves in the same embattled courtroom, uncomfortably close to crisis:

> I say in friendship, I say in comradeship, I say without malice YOU ARE ALL TRAITORS! . . . Thank you, thank you, you deny it, thank you, the vehemence I love it, lovely vehemence orchestrated and spontaneous THANK YOU BUT *(Pause)*. Things being what they are I have no choice, times being what they are I feel sure you understand in everybody's interest it is crucial I regard you all as being actively engaged in the planning of my murder — no, not really, not really, silly, but as a basis for —   (32)

Nailer interrupts in attempted restraint, but Stucley enlists his help in outlining the final phase of his religion, which deduces (as did Gassov in *The Power of the Dog*) that God is not evil but mad, 'driven to insanity by the failure and the contradiction of His works'. Stucley now identifies with his own created God in madness, exclaiming 'I understand him!', absolved from the 'absurdity of attempting to reconcile the simultaneous beauty and horror of the world'. He bursts through Nailer's explanation with his own immediacy of terror: 'THEY ARE BUILDING A CASTLE OVER THE HILL AND IT'S BIGGER THAN THIS'; and his rationalisation, 'Given God is now a lunatic, I think, sadly, we are near to the Apocalypse', suggests the imminence of his own self-destructive impulses in the light of his subjective association of himself with, first Christ, now God. This gives added danger to his turning on the audience and dismissing their importance or worth, 'juries are abolished, they are not reliable, quaint relics of a more secure time', before subsiding into personal bemused disintegration, 'I sleep alone in sheets grey with tossing, I cannot keep a white sheet white', surprisingly echoed by the usually, almost robotically impervious self-styled chunk of 'inert banality', Batter.

Skinner sights Ann and wrestles with her image, the attraction to what she was, the repulsion of what she is, confluence of love and hate: 'That all life should be bound up in one randomly encountered individual defies the dumb will of the flesh clamouring for continuation, life would not have it! I hate you, do you know why, because you prove to me that nothing is, nothing at all is, THE THING WITHOUT WHICH NOTHING ELSE IS POSSIBLE'. She feels her suffering has placed her beyond the reaches of conventional human experience and value, leaving her able to communicate only with her peers in anguish: 'Only the suffering to pass sentence, you, for example . . . *(She indicates* STUCLEY*)'* (33). This provides a surprising moment of contact between two characters, who have been exploring their agony in ranting soliloquies (and have probably been isolated in individual spots to concentrate audience attention); it recalls the unexpected sympathy between Ball and Bradshaw, or the transfixed stares of Ball and Charles, in *Victory*. But Stucley disappoints Skinner's Galactia-like ostensible hopes of martyrdom; instead of her hanging, he orders 'Tie her to the body of her victim and turn her loose'.

Now begins a series of interruptive events which constantly surprise the characters and establishes a landslide-like momentum to the play, sweeping the protagonists onward to inexorable suffering. The courtroom, and Castle, are rocked by the sound of a new unknown weapon being tested in the neighbouring castle, called the Fortress. In the chaos, Stucley is agape, and Batter shows the first signs of a significant impatience with him; and Krak enters to highlight the inevitability with which the Castle would breed other, superior constructions, presaging and necessitating 'The coming of the English desert'. Nailer is rocked with fear, but Stucley exults in the slide into the 'Extinction of the worthless' like an Old Testament God. Krak fatalistically imagines the forthcoming ubiquity of destruction; Ann thinks to contain it, Krak and their child: 'It is you that needs to be born. I will be your midwife. Through the darkness, down the black canal . . . '. But Krak identifies her search for refuge as a manifestation of what Bela termed 'The Woods Option in *No End of Blame*: doomed, futile, romantic escapism, bred of egocentric individualism. She rejects the efficacy of logic and argument in favour of the impulse to survival, but is interrupted by Skinner, in grotesque parody of her pregnancy, the decayed body of Holiday strapped to her front. Skinner and her savage humour provoke despair in Ann, who blames herself ('What have I done to you?').

Ironically, Skinner finds a strength and freedom once shackled to the rotting body of Holiday:[2] placed outside the community and normal boundaries of human experience, she is free of desire for

Ann, recognises her vanity and rediscovers an autonomy, if only to accept punishment and remain where she pleases, claiming 'I belong here. I am the castle also'. Her new-found savage wit with which she taunts a passing gang of prisoners — insisting on imagining details of human disintegration — drives Ann away, through what she sees as its hatred and pessimism, akin to Krak's. But there are consolations of varying sorts. Batter feels freed to join in casual camaraderie with Skinner, indeed seeming to regard her as part of the Castle, against which he can have no personal grudge; Krak feels he can share his distraction with her, expressing his own sexual shell-shock as his experiences with Ann have shattered his previously ice-hard points of reference ('Where's cunt's geometry? The thing has got no angles! And no measure, neither width nor depth, how can you trust what has no measurements?'); and Hush and Cant return with food, representing the section of the community who choose to heroise and worship Skinner for what they see as her strength in resistance.

Stucley confronts Krak with the knowledge that he has witnessed Krak and the rival architect of the Fortress, trading diagrams in collusion, offending Stucley's sense of ownership ('Giving your brain away . . . Whose brain do you think it is? Cock's free but brains are property') as well as imperilling the Castle and its inhabitants. Krak is engulfed in new drawings, shunning calculation of angles, bending himself to pursue new form: 'Drawn cunt . . . In 27 versions'. Even Stucley is swayed momentarily from his course: 'The representation of that thing is not encouraged by the church *(Pause. He is looking at it.)*. It's wrong, surely, that — *(Pause)* I have never looked at one, but that — '. This recalls the comic wilful blindness of Nailer wearing the tool bag; the authoritarian tendency to separate, designate something a polar opposite and then to proceed in denial of confronting its existence, inevitably produces the counter-pressure of upheaval, making war necessary.

Similarly, both Stucley and Krak depended on the division of Krak's brains from his sexuality; this separation is mocked by the upsurge of desire, which becomes a force as explosive in consequences as is necessary to surmount its opposition. Krak proclaims the Castle useless, in effect 'and an invitation to —' inexpressible horror; Stucley cries 'ONLY JUST FINISHED IT', a phrase as pathetically redundant in its invocation of form and cause as Lear's attempts at reversal or compensation in saying to Cordelia's corpse 'I killed the slave that was a-hanging thee'. Krak's malice, like their

possible fate, beggars expression: 'Spite? I do not think the word —
unless my English fails me — is quite sufficient to contain the volume of the sentiment'. Stucley glimpses Krak's contrary pressures:
'all the madness in the immaculately ordered words . . . in the clean
drawings . . . all the temper in the perfect curve'; but he tries to surmount these forces by imposing the constraints of a further self-
definition, which shatters like the others: 'But I'm not spited. If you
do not feel spited no amount of spite can hurt you, Christ was the
same, NIGEL!'

But his call for the brutal consistency of Batter instead presages
the entry of Ann; the would-be demigod's creatures and orders are
turning into their opposites, instead of the angel of violence comes
the woman of abundance. Ann has realised the futility of flight,
which only delays confrontation, 'If it happens somewhere, it will
happen anywhere'; she determines to stand her ground, 'There is
nowhere except where you are', and destroy herself and her child,
with all consequences for the focus of Stucley and the Castle itself:
'Bring it down. All this'. As she threatens her belly with a knife,
Stucley attempts a final bid at containment by faith, which is at least
partially wilful refusal to envision possibilities:

STUCLEY: You won't. *(Pause)* You won't because you cannot. Your
  mind wants to, but you cannot, and you won't . . .
  Pause. He holds out his hand for the knife. She plunges it into herself.
  A scream.

Ann's action instigates or is concerted with a wave of pregnant
women suicides, throwing themselves off the Castle walls (a grim
inversion of the Bridport women's protest through fecundity in *The
Poor Man's Friend*[3]). Batter recounts how bereaved men take absurd,
pathetic refuge in venting their rage on the broken, redundant forms
of their wives' bodies: 'Husbands want to kill 'em. Want to murder
'em, but they are murdered. Not finding anything to take revenge
on, go barmy, mutilate the flesh they simpered over once . . .'.
Cant, once uncomfortably anomalous in her belonging to neither
society, now has the confidence and maturity to question Batter's
polarised terms of male/female definition, countering his assertion 'Not theirs, birth' with 'Death is not yours either'; for his part,
he is no longer so unshakable in his brutal certainties that he cannot ask her opinion. Cant asserts (not opines, since opinion is illegal) how simplistic division is futile and destructive: 'We birth

'em and you kill 'em. Can't be right we deliver for your slaughter. Cow mothers'. Krak enters, seeking to define, as if thereby to recapture, the feelings lost with Ann's self-immolation: Batter offers the brisk reductive term 'Fucked'; Cant appreciates its insufficiency and offers 'Desire'. But she can only offer the word, not the experience, to order: Krak is left stranded in a barren present, gnawing and gnawed by his memories of irretrievable engagement, a bitter mockery for the man who had once assigned ultimate value to 'truths arrived at in seclusion'. In pain at least he is linked to Stucley as a 'dear brother in lost love' among 'The howl of men bereaved'.

Batter sees Stucley's mind is burned out to husk at the point when Stucley orders a new Castle with a different profile. Batter tries to activate Stucley's memories of a glorious past as he carries him off to kill him: this image of Batter sweeping up the regressed, incapable Stucley in his arms, 'Light as a child', is a poignant reversal of power and the final development of Stucley's boyishness: he is tenderly carried to his death like a child, exhausted by play, to bed. Only Krak seems to appreciate the import of Batter's action: he offers himself to the bemused soldiers, invites them to cut his skull through, but they remain perplexed, as he berates them for their lack of imagination, 'articulation and explanation dead all dead YOU DON'T HOLD WOMEN PROPERLY IN BED'.

The first half of the final scene has a sense of calm after a storm, tentative bids to knit damage and a consciousness of their ludicrousness. Batter and Nailer are by now familiar in their consistent insufficiency, but they attempt to bend to new circumstances with comic earnestness, which may stir in the audience something surprisingly like affection: they, like the audience, have passed through the storm more or less intact, and bonded. Like Stucley, they seek refuge in a system and offer Skinner power, comically plaintive in their notion of flattery and bid to annex revolt by incorporating feminism into the new state's apparatus ('The Holy Congregation of the Wise Womb') and bemused and exasperated at her lack of interest (Batter huffs, 'Well, do you wanna church or not?'). But the tragic strain swells again with audience proximity to and involvement in Skinner's feelings, her memory of the lost form of Ann ('She was all womb') and mingled regret and anger at the 'vanity' of her suicide and infanticide. The offer of the Castle keys, male-defined power, attracts and repels her; she defies the villagers' notion of her passive resistance as sentimental worship, sensing her own potential for cruelty: 'the act of kindness from the victim to the murderer, grey eyes serene in pain absorbed, agony knitted into cloths of wisdom WHO SAYS! Reconciliation and oblivion, NO! GREAT UGLY STICK OF TEMPER, RATHER'. Sensing also self-consumption, she wishes for the relief of death, 'The best thing is to perish in the struggle', but Krak emerges, insists on persistence, and offers his services: 'Demolition needs a drawing, too ... Krak's definition of demolition will be intrinsically male, hence Skinner's suspicion and hesitation: she 'strains in recollection', as the noise of a modern jet impels urgency, for the lost ideal, when 'There was no government', crucially wary of the terms which define even a politics to end politics.

The Castle is, by definition, not definitive. Its characters, like those of *Hamlet*,[4] are endlessly involved in attempting definition, formulating impulses to contain or commit, which fail, even as they provoke or challenge similar attempts on the part of the audience. Like *Macbeth*, *The Castle* is a terrifying, tragic, nightmarish demonstration of the inability of the imagination to maintain control over its products. Stucley exclaims: 'Everything I fear it comes to pass. Everything I imagine is vindicated. Awful talent I possess' (34). Indeed, the first part of the play bears out this phenomenon, with Stucley straining to formulate new ingenuities of injury, which occur; he desperately tries to rationalise them through developing and appealing to new inclusive philosophies of religious and political systems. But the play demonstrates that catastrophe can exceed what the mind is able to confront in possibility before its occurrence: Stucley refuses to imagine that Ann will kill herself, and she performs the unexpected. Pressure provokes counter-pressure; Stucley seeks to dissociate what Ann's mind wants from what her total self can perform, and she surprises him in her integrity. Skinner testifies to the same impulse, 'If I know all I can struggle with it, I can wrestle it to death', but she dreads the taunt to formulate, 'the imagined thing'.

The Castle insists on its characters and audiences confronting 'the imagined thing' at every turn, and permits a perception parallel to Skinner's: 'it is the pain of witches to see to the very end of things', while also being compelled to be involved, to engage and act and envision. Correspondingly, *The Castle* is an almost unbearably long play — not in its literal playing time, which barely exceeds two and a half hours, but in the range of feelings it evokes and forms it stretches, in ways comparable only to *King Lear*, the unexpectedly

long route and details by which Lear is forced to accomplish his initially planned 'crawl toward death'. Just as Lear longs for release
from worldly vicissitude, Skinner claims 'I gave up and longed
to die, and yet I did not die' while conscious that she has passed
through the fiercest furnaces of human possibility: 'If you haven't
had love ripped out your belly, dragging half your organs with it,
don't talk to me, you haven't lived!' (33). Stucley correspondingly
perceives a kinship in suffering between himself and Krak and the
other bereaved men: 'I know his filleting, I TOO WAS FILLETED'
(41). The suffering of Skinner, Stucley and Krak arises from the
intensity of their concentration on the form of Ann, similar to Lear's
on Cordelia, through placing one's world in another's self, and
finally being confronted by the broken shell of that self.

Stephen Booth has identified the gruelling distance and contrary
tensions, challenging and breaking all hopes of definite confine-
ment, yet, nevertheless, confined within *King Lear*:[5] correspondingly
Stucley yearns for 'the obliteration of the melancholy crawl from
the puddle to the puddle, from the puddle of the maternal belly to
the puddle of the old man's involuntary bladder', while becoming
increasingly aware of the fragility of reassurance in rational pattern-
ing, sensing 'all the madness in the immaculately ordered words . . .
all the temper in the perfect curve', which permitted Krak to enter-
tain and initially manage such immeasurable forces of destruction
before they slipped from his control. Krak's own rationality is overturned by the discovery that the body is itself infinite, 'no measure,
neither width nor depth', rather than the definite thing he thought
to have limited, tamed and, to most purposes, dismissed. It is probably the intense concentration of energy and faith on Ann that
buckles her sense of possible shape and drives her to define herself forcefully in death: this sense of explosive destruction through
sexual concentration is foreshadowed in Stucley's inflamed vision:
'Tumescent as the dick which splits, splashing the ceiling red with
sheer barminess' (38–9).

Stephen Booth argues that *King Lear's* effects are terrifying
through the play's compulsive shattering of forms, dramatic and
otherwise: all generic and conventional signs suggest stasis for Lear
and Cordelia when assigned to prison together, but the story continues:

> I submit that audiences are not shocked by the fact of Cordelia's
> death but by its situation and that audiences grieve not for

Cordelia's physical vulnerability, or for the physical vulnerability of humankind, but for their own — our own — mental vulnerability, a vulnerability made absolutely inescapable when the play pushes inexorably beyond its own identity, rolling across and crushing the very framework that enables its audience to endure the otherwise terrifying explosion of all manner of ordinarily indispensable mental contrivances for isolating, limiting and comprehending. When Lear enters howling in the last minutes of the play, Shakespeare has already presented an action that is serious, of undoubted magnitude, *and complete*; he thereupon continues that action beyond the limits of the one category that no audience expected to see challenged: Shakespeare presents the culminating events of his *story* after his *play* is over.[6]

Booth claims: 'If the power and intensity of our responses to the last moments of *King Lear* do not result from *what* happens, they may result from *when* and *where* it happens'[7]; Lear and Cordelia are dragged back to the impingements of chance, malice and grief, in defiance of all criteria for relief. *The Castle* gathers its awful momentum and force from similar effects: when Skinner anticipates the relief of hanging, Stucley orders her to be effectively 'reconstructed', having another body tied to her frame, and turned loose to continue living in these freakish circumstances; the appearance of the Fortress, however, proves Stucley's control to be limited and short-lived; as Krak and Ann seem resolved in their positions of resignation to destruction and hanging on to life, Skinner enters with the skeleton, and their feelings tip out of control (and eventually their positions reverse); when all the men assume destruction by the Fortress to be the worst possible eventuality, Ann and the women kill themselves and consign the men to continued life without them; when Stucley fades, Krak remains; when Batter and Nailer offer reconciliation and resolution through 'The Holy Congregation of the Wise Womb', Skinner resists; when she wishes herself dead, Krak appears to urge her to life; even as he offers his expertise, Skinner's acceptance or rejection remains indefinite, as does the very definition of the word 'demolition', and the roar of modern jet planes streak through and soar out of the play's historical framework into our own. The last scene between the 'human flotsam' amid the wreckage particularly recalls Albany, Kent and Edgar at the end of *King Lear*, where it is suggested that someone must rule the kingdom but the audience never learn exactly who does or in what configuration.

Stucley's cry 'YOU'RE PUSHING ME WHERE I DON'T WANT TO GO' could serve many of the play's characters, and also its audiences, as befits Barker's sense of tragedy as 'a constant picking away at something one knows must be exposed, then, when it is exposed, it becomes catastrophic in one's inability to acquire stability ever again'.[8] As a tragedy, the play offers little chance to assign blame, identify and displace evil, as in Barker's early plays. None of the characters in *The Castle* can be identified simply as evil: Stucley, Krak and Skinner remain true to their passions, and are prepared to be consumed by them, but their formulations of their passions are belated and redundant, pitiable like the bereaved husbands striking the corpses of their wives, one fatal moment behind seizing the truth of a moment and forcing change, rather than having it forced on them. Stucley's religious systems are similar breathless attempts to accommodate experience and proceed on its basis in future, but his metaphysical, political and perceptual structures are repeatedly found wanting. He fails to persuade others to accept the world, and thereby himself, at his evaluation — he himself is forced to collapse into surprise and breakdown. The main hope for truth seems to be in identification with the tragic dynamic itself, the shattering of old forms and our attachments to them, release from logical and emotional commitments to any given petrified moment, moving toward a recognition of a life-force expressed through the regenerative possibilities of continual revolution and revaluation. Even Skinner and Krak may be outstripped in their capacities to instigate or deal with change on this scale. But the hope of *The Castle* resides in the undefined potential to remain dynamic within Skinner and Krak — and, beyond the play, hope resides in the audience's similar undefined potential, which may be illuminated briefly, as by a flash of lightning in the ragings of a destructive storm.

Barker's version of *Women Beware Women* (staged 1986) continues the theme of the body as both focus and disruption of power, in a speculation on themes laid down in Thomas Middleton's 1623 Jacobean tragedy. Rather than conclude the play with a spate of abrupt murders and the Cardinal's obfuscating and Procrustean moralising on the wages of sin, Barker extends the play into speculation, insisting on the corrupting power of money, the link between power and sexuality, and desire as a regenerative catalyst to imagination and action. Barker's condensation of Middleton's first three-and-a-half acts into a first half, to be succeeded by his own full-blown development, again insists on an unconventional length and range of experience for characters and audiences alike, as dramatic form and characters are stretched to the point of reanimation, wrenched into wholly new creations. Characteristically Barker pursues effects of astringent sensitising to unwonted holisticity, examining the notion of the body as property or currency, the means through which men and women travel the strata of society. Barker's Sordido makes the central calculation that if the body is currency, it is also thievable: what can be sold can be stolen. Whereas *The Castle* dramatised politics as the absence of desire, *Women Beware Women* shows the infusal of politics with desire, and is not tragic. Rather its keynote is Livia's line 'It kills the soul not to exploit an inspiration' (30); desire is identified as inspirational and redemptive. In counterpoint to *The Castle's* tragic explosion of possibilities, sexual polarisation and sense of the fascination of destruction, *Women Beware Women* presents a more optimistic explosion of possibilities, sexual collusion and the impulse to change. *The Castle* demonstrates uncontrollability, *Women Beware Women* discovery. Barker:

> The Left has ignored the body. It has yielded sexuality to the reactionaries. Middleton knew the body was the source of politics. He did not know it was also the source of hope.[9]

In Middleton's play, Bianca, an upper-class Venetian girl, elopes to Florence with Leantio, a clerk. She is seen by the Duke of Florence and, through the machinations of Livia, a middle-aged widow, she is seduced by the Duke. Livia herself falls in love with the young Leantio.

Barker enters the play through Middleton's depiction of unsettling, unexpected upheavals of desire in Livia and of acquisitiveness linked to sexuality through gratification in Bianca; the exposure of Leantio's pain; its awakening of Livia's erotic pity and her own pitiful struggles to express her passion. But, though dammed, it explodes; and it is Leantio's rhapsody in release that initiates and charges Part Two with such breathless impetus of trajectory:

> We fuck the day to death. And suffocate the night with tossing. Time stands still, she says so. Rolls back, even. As for the bed, it's

our whole territory, the footboard and the headboard are the horizons of our estate, rank with the flood of flesh. Oh, beautiful odour of the utter fuck! And come? No, never come, for that's to end it.

Livia experiences the rinsing out of accumulated bourgeois limitations, the recognition and release of futility and shame: 'I have no indignation left, surprise, or petty reservation. No thing I won't yield up, nor thought ashamed to utter'. In contrast, they identify restrictive habit and meanness in the crowd below the bedroom window (provocatively identified among the theatre audience): 'REPETITION OF THE MUNDANE LIFE! . . . She'll lend a little of her hip, he'll tamper with a giggle, that one might yield her place to satisfy persistence, and him mutter as he shudders' (19). With the outside world bustling with celebration of Bianca and the impending royal wedding, Leantio and Livia discover a regenerative dislocation from triteness, 'good riddance to their sense, their swap of stale banalities!', and realise that extremity of love correspondingly enlarges capacity for, and facilitates crystallisation of, hate: 'Those whose love runs deep dispense no charity . . . Through pain of longing we have trod down sickening conviviality'. It is informative to compare Skinner's experience of desire with Livia's: Skinner found a perilous, narrowing concentration on the form of the loved one, and sensed painful brittleness: 'That all life should be bound up in one randomly encountered individual defies the dumb will of the flesh clamouring for continuation'; rather than this implosive near-paralysis or danger, Livia experiences explosive autonomy, release into new potential and impulsion to action: 'Beloved man, if you perished tonight in some backstreet stabbing, I would say even this little was enough, this was light and transformation. It made me hate my life. All hate your lives and change the world!' (20).

The Duke and the Cardinal observe the ecstatic couple with bewilderment, ironically reversing the Duke's usual position of power as object of voyeurism. In *Victory*, Clegg's nuptial verses celebrated how 'The aristocracy unite the nation/Flesh and gold's infatuation' and Charles thrived on the appeal of orgiastic association, where the courtier 'grasps your flesh, he shares your monarchy'. The similarly decadent and debauched court of *Women Beware Women*, however, lacks Charles's bluff, though circumscribed, anarchy. The Duke's power is absolute, egocentric and opportunistic, and the people condone and worship the ruling class in all its contemptuous hedonism, as the Cardinal has learnt to appreciate: 'Who rips the sheets with him, and who was grappled half way down the stairs is all public speculation, keeps the masses warm with itching. It's the entertainment of the modern state and the proper function of an aristocracy!' (20). But the Cardinal also glimpses in Livia and Leantio's union something beyond the Duke's relish of culinary fuckery: 'That two might lock, and in locking, undo whole cliffs of discipline'; that sexual upheaval might unhinge the civil state, and desire flood over into politics.

Under Barker's cultivation, the Ward, a rich young heir married into aristocracy through Isabella, is allowed a self-awareness and existential pathos beyond his frivolous clowning in Middleton's play. Barker's Ward has a sense of irony at the conscious absurdities of his conventional marriage, how its proferred image of identity for husband and wife alike merely cements them in support and supplication of the established hierarchy: 'I think it is a dirty world, where we are stuck together by some senile whim which thinks our youth will match their sentiments, and our fucking lubricate their arid transactions' (21). But the Ward's sarcasm guards him against his essential sense of impotence, 'I find my only comfort in the mocking of their shallow ardours', and an awareness of the artificiality of postures struck by Isabella and other women of the court. Invigorated by the arrival of his companion Sordido, the Ward admits his recognition of loss of purpose and value in their society's emphasis on stimulation of frivolous appetites and addiction to gratification: 'WHAT IS BLISS EXACTLY? I thought of hanging myself with a tennis net, to carry my act to the end' (22). His playing the dunce is itself a posture of licence, but adopted out of pain not ignorance, and his imagination hungers for a mission amid the sated complacency and smug luxury, a scheme to free him from his spiritual shackles of silk. Sordido can satirise with more inventiveness and edge, and has more sense of satire's limitations; unlike the Ward, he also senses the fragility of social transactions which bolster and debilitate, and can envision rupturing the façade of compliance. He conceives of striking at Bianca, society's conductor-mannequin of envy and worship, who embodies both sexual invitation and regal inaccessibility.

Bianca has embraced her leading role in the pagaent of power, wryly mocking those, like Leantio's mother, whose frustrated impulses she enacts and stifles. She justifies herself by generalising Leantio's indignation in dispossession:

The little conscience lurked, did most certainly, until your son abused me. Then I saw, under his little charm lay hatred. Undo the rope of love just once and like a sack of dead and rancid cats all stench pours out over your knees and feet. I do not think men like us, though they sweat with wanting, or if they like us, can't fuck except with jogging fondness. No love without hate. That's my discovery to date.   (24)

The Duke is a cheery vortex of lasciviousness, not a creature of essence, and society remakes itself in his configurations. His power is that of counterfeit: 'I am not ugly. I am the Duke . . . I could go like the lice-infested tramp, all fingers in the arm pits, and assure you, all the blades would call it fashion and go scratching likewise, and all women would say, how well he scratches, he is the essence of manhood!' (25). His government is populist and brutal, 'Tinsel to the nostrils and a spike at the arse', debunking Hippolito's cautious injunction to 'respect', such as he uses to cloak his liaison with Isabella, his niece. The Duke's nakedness of intent makes him impervious to satire, withering it into redundancy, and his simplistic heartiness shrinks the Mother's allegation of 'evil' into 'the leisure to refine lust', asserting that the only human difference lies in opportunity, secure in the people's belief in this as well as his own. Thus his sole responsibility is to annex beauty, 'what all men collude in desiring', having persuaded the people he acts and enjoys on their behalf, and that they in turn are validated — at a crucially metaphorical remove — through his possession of Bianca, 'flashing like some encrusted gem, blinding discontent and dazzling the cynic'.

Again, the Cardinal detects a niggling chink in the edifice of association, through the wedding service's acknowledgement of a diffusal of complete subservience to God and society, in the lines 'With my body I thee worship'. The Cardinal sees the subversive potential of this pocket or repressive tolerance: 'What says the Almighty to this other faith? Is he not a jealous god?' Bianca refuses to confront the contradiction, eagerly developing the ducal and populist lack of curiosity: 'You would have scientists put microscopes to women's breasts and weigh them in the scales, and come out only with the circumference or gravity, not one smatter wiser why it drives a prince to melancholic death he cannot touch them. Mystery! Adore it!' While she correctly identifies the breakdown of rationalism in the face of instinct (as discovered by Krak), her rejection of enquiry and sense of consolation in opportunism are grounded in slavish superstition, which she colludes in furthering: 'I only repeat what clergy tell me, that we all swill in sin. I have trod by beggars and thought, not, oh, charity, oh, alms, but oh, fragility of consciousness, give me a man who finds me in all this horror — divine!' (26).

In contrast to Bianca, dazzled by her own sanctified reflection in others' eyes, Livia glows with new-found authenticity in desire, which unsettles surrounding colluders in restrictive unanimity, consciously or unwittingly retrenched in institutionalised shame, even as she shines in her fundamental challenge of encouragement. She is exulting in her sundering from 'The geometry of servile continuation' in the street, outraging the guilty insecurities of Hippolito; she turns on him: 'I see you are the man you were. Therefore your love is drivel . . . IF YOU HAD KNOWN DESIRE YOU WOULD NOT LOOK AT ME LIKE THAT!' Hippolito mourns her former self, presiding over tinkling witticisms and parlour game needlings, teasing society in guarded security. Livia's distinction is crucial: 'Teased it, yes, but altered it? I would not go to my grave with such an epitaph as this — she had her salon, she had her wit, she had her teacups and her gin. No, I loathe wit, the rattle of dry words and poets licking one another's sisters. I think we lived an elegant and disgusting life'. Her rejection of irony is recognised and appreciated by Sordido, bandit scholar and virginal bachelor of artful instincts, but she rejects his sexual overtures, not out of loyalty 'but hunger for one only, that's proper chastity. I swear nothing to priests or civil servants' (27). Sordido is returned, though aroused and self-knowing, to his enforced irony: 'Unfair world, he muttered ritually'. Livia insists 'No democracy in love', and Sordido accords, 'None and I'm no democrat'; as he ranges streets where 'democracy is clapping' and ordained adoration of the Duke, 'HIS CHARM, HIS LOVE OF FUN!', he feels an upsurge of instinctive resistance.

Sordido next collides with Leantio, as they watch Bianca and the Mother indulging a crowd. Sordido believes the crowd see Bianca 'naked in their mind's eye' but Leantio opines 'They think her pure, they cannot imagine such whiteness on its back and yelping' (28), knowledgeable that Bianca's virginity is trumpeted as a counterfeit sop to sentimentality. *'Their eyes are locked'* in mutual exploration and speculation, and Sordido outlines his plan to engage in his own hazardous transaction, to realise however unforgivably, the abstraction on which the society's political and sexual power converge and depend — with surprising fragility, as he realizes. Bianca is enshrined as public property but society depends on the public not acting on the implications of the offer; she has acquiesced in becoming an advertisement, the citizens are happy in the sense of enjoying a metaphorical relationship with her. Sordido determines to seize Bianca and commit the sin of acting on their society's unacknowledged temptations, closing the circuit of its implicit, paralytic promise.

Sordido mischievously demolishes his professed plan — 'There, forget I spoke . . . I am liable to visions. Comes of poverty and weird alcohols' — but its foundations have taken root in him, Leantio and the theatre audience, leaving the latter two to consider its implications, shrink from or engage with them. Leantio seeks refuge in sexual escapism with Livia, deeming Sordido's scheme 'A dream not fit for telling'. As in *Macbeth*, the audience may be imagining the consequences of a prophecy, running ahead of the characters. Livia insists 'Desire's truth, Leantio, and compels it speak. All the rest is fucking. Our union is not a place for hiding in, or a sink to vomit temper'. But Leantio is reverting to a clerical fear of risk, maintaining he 'dare not' see more of Sordido for fear of the power of his imagination: 'HE MADE ME LONG FOR VENGEANCE ON THE DOLL WHO WAS MY WIFE' (29). Livia, rather, wishes to pursue the unknown consequences of enflamed instincts, and the Cardinal intuits the widening of the flaw in his society's paste jewel: 'Oh, easy lust or nagging marriage, this we know and manage, but imagination . . . ! BIRTH OF AN IDEA THERE!'

Livia and Leantio join forces with Sordido, The Ward and Isabella, other characters whose wants are not smothered or intimidated by the 'stink of the nightclub and brassy odour of the stock exchange'. Leantio draws back from the brink of their mission with humanist misgivings and shameful unease ('I would not have my basest urgings played to'), which Livia denounces as bourgeois timidity and precious, redundant individualism, which she had thought scorched out of him, loving him for his hunger, not his decency: 'What we have found in love doesn't come to clerks with consciences, all "does this please you" and "forgive me, does that hurt?" No, but taking, from the depths of unkind longing' (30). Leantio careers through a series of traditional arguments for breaking impulse from becoming executed action, such as realism, which Livia identifies and dismisses as the surrender of the right to determine possibility (as Tom Downchild saw the invocation of maturity as 'a con to rub the edge off a decent blade'). But Leantio fears enthusiasm is madness and accuses Livia 'You hate Bianca and dress up revenge as politics'. Sordido's intervention is timely in reminding Leantio that the influences of Bianca's complicity range beyond the immediately personal: 'her protesting mouth was stopped, not by a fist, but greed and glamour choked it'; and Livia urges 'a thing is vile, not in itself, but only in relation to its uses' (31) — though Leantio holds back from countenancing, or possibly considering, this. She also intercedes for the Ward and tells Isabella he plans to remarry her, with Sordido as witness, at Bianca's wedding, and proceed to consummation. Livia pauses alone, wistfully reflecting on her organisational instincts and the ubiquitous confluence, 'for all my travelling in love, through hurricanes of difference . . . I believe I'm even better at it', like an elder presiding genius of a Shakespearean comedy equipped with the harsher, sharper knowledge of incisive resistance, a 'no' at the core of her affirmation.

In the palace, Bianca continues to be intoxicated by her effect on others, relishing envy from without rather than inward change: 'Do you think — she is pretty as a doll — she is so pretty she is — scarcely human — or rather, at some point she is naked under that?'. The Cardinal proclaims her 'a symbol of the state', and indeed power seems to be hollowing out her character until she is as literally vacuous as the Duke, a whirlpool of subjectivity. As she senses, 'there must be poverty, if not of life, then of mind. Or we could not love ourselves so much'; the Mother's compliments send her spiralling inward, drunk on narcissism: 'I am everything. There must be me, mustn't there? There must be me, or they would all —' and Sordido completes the phrase, 'Despair?'. He insists on the rightness of his explosive attack, 'THIS IS MY ENTRANCE'. Livia, though trembling worse than Bianca, maintains 'I must, who makes dreams come to life, witness the occurrence. Don't call me hypocrite, what I have dealt in I attend right to the finish'. However, Leantio is fearful for the 'dear girl wife, who clung to me in perfect innocence', grasping the glorified corpse of an ideal like Scrope appealing to the ghost of Richard Bradshaw; Livia proclaims 'IT IS NOT HER' (33); his emotion is as redundant as the anger of the men mutilating their wives' corpses in *The Castle*.

In the social context of *Women Beware Women*, Sordido can only take, not give, sexually; and Bianca is denounced by the Duke as a defiled possession, 'a pitch of muddy squalor', having sold her right to self-determined essence. Her intoxication shattered, she is once more capable of self-determination, averring 'I'll not act the coronation', and risking the Duke's rage in search of truth, 'for if I loved power, and power was my dream of male', Sordido 'had it too'; Livia claims Bianca confused the Duke's costume for his sex, and these impulses to locate essence beyond superficial, dead or artificial husks are continued by Bianca disrobing, rejecting the costume of her sex, as designed by the corrupt state to be her sole claim to existential veracity and to be her observers' false standard of the desirable, the female *objet de luxe*. The Duke surprises even himself by being unable to kill Bianca; like Krak in *The Castle*, he finds beauty 'rots all calculation'.

As at the end of *The Castle*, there is question as to who shall, or will, govern the state. The Ward rejects the opportunity, unable to reach beyond his skills in irony: 'I would tell the truth in such a way as to make it unbelievable, and then they'd all rejoice to swallow simple lies'. Rather he thinks Livia's manifesto 'I LOVE AND I HATE MONEY' makes her 'fittest for a dynasty'. Isabella moves from him to support Bianca. Sordido lies dead. The Duke nominates Leantio and Livia as 'new duke, new duchess' and adds a warning, 'Don't love . . . ! Don't love . . . !'

Livia seems the most capable of crucial revolutionary insight, as when she harangues the Cardinal: 'Get Christ out of your pocket. He knew money strangled love, and love's corpse stifled imagination, and dead imagination was the ground from which more money grew. Money, death, and money!' (36). The Duke's final caution against love is, more precisely, against love's corpse, under Livia's terms; certainly, Leantio has suggested an increasing, debilitating predilection for this. Discarding a state built on money may also involve shedding the corpse of their love.

Defending the continued use of Middleton's title, Barker tells his dead 'collaborator': 'In [your play], a woman engineers the fall of a woman, for a man. That is the role of women in your time. In mine, a woman engineers the fall of a woman, but for her own enlightenment. But the pain is terrible. So the title finds an irony it never had in your play'.[10] There are also further ironies, in the suggestion that women should beware women like the corrupted Bianca, who sell their bodies and selves for personal power, gained through complicity in stifling imagination; and that these women who assist in the confusion of sex, and flesh, with costume thereby mock and sacrifice any claim to sisterhood to save them from women like the transformed Livia, and the revenge they may wreak or facilitate.

Barker does not lose his interest in power, but moves from the early work's exploration of institutional and party political power, frequently mediated or manifested in sexuality, to the dynamics of the personal acquisition of power, and its location in the body. The regenerative possibilities of desire and imagination become vital resources of resistance to the imposition of prescriptive ideologies. Authority is identified as the enshrinement of systematic lies, which nevertheless implicitly generate a sense of dissatisfaction or dispossession, like the advertisement which makes associative promises that its product cannot fulfil. The liberating action or agent — often branded 'mad', 'obsessive' or 'impatient' — anticipates identity, insists on complexities of vision and instinct, and their relation to each other. Thus, institutionalised and habitual limitations and definitions are demolished, and the truth is continually and ruthlessly re-defined.

The Castle and *Women Beware Women* examine the convergence of political and sexual power, systematic and personal injunctions. In both cases, surrounding characters seek to define and possess a central human form — Ann, Bianca — which is shattered by the pressure, and the characters have to remake and regroup themselves after the ubiquitous damage; Bianca has the opportunity to remake herself, in *Women Beware Women* only Sordido does not. But he is neither embittered nor repentant, and has avoided regret and petrification, breaking the lie of innocence. Krak and the Duke believe they can define and control the body, but their plans break down, as do Stucley and Bianca's misplaced faiths in their definitions of themselves, of which they seek to convince others, and thereby control them. But while the characters in *The Castle* are tragically short of seizing the truth of the moment and consequently have change forced upon them, Sordido and Livia in *Women Beware Women* succeed in forcing change. They achieve this by refusing to cling to the corpse of dead love, which stifles imagination. Krak and Skinner may or may not be capable of this, even as Skinner is ironically festooned with the skeleton of Holiday. Rather than seeking to possess another, like the Duke and even Leantio, Livia and Sordido voice their preparedness to acquiesce in their own destruction, knowing that change has taken place, on a personal level, but which has political reverberations.

The dynamic of desire proves surprisingly similar to that of tragedy: the shattering of old forms and our attachments to them, release from logical and emotional commitments to any given petrified moment, moving toward a recognition of a life-force expressed through the regenerative possibilities of continual revolution and revaluation: both forces move toward the hope for truth, in a movement through and away from the definite form of the single body and its restrictions, toward a sense of the infinite: like Livia, discarding her limitations and loneliness, with the cry 'I will not be animal but ecstasy!'

9

Every Man's Evil
Expresses Me

DON'T EXAGGERATE, THE BREATH OF THE CROWD

Every time someone looks in our eyes, we wonder, could this be
the man, the woman, who will make me different?

Crimes in Hot Countries

Imperceptible redefinitions occurred
Which at a later date may seem significant

Gary Upright

'The delicate and sometimes brutal relations we weave with strangers' provide moments of elision between spheres of experience
conventionally and schematically termed 'private' and 'public';
these relations are particularly fundamental in daring to enter
a theatre, or to walk onto a stage, or to write a play, all of which
involve self-exposure to the unexpected revelation or reaction.
They offer a sense of the riot of possibilities through interpersonal
expression, depending on the force of circumstance and individual openness, or want. Such is the importance of Axt's encounter
with Drum in *A Passion in Six Days*; and Stalin laments his personal
elevation beyond the reach of accident and surprise, the chance to
meet a woman on a train, in *The Power of the Dog*. In *Women Beware
Women*, Sordido speaks of the way strangers catch signals from each
other in the street, stirring withdrawal and sympathy, occasionally
the glimpse of a want which completes a personal chord, major or
minor:

LIVIA: It was not arbitrary, your coming across.
SORDIDO: How could it be? In this state we are all linked by hate, by
little quirks and signs, and eyes to eyes direct when looking down
would be collusion with the great unanimous approval. The word

which characterizes everything is YES and no is only fit for whispering — *(He grabs a passer-by by his lapels)* Say yes!
MAN: Yes. . . .
SORDIDO: He says it! See! *(He turns back to* LIVIA) You are a no, or
you could not fuck like that . . . good day. . . .   (28)

Barker's first two volumes of poetry, *Don't Exaggerate (desire and
abuse)* and *The Breath of the Crowd*, thematically foreground one or
two individuals against the mass, in actions or observations which
'provide focal points in what is both an affirmation of our common
lot and a demand for the right to private culture in the age of the
populist state'. In an extension of this process of mutual confrontation and examination, Barker's poetry is conceived for public performance: the narrative *Don't Exaggerate* and the cycle *The Breath of
the Crowd* being written for actors Ian McDiarmid and Maggie Steed
respectively. This is a unique development of what is conventionally and limitingly considered as the genre of private reflection,
conducted in isolation. Barker:

> I prefer the actor's voice to the author's. Nowadays it is an arti-
> cle of faith that poets read their own works. But the gap between
> intention and execution in the untrained voice makes the poet's
> rendering of his own material more false than the rehearsed
> actor's. If I can trust an actor to read a speech in a play there is no
> reason not to trust him with a poem. A poem can be read differ-
> ently on different nights, as a play can be. There is no authentic
> version.[1]

Indeed, many of the poems focus on dislocation, and the personal
challenge and speculation which can be generated as a result, particularly in the recognition of impulse, and its favourable reception, involved in desire — the moment and movement of personal
revolt and upheaval where, in Barker's words, 'There is discon-
nection from the mundane in the chance collision that brings
knowledge; showing how life in the station concourse, the football
stadium, the way we behave in public, is actually a lie. Our behaviour towards each other is cemented with sterile conventions. Only
desire can undermine them, in the look — the seized look — the
touch — the moment of emotional confusion when perceptions lead to
disarray'.[2]

Barker's poems also investigate impulses to cruelty, and the importance of confronting malice in the self rather than recoiling from its presence and attributing it exclusively to neighbours and enemies. This is another form of the recognition of possibilities before proceeding and progressing, seizing the truth of a moment in a way that might transform private history, and consequently public history, in consequence — movement involving the incorporation of opposites, and awareness of the limitations of the single perceptual viewpoint through confrontation of the conventionally and habitually forbidden. At this point, morality is recognised as custom developed under a community's rules for its own preservation; and the individual may realise that this clashes with his/her personal drive to preservation, and *be essentially driven* — not *choose* — to act in defiance of moral tradition and prescription, which involve the surrender of rights to individual valuation. Here the community and the individual are at odds in notions of what is 'useful' and 'not useful', with the overturning of secure pieties often being identified as 'evil'. But such may be the feature of re-evaluative poetry and drama, as when shock occurs through the narrator of *Don't Exaggerate* speaking of a 'too-long peace' and challenging a liberal consensus of desirability through being severed from the contemporary community's practical restrictions — much like Murgatroyd in *Pity in History*, who is beyond punishment, beyond control and beyond restriction to historical moment (as he says, 'you can't control me 'cos you can't punish me! What are you going to do? Take my leave away? I'VE LOST MY LEAVE FOREVER YOU!'). *Don't Exaggerate* involves a similar self-conscious corpse who refuses to lie down in his hole with quiet submission, in the interests of surrounding and future smoothness and symmetry (compare Katrin in *The Europeans* and her resistance of the State's bids to encompass the pain of the individual).

Don't Exaggerate: A Political Statement in the Form of Hysteria (first performed 1984, Thoughtcrimes Festival) comprises the reflections of a resurrected Hungarian soldier killed fighting the Russian army in the First World War. He is a self-conscious misfit in the imperial army of the Habsburg Empire, conscious like Pain in *Crimes in Hot Countries* that 'an army is a fallacy sustained by a contradiction'. Liberated from limitation to historical moment and mortal body, his viewpoint ranges through 20th-century European history, critiques of failed democratic idealism and Leftist positions of rigour, in an arc which finally brings him to focus in on England, London, Leicester Square, and a fellow misfit, who is silhouetted against the tawdriness of populist capitalism and who decides on suicide. Poet and characters realise desire as an essential regenerative force conspicuous by its absence among the array of decadent posturing in which they cannot submerge themselves.

Don't Exaggerate thus emerges as an individualist manifesto insisting on the revolutionary potential of desire, springing from the painful tension and irony of existential pathos — realising that the self does not accord with any of the ideals and definitions, with which given societies are attempting to oppress its members into association. It is an expression of resistance of social current and redundant form, which Barker thinks 'suffused with sorrow rather than anger: but not sorrow as a state of paralysis'.[3] Fuelled by pain, its pistons of performance are outrage in search of expression, relentlessly exploring angles of shafts of expression: the opening pained explosive utterance, 'Oh the bastards', immediately qualified with consciousness of its inadequacy, 'For want of a better word', relishing the expletive while conscious that 'The truth lies somewhere between/The coarse emotion and the calculation'; amid numerous invocations of the truth, the Exaggerater does not purport to hold or communicate it, thus rejecting the appetite for authority dependent on the illusion of a sole custodian of the truth (compare Old Gocher berating Leary at the end of *Fair Slaughter*, 'Think for yourself. They stuck Lenin under glass, and look what they have done in his name').

This illusion fosters idolatrous faith in leaders, teachers and even artists; he rejects theory and fact for abuse and exaggeration, better fitted to those 'Who have lined Europe with their teeth' and thereby given a right to express evil, as it is defined by geographically and historically local communities; he is severed from responsibility to them by death, ironic as he has died on behalf of his community (particularly its rulers), its web of responsibilities and pressures of integration which never completely satisfied or enslaved him. Rather, he is defined by a sense of thwarted possibility, 'I am the dictator who never was' — not, as some might romantically hope, the liberator or hero — scornful of 'The eternal habit of submission' to ideals because freed of both guilt and pity. He proclaims himself awoken by argument, its diffuseness and redundancy, the academic 'avalanche of falling categories' which leaves things fundamentally unchanged: he proceeds to give the audience his own forceful variant on the history lecture, complete with personifications of the inanimate and digressions, which are embraced in their liberations of imaginative possibilities over the debilitating restrictions of argument and fact.

As a kernel analogue to social inertia, he alights upon 'the kerbstone', witness to human flux in all its intoxication and disappointment, of which the keynotes are false laughter and shame as cultivated by bad acting and a theatre given over to sordid and demeaning transactions of fundamental impoverishment; he adds a contrary sense of the highest moment of consciousness in suicide, which is linked to knowledge, but the connection is as yet undeveloped. Debunking the restrictive pressures of education, he clowns savagely in mocking parody of his listeners' impulses to dissocation 'DON'T EXAGGERATE/YOU ALWAYS EXAGGERATE/YOU KNOW YOU DO', then jolts back into details of his re-emergence and its symbolic European centrality of position ('The intersection at which swung compasses would meet/The points placed on/The tip of Norway/And the floor of Crete'). This unconventionally untamed, articulate and demonic Unknown Soldier anticipates and debunks sentimentality in gathering his forces, 'The wind moaning not/Old songs of peasant labour but/Spent propaganda', converging in defiant essence and the shout:

I!
I!
I!

The 'Ex-actor/Rifleman deceased' marvels at his own new-found 'smoothness' in the 'level travel of the ghost', as a sense of his isolation dawns: 'Oh would all Europe's [dead] resurrect/Or only me'. But isolation is scarcely new to him: this embarrassingly intellectual and imaginative ex-thespian could find no niche in the army beyond 'Chess Champion of 42nd Guards Reserve' and was deemed 'mad by general agreement of the troops'. He recalls the battlefield, its unlikely beauty ('Aurora borealis of bombardment') among the shatterings of human bodies, trappings and forms of thought; a war and historical moment which enveloped Wittgenstein, Reich, Kokoschka, fearful of their own thwarted possibilities: 'In pits the geniuses twitched/Lest death should overtake the writing of the book'. This imperilled concentration of future oracles of Language, Sex and Art breeds pain and pathos ('Europe, oh') suddenly disrupted by a comic change of viewpoint, insisting and demonstrating that 'There are limits to consciousness': 'I assert you can be both/A sex therapist and a monarchist'.

The Exaggerater's loss of hope makes him capable of resistance, like Attila in *The Blow*, observing and imitating elemental indifference: 'It rains on all the graves so what/It rains on all the books so what'. Like Toplis in *Crimes in Hot Countries*, he stands 'in the greatest contempt of mothers' and of the invocation of the family to enforce collusion in sacrifice, wryly commenting on the irony of bereaved passivity ('Bereavement did bring out their best/They wept') while the ruling class is fundamentally unaffected — except perhaps at officer level. One such officer mocked this ex-actor, thereby bolstering the other soldiers in their relative power and hierarchical security at his expense, demonstrating the double-edged bonding and severance of integrationist laughter, secure in its malice. But this security is fatally limited, as the butt of humour recognises his mockers' proximity to death. He wryly glosses such events as 'Passages from Imperialism to Communism', and significantly qualifies the ideal, 'Communism of a sort', paying tribute to a moral communism prior to mechanistic ideologies and their debased manifestations:

Please say the word
Not Marxism
Not the argument
The feeling
Not the analysis
The hope
COMMUNISM

But with the passage of time, the landscape, like the kerbstone, remains a relative constant beyond human endeavours and aspirations like those of the soldiers, 'idiots/In love with death'; but the present-day landscape is not blank, as the revenant Exaggerater spots 'A man under the bonnet of a car' which may be partially recycled gunmetal: such are the ironies of events perceived from a viewpoint beyond human limitations. Unfamiliar configurations of concepts, such as the country 'Poland', do not obfuscate his awareness of continuous suffering, the endless repainting of Europe, 'Death's estate', with human waste. The Exaggerater perceives a collusion in fatality, like Ilona in *The Power of the Dog*, from the outset of life: 'All babies have [Death] in their eyes', as he recognises from kissing his own picture under barrages, 'Pretending to be my own child', lending those around him a mistaken sense of his normality and docility, 'He loves and waits to die', in circumstances where ideals of love are used as clarion calls to death. A conventionally unperceivable geographical irony is that while the gun fires on and kills men in trenches, its 'draughtsman sits among his heirs in Pilsen', enjoying the privileged security of idyllic family life, to which the soldiers may think they are defending their own right, mistakenly. Such is the human disinclination, exacerbated by a sterile society or ideology, to pursue chains of enquiry; as is demonstrated by the car driver's limited attention and self-absorption:

> And so I helped him push the car
> But did he say
> Did he
> (Really you must admire the lack of curiosity
> That distinguishes man from animals)
> Your eyes are holes
> Why have you holes for eyes

The Exaggerater mischievously constructs an idyllic background by which the audience might locate, define or seek to understand (and thereby dismiss) him, a picturesque home and mother in national costume singing with hearty rusticity; then demolishes it (like the Ward and his illusory riverside encounter in *Women Beware Women*), exposing audience readiness for romantic fictions, indeed their dependence on them:

> The greatest lie being the lie
> You tell yourself
> That is the beautiful
> The immaculate lie
> You know the lie
> You do

From personal challenge, he snaps back into self-description like Sordido with Leantio in the street of Florence, leaving his idea implanted and offering consciously fake reassurance, in the thought of 'Murderers and child molesters' dying in war; but then he stretches the catalogue of death to include the self-important and self-preoccupied, poets, professors, minor officials, revolutionaries, writers, no longer the controlling centres of their own worlds. This leads to another core statement: that there is no enduring core of certainty:

Truth is not stable
Any more than passion
Truth will expire
Just as quickly as desire

He parodies the recoil from the implications of this assertion, 'Oh don't exaggerate', and the preference for attention to seek refuge in expressions of 'benign materialism' as advanced by the paternalist or maternalist state: workers' flats, teak benches and concrete flower tubs. But the Exaggerater characteristically extends a line of argument past its conventional limits to expose its essence: 'mothers on/Returning from the creche may sit on teak benches and/In the scent of blossom':

Dream of being somewhere else

From dislocation, deduction — and counter-assertion:

It is not the end it is the struggle which dignifies

He proclaims the flats to be on the formerly forested site of his conception, and ironically speculates on his parents' lack of foresight in not anticipating, and preparing him for, a populist era of inverted attributes and attractions:

The fascination with the ugly
The lure of criminality
The worship of the squalid act
Which characterizes the educated and artistic

THE DEBILITATING MENDACITY OF THIS AND EVERY TIME

Thus he bursts through to present day populism and addresses the audience's unawakened hopes:

You know what I mean
What wouldn't you give for one bit of
Not debating heroes of the universities
Or thirty volumes of intentions
Giggling celebrities clutching one another's
Parts beneath the desk
BUT ONE BIT IN YOUR FIST OF
WAIT
I'LL GIVE IT TO YOU
WAIT

Significantly, he never does, nor says what it is. Thus the audience are invited to formulate a possible counterblast to redundant superficiality, and implicitly chastised for putting their faith in someone else to do it for them. The missing word might be 'truth' — which then again invites imaginative effort to envisage in its purity or establish in a practical context. The Exaggerater takes his cue to reel through a catalogue of Leftist idolatrous idealism, 'Perfectly Correct Stuff', identified as sentimental worship of an icon deemed valuable in its distance from the worshipper, more debilitating mendacity:

The ease with which you can identify
With the oppressed
Does not excuse the adulation
Of their banality

Similarly he denounces theory as a distraction developed to bolster authority in its essential insecurity, 'The complexity of theory is a/Professorial regime', where language is used like capital to reinforce the distance between owners and dispossessed:

Free words from
Louts
And
Professors

Having railed against the retrenchment of expression, he launches into the rhapsodic evocation of another doomed idyll, on the banks of the Dneister River, then lightly exposes its powers of attraction and the mechanics of popular deception:

You can always take an intellectual for a ride
If you stare into his eyes
He is so hungry
So hungry for a bit of
ACTUAL LOVE

Someone to kiss who cannot quote
Whose dreams have not been ravaged by fiction

But this digression on the nature of the species may not absolve
him from susceptibility to pity: 'The field brought tears into my
holes'. The simple persistence and continuance in growing turnips
expresses a sense of right to survival that is threatened. Again, the
Exaggerater parodies, and pivots — turning the threat into a sense
of doom worship which his multi-historical perspective finds ludicrous and offensive:

It thrills you to say
You love to say
Who have been so protected
And drunk orange juice from poor countries
This is the worst time you have known
It thrills you

He teases them further with a denunciation of the popular press,
apparently a relatively safe and easy target ('The newspapers are
lies/The newspapers obviously'), but again the implications are followed through with disconcerting persistence. The urge to 'Hang
the editors' might at least be entertained; its extension to hang
the printers and readers is more likely to shock, and this shock is
anticipated and indicted: 'Do they not have souls too?' Similarly, he
anticipates and refutes a demand for evidence behind his association of lies with cancer, and extends complicity and disease beyond
editors and printers to 'readers who longed to be lied to', while
darkly suggesting 'The liars operate in imagination too'. A glimpse
of London and its roadways affords the opportunity for reflection
on trivialisation and materialism which prevent people considering
the implications of 'The movement of troops' and 'The movement of
rockets', through the shower of consumerist pressures and injunctions which break attention and trivialise wants, just as a plethora of

facts are invoked to disrupt and distract attention from a causal chain of events:

> But I am not here to tell you facts
> Only to exaggerate
> Long live exaggeration

> It brings you somewhere near the actual horror

The audience are implicitly indicted for their lack of enquiry, the urge to see and think with unrelenting linear determination and recognise a pattern of motivation and consequences beyond familiar seductive superficialities. The distortion of that surface through 'exaggeration' stretches familiar forms and expectations to reveal an essence which is malign, and possibly its ostensible opposite in terms of conventional definition, in which their collusion is highlighted. Hence the predicted resistance of the impulse, 'DON'T EXAGGERATE', here incorporated and mocked. Exaggeration becomes an art form attempting to distort lies into truth and dislocate conventional injunctions to people to brake themselves — failing to question, pursue a line of enquiry and act on the knowledge gleaned; the Exaggerater might represent the ruthless 'bad self' which Bela recognised but drew back from in the first scene of *No End of Blame*.

He presents another version of his conception, a bedroom union between 'The Viennese optician and the carpenter from Pest' replete with idyllic sexuality ('Such was their sympathy/Breathed in unison the word/Hosannah'), and challenges the audience to disbelieve ('IT HAPPENED AND WHY NOT'), adding more mundane details in support — then richochets into further ironic observations on the paradoxical existence of an iconography of insurrection:

> They pass from left to right with banners
> Pure anger
> Pure
> Pure stuff

But the recognisable is extrapolated into the challenging: 'We all like mutiny but revolution'; 'Revolution is the redemption of the secret police'. This in turn gives way to a foreigner's perspective on England:

Where the coinage is not convincing
The crowd are violent with debt
And the passion of the populace is not for love
(That is the property of princesses with tooled smiles
Or teenagers who run away to die)
But
Fun

The idiosyncratic veneration of 'fun', with its associations of inherent triviality, cheap gratuity and peripheral indulgence, envelops the fearfully restrictive English definitions of sexuality and its potential:

And men and women touching one another's flesh
Who dare not call fucking anything but
Let's have a bit of
FUN

Though the imminence of class warfare is pronounced 'routine as clockwork', England remains secure in stasis; as under all authority, the brutalised and brutalising facts of predetermined form are valued higher than imagination, which seeks to anticipate form and identity, subverting definition; it is therefore resisted or marginalised:

The only thought afforded status
Is that which in the end accords
With what exists

While a self-congratulatory inclusiveness is extended to isolated or untroubling enthusiasts, the Exaggerater recognises that this strengthens the force of exclusion to be levelled at any fundamentally questioning voices, and he parodies their castigation as 'THE PARANOID EXAGGERATERS OF DESPAIR', 'You elitist snobs/You are all fascists underneath/If you do not love fun/You must be one'. Death provides opportunities for the 'reclamation' of such voices, when the agents of official definition can place anger 'in perspective' and trivialise challenging ideas through reference to personality:

Despite the severity of many of his statements
We can confidently assume he did love

Fun

THUMP

Mimicking the field gun, the Exaggerater blows away the tactics of belittlement with a final reference to the battlefield as repository of thwarted possibilities, and focuses on Leicester Square, 'Roost of the Happy':

Who did not swerve at my condition
(Really you must admire the lack of curiosity
That distinguishes man from animals)
And saw how numerous you are
(We too were numerous but that only went against us)

Amid 'the ambushes of laughter/which was false', he alights upon an imminent suicide, insufficiently intoxicated by the tawdry gratification offered in the West End, and the early mention of knowledge, 'The highest/Moment of consciousness/In many minds at least', is revealed as the shattering revelation: 'Everything he had been told was false'. With the suicide poised on the brink of his final action, the Exaggerater offers an analogy, by means of digression:

Art brings chaos into order
The actor must destroy
The writer must demolish
All previously held notions of performance
All previously held notions of reality
All clamour for comfort
The accusation of the cultivated philistine
That the work gave them nothing
WHO SAID IT MUST GIVE YOU SOMETHING
It is like love you have to want
Do you want to be saved said Christ
Do you want it
Do you want

Thus he scourges the prevalent posture of passivity in unquestioningly consuming 'art' rather than engaging with it as a problem, a question difficult of solution yet demanding solution. He then releases the sequential narrative to permit the suicide's release into death, with the kerbstone as indifferent witness to the realisation that individual life is not precious in a populist social context, 'The worst lie is the sentimental':

> We are brothers for example
> Are we brothers
> Are we or not
> WELL ARE WE

In his dislocation from temporal, geographical, mortal limitations of viewpoint and experience, the Exaggerater is empowered to turn on the audience and defy them to empathise with or include him in conventional humanist terms; the powers of exclusion are now his, and he adds a Christ parallel which hangs between pity and chilling mockery: 'I am the reconciler who never was'. He launches into a final account of his conception, which is not idyllic, in a rush of detail which builds into a rhythmic striving parallel to the act described, resolving itself into his one expression of sympathy: 'Oh English suicide'. The cry, 'Oh the bastards', which may initially have seemed incomprehensible or gratuitous petulance, is now heard in causal context, a final cursing of 'the unchanged world', a recognition of the suicide's insight that he is beyond possibilities of regeneration and renewal as constituted by his context, which has excluded him from the reach of

> The great breaker of moulds
> The great solvent of opinion
>
> Desire
> Not sex
> Sex being part of the happiness racket
>
> Desire
> Would not touch you
>
> So why persist?

The question hangs in the air for the audience to attempt to answer.

Don't Exaggerate is intensely and thoroughly tragic in its unrelenting exposure of the cowardice of idealism, and in its painstaking anticipation and demolition of all structures of support whereby an audience might seek to distance itself from its essential questions. It involves performer and audience looking as long and deeply into each other as Sordido and Leantio in *Women Beware Women*, where a man animated by pain and hate defies his witnesses to imagine, and challenges them to pursue rather than to shrink from the implications. The performer has to negotiate the poem like a tightrope, balancing between engaging and offending the audience, drawing them into his perceptions and forcibly returning them to a consciousness of the restrictions of their own perceptions. It is illuminating that audience resistance often occurs at the section beginning 'Art brings chaos into order', when they glimpse the extent of the assault on all previously held notions of performance and reality and all clamour for comfort, and the relocation of responsibility for the work to 'give them something', referred back to them. The audience may see this as a breakdown of the conventional performer/audience contract, as it is, and feel embarrassed or short-changed; on the other hand, it may stir them into a heightened self-consciousness of the importance of their activity and contribution, 'It is like love you have to want' — it asks them to acknowledge their own want, their own pain, and thereby progress to an awareness of their own relative possibilities of experience, compared to and alongside the Exaggerater and the suicide, in a painstaking uprooting of 'the lies you tell yourself'. This opens a fissure in the self-defined limits of the self, to allow in pity, through the final understanding of the suicide's progression to his self-immolation: an awareness of participation in the evil of compounding isolation, which, from another point of view embodied by the Exaggerater, we may be unable to forgive.

The performer must prepare for — and delight in — the scaling of great crags of language, incessantly reaching for new entry points by which to engage and surprise the audience; part way through a headlong rush down along the trajectory of a meticulously assembled scenario, he has to be prepared to arrest, pivot and mock or demolish it, causing a jolt of nausea in the audience through the denial of expectations — the dramatic equivalent of hitting pockets of air turbulence. Rather than be simply alienating or simply pathetic, he has to engage the audience in a dynamic of challenge, control, challenge, release, renewed challenge, which has distinct parallels with the sexual dynamic. If he achieves a wished-for breakthrough in his and their senses of limitations and separateness, this is immensely rewarding — if failure occurs, and he and they are confined to and driven further down into a sense of innate isolation, this is immensely dispiriting. The opposition of performer and audience in performance of the poem is analogous to its opposition of individual and crowd.

Don't Exaggerate is also remarkable in its thorough linguistic exploration of evoked scenes and concepts, and in the chronology of its circuitous narrative spiralling between the twin poles of the Exaggerater's conception and the suicide's death, which are touched on and circled around several times. Surprising but relevant parallels are afforded by Tony Tanner's consideration of Joseph Heller's savagely comic 1961 novel *Catch-22*:

> Sentences undermine themselves, cause and effect are dislocated, logic goes awry, propositions are negated as soon as advanced and truth comes in strange forms . . . This is all symptomatic of what happens to language when the dominating people use it, not as a way of discovering truth, but as a tool for manipulating people . . . In the language situation of this book you have to be an evader if you are to tell any sort of truth . . . as though by making the available language reveal all its capacity for perpetrating perverted formulations [Heller, and by extension his protagonist] is at the same time demonstrating his own freedom from his false patterning . . . [refusing to be] trapped in the deceptive orderliness and misleading coherence of conventional plot structure.

But Heller the author and Yossarian his character are drawn to confront the truth of death 'under all the falsifying forms and patterns and paper facades of this world', only to recoil from it. Tanner calls this counter-movement a celebration of 'a sort of private dance of life', though he acknowledges 'The dance on the periphery may not be leading anywhere'.[4]

Barker the poet and the Exaggerater his character — and their audience in performance — confront death but do not recoil. The Exaggerater is to some extent excluded from involvement in the existing structures of reality as it surrounds suicide and audience, and is not subject to conventional human definition (his viewpoint is akin to that of the Witches in *Macbeth*). Barker, more optimistic about the possibilities of language than Heller, moves from savage comedy into tragedy:

Because they try to debase language, the voice of the actor becomes
an instrument of revolt.
The actor is both the greatest resource of freedom and the subtlest
instrument of repression.
If language is restored to the actor he ruptures the imaginative blockade of the culture. If he speaks banality he piles up
servitude.
Tragedy liberates language from banality. It restores the power of
expression to the people.
Tragedy is not about reconciliation. Consequently, it is the art
form for our time.
Tragedy resists the trivialisation of experience, which is the product of the authoritarian regime.[5]

Don't Exaggerate demonstrates how language, like the actor, can
be the greatest resource of freedom as well as the subtlest form of
repression, as the means to tragic confrontation, rather than reconciliation and trivialisation of experience. What Tanner identifies as
Heller and Yossarian's private dance on the periphery of reality's
structures is fundamentally a limited avoidance, a recoil into idealism; Barker rejects the peripheral and central dance on the terms
of imposed structures, in the poem 'Refuse to Dance', which urges
resistance in a time of ordained dancing and laughter, where 'the
body is annexed' and the landscape is filled with 'the endless shuf-
fle of acquiescence'. Again, a character stands out against a crowd,
'splendid wallflower'. Correspondingly, the painter in 'The Artist Infirm' discovers pity and vision in pain of illness, but also 'The
necessary contempt' for 'the dispensers of patronage and love':

So not hearing wit he witnessed cruelty
And missing flattery he recognised lechery
And deaf to excuses he saw the act for itself
And painted himself not as
He Who Understands All
Compassionate in old browns
But as untrustworthy
And thereby made his face the mirror of the world

Several other poems in the collection *Don't Exaggerate (desire
and abuse)* concern the honing of the self into autonomy through
ruthlessness in exposure, discovery and rejection of limits, as

determined and defined by social pressures to conformity. The assault on prescriptive definition (with its implicit Latin root finis, a limit or end) is a keynote at every level of Barker's work, not only in the length and scale of the experiences which plays and poems range through, but also in such crucial small-scale linguistic effects as the use of the word 'but' at the end of a sentence or section to expose the insufficiency of definition by every word and concept that has led up to it: as in Skinner's line in *The Castle*, 'we all bring to the world, inside our skulls, inside our bellies, Christ knows what lumber from our makers BUT'. Similarly, Stucley thanking the jury for 'lovely vehemence orchestrated and spontaneous THANK YOU BUT'; and the Exaggerater's 'The erudite is all very well but/I shall be erudite but' and the unfinished 'Not war/Not chaos/Has broken you/But'; and the title of one of the plays in *The Possibilities*, 'She Sees the Argument But'. All these effects involve and demonstrate an undermining of faith in supposed objective or rational assessments of situation and motivation, and the suggestion of an undefined potential which negates or overturns it. Its tragic use is in demonstrating that human attempts at all-inclusive definition, like Stucley's, are doomed to fail; its positive sense is in the resistance of external imposition of all-inclusive definition. The writer or speaker prises open a fissure in authority on the basis of this tiny chink of a syllable, 'but', which recognises that official, rational, logical and objective definitions are nonetheless not exclusive or all-powerful reflections of human potential and its lurking capacity for, perhaps insistence on, resistance, upheaval and change.

The development of the 'but' in the self, the capacity to assert individual rights and difference within a collective ideal, is increasingly important in Barker's work, as is the capacity for imagination, individual revolution and resistance of the lures, values and prescriptions of the philistine populist state. The poem 'Random Stabs from a Victim of Maternity' is an oblique but demonstrative expression of gratitude to a mother for encouraging, however unconsciously, a child's development of ruthless autonomy and self-determination, which correspondingly has to be enacted and pursued through characteristic use of the imagery of physical cruelty:

I see it now
This is the time
My mother

To see your corsetry undone
The flesh undimmed
Not as the lover
Nor the doctor
But as the mortician's apprentice
Who slashed the fat unscientifically
And left disordered viscera over the floor
So shall I hack you out of love

Thus, the child thanks the mother for being forced to turn into the parent's opposite or complementary (recalling the relationship between Bradshaw and her consciously-moulded son McConochie in *Victory*). Beneath the cruelty — indeed, exposed by cruelty — is a poignant acceptance of self and other by the child, who learns 'From numerousness/Differentiation', and the traps inside hopes from her gnawing invocations of them. The child defines himself in negative of the mother's qualities, as suggested by the sections of her description which end 'but he'. And the final assertion is that many things 'She understood'.

'Scenes From the Rise of Our Fascism 1' examines the effects of failure of imagination as a national characteristic, inability to sense or realise 'The unlived life'; and wonders how long before

The preference for control
Which characterizes us
It suits them to suggest
Is seen
Not to be dignified
The discreet manner of an ancient race
But
The obscenity of collusion?

Here the 'But' is a pivot, on which the reader is invited to recognise the trap and effect of official definition. The hinge of surprise and reversal is also used in 'Three Huffs at a Lost Woman', of which the first is a superbly compact example:

I made a place for us to kiss unseen
But you have gone and married
Clearly your imagination did not coincide with mine

This discovery of unexpected personal difference also occurs in the other two 'Huffs', wryly humorous at the expense of the narrator's own limitations of knowledge. The dislocation of imagination is also central to 'An Acolyte' and 'Fat Actor', which hinge on reversal, comic and surprising, through juxtaposed events and the word 'Then': in 'An Acolyte', the theoretical reverence of a cerebral admirer is disrupted by the glorious insurrectionary effect of a 'cruelly articulate/Warm hipped woman'; in 'Fat Actor', an awkward man suddenly demonstrates his capacity for willed transformation, becoming 'Implacable in borrowed form,/Only self in the imagined'. In 'She Bares her Arse to the Soldiers', a woman similar to Skinner in *The Castle* dislocates the security of sexual role through her mocking gesture. 'Infatuation of the Torturer' details how a professional perpetrator of licensed atrocity armours, and perhaps justifies, himself through the displacement of romance (like Ball in *Victory*). 'The Evangelist Addresses Millions' locates the preacher's power in his imaginative stirring of the unlived life with the word 'Unfulfilled'. 'Mr Kurtz His Bonus' traces the effort of willed evil in the world of Conrad's *Heart of Darkness*, as the agent of the Company pushes himself to new ingenuities of butchery as an index to efficiency. In 'Second Poem to Valls' the butchery is of words, the Cuban state-ordained destruction of conceptual and verbal nuance in sacrifice to banal unison of music and slogan, which nevertheless fails to overcome isolated individual resistance:

But you
Would not kiss offal
The relatively valid
Nor stoop to rinse
Your mouth with blood
The conditionally true

However, the rareness of the determination to move against the grain of the vengeful crowd is the ruefully philosophical discovery of a Japanese dancer and lover, in 'Genshu Hanayagi', who has dared to mock 'The tortuous symmetry of the factory life'. As in *Women Beware Women*, individual action shared or witnessed has proved itself capable of upheaving official definition: Genshu knows that 'In my eyes men learn the world unlocks' and awaits the vengeance of the viciously insecure guardians of an exclusive truth, who will not permit the existence of the man who acts 'But' and has 'set the poor to questioning':

> I have said that god is a murderer
> So god's cohorts yell revenge at my gate
> They scare my students away
> My students who say
> Let us enroll at another studio
> Perhaps after all Genshu's style
> Is out of date?

Thus, 'Genshu Hanayagi' reflects the converse of Thomas Middleton's hopeful suggestion in his dialogue with Barker that 'now, as in my time, the more ferocious the imagination, the more loyalty it commands'.[6] The poem delicately suggests the melancholy awareness and acceptance of isolation alongside unrepentant pride in self-willed achievement.

The Breath of the Crowd (first performed 1986, Cheltenham Festival) is reactive and romantic whereas *Don't Exaggerate* is active and tragic; it stands as a similar converse to its sibling poem much as *Women Beware Women* does to *The Castle*. The reactive element was expressed on its first reading by Maggie Steed discovering the book on a park bench, reading from its pages and becoming increasingly engrossed by its testimony of experiences and observations, then leaving it on the bench for the next chance encounter.

The Breath of the Crowd shares with *Don't Exaggerate* the aim and scope to reach through 'false celebration', 'imminent colonialism' and 'selective memory', print, film and drowning music, to describe 'Europe's deeps', strata of pains and unpublished griefs, the excavation of the unspoken will and truth, unheard assertions and debates which do not correspond with repressive invocations of popular beliefs or conventions. The mother's discriminations and bans teach the child to nourish 'the horror of others' (poem 2), but the pebble of resistance in his gut produces secretions, 'which made pearl/Of curiosity', proving him 'the crowd's child also'. This divergence from 'the lack of curiosity' which the Exaggerater claims 'distinguishes man from animals' defies the populist suppression of interest in the search for knowledge, hence the movement 'contrary to tides' (poem 3) in 'Unutterable passion/Clandestine hunger' and delight in disintegration of the familiar: 'Intimacy I reserved for the rot/Of the public thing'. But unlike the crowds in *Women*

Beware Women and *Don't Exaggerate*, the Breath of the Crowd is here also associated with witness, movement and untapped potential, as opposed to merely furtive shame and inane self-absorption; the wind blows through evidence of human striving and absurdity with less studied indifference than the rain beating down on graves, books and mothers in *Don't Exaggerate*, though still mocking burdens of 'borrowed/chanted/coagulated/opinion' and configurations 'Where politics were glued/As the wafer is jammed to the toffee'.

The Breath of the Crowd's central reverberative incident is a man and a woman meeting as strangers on a train and discovering 'To copulate in a public place may pass for adventure in a/society where risk has been minimized in the interests of/welfare and polar explorers are considered absurd'. Those around them are literally cushioned and circumscribed in their private compartments, while

She unhitched
She disordered
She exposed
.   .   .
And copulating
They
Beat
Back
The clammy cold of a polite democracy

By disconnecting from the mundane, the man and woman expose 'The rigidity of the congregation' where 'The crowd is a lie', the habitual repetition which Livia in *Women Beware Women* dismisses as 'the geometry of servile continuation'. Their coupling mocks unspoken conventions of commuter interaction, where physical proximity is permitted and excused through rigorous 'privatisation' of the self, avoidance and indifference elevated to the systematic. Similarly, poem 6 focuses on the conceptual rigidity nevertheless present in flimsy separation, where the central voice tells 'I lay alone on the hotel bed', hearing and observing parallel lives boxed together in what a subsequent poem terms 'hired space', as in fearful avoidance: '(They feared the view, the wolfpack/On the boundary)'. As the central figure reclines alone, outside 'encumbered women/Narrate the slipping of life', finding relief in the barest of consolations, reappearance and recurrence.

Poem 7 is an excursion into parable form, describing a poet in a garden near Salonica, who (like Krak in *The Castle*) values and pursues truths arrived at in seclusion, exploring personal epiphanies in the costly privilege of his garden's silence. But silence, food supply and garden wall break down when the poet's fortune is spent, and the beggars invade his boundaries: 'This earthquake of flesh/No wisdom prepared him for/No insight armed him against'. Scholars, 'shamed at sudden impotence', declare the poet's 'terrible' truths incomprehensible after his suicide, extending the pattern of reluctant rebuke in failure to communicate. Like poem 10, poem 7 implicitly criticises the isolation of genius from the bruise of public encounter, where self-absorption leads to an impotent obscurity. Conversely, a boy and a girl copulate on a tomb, in poem 8, as if in a long delightful insult to the dead, who endure their own ironic subterranean juxtapositions, in a submerged history which recalls Richard Bradshaw's brief repose, broken several seconds into the play *Victory*.

Poem 9 details the prurient, censorious watchfulness of a bald man, sleepless in the failure of boredom, having 'more/time/ than/ imagination' and 'neither/love/nor/power', driven back into himself by the sound of chiming towers and barking dogs: 'The stir of the pack rekennels him'. A passing woman shows contrasting purpose, 'She possesses a destination/In this she's rich'; though this may be imaginary armouring against others and self, walking to a selected paving stone only to return; she tautens, he seethes, both driven further into their isolations by the sense of an other. Cultivated distance recurs in poem 10's portrait of an artist-academic, smug in his sense of power among staked roses, asserting in imitation of an ancient emperor 'PEOPLE WILL FIND VOICES' but withdrawing the benedictions of his intellect from any student who might dare to argue 'past a certain point'. This vignette is a finely observed illustration of the professorial regime in its circumscriptions, vulnerability, vanity and dependence on distance between theory and practice.

Poem 11 opposes the statements 'You can lend too much room to opposition' and 'All men should be heard'; the first notion is identified as systematic of the reductive ideology and stunting imagination of the party hack, born of the plaintive if childish idealism, 'IF ONLY TRUTH WERE STABLE', and capable of extension into committee-room discipline and oppression. The variety and artfulness of human resources illustrate the need for continual reassessment, a theme developed in poem 13, Barker's response to Donne's line 'Every man's death diminishes me', which prompts reflections which might provide an epigraph for Barker's work as a whole:

To affirm the sentimental
To reiterate the doctrinal might not

Damage

But wholeness remains the harder thing
Bitter as probing the calyx of wounds

Pronouncing a kinship with 'Every man' extends to a kinship with old vagrants and young warders, whom the party hack of poem 11 might subsume into 'the masses' with expedient clumsiness only to disclaim representation and shun contact. Barker realises personal investment and commitment must be total, 'Is the point of departure/The locking of self to the wheel', and deduces 'Every man's evil expresses me'. The Viennese professor's son of poem 15 howls for blame with the intransigence of Leary in *Fair Slaughter*, identifying pity as the blunt stick 'Every cringing and falling enemy/ Wields against the just man's temper'; in the simplicity of his bitterness, he would denounce the ageing East European teacher of poem 18, required to live through 19 governments, with voluntary and enforced changes of belief which his vehement youthful stasis would deem unforgivable, impatient with her own 'weight of unkind memory' and parallels to her behaviour beyond the obvious: 'MARRY YOUR ENEMIES/But that is universal practice/ FEED YOUR FOES/Is that not the rule of every kitchen'. The poem extends a rare example of sympathy to her in perceiving such parallels to her cardinal sin, of offending ideological and theoretical dogma: 'If she betrayed/Do you not think she also once believed?'

The theme of vital fracture of routine in personal contact re-emerges in the cycle, particularly focusing on the way fear of strangers dissolves 'in deprivation/in uprising/in imminence of death' but 'Carbonizes in property/in repression/ in predation' (poem 16). In poem 17, a woman finds herself bearing 'The stranger's child', with all the fearful and fascinating paradoxes involved in literally conceiving another within the self:

> Her body yielded all authority
> As the servile instinct offers
> Its poverty to the invader

Her rational mind can no longer command her body's mutiny: 'A queen in a tower/Idiotic/To the boiling river of the crowd'. Resolving to give birth to the child involves and brings an awesome but complete acceptance of wholeness: 'Any man might be my husband/And any child my daughter'. This second 'pearl of curiosity' has a father associated with the memory of variety and chance ('The crowd moved in and out of him/A tide'), and embodies, with appropriate independence, fruitful disruption.

The converse of this is examined in poem 19, where risk is extirpated in favour of programmatic calculation. In a bid to breed the perfect citizen, 'The kind man married the sane woman/And of their union came a silent child', who is devoid of curiosity:

> She had no temper to explore
> No pain to bless
> Or rinse the inanimate in

The cycle ends with an apt return to the essential fading and impulse towards contact in each human individual, an acknowledgement and acceptance of missed and exhausted choice, separateness and interdependence:

> Old mother
> Place your rumpled hand on your son's balding head
> Part your daughter's greying streams
> With fingers smooth from folding

Don't Exaggerate frequently depicts crowds illuminated by aurora borealis of bombardment, or splashed with chill, garish neon, bound by their own limited spans of attention and absorption in the moment, shuffling in acquiescence toward a soporific death; the spirit of enquiry is withered to the anglepoise lamp of the tutorial room, or the stark light above the butcher-mortician's marble slab. But the observing voice refuses to be entrenched in the indifference of pessimism; the pain of witnessing meekness and outrage drives him to slash the fat unscientifically and hack the living and dead out of love. Conversely, the moonlit, moonstruck speculations in *The Breath of the Crowd* testify to reflections and discoveries of wall-flowers, realising secret lives in defiance of a society where risk has been minimised in the interests of welfare; walls tumble, lovers rich in impertinence copulate above or around the dead, and, even in recognising the slipping of life and imminence of death, the word 'stranger' dissolves.

Don't Exaggerate's images of anguished retrenchment expose and burst faith in historical definitions and limitations; *The Breath of the Crowd's* images of lost and perfectly exhausted choice expose and burst faith in personal definitions and limitations. The Exaggerater's stark, tragic harangues join with the hunger of the lovers' thrusts in mutual reinforcement of the assertion that, in making and re-making our selves, we make and re-make those around us; in the closing words of *The Breath of the Crowd,*

Look
We pass in and out of one another
We pass in and out

10

Pain and Breakthrough

THE BITE OF THE NIGHT, THE EUROPEANS

'WHO THE FUCK IS THAT IN MY FILM?' the Director bellows.
'GIVE HIM THE TREATMENT.'
  So they did and it backfired.

William S. Burroughs, *The Place of Dead Roads*[1]

I have restored you to your pain . . .

The Europeans: Struggles to Love

In the first chapter, I wrote of Barker's characters re-telling and re-experiencing pain, in pseudo-historical ages when the acknowledgement and infliction of pain are two of the few methods of self-definition left. This does not prescribe or endorse sadomasochism (I remain mindful and respectful of individual choice), but involves an imaginative cruelty such as Artaud sketched an artistic need for.

When people are given the term 'outlaw', they will take it on, hopefully, as do the uncontrollable, evil Exaggerater, Murgatroyd in *Pity in History* and Skinner in *The Castle*, who realise 'they have made me like this' and find that excommunication is liberation, with possibilities of surprising, unorthodox beauty. Once removed from the conventional terms of society, told 'you are no longer one of us', they are freed from the continual pressure of trying to be 'one of us' ('do/buy this to be a *good* member of a *good* society'), or attempting to realise their selves conventionally. Stucley inadvertently gives Skinner power through carrying torture and pain too far, past the point where pain is experienced out of principle on behalf of others to where it becomes a matter and ingredient of unassailable personal dignity: the sufferer does not resist/submit/speak/remain silent for others, but for self. Torture attempts to refine pain to take the self to breaking point, but there is a point at which pain creates, makes, individualises the self. Stucley, in the mistaken belief that you can break anyone, makes Skinner, and breaks himself: he reaches a point of psychological exhaustion and finally goes mad (as did Bela, briefly), whereas Skinner, Gay and Katrin and other characters in *The Bite of the Night* and *The Europeans* decline

210

to be insane. Their pain is not digested into conventional notions of 'maturity' or 'experience'; in Skinner's terms of self-description and self-definition. 'Oh, she is not dignified, she is not charitable, the act of kindness from the victim to the murderer, grey eyes serene in pain absorbed, agony knitted into cloths of wisdom WHO SAYS! Reconciliation and oblivion, NO! GREAT UGLY STICK OF TEMPER, RATHER'. In this way, she blocks the conventionally defined linear process of history, by which a control-oriented society registers and absorbs people's pain, bereavement, mutilation or humiliation.

Rather than be reduced to a social museum exhibit, or be bandaged up to the point of unrecognisability like an Egyptian mummy, Barker's characters triumphantly insist on the right to personal definition: they keep their pain public, portray, enact, perform and re-experience it at all points, tearing away at all dressings. Burroughs:

> Castaneda would describe it as a sudden eruption of the Nagual, the unknown and unpredictable, into the Tonal, which is the totality of prerecorded film ["reality" as conventionally defined]. This violates the most basic laws of a predictable control-oriented universe. Introduce one unforeseen and therefore unforeseeable factor and the whole structure collapses like a house of cards.[2]

With Holiday's corpse strapped to her, Skinner discovers a form of liberation and a form of wit, and unsettles the society's terms of definition through her effect on others. The legitimacy of society's control depends on its possessing history, convincing the masses that they are subsumed in a process based on endurance which will bring benefit/wisdom/maturity; but Barker's characters insist on a right to personal definition through permanently asserting their own biographies, saying '*no*, this is about me, what I went through on one particular afternoon', and discovering their unsettling power of anti-history, exposing the gap in theoretical definition, achieving the breakthrough of knowledge.

THE BITE OF THE NIGHT — THE GASH OF KNOWLEDGE

DANCE ON THE SKIN OF KNOWLEDGE but don't fall through, you'll drop forever

Act 2 scene 3

Barker's play *The Bite of the Night* (written 1986) pursues the theme and experience of *knowledge* — recognising and rupturing the illusory nature of definition or perceptual structure as generally prescribed: not the accumulation of facts (personally unrealised theories or non-experiential data), but the glimpse of unstable and destabilising truth gleaned through re-perception of superficial familiarity in such a way as to illuminate self and others past the conventional limitations of imaginative vision. *The Bite of the Night* dramatises the dangers and fascinations of this pursuit through the experiences and self-excavations of Savage, a university lecturer who has realised that knowledge lies behind pre-digested or pre-recorded catalogues of facts or traps of kindness, in belief derived from personal experience, locating and exposing the self; he accordingly pushes himself further and further, no matter what risks, opposition or awful discoveries entailed. *The Bite of the Night* does not offer the apparent comfort of being grounded in history, like *Victory* or *The Power of the Dog*; rather, Savage and his student Hogbin tear through their world, 'The Ruins of a University', into mythic Troy and psychic essence; play and characters plunge beyond contemporary socio-economic criteria of historical verification into an excoriation, realisation and expression of kernel selfhood in all its defiantly contradictory and anti-social manifestations; and the dedication to the pursuit of this knowledge proves magnetic, alluring and destructive, for self and others.

But this dramatic approach yields a sense of liberation as personal exploration produces searching political exposures unavailable to ideologists of whatever colour or system: *The Bite* is crucially anti-systematic, a three-act play with three obliquely relevant prologues and two obliquely relevant interludes, designed to operate on the imagination in ways that are non-linear and non-developmental. Indeed, *The Bite* and *The Europeans* might be termed non-narrative plays, aiming to break through to a sense of raging freedom, conscious liberation texts (I would draw a consciously imperfect parallel with the resistance of 'narrative sequence' as in the novels of Burroughs and Kundera, which offer something more akin to variations on themes, metaphorical effects conventionally associated with poetry).

In *The Bite of the Night*, as in *Don't Exaggerate* and *The Breath of the Crowd*, insight requires recognition of the capacity of the self for what christian-humanist conventions of art and perception shrink from as 'evil', or deny the possibility of its existence

(Burroughs: 'people are not bribed to shut up about what they know. They are bribed not to find things out')[3]. Significantly, this does not preclude *The Bite*'s capability for social analysis and speculation, though the play does involve a movement beyond the documentary vision of social organisation which informed even the heightened realism and grotesqueries of Barker's 1970s plays. In *The Bite of the Night*, numerous Trojan political systems spring up, imperfectly ideological in organisation: rather than being founded on systematic evidence or an economic basis, the successive models of Troy are manifestations of one individual psyche — usually sexually conditioned — supplanted by another, though these personally ordained configurations of power demonstrate unsettling parallels with contemporary and supposedly corporate prescriptions. *The Bite* extends the post-catastrophic atmosphere of *Victory* and *The Power of the Dog*, where life extends beyond the guidance of mortal and moral reference points, and survivors struggle to reassert morality and redefine possibility; but whereas in the earlier two plays, the idea of society has been apocalyptically shattered or reduced to redundant corpse-like twitching, *The Bite* depicts successive incarnations of a monstrous and voracious social force, desperately and hysterically out of control, assuming protean shapes in search of an illusory centre or fixed point, annexing, battening and preying on individuals such as Helen, consuming rapidly and seeking new grist. There is an increasing sense of urgency and limited time, in that only so many Troys are believed to be permitted before Troy as an experience ends, leading to a feverish exhaustion of form and imagination where politics consists of the imaginary results of tension: tension produces a system, which collapses, another asserts itself, as the pressures increase.

The lack of shared reference in characters' separate and subjective personal drives contributes to the play's sense of a splintered panorama of dislocated, fragmentary sensibilities and the powerfully authentic note of hysterical momentum in the characters' reactions. These human tempests are nevertheless uncertainly contained by the cumulative postulations of a malevolent Society which the characters seek to define, understand or move in sympathy with. Thus, human disintegration precipitates attempted characterisations of self-justifying dominant social force and order, which develop as responses to attempt the offset of, or integrate, the disintegration. The inadequacies, partialities and atrocities of such attempted characterisations heighten the sense of strain and terror among the characters, who do not 'develop' in the conventional dramatic way; rather we are presented with the more disturbing or unusual sense of characters weathering a range of experiences beyond even those spanned in a 19th-century three-decker novel, reducing and reconstructing themselves, or being forcibly reduced or reconstructed.

Our engagement with the play is less through customary sympathetic identification with these characters than through the horror, which we share with them, at the insistence of the atrocities (as in *Titus Andronicus* and *King Lear*, apparently every atrocity which might occur does so, to the point of surpassing any former sense of possible destruction and persistent experience of this destruction),[4] and through the cumulative positings of a Society superficially benevolent in its pandeterminism but essentially insensitive and inimical to individual human perspective. As in *Titus Andronicus* and *King Lear*, the insistence of atrocities, and moreover of their survival, defies comprehension by imaginative limitations while paradoxically insisting that attempts at imaginative comprehension be continued.

The Bite of the Night is the most existentially individualist Barker play to date; its central impetus is the headlong drive down into the core of Savage's self, where he hunts out the essence of knowledge and infatuation. The play's breakthrough is not the recognition of a political conspiracy as in earlier works: Savage negotiates changes in political climates but remains at one or more removes from their instigation, participating only in pursuit of what he thinks of as personal peace or power. He seeks breakthrough to a knowledge within himself, pursuing his drives singlemindedly at whatever cost to those around, even countenancing the rejection, disfigurement and destruction of loved ones in order to explore, or eradicate himself from, their power: there is a Faustian-Kurtzian glory and horror in his compulsion to will himself on to further self-exposures, and irrevocable sacrifices of stability, while those around him career into ideologies, impelled by the fearful strain of living with contradiction: and also a profound questioning of the human essence, the malicious allures which exist prior to shame or civilisation — with what may be troubling consequences for the possible correspondences between these two self-restrictive forces? Free of guilt and pity, Savage is as uncomfortably unassimilable and uncontrollable as the Exaggerater, who recognised and announced his own capacity and impulse to be 'the dictator who never was'.

The Bite of the Night opens with a First Prologue by MacLuby, who correspondingly questions the essence of drama ('What are theatres for?') in his description of the cemented habit of entertainment, with its consequent enshrined smothering of imagination, concentration and attention. In the face of simplistic populism, he insists on the revolutionary nature of offering, and wanting, complexity, search and struggle, 'THE PAIN OF UNKNOWING'; rather than invoke the reassuring tyranny of the familiar, MacLuby and Barker encourage the 'hard work' involved in the persistent 'reach down beyond the known', bypassing 'CLARITY/MEANING/LOGIC/AND CONSISTENCY'. Appropriately, the reiterated keyword is 'Beyond' in a self-consciously 'IMPOSSIBLE' but undeterred striving for breakthrough to the 'honour' of mutual surprise, rejecting the patronising condescension and Procrustean injury of theatre, as the medium of fearful ignorance and slavish trivialisation of human potential and experience: he affirms that the process of discovery is compulsive, and hopeful in its bid for recognition and engagement: 'IT'S AN OBLIGATION . . . !'

In a second prologue, Creusa, Savage's estranged wife (though classically the lost wife of Aeneas), proclaims her conscious choice to 'get lost' rather than continue their marriage in another place (an alternative history to Virgil's *Aeneid*). Frenzy and hazard 'notwithstanding', she absconds, but is still forced to wrestle with the urges to reach out to/withdraw from Savage, 'boy in hand and dad on back' forming a triangle of male bodies, 'The three degrees of man'; but she overcomes herself, vomits shame and self-disgust, to stand up 'frail but light' with the power of self-determination: 'Widowhood is grief but also chance/And falls of cities both finishes and starts'.

Creusa's hesitant edging to autonomy and final release into shedding old selfhood provides a counterpoint to Savage's sense of seething restriction in a 20th-century world. His resentment bursts into embittered stabs at his son, whose well-meaning but imperfectly comprehending repetitions of his father's familiar complaints only compound Savage's sense of claustrophobia: domestic routine and the promise of 'avenues where they sleep the sleep of family love' have ossified into encumbrances and taunting false idealisms to which he is nevertheless shackled at a self-gnawing ironic remove. Savage's pupil Hogbin, last student in a defunct university, defines himself in opposition to his own background through a combination of erudition, theory and cynicism, but Savage emphasises the limitations of facts not grounded in experience: 'You read it. You did not believe it. Knowledge is belief'. Though infuriated, Hogbin recognises validity behind his lecturer's insistent perversity and urges 'GIVE US YOUR INTUITIONS AND STUFF THE FACTS'. MacLuby, a soap boiler, recalls the collapse of the university, hastened by the casual, indifferent destruction of 'demolition cowboys'; Savage wryly admits the buildings' vaunted dedication to, and representation of, knowledge proved pathetically vulnerable: 'It was a paper overcoat against their spit'. MacLuby's Mephistophelean request for the Boy takes root in Savage, who prepares his son for an apprenticeship in the soap trade: Savage's attempted armouring of Boy and self against feeling is a pitiful adjunct to their self-consciousness and mutual understanding (as the Boy says, 'You are so unhappy. And I can't help'). The Old Man's well-meaning suggestions turn into grating platitudes on contact with Savage's churning loathing of world and self: Savage uses them to spur himself into increasingly ruthless self-expression and self-definition, consciously at the expense of his father, who takes the cue to action with apparently boundless loving unselfishness, which impels Savage to chase it to the last boundary:

(The old man withdraws some yards behind Savage, and sits)
SAVAGE: Knowledge is total. It is simply hidden behind obstacles.
   (He breaks the plate)
These obstacles we ourselves erect.
   (He takes a shard)
The conspiracy of the ignorant against the visionary can be broken
   only by the ruthless intellect.
   (He undoes his vest)
Pity also is a regime.
   (He attempts to cut his throat)
And consideration a manacle.
OLD MAN: Trying . . .
SAVAGE: Manners —
OLD MAN: Trying . . .
SAVAGE: Loyalty —
OLD MAN: Trying, fuck it —
SAVAGE: Responsibility, IRON BANDS ON THE BRAIN.

Hogbin's horrified witnessing of the process deters neither the Old Man nor Savage ('KNOWLEDGE IS BEYOND KINDNESS YOU

KNOW'), and the tableau of clasping tutor and student, while the Old Man posthumously soliloquises on an idyllic epiphany from his lost airforce days, reverberates with simultaneous cruelty and love in a forceful unorthodoxy of dramatic experience which defies dissociation, to an extent unique in Barker's drama or elsewhere. Savage's purposeful speed and bankruptcy in expressing grief ('The death of my father necessitates the cancellation of our next tutorial') continues his unwavering self-invention which defies audience belief or indifference. This process extends into MacLuby's reflections on the Boy's ineptness at play: Savage adds a further twist of self-exposure tempered and decisively shaped by self-determination: 'A FATHER ALSO LOVES BUT THROUGH A GRATING. Tell him that . . .'

A parallel taunt to release pervades Helen's soliloquoy of self-establishment — 'BURST MY FACE OR I SHALL GO ON TALKING' — as she recounts her path to becoming ensconced with the Greek King, her former husband, Fladder (classically, at the fall of Troy, Helen is restored to Menelaus); he is attended by his soldiers, Epsom, Shade and Gummery, who stew in resentment. Fladder is fascinated by Helen, 'The word' and 'The idea' in conjunction with the physicality of the woman; Creusa has taken up with Shade, in a mood of undeluded resignation ('Not the worst thing in the world, to have no choice . . . The worst thing is . . . To imagine choice exists'). Helen and Savage recognise each other immediately, as twin repositories of the anguish of others; Savage similarly understands Fladder's decision to stay in Troy, having invested so much pain in it ('Where so much hate has concentrated, that must be home also'); Troy is sustained through redefinition by Fladder, 'Paper Troy', with Helen and himself still presiding. The sight of Savage, nominated as constitution writer to Paper Troy, again fractures Creusa's poise of indifference, and they instinctively fly into harangue; it is Savage who manages to perform indifference, resigning Creusa to Shade, and Creusa perceives both the distance and the cost in the performance (her remark 'Oh, you mad and forlorn bastard' bleeds out in expression of pity). Shade insists on his own levels of invention, in rivalry, with ludicrous but sincere baroque paeans to his own mind; Hogbin recoils into hope of a world elsewhere, but Savage knows, like Ann in *The Castle*, that there is nowhere except where you are: 'NO KNOWLEDGE ON THE HOOF . . . To go beyond. That's our hunger, that's our thirst. To go beyond, you must stand still. FIRST PARADOX OF ALL GREAT JOURNEYS'.

Just as Stucley decreed that the Castle's 'fifth wall is the wall of morals', Fladder builds Paper Troy through prescription and its adoption, and Savage composes a suitable constitution for a civic institution based on deconstruction, celebrating subjectivity in an essential gesture of impotent shame. However, Fladder senses the personal implications of the process he has instigated:

FLADDER: Knowledge is a suite of rooms. Dirty rooms, unswept as museums in the provinces. And to enter each room you must leave with the woman at the door some priceless thing, which feels part of yourself and your identity, so that it feels like ripping skin. And the keepers sit in piles of discarded treasures, like the pelts of love or children's pity, and at each successive door the piles are less because few stagger such a distance, until there comes a door at which there lies a small, white rag stained as a dishcloth which may be Sanity AND IF YOU THINK THAT IS THE END YOU ARE MISTAKEN IT IS THE BEGINNING.
(Pause)
And people say, 'I know myself'. Have you heard that? Never! They know the contents of one room.

Savage knows, like Livia in *Women Beware Women*, that a thing is vile — or beautiful — not in itself, but only in relation to its usage. He finds his comment 'All my life I have searched out Helen of Troy. And if you stuck a bin of offal there and called it Helen' literalised — he is chained to a dustbin scarcely the words are out of his mouth.

Helen's daughter Gay is another character who wills her self-creation, determined to enact the carefree airiness of her name in defiance of the atrocities she has witnessed during the war, which thereby give a pitiful substance to her childlike mixture of offhandedness and intentness ('I have seen the lot, I can assure you, and I thought to myself, Gay, they want you to go INSANE. So I decided then and there I would not. I DECLINED TO BE INSANE'). As Hogbin skittishly exults in his own liberty and nestles up to Creusa, Savage gnaws the terms of his self-appointed mission as substitute for warmth ('I know what Helen is . . . I trawl, I dig, I excavate! Under your half-truths!'). But Fladder requires his services as magistrate, having resolved to carry his personal guilt to its logical extreme of self-persecution; Savage takes to his role with inspired improvisation, secretly wondering at the licence of his position: 'If every man is ashamed, and you are not ashamed. If every man is guilty, and you refuse guilt . . . WHAT THEN!' Shade provides the answer, in thinking Savage 'a god'. Savage's refusal of guilt characteristically extends to losing his child and helping his father die: again, Creusa experiences an impulse of erotic pity, mindful of the cost of his clarity, 'Hold my hand, you terrible mouth, biting the concrete, your gums all shredded and your lips all torn . . . terrible mouth', reassuring Hogbin 'these are old bruises we have to bruise again'.

Fladder decrees 'In Paper Troy the only crimes are crimes against the self', and in his exhibitionistic drive to 'Vomit the self', delivers himself for punishment, which Shade devises: 'The worst thing that can 'appen to a compulsive apologist I think, is to lose his tongue'. Shade installs Creusa as queen and founds Laughing Troy, based on populist unison and celebration of banality, a forbidding of introspection.

On a beach, Savage encounters his own god, the lecherous but otherwise unmoved Homer, from whom he begs knowledge, like Scrope before Milton in *Victory*. But both Gay and Hogbin are unimpressed by the poet, and Hogbin's sceptical anatomising of man using the contents of the bin of offal is interrupted by Helen's playful propositioning. The infantile vengeance and anti-intellectualism of Shade's regime is demonstrated in his abasement of Homer ('I think with vast and bloated genius, to stoop is healthy'). Savage fuels Shade's propaganda (suggesting the centrality of the words 'US and MUST. The unity. The necessity. The twin pillars of history'), and even performs the dismissal of Homer, striking attitudes in service of survival like Bradshaw in *Victory*. Creusa offers herself to Hogbin with a self-explication of painful infatuation, moving and pathetic in its explicitness compared to his non-committal monosyllables 'Cold today', which she picks up and fetishistically spins out with the whirling, fractured consciousness and self-abandon inherent in desire (compare Stucley with Ann in *The Castle*, Scene One, fearfully imagining the words which his torrent of explication might permit, if dropped): eventually she runs out of verbal defences and cracks before the realisation 'Oh, God, you have met someone else' which she can no longer fend off from recognition. This mobilisation of defensive, vulnerable, exhaustive self-explication against awful, implacable, secretive silence displays a terrible but compulsive depth of self-deception redolent of wrapping a bullet in paper to diminish its power to hurt. Creusa becomes profoundly pitiful in the inevitable failure of her necessary bids for the avoidance — which she knows to be doomed and illusory — of his separateness. His ominously sparse utterances posit a fissure in her would-be exhaustive definition of possibility. The fissure yawns open, pain floods in.

Shade's programmatic definition of Laughing Troy strives to furnish an inclusive ideology which, like others, depends on a measure of exclusiveness ('What isn't written can't exist'). His narcissistic account of possibility is appropriately accompanied by the ex-soldiers' joint speech to a mirror, as they seek to read qualities out of Shade's face as part of his reinforcement of self-justification: 'They bay, but I think they want me to be cruel. I think even the beaten man wants to be beaten'; Savage recognises an element, if not a mandate, of acquiescence in subordination, 'The governor is the nightmare of the populace', hence his authority. Like the Boy, Shade has assumed aspects of Savage's terminology, dismissing his former fellows as 'molluscs' — but more selectively and deliberately than the still-vulnerable child: Shade takes up only what justifies or serves his own ends.

Savage, in turn, seeks knowledge through Shade, like Livia using Sordido in *Women Beware Women* for her own enlightenment at personally diminished risk: Savage is content to remain the dictator who never was, by deliberate choice, and awareness of self: 'I DON'T BELIEVE! I CAN'T BELIEVE! I WANT BELIEF BUT EVERY TRUTH CONTAINS ITS OPPOSITE!'. Savage feels this capacity for perceiving contradiction excludes him from the stable and systematic (as if these were qualities of truth), making only ironic relationships possible. The expiry of his passion for Creusa militates against his own wish for the eternal nature of truth, which is thwarted by his knowledge that 'all hatred is sandwiched in dead desires'. Shade picks up a phrase dropped by MacLuby, whose brief reappearance recalls Faust's Bad Angel even as he reminds Savage that he is weaving hatred into the constitution of Laughing Troy (as Krak ensured the Castle would be a 'magnet of extermination'); but the explication of the phrase 'The pruning of Helen' falls to Savage who, like Macbeth and Stucley, is horrified and fascinated by the tendency for his worst imaginings to be instituted, vindicated or even surpassed: but rather than act to warn Helen, he peers into Shade's mirror for 'Knowledge', misinterpreting MacLuby's gnomic assertion that 'Knowledge lies within' by staring at surfaces.

Hogbin's attempts to save Helen are hindered by the simplistic solidarity of jubilant conga dancers celebrating their own intoxication: even Hogbin realises its lure ('alf of me says "dance Kevin! The beat!" An' 'arf says "put wax in yer ears! Tie down yer feet!"'). Homer stands fixed, believing 'The first duty of the poet is to survive', but in singing his Heroic Life of the Citizens of Sacked Cities Or The Ruinad ('You ask me to believe/In the mercy of the gods/I say their mercy is only/A refreshment to their malice') it is possible that he distracts Hogbin from his search and enables his fatalistic prophecy to be fulfilled. Helen enters with her arms amputated,[5] occasioning a brilliant moment of savage comedy:

GAY: Has anybody got the doctor?
HELEN: It was a doctor did it.

Homer astutely and unsentimentally defuses her request for death: 'You don't mean that ... why ask? There are cliffs. And ponds. Mine shafts. Railway tracks, and dynamos — Hogbin seizes the power of advantageous pity, which ensures the indispensability of the donor's influence, by offering to fulfil the functions of her missing arms. Her loss of motor functions lends her the power of archetypal erotic icon, so that she becomes, not only a construction of Homer's imagination, but also something of a construction and flattery of Savage's imagination, Hogbin's imagination, and male imagination in general.

In the First Interlude, Gay, in a different historical plane, orders the execution of two cartographers, Yorakim and Asafir, with all the implacability of Venables in *Pity in History*, an illustration of the capacity for cruelty springing from her sense of unlived life, preventing her sentimentalisation — especially in her mercilessness toward the more likable, comic, laconic Asafir, whom she sends to death with the momentary delay of a kiss, wringing every nuance of satisfaction from revenging herself upon the unresourceful innocent. MacLuby's Second Prologue takes up the theme of the fragility and redundancy of appeals to mitigation before the cynicism of ensuing generations, and notes how even those who commit atrocities may sense a short-changing in the transaction, 'with the draining out of this joyful/Malevolence [they] experience depression such as the/Act of an unequal love induces'; for, as Savage has perceived, 'all hatred is sandwiched in dead desires', and yet falls fatally and painfully short of reviving and fulfilling them.

Act Two opens with Savage relishing shameless corruption, 'SUPREMELY VILE', accepting himself in depravity, 'I no longer sit on the edge of the chair, my arse spreads and occupies', and freed from his bin. But Helen and Hogbin can still expose a fissure in the terms of his peace: as Hogbin slyly puts it, 'Pity makes your cock big, but pity's only power', inviting the imaginative formulation of sex and power's shortfallings. Hogbin's pantomiming actions as Helen's arms infuse atrocity with irresistible comedy, undermining Savage's profession of desire; but he persists, exposing his painful severance from erotic ideality, 'WORSE THAN AMPUTATION WHAT I HAVE ... IT HURTS TO LOOK AT YOU, I would chuck reason in the ditch and bury it for one moment of your sad mouth against my sad mouth'. Helen finds 'Nothing new' in his description of the universal poignance, and maintains her allure lies in her status as 'SPEC-TACLE OF PAIN'; Creusa adds a comic coda to this on discovering Hogbin enacting an embrace of Savage from behind Helen, exploding 'I'LL THRUST MY ARMS IN A REAPING MACHINE, WILL THAT MAKE ME POPULAR?' It is a characteristic black irony of the play that her frustration ushers in her personal apotheosis of power, which nevertheless fails to achieve alleviation. Creusa decrees a matriarchy, Mum's Troy, and Epsom and Gummery debilitate Shade; accordingly, Savage asks Shade with pointed redundancy 'I must betray you, do you mind? . . . Because only the traitor comes near knowledge. I am a traitor by instinct, because to doubt is treason, and I doubt commitment even as I utter it'. He survives, chameleonically unfathomable and undetermined by anyone or anything but himself. But this is only power.

Gay foresees that the regime of 'LOVING MOTHERS' breeds a destructively infantile sense of the priority of personal appetite, as surely as aristocracy and democracy licensed slaughter in their turn. Recalling Hladder's parable of the suite of rooms, Savage wonders if he is mad or has discovered truth is madness, unaware that he has many more rooms to negotiate. His proudly expert self-definition admits to a nagging cavity which mocks its achievements:

> Because I was an intellectual I chose to follow thought, thought to the finish, that is the duty of one, isn't it? The finger of thought beckoned me past the frontier post where others who had been my equals stood or waved me through, YES, YOU STAY BEHIND AND COURT YOUR ADMIRERS, oh, the teachers with their followings, the gifted with their cliques, they

carve their names in wet cement to the sound of the acolyte's gig-
gles, DANCE ON THE SKIN OF KNOWLEDGE but don't fall
through, you'll drop forever.

(Pause)

It's lonely here. HELEN!

(Pause)

It howls here and no cunning girls of seventeen think I am fascinating, no youths can be seduced in my dim study or learn
the trivial habits of depravity over set texts, KNICKERS AND
KAFKA, MINGE AND THE GREEKS! HELEN, IT'S LONELY
HERE!

Helen appears and quizzes Savage, her 'shapeless adorer', as to
what shape she might be forced into or out of in order to sustain
or amplify his fixation: 'would you hack my legs off also? Legless,
would you desire me more?' She wonders as to the extent to which
others might seek to make her shape reflect or express their own
essential existential nausea: 'What joint or knuckle, what pared-
down shredded section would be the point at which your love
would say stop, ESSENTIAL HELEN? Slithering over rocks, some
slivver of cheek or gum, there! Saw her! Flap of appendix in the
rock pool!' But she is also attracted and repulsed by Savage, urging (and foreshadowing Katrin with Starhemberg in *The Europeans*)
'Don't come near me. I want you more the greater the space between
us, it conducts my heat'. She survives shamelessly, although con-
strued as a living insult to Mum's Troy, which even lures Gay into
complicity as she arraigns Hogbin and his professed lack of will or
desire, 'Look, pregnant women get three ration books. That's will.
I got my legs open. That's desire. Now do it'. Childbearing holds
sway as a prescribed consumerist apotheosis: Gay complains of
Hogbin's reluctance, 'The happiness I'm entitled to, you are frus-
trating it'.

Creusa upholds innocence over reason in Mum's Troy, where
a baby is 'not a baby' but defined as 'an adult in a state of moral
excitement' and consequently the adult's authoritatively pure
superior under 'the liberating coercion of pre-articulacy'. In killing
her child, Helen is accused of betraying 'the sacred trust of motherhood' and stifling innocence, but she insists the child was guilty
of 'Aborting love' by its birth: 'It would have been a killer, too, of
the love I suffer for its father. It would have seduced me from my
man. You know the appetite of babies'. This statement is a cardinal

sin amid the babies' tribunal of Mum's Troy, a one-party state where the masses are interpreted. She is led away for her anticipation of further dismemberment to be realised, and Savage checks Hogbin's horrified attempts to deny her pain (foreshadowing Starhemberg with Katrin in the marketplace scene of *The Europeans*): 'You want to save her. But she can't be saved. Nor does she want it . . . I KNOW WHAT HELEN IS . . . What do you think she wants? A rose garden? A pond of frogs?' Knowing that he can and does 'know too much', Savage hopes to fashion himself back into relative innocence and calls 'Give us an old self, MacLuby'; but history will not reverse, and recurrent details only mock their altered context: Savage's son appears, having forgotten him, and Savage lapses into his reflexive scream to, and initially described by, Creusa.

Helen, now legless as well as armless, remains unashamed, refining her self even as her body is curtailed: 'THE MORE THEY INJURE ME THE MORE THEY HATE . . . They want to pity me, it is their only hope, but I am not pitiful, am I? I cannot think why they neglect my face, it is the obvious starting point, but perhaps they want to see me weep? . . . I WON'T SATISFY THEM'. Hogbin feels his senses turned by the weight of experience, claims 'I am losing my mind', but Helen insists on the capacity to move beyond conventional definitions rather than be limited by them: 'Which mind? . . . Do you think you lose your mind? You find others. Do you think you lose your sight? You see by other channels. And the legless also manoeuvre! . . . You want your mind, but why? To spare yourself the pain of knowing?' Helen's power of refusing satisfaction is demonstrated by her unperturbed agreement with Creusa's intended condemnations of her, which only infuriates Creusa and further unsettles her own security of self: like Dawkins in *Heroes of Labour*, Helen accepts the terminology but not the values of her society, and thereby disturbs its equilibrium by exposing flaws in its capacity for definition.

Hogbin also becomes the subject of wrath for his part in creating a flaw in Mum's Troy: Gay's child is born without arms. To protect himself from the charge of 'genetic criminal', Hogbin offers a counter-definition of himself, 'I am the Accountant and therefore the dispenser of all life and death, all marriage, surgery and literacy 'ang off my calculation', and blames Helen's continued existence for any variety of existential pathos Troy's denizens may experience: he convinces Epsom and Gummery of her culpability, but to his horror they trust her punishment to his paraded capability. However,

Hogbin petrifies and expires rather than practises cruelty, unlike Savage, who continues by it: Savage claims Hogbin refutes the argument, not by counter-argument on its own terms, but by ignoring them in favour of his own separate terms, which call a halt to his experience; 'he wanted . . . not knowledge but MORALITY, which I don't teach'. Savage, like Homer, contrastingly believes survival is the first duty to oneself: 'I thought he'd learned a trick or two, but no, he's dead'. Though Hogbin has imposed his own limit on himself, Gummery sanctifies his memory and extends and projects it into the messianic figure of Hyacinth, come to lift all from their secret cess into fragrant grace. Gay dismisses Helen's knowledge as transgression unsupported by order, hence her exposure to violence; Savage has hitherto managed to scramble into a niche just inside, but not too central to, the forces of order, but in Clean Troy, a regime of essences where even Savage's son might boil his father to make soap, he senses his vulnerability.

In a second Interlude set in 1900, the German archaeologist Schliemann seeks the seeds of European culture on the site of Helen's bed in Troy. His labourers (the Mohammedans Asafir and Yorakim, re-activated from the First Prologue) discover an armless baby. Schliemann is disgusted by its imperfection, trains his thoughts on the day 'the birth of monsters will be an impossibility, such will be the spirit of science . . . and all pain abolished'. Schliemann's qualities of civilisation make him shrink from either adopting or killing the child. Asafir has no such qualms and dispatches it with a sickle: Schliemann exclaims 'THERE WOULD BE NO KNOWLEDGE IF PITY GOVERNED, WOULD THERE, ASAFIR, YOU KNOW', and pays him off with a tip. MacLuby's Third Prologue takes up the theme of navigation by ruthlessness rather than shrinking from pain: 'REFUSE TO BE WRECKED/I do . . . I say/This is just another death I am singularly/unimpressed I look you in the eye whilst not/reducing one iota my walking pace'. The 'weak brains' and 'frail imaginations' pop under the pressure and 'THE GROWING STRAIN OF CONTRADICTION' of revolutionary situations, where the youth are to the fore; MacLuby seeks a laugh, not of solidarity, relief or integration; but rather, a laugh containing the absolute in horror but also the defiant self-determination of one who wills to continue (like McGroot in *The Power of the Dog*, insisting 'Ye gotta laugh, ye gotta laugh'); a laugh which mocks previous limitations of endurance and propriety: a recognition of surprising victory and self-overcoming:

Let us batter out a modern laugh
A laugh for the era
Not a boring howl
But something growing from the bowel
HA
It's only the madwoman skating
Exquisitely skating on the suicide's gore

Act Three opens with Helen and Savage imprisoned in Clean Troy, forced to wash incessantly in service of the dominant puritan horror of the body, using soap derived from, or at least named after, the mythicised Hogbin, transmogrified into 'Hyacinth'. The regime further demands that Savage remarry Creusa and perform a sexual consummation, in public, on a bed of twigs. This ordeal is designed to focus a number of allied prescriptions, such as the abolition of desire, the restoration of family, conjugality and fidelity as the answer to crisis, in a celebratory reassertion of traditional familial and sexual values. Savage is appalled and admits to being exhausted by 'THE PLUNGING LIFT OF THIS INFATUATION' with Helen, desecrated muse of pain and knowledge, but she characteristically urges 'NOT RENUNCIATION, PLEASE'. Savage tries to convince himself 'I think . . . you are a barrier to knowledge now, where once you were the absolute condition', but Helen perceives and mocks his flagging spirits 'What are you learning? That you hate me . . . and could punch the sight out of my eyes . . . The feeling out my lips'. Gay imputes Clean Troy's politics of shame to the experiences of dumb Fladder, though he mutely refutes all she says; Gay begins to perceive the reason for Helen's power and command of undying love, 'Is it because she's unashamed?' Gay tetchily attempts to remain gay through studied ignorance and extirpation of curiosity, defensively denying the lurking possibility of alternative life: 'I AM TIRED OF THIS IDEA THERE'S SOMETHING ELSE. IT'S USED TO BULLY ME, TO HIT ME ON THE BROW AND BRAIN . . . There's nothing else!' However, she later finds herself with Savage, admitting to a hairline fracture in her certainty, which widens into the abandonment of risk:

> *(She stares at him, then with a gesture of profound despair)*
> GAY: Look, I don't know if this is desire or not . . .
> *(She kneels, despondently)*
> I don't know if it is, or not . . .

(A chasm of silence)

But Savage is incapable of reaching out to her, or unwilling to do so. He is forced to submit to the 'affirmation' of the public consummation with Creusa, thus demonstrating what Gay holds to be 'the utter CIRCULARITY OF LIFE . . . That if you walk defiantly away from a fixed point, the earth's roundness ensures you will return to the same spot, no matter how terrible the journey! THE LOOP OF KNOWLEDGE!' MacLuby laughs demonically at the spectacle of Savage's discomfiting range of experience, and its perverse definition and absorption.

The Boy expounds to Helen his ideology and profession grounded on soap, and admits that it is in the interests of his system to incorporate an element of beauty, 'it stirs the blood, and yes, it is a truth of sorts'; Helen refines, 'It's a lie . . . It is simply the best available lie on the subject of truth'. The Boy persists, planning to boil and transmogrify her like Hogbin, into an ingredient of vicarious life (the antithesis of knowledge): 'To give all women, so all women may be, at moments of their choice, Hellenic . . . the lending of transgression to the ashamed, the loan of passion to the guilty, the licensing of total love to the domestic'. She registers horror at this lubricated compartmentalisation of the self; he condemns her as elitist and unforgivable (drawing the insistence from Helen 'I want to be unforgivable! How could I ever forgive myself if I were forgivable?'). The regime attempts a second spectacle, Epsom's murder of Helen: Savage looks on, hypnotised by the prospect of experience and the range of imagination, proclaiming to Epsom 'I AM WHAT YOU ARE ONLY IN YOUR DREAMS', but his pride is punctured by Helen's revival and Epsom's capacity for surprise, in deliberate incompetence ('I take life and I'm criticized, I give life and I'm criticized, CAN'T I PITY SOMETIMES, TOO?'), which Helen momentarily and mistakenly took for lust: unlike Savage, she can laugh at her own vanity.

Savage determines to write a book, in order 'to spread unhappiness' (or perhaps, more charitably, to spread pain as the only antidote to fragrant self-limitation); Hogbin and Gay's armless daughter Charity stands by to receive the oral epic narrative. Gummery and his officers maintain 'WE ALL SAW HELEN DIE' (in unconscious parallel to MacLuby's Act One line 'WE ALL HEARD THE LIBRARY CRASH'). They interrogate an armless and legless Old Woman on suspicion, but discount her as 'far too sensible' in her clowning to be Helen. The aged Creusa experiences contractions, heralding the birth of her 'miraculous' child conceived at the public ordeal; with Savage distracted, Charity articulates the first line of the book, which affirms 'Refusal' as the only way to learn knowledge; and the tongueless Fladder articulates the apocalyptic threat of the people, that Troy will be razed as low as a yard. The Old Woman darkly pronounces 'First Troy was burnt by foreigners. But Last Troy the people burn themselves', as Creusa leaves Savage, loses herself once more, this time taking her child. Gummery's officers outlaw and arrest youths who claim to 'have seen Helen and enjoyed her', implicitly threatening the regime.

Savage identifies the Old Woman, toppled from her trolley in the rush to vacate Troy, as Helen, though she insists on the instability of identity: 'No Helen but what other people made of her. I deny the body exists except within the compass of another's arms'. Gay urges 'Bury my mother now. And then love me'; MacLuby flings Savage a spade and he complies; '(*Finished, he flings down the spade, stumbles to Gay, who opens her arms to him. He slides to his knees. She takes, in a gesture of absolute love, his head in her hands)*'. This might be indicative of Savage's corrupt complicity with Gay and Clean Troy's bid to extinguish Helen's spark, utterly and forever; or else, it might represent her merciful release, and Savage's — in the sense that she is his muse, dream and imaginative construction more than an actual woman (compare Bianca as doll of the state in *Women Beware Women*); in burying her, Savage closes the doors on madness, rising to the challenging offer of Gay's desire and to the innocence, as well as the cruelty, which she represents as the incarnate nightmare of Troy's siege. Tragic retrenchment or romantic relief?

The Bite of the Night incorporates as well as depicts the glories and horrors of the search for knowledge, in an extreme refinement of Barker's tendency to stretch his material beyond the hitherto-deemed unbearable: it is an immense, exhausting and exhaustive challenge to an audience's physical and mental capabilities, implicitly asking them, like Helen with Hogbin, 'You want your mind, but why? To spare yourself the pain of knowing?' Act One Scene Two's explosive exposition bursts all forms of containment and comprehension — familial, sexual, national, intellectual, historical — and the play sustains this motion and consolidates it with relentless exploration of the characters' selves in their astonishing extent of configurations and experiences, hunting down essence and battering out a modern laugh in its breakthrough to the will to continue, the theme developed in *Gary Upright*.

THE EUROPEANS — CRACKED STATUES
I speak as your adviser in whose pain you may see real beauty
Act 2 scene 6

In the Second Interlude of *The Bite of the Night*, Schliemann reflects on how 'The Asiatics took Helen into Asia. The Europeans took Helen back again. At that very moment they became a culture! . . . And the Asiatics came again. To the very wall of Vienna. Were they seeking to take Helen back again?' He also looks forward to a time when pain and physical imperfection will be things of the past, and shrinks from Asafir's casual murder.

This is probably Barker's starting point for *The Europeans: Struggles to Love* (written 1987), in which the figure of Katrin forms another desecrated icon of pain and knowledge and takes up self-performing qualities similar to Skinner, Helen and Gay. As *The Bite* stresses discovery of self, *The Europeans* focuses on invention of self as an existential process. The play opens with the Turks, having besieged Vienna, being driven out by the Poles. Starhemberg, Imperial General and defender of the city, welcomes the return of the Habsburg Emperor of Austria, Leopold, who performs instability like Charles in *Victory* and Genshu Hanayagi, in whose eyes 'men learn the world unlocks'. The audience's first sight is that of Leopold's compulsive disruption of conventional response on a plain, following a battle: he exults 'I LAUGH' and glories in the thought of 'Muslim flesh' manuring 'Christian ground', 'This pain which soddens every turf', and crowing over Turkish prisoners 'YOU LOST', nimbly disarming an attendant Painter of his standard presumptions. Leopold greets Starhemberg with characteristic complexity and truthfulness:

I slept in lovely beds while you thrust corpses into breaches of the walls, I do most humbly thank you and of course simultaneously hate you for showing the dignity of character I was not endowed with but how was I to know the Europeans would suddenly unite? It is the first and I daresay the last occasion we have managed so fuck you and thank you!

(They embrace, swiftly, and separate)
Now slaughter this lot.
(He indicates the Turkish prisoners)

Katrin, a Viennese citizen, recounts in a convent how pain was forced on her by Turkish soldiers raping, impregnating and disfigurring her: she presents her recollections of the moment, 'the CASCADE OF IMPRESSIONS', in a speech of fractured consciousness which demonstrates the unsettling power her self-obsession gives her, anticipating and playing against response (like the Exaggerater, Skinner, Helen and Gary), constructing and demolishing idylls and denying humanist reconciliation from outside a sense of community:

Listen, this is madness, this is proof! I dream, I passionately dream, of some pretty valley in the Danube where a Muslim girl is kneeling to the East. She bows to Mecca, she spreads her Turkish things, her Turkish mirror, her Turkish mat, and threads the Transylvanian flowers through her hair when down like wind swoop Christian troopers rancid with the saddle and STAKE HER TO THE GROUND WITH KNIVES, her naked haunches, her perfect breasts they slash into a running sieve of blood, all channels red, all drain of horror, what satisfaction could I have from dreaming only my Turks die? No, revenge must be upon the innocent. Now, am I mad?

Her sense of exclusion from the human endows her with hate and uncontrollability, bursting concepts of integration like 'home' and reversing the assumptions of those around her, like Murgatroyd in *Pity in History*, telling her sister Susannah 'at least you are unhappy, thank God for that, I could like you, given time', hurting her and baiting her with the unanswerable authority of evil insights:

. . . home is the instrument of reconciliation, the means through which all crime is rinsed in streams of sympathy and outrage doused, and blame is swallowed in upholstery, home is the suffocator of all temper, the place where the preposterous becomes the tolerable and hell itself is stacked on shelves, I wish to hold on to my agony, it's all I have.

But when Orphuls, a priest, remarks on her boiling and fuming, Susannah adds 'She always did. Her ordeal has made no difference.

And of course I hate her, too'. She offers herself to Orphuls in the hope of a loaf, which Starhemberg puckishly provides, giving Orphuls the prize which Susannah has to win from him.

Leopold describes his restored monarchical method to a mob of courtiers, in a formulation which might serve for description of Barker's own dramatic technique. He topples a chair, perches on the result; they shift uncomfortably, he declaims:

> Sometimes, you will want to laugh. And you will feel, no, I must not laugh. Sometimes you will suffer the embarrassment of one who feels exposed to an obnoxious privacy. You will feel, he should never have shown me that. And sometimes you will experience the terrible nausea that accompanies an idiocy performed by one for whom you felt respect. As if the world had lost its balance. I can only tell you, all these feelings I permit. So laugh when the urge seizes you, and then, be ashamed of the laugh. The Emperor only acts the insecurity of all order. Do you accept the truth of that?
> *(They shift uncomfortably)*
> No one understands! Nihil comprehensa!

His power to surprise and disarm through self-exposure is further demonstrated in his exchange with the Painter:

> LEOPOLD:. . . I speak everything, like one variety of idiot. And you are silent, like the other. Draw me now. I pose.
> *(He kneels on the floor like a dog)*
> I pose. And thus cheat your imagination.
> PAINTER *(TURNING TO A FRESH PAGE)*: How?
> LEOPOLD: Because the artist hopes his portrait shows a secret truth, and I show my secret. Call this He Comes Back to Vienna.

The Painter grapples to comprehension and points out his misgivings: 'I think you want to control everything. Even the way you are seen. I think, by discarding the formality of monarchy, you think you disrupt criticism, and by playing the fool, disarm any who would call you so, and thereby flatter your intelligence. I hope I am not offending you. An act remains an act, however it serves to fend off malice'. However, he fails to grasp that such an efficacious performance does not diminish its effect through its nature, as performance; rather, fending off malice is one of the most useful functions of performance. When the painter glimpses and sketches Leopold's fleeting moment of despair before Starhemberg, Leopold stops him and tears out the page: 'We must have pain, and keep it ... They will clean it all, and make suffering a museum'.

Leopold remains in control of his self-definition by clowning and displacing pain, whereas Katrin flourishes her pain at every turn; Starhemberg is the third self-defining figure, who understands them both and continually eludes external definition, thus making himself fascinating and authoritative, enigmatic in such a way as to be heroic and inspirational for others. As Leopold says, Starhemberg is 'unobtainable' but purposeful, loathing the crowd and thereby capable of 'forcing freedom on them', flawless in his selfishness but burdened with hate, as the Emperor perceives: 'In the bone, is it, this hate, crying from the marrow, night and day? ... Starhemberg, my maker, you are ill'. These observations seem to strike home, as Starhemberg divulges his realisation (like Bradshaw's in *Victory*) that 'The innocent are not innocent', and therefore their conventional definition as such holds no appeal or defence for him — and also that his immaculate self-definition is, in one aching respect, something of a limitation compared to the essential hope of engagement with another: 'I love a woman'. But he is soon back on guard, suggesting his statue should have no face.

The Empress is even more perceptive than Leopold: 'He thinks his boldness will win our admiration. He is very near offence, and thinks we will admire his subtlety ... I think you are a cold and wonderfully imagined man, I mean you imagine yourself, isn't that so?' She realises that his existential talents to be his own example are a necessary form of knowledge at this juncture of history, and should be similarly cultivated by others; indeed, they inspire her to new heights of inventive improvisation: 'You see, I can match all your gestures. No real man is worth the effort, but one who invents, and re-invents himself! He can keep us heated! ... Starhemberg, we must invent the European now, from broken bits. Glue head to womb, and so on. And fasten hair to cracked, mad craniums. And stop being ashamed. Now, go, you excellent actor, do go ... '

Having related her experience for the ecclesiastical records of the period, Katrin goes on to reveal her mutilations to a group of surgeons, but rather than simply be an anatomical freak (like Prodo in *Scenes from an Execution*) she asks for drawings of her condition to be printed and published throughout the Empire and demands a public square in which to give birth to her bastard. Her impulse to destabilising exposure is thus more reminiscent of Galactia, though Katrin performs and develops her own pain rather than paint others'. Meanwhile, Starhemberg gambles on Susannah consenting to a contrasting self-exposure, 'Your succulence, and her aridity', and he glances from the conventional perfection to the atrocious desecration represented by the two women's bodies. Katrin rejects pity, 'You only rub your grief against my flesh, as if it would come off', and maintains her essential wholeness and control: 'None would look me in the eye ... My eyes remain unravished ... like unentered rooms'. The challenging pride and implicit promise of this provides Starhemberg's cue to surprise her out of her poise: 'Let me father your child'; but she ducks out of his slipknot, claiming 'But it won't live!'

Orphuls the priest expounds on crisis as encouragement to regenerative impulses, 'Every morning when we awoke, we felt the possibility of UTTER TRANSFORMATION, rising with the sun'; Starhemberg finds his essential vanity appealing. Sensing the appearance of an apprentice, Orphuls compromises — states then retracts — the feelings of emburdenment represented by ageing parents, which Savage exposed and pushed to their apotheosis. Orphuls's mother tyrannises him with shame by centring her world exclusively on him: 'You love me, that's what kept me whole ... You must do or you wouldn't tolerate me', she tells him, challenging any counter-assertion with oppressive details of dependency and infancy, adding 'Mind all these women' in a jealous guarding of her own control; she is the most extreme development of Barker's restrictive mother figures who mould their sons in debilitating postures of conventional 'ambition' (her genesis lies in Mum in *Cheek* and Mrs Egdon in *Edward — The Final Days*). Accordingly, Orphuls goes part-way towards Susannah but prefers to exist at one fetishistic remove, excited by the preservation of distance between them.

Starhemberg teases some Viennese beggars in a scene which refuses to heroise the underdog proletariat, in performance of the suggestion that 'The innocent are not innocent' and that self-abasement before poverty is another form of fetishism; rather, Starhemberg plays out his resolute control and appeal in a mix of taunt and charm, and exposes the implicit comfort in the stability of separation between rich and poor (predicting the poor will burn the houses of the rich 'again, and again, or how else could the rich feel happy?'), highlighting the way in which populism is efficiently restrictive through the certainty with which it provides self-definitions for all concerned. Starhemberg has the knowledge to elude its lures; as he puts it, he 'suffers clarity', experiences the isolation this knowledge brings, but remains defiantly unashamed and therefore independent. However, he feels compulsion to visit an old woman who may be his stepmother or his mistress, and their invention contrasts with the reassurances of shame which structure Orphuls's relationship with his mother. In an exchange with the Empress, Starhemberg suggests the Turkish habit of disfigurement springs from a fearful recognition of, and attempted extraction from, the victim's power of allure: 'They are afraid to love'; but the Empress recognises the ubiquity of this posture: 'Aren't we?'

In a subsequent meeting in a park, it is Starhemberg's turn to suffer taunts, under Katrin's gaze: 'We meet only in public places. Is that because you follow me? Or do you feel you can be more familiar in a park?' But her control is imperfect, and she lets slip two admissions of pleasure in pain, for all her armour of hate, on which Starhemberg can play: 'Starhemberg, I am frightened of everyone, including you, and I would not be otherwise. I am so alive with fear, I am skinless, I am flayed, and the nerves tremble on the slightest passage of another, like leaves on birches flutter at the poorest breeze'; and when he claims a similar sensitivity, she says 'Good. To fear is to be alive'. He might also derive encouragement from the depth and pitch of feeling (rather than aloof indifference) which she admits he stirs in her ('I would shudder if you touched me and some cry would issue from the very bottom of my gut like after-birth sings in the grate or a green log screams'), for all her baroque assembly of a fictitious ideal male. He attacks her on the similarly fictitious detail of pleasing her mother, which he demolishes, and adds a personal thrust and twist with the second half of his line 'Your mother perished on the same day as you'.

Katrin is incensed by this imputation that her self has been smothered; in retaliation she claims her essential reconstitution by injury, 'HOW DID I PERISH, I WAS MADE', effectively positing herself as a walking abstraction of Injury. However, her imbalance is exposed ('the park fills me with despair') and she spins out an inventive set-piece satirising bovine fecundity in her fellow citizens, before regaining the confidence to taunt Starhemberg in a way that betrays a relish of detail and challenge: 'All right, kiss me, if it helps you, press your thin mouth to my thin mouth, all cracked with wind, we'll bleed together, the blood will mingle and drop off our chins . . .'. With a sense of danger and triumph, she recoils into her inanimate, abstract identity: 'How well am I known now? Is it selling, my print?' Starhemberg is losing, and gambles on self-exposure and vulnerability: 'Help me, or I think we'll die alone'; she stabs with mockery, 'Why not? Why not die alone? How would you die? To the sound of violins and the sobs of infants? With your children clinging to your feet as if your soul could be pulled back through the ceiling?' Thus, this intensely charged scene ends with her drawing the more blood, but provides Starhemberg with details he will later seize and reinvent.

The next scene provides a comic-analytic interlude (with formal but not tonal resemblances to the satirical bankers' scene in *Victory*), in which Leopold seeks to establish an artistic mandate, with characteristic idiosyncrasy: 'I call upon you to elucidate the principles of a new art, because the stir of Europe from its sleep commands a terrible and unrelenting movement of the soul. I have only half an hour'. He dismisses Arst's proposal of 'A People's Art' with 'No. Anybody else?' But Arst persists in his ideological veneration of the people insofar as he is able to articulate their wants on their behalf, drawing out the violent fury of his fellow academicians, and scornfully withering the painter for his vulnerably simple reverence of Carpeta (the fictional Italian master from *Scenes from an Execution*). Hrkaly is the only intellectual who does not shrink from contradiction ('The apparent logic of my position is only the dressing of flagrant incompatibilities'), and is mindful of his probable isolation, hence his distinction:

What I want. And what there will be.
I want an art which will recall pain. The art that will be will be all flourishes and celebration. I want an art that will plummet through the floor of consciousness and free the unborn self. The art that will be will be extravagant and dazzling. I want an art that will shatter the mirror in which we pose. The art that will be will be all mirrors. I want to make a new man and new woman but only from the pieces of the old. The new man and new woman will insist on their utter novelty. I ask a lot. The new art will ask nothing. I am a Hungarian, and we have been ridden over, and ridden over, and ridden over . . .

However, the Empress finds nothing offensive in the thought of the imminently dead 'mouthing sentiments of banal happiness', and the sound of a popular march rises to a crescendo.

Act Two opens on Susannah, maddened by Orphuls's self-restriction to sending her little notes by way of 'half-hearted penetrations', and Katrin's counsel that she should remake herself with knowledge; shrewd politician that she is, Katrin describes this in the terms 'Build your walls!', urging a self fortified against love or change. She anticipates her involvement in 'the criminality of motherhood', in images which recall Creusa's Mum's Troy, of the parental license to selfishness by proxy, through the infant. Susannah finds Katrin insensitive and tells her 'I think you must learn to be hurt', but Katrin is conscious of the dispossession which has been carried out under this prescription, 'Is that what they call — history?'

Starhemberg skulks through alleys filled with the crowd's self-reassuring fearful laughter, anticipating the public birth of Katrin's child; he conjectures that 'pain's divisible, there's pain for something and pain for nothing, so birth's tolerable and torture's sheer disintegration', but remains restless, 'Every bastard I meet furred and flannelled has a better reason for existing than I do'. He is gnawed to thinness while Orphuls swells on his ecstatic sexual deprivation and growing religious authority. Starhemberg strikes clownish attitudes, which Orphuls deems unbecoming in context of his public associations ('STOP IT, YOU ARE STARHEMBERG!'); even Leopold senses the danger to stability, urging the renegade general 'Make your moods into policies, what else is government?' Leopold worships Katrin as an icon, 'Oh, to be as unashamed as she is . . . she has no secrets . . . neither in her body nor her soul', but Starhemberg insists 'Of course she has', denying her monolithic immaculateness.

The state is here pushing towards total incorporation in the guise of total humanism (where no 'sick' person can be permitted to die, no child, even the bastard of rapes, can be excluded from the patriarchy). Starhemberg perceives the falseness of Leopold's humanism, and forms an agonised alliance with Katrin in her heroic project — he defends her right to give birth unaided and possibly die in the process, in an aesthetic rebellion of intense sensitivity to the freedom of the woman he adores. This embarrasses Leopold as monarch if not as man and drives him to attempt further assimilation: 'Starhemberg, I offer you a choice. Either join the government or go to jail'. But Starhemberg remains both passionately uncomfortable ('I do not pretend a single thing, and this, I assure you, is no luxury. The pretence is, oddly, easier') and conscious of his potential power:

Christ also suffered the intensest hate or he could never have found charity, do you think he was simply good? Never. The simply good have no purchase on the memory, who would follow the innocent? No, you follow him who triumphs over himself, who boils within and in whose eyes all struggle rages, him you follow to the water's edge, and no other!

Despite her revolutionary, defiant and positive attempt to resist historicisation by insisting on her status as political victim, Katrin finds she has nevertheless been assimilated — 'HISTORY THEY MADE OF ME' — but Starhemberg promises 'revenge'; his dangerous shamelessness and capacity for improvisation are subsequently demonstrated by his treatment of an abusive midwife, licking blood from her hand and ordering her to be hanged as a witch, in reversal of the fate to which she referred him; and he subsequently duplicates this freeze into lethal resolve with Orphuls, suggesting that after burying Starhemberg's deceased mother, they might kill Orphuls's (a suggestion which has the same deep look and implanted vision effect as Sordido envisioning Bianca's fate for Leantio in *Women Beware Women*).

Katrin becomes the focus of numerous admirers, including Hrkaly, who explains 'I think by acting as you do, you make many hate you, but some of these see through their hatred, and find that it is love'. She treats her daughter Concilia with a studied lack of kindness, hoping to make her 'an original woman with the keenness of a starved wolf'; as godchild of the Emperor 'They have made her a symbol. That is how I treat her'. Katrin denies effort in this:

KATRIN: . . . I was made, as we all are, brick arches on which the state may rest. And I unbrick myself. I shake. I inch the mortar out between my cracks, down come the dressings, down comes the quoin, I am a heap of fallen bricks, and then -
(*Pause*)
But I'm not there yet. Rebuilding in a different shape — that's another matter . . .
STARHEMBERG: Walls?
KATRIN: Walls, naturally. All shapes are walls.

Though Stucley and Krak (before meeting Ann) would agree with her, Starhemberg knows differently, and is capable of forcing the unexpected which is comic at Katrin's expense: invited to kiss her hands ('the palm, which is sticky, not the arid back') he goes a step further: she explodes in fleeting but significant disarray, 'HE LICKED ME!', tricked into revealing she is still capable of surprise. Then Concilia interrupts their stalking one another round the room, and Starhemberg explains 'Your mother is insane, and so am I!', instructing the child to recognise the baits of authority: 'Do you hate the grown-up world? It is a paradise for the sentimental, they always win the day! But the truth-tellers, OUT WITH THEIR EYES! . . . First lesson. Never trust the man who gushes over you. He is the torturer'. Such initially apparent paradoxes are characteristic of the figures in *The Europeans* who possess knowledge, which is, as Savage recognised, beyond kindness.

Orphuls has taken his own step in this direction and killed his mother, experiencing a sense of rebirth: the Empress's existential instinct surpasses her taste in music and decor — she tells him 'preach. What you have learned. Not murder, but what came of it', and recognises goodness in a Labourer's unsentimental sympathy. As knowledge is beyond kindness, Susannah perceives that love has obligations beyond pity (though pity may initially kindle desire) in demanding — indeed, forcing — the breaching of barriers, and that she is capable of this in relation to Starhemberg, and that he is capable of it but not in relation to her. Her self-exposure before, and adoration of, Starhemberg, is however an experience complete in itself, for her, in terms of her self-overcoming; she tells him 'I think whatever you may be, I need not know it'. They create a novel definition of the act of love, which is not predicated in familiarity, but in rigorous denial. Starhemberg further demonstrates his capacity for inculcating self-exposure and self-overcoming in making an Officer invent a dream-like tale of pain which involves Freudian tension, pressures of individuation and final defiant self-liberation from authority.

Feverishly loquacious and rawly instinctive because of an infection, Starhemberg receives a Turkish commander, Jemal, in the Habsburg fort in Wallachia, and quizzes his hostage emissary on the topic of mutilation, previously broached with the Empress: 'this slow hacking has not even the decent motive of the butcher, this blinding and dismemberment, does it have a philosophical interpretation, I have yet to explore the religion of your lot'. Jemal stands on his honour and formally refutes imputation with systemisation of 'the occasional atrocity with which all armies are inevitably smeared'; Starhemberg opines once more, 'I think it is to do with fear of love, which is greater than the fear of death', and achieves personal breakthrough to Jemal through exposing the Turk's private enthusiasm for playing the organ, then swings back into a digression on frozen resolve: 'In the very moment of the coolest torture, I believe the perpetrator suffocates the possibility of freedom in himself. And thus it becomes habitual, a narcotic. Do you not find the cruellest acts are done without real hatred? . . . No, the essence of horror must be its casualness, which I have only slowly come to understand'.

Thus he prefaces his donation of the reluctant Concilia to Jemal, who cannot refuse on pain of death. Starhemberg is conscious of her grief, and of his addition to the pitiful and repetitive carnage of Europe, 'the great chaos of this continent, the beating of lives in the bowl of quarrels, the batter of perpetual and necessary horror'. But his act of aesthetic cruelty seeks to rupture History — which by Barkerian definition constitutes the rationalisation of pain in ideological forms. While Katrin may have feminist reasons for treating Concilia like a symbol in order to make her 'an original woman with the keenness of a starved wolf', this is contained by — and is here supportive of — the false humanism of Leopold's state. Starhemberg seeks the demolition of Concilia's symbolic role within the state pageant, and thereby of Katrin's symbolic role: 'How do you escape from History? You reproduce its mayhem in your life'. There are analogues with Sordido's project in *Women Beware Women* in terms of the hijacking and disruption of political symbolism. Starhemberg insists 'Catastrophe is only —' and Concilia breaks down, unable to supply the word of completion, 'birth'.

Leopold walks, like Henry V, in civilian disguise among common soldiers, who arraign him for refusing to participate in ordained celebration and laughter for a recent victory, with which the Viennese park is otherwise awash. Leopold answers with a laugh of terrible despair, and asks 'What good is goodness?', ironically conscious of the futility and harm of sealing up perforations in order at so many junctures of history; the Empress dismisses this as a mood, excited by the thought of her own monumentalisation, 'I think we think our underwear should lie in the museum, and our shopping lists go into print'. Hrkaly correspondingly reflects on fireworks as a trivialising mimicry of battle conditions, 'suffering as exhilaration', but shrinks from Starhemberg's appearance in outraged humanist horror. Taking Leopold's announcement 'NO MOMENT OF UNITY IS EVER TRUE' as his cue, Starhemberg steps out of darkness to perforate the roar and laughter of the crowd with disruptive horror, revealing to Katrin his restoration of Concilia to the Turks, challenging Katrin's assertion 'you make a thing out of me, you hack me out of horror like a mason carves a mask from stone, I CAN BE WORSE YET AND NOT SPLIT', pushing her to her boundaries of definition.

Like the Duke's intrigue in the final scene of *Measure for Measure*, Starhemberg's execution of his plan has an aesthetic formality and an experimental gamble that the people he guiltlessly stage-manages will respond as he hopes. Katrin maintains her individuality and control, formulating the process with an effort of concentration: 'You . . . made — restitution of their — property — for which — I merely was — curator?', and adds with relief of tragic achievement 'How well I can express my suffering, as if expression took the teeth from it' (compare Edgar's crucial lines in the tragedy of *King Lear*, 'The worst is not/So long as we can say "This is the worst" '). As Katrin acknowledges, the expression of her pain

> also is habitual, and there's the actual tragedy, not in pain, but the unflinching tolerance of it, did you expect I'd kill you, thrust some woman's blade into your eye, or poison you at breakfast? No, no melodrama, me. All woven in. All swallowed, and digested, look.
> *(She stares at him, in a state of utter stillness)*
> Now, that was a splendid –
> *(A burst of firework drifts down the sky)*

Starhemberg acknowledges his speculative risk in their duel of control and abandon, 'I think if only you would tremble, then so would I', but she defines herself in opposition to him, 'Never. It would wash away every arch on which my sanity is built . . . you the river . . . me the bridge'. In a bid to unbrick her walls, awaken her capacity for surprise (as when he licked her hands), he realises her previous invitation in the park setting ('press your thin mouth to my thin mouth, all cracked with wind, we'll bleed together, the blood will mingle and drop off our chins'):

STARHEMBERG: I have restored you to your pain . . .
> *(He kisses her)*

LEOPOLD: CON — CIL — IA!
  (Burst of lights)
CON — CIL IA!
  (They trickle down the sky)

This call for the absent symbol of reconciliation completes another of Barker's most complex and memorable stage tableaux, where the self-styled agent of disruptive knowledge physically merges with the self-styled figure of tragic injury, both supremely conscious of their simultaneous self-definitions and flaws of pain. They stand alone together as two revolutionary renegade figures who refuse annexation by the museum of the state, which acts as repository of experience and the political requisition of private pain: instead the keynotes of the play's conclusion are mayhem, breakthrough, refusal of reconciliation and the demonstration of the insecurity and instability of all order.

The Bite of the Night and *The Europeans* develop Barker's interest in creating characters who lecture, expound and digress, who risk truths and profound insights to which the audience is impelled to listen. A character talks imaginatively, makes words his or her own, and this activity is legitimised dramatically by a pupil or acolyte figure, whose incomprehension relieves the audience of embarrassment: examples are Savage and Hogbin, Helen and the Boy, Starhemberg and the Beggars, Leopold and the courtiers, Katrin and Susannah, but also Downchild and Stoat, Gaukroger and Pool, Toplis and Music, Sordido and the Ward or Leantio. For all the positions of unequal power, both need and want the other as well as resisting them, testifying to Barker's recurrent interest in the dynamics of knowledge being passed on through history. The forceful severances from parents and children which recur as motifs in both *The Bite* and *The Europeans* also develop Barker's interest in themes of mutual influence and also drives to independent, immaculate self-creation, broached earlier in Chapter 3, revisited and re-invented in these two plays in more complex, mythic and psychic terms.

The *Struggles to Love* in *The Europeans* are national and general, in the face of overwhelming evidence that fellow human beings are not lovable, particularly under the European burden of shame in relation to other nations, through its association with colonisation.

By starting from the point at which Europe has partly escaped colonisation by Islam, the play reverses this association to examine the complexities and cruelties involved in a European state of identity, shifting conventional structures of perception to expose certain bindings of people through pain which they are not encouraged to acknowledge — which, in fact, the manipulation of state history, liberal or communist, discourages. This anti-history might represent a strain of knowledge that people are as yet unprepared for, and Barker attempts to challenge these boundaries of self-consciousness, as pain comes to the forefront of people's experience and exposes the instability of post-war pseudo-democratic attempts at integration.

The *Struggles to Love* are also necessarily personal and sexual, as when Starhemberg and Katrin tremble on the edge of a breakthrough in the seized look — the touch — the moment of emotional confusion when perceptions lead to disarray. Proudly self-defined, self-performing and trying to elude being monumentalised into statuesque abstractions by those around them, they nevertheless expose cracks of pain in each other's marbled senses of definition and possibility, and bleed together.

11

Catastrophe is also Birth: Inconclusion

Catastrophe is also birth. Out the ruins crawls the bloody thing, unrecognizable in the ripped rags of former life. Ghastly breaths of unfamiliar air! Like the infant, expelled from the silent womb, screams red its horror, then tastes oxygen. I have to find my life!

Women Beware Women

This book offers a structure for perceiving that perceptual structures are illusory. The offer is an obligation, and a challenge. It asks, do you want? Can you embrace, do you want to be able to embrace that want?

Barker's drama and poetry seek to demonstrate that the dominant conventional social terms of definition of possibilities are neither exhaustive nor complete. His writing works through passionate insistence on the human consequences of power: pain. Pain is articulated in all viewpoints on the political act: in the political victim (Katrin), in the renegade hijacking and disrupting the symbolism of state (Sordido, Starhemberg), in the managers of the symbolism of state (Stucley, Leopold), and in the symbolism of state itself — instances when the symbolism of state is human (Bianca, Concilia) being particularly troubling. The imaginative conviction with which Barker renders these voices is not, however, dependent on or associated with a spirit of liberal humanism, which the work frequently identifies as pernicious.

Whereas Christianity promotes an ethic in the present and promises a good life in the hereafter, and Marxism promotes the value of struggling and suffering today in order to achieve future perfection in material terms, existentialism insists that we are creatures of infinite possibility with an obligation to self to live in the present, as a priority to creating community: this is the position towards which Barker's writing has moved during the period under survey. While the effect of seeing the work is to shock, it also engages the audience, pulling them as a body (and not a minority) into territory which causes worry and conflict, and the subsequent re-examination of ideas about theatre's permit. His work emerges as a liberationist endeavour, post-ideological and to many people passionate and mesmerising. It is not in the conventional sense a heroic theatre, speaking to would-be heroes, but a democratic theatre which refuses the minimal life of licensed feeling.

A key line is Bradshaw's exclamation on her victory, 'I have broken myself into pieces to do this'. Another crucial exchange occurs between Leantio and Livia:

LEANTIO: I hate this life which wrings such changes! (*He weeps on* Livia) Give me the lie of innocence, always the lie —
LIVIA: No, life is alteration, the shedding of all things until at death there's no regret, but all's been spent, discard, discard or petrify!

Barker's characters achieve moments of terrible splendour and beauty when they reject 'the lie of innocence' in pursuit of their own new, raw truths, a process analogous to writing, acting and sexual desire: the compulsive, passionate pursuit of discovering possibilities, imaginative exploration through engagement with alternatives, shattering the cement of habit and convention. Barker's characters can be inspirational in self-overcoming, flaying off the dead cells of the self in endless breakthrough and renewal, despite the often terrible cost; like Downchild, they resolve 'No dignity. No wisdom. Serenity. Or peace. Kick to the finish!' Their experiences of pain and knowledge can inform the 'choices in reaction' of audience members by providing them with tools for analysis of motivation and situation. Audience members may be ready for, and want, change but be unable to reformulate themselves alone, and a production can illuminate their own capacities, the constellation of abilities, opinions and beliefs that constitutes their personalities, and assist realignments in it, articulating and perhaps even habituating want in the self, through the demonstration of alternative life.

In the eponymous poem, Genshu Hanayagi claims:

Forty is the age of truth
And death not being altogether preposterous
An age to choose or to refuse the obligation
Sensibility bestows and art exemplifies

The achievement of Barker's work has been its exemplification of the obligation of choice or refusal for the audience and performers (and, indeed, the directorial and production team. It is worth noting the increasing incidence of challengingly non-specific stage directions in his work, such as '*An effect of rain and time*' in *The Castle*, '*A HIATUS OF PITY*', '*A GESTURE OF PROFOUND DESPAIR*', '*A GESTURE OF ABSOLUTE LOVE*' in *The Bite of the Night*).

This works by throwing their sense of experience into flux, through drama which pushes to the boundaries of the tolerable and explodes them. The relentless refusal of the expected, and the excess of transforming experience is the essence of the dramatic experience, involving the bewilderment of the audience in the face of persistent dislocation. The sense of having witnessed too much is crucial. It leads not to a drunkenness or a reeling exhaustion, but a roaring sense of possibility and a rinsing out of accumulated expectations. Barker's own title for this form of theatre is Catastrophism, and *Victory* marks his breakthrough into it.[1]

The moment of the flux of possibility often occurs in striking tableaux, such as Savage pushing his father into death then embracing Hogbin in *The Bite of the Night* or Starhemberg kissing Katrin at the end of *The Europeans*, where the force of the image glues audience concentration beyond conventional limits of linguistic compulsion (considerable as these are);[2] and in moments when characters such as Ball and Charles, Sordido and Leantio, 'look deeply into' each other, demanding acceptance of other, and of self. Though Barker's characters compulsively voice their feelings, these moments of eye contact testify to a raging conflict of contradictory feeling which defies articulation as its offers the explosion of possibilities, when history can be transformed. Helen's lines in *The Bite of the Night* provide the best formulation of Barkerian eye contact:

> I will tell you what a look was. It was a thing as solid as a girder, down which streamed all the populations of our forbidden life.

R. D. Laing writes thus on overruling the veto against possibility:

> It is impossible, therefore it is not. It is not, because it is impossible. It is, therefore it is possible. If it is, it cannot be impossible.

But. It is: but it is impossible. It is possible, but it cannot be. It is impossible, but it must be. It would be impossible, were it not so . . .

In any event, whatever we make of them, stories of experiences we continue to regard as impossible continue to well up from the very depths of ourselves! *We* are impossible.[3]

It is characteristic that Barker should write ten short plays collectively entitled *The Possibilities* (written 1986) which dramatise supremely that conviction and subsequent action overwhelm logic or rationality. These plays initially invite parallels with Brecht's *Lehrstücke*, or instruction pieces, but this comparison is artfully invited only to be disrupted: *The Possibilities* might more aptly be titled *Zerreissükke*, discord pieces. They may spring from this exchange in *Scenes from an Execution:*

PASTACCIO: Please, argue the point.
GALACTIA: No.
PASTACCIO: Why not?
GALACTIA: Because you'll only win the argument.

Apparently a verbal riposte, this is a crucial affirmation of spirit versus logic and rationalism at the service of ideology. It reappears in many of *The Possibilities*, where the apparent possession of irrefutable 'truth', as conventionally and ideologically defined, is exposed as insufficient reason for acquiescence, under personal terms of definition, on the hinge of the 'But': The Woman in 'She Sees the Argument But' will live sexually even if she is told it is irresponsible to do so; 'The Philosophical Lieutenant and the Three Village Women' suggests the illogicality of resisting superior force, but also the compulsion to do so; 'Only Some Can Take the Strain' demonstrates the obstacles to seeking out knowledge, but also the Young Man's insistence on doing so; 'Kiss My Hands' depicts the illogicality of opening doors to possible agents of catastrophe, but the resilient human impulse to overcome fearful recoil.

Barker's poems *Gary the Thief* and *Gary Upright* (written 1987) develop the theme of the individual foregrounded against the crowd. *Gary the Thief* begins as a monologue of conscious, deliberate, self-proclaiming evil, in which the eponymous figure defines himself in defiance of the community and audience, 'I tread your consciences like a brass heeled/Titan wades a sea of eggs'. He realises Downchild's simulated killing of a baby in purposeful outrage of morality, and fleeting sense of reproof; even arrest does not crack his poise, 'And to the cells he marches dignified as the/Plenipotentiary of powers momentarily overcome'. An undigested shred of unkindness may have 'made Gary the thief' and created a pearl of 'no' at his core (to thieve an image from *The Breath of the Crowd* 2), but Gary disdains 'the damaged character as cause'. Rather, he describes himself as essentially posited in inevitable contrary pressure to society's edicts, 'My defence lies in your opulence':

> I am only
> I am simply
> I am the crow of the city
> Silently descending

An incarnate realisation of the forbidden, his shamelessness strikes others into shame: 'for the absent truth erect/He looked from eye to faltering eye'. In prison, he 'Does not degenerate/Or shred himself in tempers' but holds firm to his own essential terms of definition while performing acquiescence with mischievous virtuosity. He is an opportunist, seizing others' terms of definition; for example, he annexes infantile left-wing rebel chic and ideological distortions which suggest all criminals are heroes. He dodges the Party Theorist and the District Organiser who seek to 'Reclaim' his destructiveness and make him 'Weave out of old hates/A proper class analysis', extracting 'a secret pleasure/From his elegance' and sly, casual instinctiveness; inwardly, he sprays them with his customary contempt, defiantly eluding them with anarchic nimbleness: 'I ride History lightly as a leaf'. However, this is to take Gary at his own valuation of himself; and, like all definition, even his frozen certainty can be cracked, and he experiences a 'plunge of mortal horror'

> Through
>   every
>   net
>   of
>   habit
>   fiction
>   or
>   relief

making his self 'unreflected', 'All brittleness and dispersed possibility' like a blown egg, displacing his talismanic self-identification and leaving him 'Gary the robbed', uncharacteristically desperate for some other to 'fix infinity' on his behalf: an ironic position for the former proud smasher of definition (self-styled). He seeks knowledge by stealing the brain of a dead prisoner and professor which he keeps in a jar, reminiscent both of Gocher severing Tovarish's hand and of Krak, shellshocked and hypnotised by the unfathomability of 'cunt's geometry'. But no answers come quickly to 'Gary the dispossessed', who wonders 'If I do not inspire fear . . . What am I?' He buries the brain and, next morning, awakens into newfound resolution:

I shall go forth and be a prophet
Says Gary Upright

He plans explication of self and others with words to 'press in the wings/And burst like actors flooding a stage', and listening in order to 'mirror the pains/Of a life of opportunity', determining:

I shall reveal

Gary Upright takes up the enactment of his new mission, with the apt announcement:

I come to you without anger or exaggeration
I proffer myself

He becomes a public lecturer, who recurs daily like the women in *The Breath of the Crowd* (6), but rather than 'Narrate the slipping of life', relieved by simple recurrence, or persist 'encumbered', he offers slightly different perceptions and knowledge every day, offering his philosophical wares:

I will teach you how to live and die alone
I will make you this gift free of charge
.   .   .
I have a message of course

Pity the man who has no message
And the woman who refrains

Pity the man who finds no madness
And the woman who refrains

Pity us all whose flesh is not the subject
Of campaigns

He reinvents some of his old thievish defiance, defining himself against his background: 'This incessant fog obscures everything/ Except my voice/My voice it magnifies', teasing his audience:

You think he is not here yet
The spectre of Gary
He must have overslept

No

It is only the fog's bargain with mischief
Its old dalliance with our hidden self
I'm here as ever
If anything more so

This glorious declamation of artful contradiction and self-redefinition acts as prologue to his text, 'Gary chapters 1 to 3' (an insistence on personal right to knowledge comparable to 'Murgatroyd verses 1 to 18' in *Pity in History*). Gary announces:

I narrate disintegration among rulers
And the kindness of the enemy
I report the speed at which fear grips the innovative
And the intolerable loneliness of the habitually free

He invites the audience 'Observe the practices of one who/ Stands before you unashamed', which gives him 'the attributes of a god unnamed/Which you are also', but exposes their lack of want, 'since you won't affirm your deity/Since you will smother/ Since you will obscure the light with your hand'; he exclaims 'I forgave myself so long ago' and exhorts his audience to throw off their encumbrance of shame similarly, 'Forgive yourselves also'. Rather than merely physical exposure, he asks to uncover the very self, 'Allow me rather strip/The public off your pale tenderness', and addresses himself to the first of three clichés of common received 'wisdom' which he proceeds to demolish: *'We came into the world not of our own volition/True or false?'* This takes up the theme broached in *The Europeans* through Concilia, the idea that even the unborn will their creation: Gary describes a plummeting airman, and asks

> Did the two parts of him not plead
> Did the two parts not ache
> Pressing the flesh into service
> Conscripting the separate shapes
> And beating them together like pugged clay

He insists 'I tell you this/Because you need to know', that even among idleness which licenses 'uncontested criminality', 'The smothering of a democracy' and 'Another act of unfelt love', hope persists:

> But equally a disarray might yet be born
> In the time it takes the hand to travel
> From the ash tray to the yawn
>   .   .   .
> I tell the possible
> Which must have effects
> I never doubted it would have effects

Thus Gary continues, 'erect for the absent truth' in a more philosophical sense, and turns to the proposition *'You've only got one life/True or false?'* He tells of a suicide, like the one in *Don't Exaggerate* who realised 'Everything he had been told was false', saw the world and self as unchangeable, and so fixed on his terminal 'No'; Gary's subject also experiences apparently irrevocable decadence: 'Nothing had progressed'; 'Something had substituted itself'; 'Everything had failed to be necessary'; but rather than immolate his self among the 'ambition's wreath' of laughter, he resolves to reinvent his self and thereby redefine others, however minimally, but significantly, rather than throw himself under a train: 'at the moment of decision chose not to lie but jump' into 'The usurpation of a second life', disassembling the former 'arches on which his purpose stood':

> Knew he might be unkinder
> Less loving
> Suffering fewer fools

More leather than sponge
More oak than cork
More slub than lace

And thus, like Genshu Hanayagi, finds self-respect despite the inherent isolation of his position, akin to 'A shepherd in the city/A fishmonger in a landlocked country/An unfathomable grinder of lenses'.

Gary turns to the proposition *'You have to die some time/True or false?'* (recalling the Old Woman in *The Europeans* telling Starhemberg death must find him, because 'it finds everybody else', and his counter-assertion 'That proves nothing'). He tells how, rather than concession to 'the authority of disease' by way of 'escape', a woman prisoner applies herself to the willed ability to 'stop her heart whole minutes/Dying over and over again in solitude':

And learned that death does not choose us
But is ours to choose

Gary himself admits to discomfort, but never exhaustion:

But I am not tired
I am not broken yet

Not yielding to the burster of the little vein
Not yielding yet

Rather it is true we have to live some time

Thus he spurs self and others onward in defiance of almost ubiquitous and institutionalised discouragement:

Not only gravity would pull us low
But the philosopher who lives under the stairs
The servers of fictions
The fixers of elections
The chairmen of factions
The ageing hawkers of perceptions
Keep telling us that we must die

Which I deny
Emphatically deny

Since to accept the power of the obvious
Is only sometimes the mark of the wise

Thus, *Gary Upright* identifies and glorifies the compulsion of instinctive forces to surge and burst through imposed form – but rather than at a social and political level, as in *The Castle*, this compulsion is traced at a personal, individual level, where even the self may be divided to debilitating or fatal effect, smothering the 'light' of possible life. In the face of rational arguments for, and experiences of, exhaustion and extinguishment by overwhelming logical odds, *Gary Upright* provides a passionate demonstration of the incontrovertible resilience of instinctive impulses to generation and regeneration: the 'cry of the blood' which instigates the birth of children, the ability to remake the self in defiance of a whole lifetime's experience up to the point of change, the determination to stare out exhaustion until all imaginable (and therefore infinite) purposes are fulfilled. Gary Upright is the distillation of Barker's characters who display a Faustian or Mephistophelean energy, from the limited conventional point of view, in affirming the possibilities of 'a god unnamed' in every being: beneath the shroud of shame lurks an essential spark of vitality, compulsively resilient if recognised (Barker's conceptual framework is crucially existential rather than nominally Christian like Marlowe's). Barker's 'Lullabies for the Impatient' continue the theme of the importance of not dividing and pitching the self against the self, but allowing the self to breathe and flourish to maximum effect, and thus swelling to resources forever striving to a state of unstoppability, where personal disease and rational argument are overwhelmed. In the final words of 'To the Aberystwyth Students', this collection of poems concludes on a uniquely but necessarily, defiantly positive note:

That must be the purpose of art
That must be art occurring
Its discomfort is considerable
And yet we return

Gary Upright, the most concentrated, direct, stirring and valuable of Barker's dramatic poems to date, stands as testimony to the persistent urge towards redefinition and regeneration in the individual self, identified as the kernel hope from which change might radiate. Barker's writing is explicit evidence of compulsive self-overcoming and persistent imagination, and inevitably many theatrical and critical[4] institutions are fearfully dismissive of the challenges it inherently poses.

But seekers for knowledge, love, or some form of personal truth might learn some things they need to know from Gary Upright's ceaseless listening, speaking, self-redefinition and persistence in the essential hope and instinct and insistence that the world unlocks:

You have gone home
In a rattle of feet
Receding like a flock of starlings
A rising up of a black sheet
At the hand clap of five o'clock

I admit the probability that nothing entered in
But I refined

Imperceptible redefinitions occurred
Which at a later date may seem significant

The rehearsal was a good one I judge

And I will be here tomorrow assuredly
Oh, assuredly

I trust

But sometimes poets lie, as do literary critics . . .

Appendix: Conversations

Penny Downie
Ann in *The Castle* (RSC)
July 1986, Stratford-upon-Avon

PD: We spent days rehearsing the first scene of *The Castle*, looking at the figures of Ann, Cant and Skinner with the question 'do we present the world of the play as it is at this moment — falling apart anyway — or do we present utopian women?' We were very keen to give some sense of the structure of the society and that it hadn't been perfect, that no unisex version of society is, by definition. We never see the 'womanly times' Skinner talks of. I think Howard believes deeply in the effect of women on men, and women on society, that the fact is that women and men make a society, but that in no way is it whole or complete if unbalanced. For example, as soon as the men come back: the society worked because the men weren't there: the first thing Skinner says is 'Stab him'. Is that polarisation at that time, of those personalities? Had Skinner never raised a knife to a man in seven years? I actually felt they all revert, inside, to the truth, however raised and heightened over seven years, of who those women are. Cant is immediately struck by her desire for men. Ann is equivocal but I think senses this is the beginning of the end — as soon as she sees Krak, nothing can ever be the same again. I think Ann is a realist, but tries to be an isolationist towards the end. As threats of destruction build up, because of her pregnancy and desire for Krak and arrogance, she says 'We find a rock', we abscond. But she comes to the realisation that finally 'There is nowhere except where you are' — not meant in the romantic sense that there is nowhere except where Krak is, but there is nowhere for the individual but the here and now — 'Thank you for truth'. But she comes to it out of a petrification, becoming rock in herself. You can only say those things out of a complete bitterness with life, which is what I think Skinner passes through, but because Skinner has always lived on the outside of life, first as a witch and later a criminal festooned with the skeleton, therefore her passion

254

is tempered by an objectivity; whereas Ann had the objectivity but not the passion. I don't think Ann is a passionate woman, until she finds Krak, and learns passion. It's as if their two journeys are the antithesis of one another.

DIR: All the characters are very true to their own codes, it strikes me. Stucley's code is an outdated one, that's his downfall. Skinner remains true to her own code, which involves pain. Krak *thought* he was being true to his code, building the Castle, but then he finds out that 'Truth is not stable, any more than passion/Truth will expire, just as quickly as desire' . . .

PD: That's what Ann finds out as well. In her speech to Krak, 'your grey misery excites me', she actually relinquishes her objectivity, the passion takes over, and it's like a descent into hell from which she can never return.

DIR: It has to be, because the first thing she recognises is 'You want us all dead'; she says 'Success appals me, but pain I love', suffering attracts. Presumably that's why she embraces Stucley, even momentarily, when he weeps in the first scene. His boyishness is coming through again, and his boyishness is his charm.

PD: And that's what he partially lost abroad —

DIR: 'I did love boyhood more than anything'.

PD: And Ann kept him there. And in other ways she kept Skinner where Skinner was. Ann contains and controls. But as soon as she actually feels the power of letting go her control, and this enormous passion, she's swimming around with the rest of them, and can't cope. She tries to believe she can contain the disaster, escape to the rock with her baby, which is so arrogant. Skinner is deeply passionate, but survives —

DIR: So does Krak — in some shape. I find Ann the most opaque character in the play — so do Stucley, Skinner and Krak, and find her unpredictability maddening . . .

PD: She can't tell Skinner 'I love you' because she no longer does. I think it's Ann who ruled the kingdom, in effect, during the men's absence.

DIR: Our Skinner, Suzan Holding, surprised me in rehearsal by playing the role more vulnerably than I expected;[1] she said 'It's Ann who is strong and hard, Skinner acknowledges her weakness in being so dependent on Ann'.

PD: I agree. Ann says 'I don't declare my feelings. You can't be forever declaring feelings'. She plays with people — not maliciously. She has control as the one who is always admired, always loved, always equal. She has never *put out* feeling — people come to her. All of a sudden, she is *putting out*, towards Krak, but wanting to control it —

DIR: And be away from the others, on the rock. She wants her little idyll with the baby and Krak — God knows how long that'd last. So — to the knife.

PD: Again part of her arrogance. Suicide, let alone infanticide, is the most selfish of acts, looked at objectively. It is necessarily self-absorbed —

DIR: It proclaims the universe is in one's own shape, which prompts the determination to 'bring it all down' . . . But it's not complete nihilism. It can't be, because it sets off a chain reaction in the other women through its essential thwarted idealism.

PD: That's the contradiction in all of the characters. When Batter says 'Come for a walk', Stucley says 'you are taking me where I don't want to go'. They all contain the contradiction that they see what's going on, but don't or can't prevent it. Ann believes her suicide will do good, she has power and knows it, perhaps more than Skinner, even in death. Except Skinner has always been on the outside looking in, no matter what the relationship is, and she therefore survives. Likewise Krak, who is kept a prisoner but feels he has control of this edifice being built; it's the passion he can't control. Ann tries to control her passion, or the results of it, and sees her suicide as the ultimate control because she believes it will change things. She is one of those people who believes 'If I tell the truth and look after myself, I expect everybody else to do the same thing'. That's frightfully English. She expects everyone to 'behave well'.

DIR: Like Annie Axt. Is this innocence, in a different form to Stucley's?

PD: It depends whether you see it as innocence or arrogance. I don't mean arrogance as a vice, but the ultimate in self-consciousness. She believes the world revolves around her, which it has. She's been at the centre, in control. So what happens without her in the last scene?

DIR: You tell me what you think happens, then I'll tell you what I think —

PD: No, you tell me what you think.

DIR: We're playing with the idea of, instead of Skinner's hands poised over the keys as final image, closing on a fade down to two spots[2] on Skinner and Krak, looking at each other, the two outsiders. And I'm hoping for an echo of the end of *Women Beware Women:* 'New duke? New duchess? Don't love. Don't love . . . ' — posing the question as to what happens next.

PD: What do we hope, at the end of this play, as an audience? Do we want hope? Do we want her to pick up the keys?

DIR: I think the audience at the Pit wanted her to pick up the keys, as the cheers at curtain call suggested when I attended, but I think the production led them into too easy an option. I'm conscious of conclusions of other Barker plays where former opponents end up colluding, outsiders recognising their common marginalisation and suffering.

PD: Yes — because they've both been on a journey, they're entitled to do that, otherwise what hope is there?

DIR: Instead of asking 'Does she or doesn't she pick up the keys?' I want to poise it like the end of *King Lear* — in what sort of configuration will the survivors try to work?

PD: To me, the end is in Krak's line 'Demolition needs a drawing too' and Skinner's reply 'Demolition? What's that?' Because once you've created a nuclear weapon you can't unmake it, that's the dilemma of our — of any — society. Once something is created there's no going back.

DIR: Ideally we need to get by without the Kraks, but unfortunately we can't seem to do so.

PD: If not optimism there's a sense of ongoing humanity — we can't destroy what we've created, we must get by as best we can, hopefully learn. But 'Does anyone remember? There was no government'. As long as there is memory, is that positive? I think Skinner's naïve there.

DIR: Harking back to a 'golden age lost, but yet to come', like the end of Brenton's *The Romans in Britain*?

PD: That's the positive view of it — as long as you can remember a past, there will be a future. Ann doesn't have that love for a future. You can only commit suicide if you do let go of other people's needs. 'I thought this child was different because it came from love. But I thought wrongly.' There are no lessons learnt. That's her, hoping to make one just action in killing her child and herself. But actually at the end, Skinner and Krak are left and, however much they're stumbling in the dark, they have learnt. That's my view of the end. The power of the play is that it presents the audience with image after image, about which they have to decide, to which they have an emotional response

— unlike plays where an author pushes his or her point of view —

DIR: 'Choices in Reaction' —

PD: Exactly! *Victory* is one of my favourite plays. Whereas most plays try to shunt the audience in a particular direction. That's like designer's theatre, which implies that it's complete without the actors. And dead. As opposed to the designer Hayden Griffin who never feels his set is complete until he sees an actor walk across it, onstage. Taking that one step further, with Howard's work — it should always be like this, but *especially* so with Howard's work — the audience provide the completeness, they actually have to engage, whereas with so many plays they can sit back and take it in like a film. I think that total engagement is the secret of doing his work. That's what I loved so much about *Victory*, it was a matter of choices we made as an audience, we were as much a part of that production as the actors. And when we began rehearsing *The Castle*, I remembered *Victory* and decided not to panic if I couldn't come to a clear idea of who I thought Ann was. I just thought, play it, play the moment for what it is.

DIR: The contradictions in the characters enliven —

PD: Yes, for me never more so than in *The Castle*. It's like a personal journey and it's a matter of how you work through it. This is what I learnt more than anything from the play, that the Stanislavski idea of working in a totally logical set of progressions — 'if she eats this for breakfast then obviously she will be like this at lunch' — the questions 'who am I, what is my process' are useless. With Ann, you are a walking set of contradictions, which *create* your character. It's not logical, it's very, very dangerous. Unless you've got danger — which is sexual energy onstage, to me — you're depriving an audience. To me, the most important thing is a character's sexuality, and therefore the way they think, it's extraordinarily dangerous. Your character becomes the sum total of the contradictions within it — you *are* your contradictions, you're *not* your logic — because if you always know how you're going to react in any given situation, you may as well just telephone it in! It's made me completely reassess how I play a part. It's difficult, because it is a matter of letting go all your preconceptions and logic and, once you've made some preliminary choices, going onstage every night open and blank to some extent. You have to play the *scene*, rather than worry about the *play*. Harriet Walter's greatness in the role of Skinner was I think something to do with the fact that she'd made a lot of choices, she'd done heaps of work, technically, emotionally, examining possibilities and all of this was 'on tap', but was, on each night, *open* — that's what makes it wonderfully *clean*. That really is flexing an actor's muscles. Janet McTeer also has that, from moment to moment you don't know what she's going to do next.

DIR: Jonathan Pryce has the same electricity, for me —

PD: Yes, it's not that the work hasn't been done, but there is still danger and sex and imaginative agility. I actually believe one of the best things you can work out is at what speed your character thinks. Maggie Steed says 'Acting is basically two things — knowing why you speak and knowing why you shut up'. Ann's silences are interesting and important. She leads Skinner such a dance, but not consciously. Ann just no longer loves what she loved in Skinner, but how do you say it? 'I think you are obsessive', not 'I don't love you any more'. When you get down to it, what is love, what is passion? And is passion better at all costs than other considerations? What matters is the reaction at the time, on the moment, as when Skinner sees a man and says 'Stab him', you get the absolute raw core of the character at that moment. I'd love to play Skinner or Bradshaw — I feel I've been compartmentalised into 'good woman' roles, sold as that commodity, as everyone is to some extent. In many ways, Barker characters are ageless. And someone expressed sympathy with the problems of playing Ann, 'Aren't passive parts difficult?' — I've played many passive parts in my life, but Ann wasn't one of them!

DIR: I don't think there is a 'passive part' in Barker, is there?

PD: No, there isn't. The possibilities are endless. It's down to the person you are, what you bring to it, although you play a role. It's wonderful, but it does make you feel completely raw and open to all possibilities.

Paul Freeman
Bela in *No End of Blame* (Oxford Playhouse & Royal Court), Toplis in *Crimes in Hot Countries*, Krak in *The Castle*, Scadding in *Downchild* (RSC)
December 1986, London

PF: Virtually no one beyond Barker is trying to say such things on such a large scale, or even trying to change the form of the theatre very much. People can't seem to accept the liberties they have, with narrative jumps. It seems to me that if people can follow a Shakespeare play, they can follow a Barker play.

DIR: Have you as an actor found any particular approaches to his work advantageous?

PF: Well, I always come at it from the political point of view because I agree with what he's saying. The problem is, the plays are sometimes obscure until you start working on them. They're wonderfully constructed plays, it's just that there are deliberate gaps in the narrative — which is a quality of the plays. As an actor, you have to ignore that. In *No End of Blame*, the question arises, what do you do about ageing from Bela at 18 to him as an old man? The answer is really to ignore it and just play that scene, then try and make the next one absolutely different. Actors should always do that, but few plays force you to make that journey — whereas you should always be coming in on a different note, like the play itself.

DIR: I remember from my own experience of playing Scrope in *Victory*, what a gear shift was required from playing the estuary scene to being shown round Clegg's garden, indignant but contained . . .

PF: It may be that's what audiences find difficult to take.

DIR: Possibly. It does demand speed from actors, directors and audiences. Not only the speed with which Barker tackles subjects, but the amount of subjects he tackles at that speed — this is totally contrary to what we are taught is viable.

PF: Also the humour is distinctive. When you're in a scene you would expect to develop tragically, it's made into a comic scene, and vice versa. There's hardly a scene in *No End of Blame* that isn't comic, even though the import is extremely thoughtful and serious — the exception to the comic mode being the scene with the Fourth Comrade (I.5.) with its final exchange on imaginary touch — which leads straight into Bela arriving at Dover as an eccentric foreigner! And what you expect to be a scene about what happens when Bela is hauled up in front of a committee suddenly becomes a comic scene about how committees are run, how people have favourite chairs. It's an immediately recognisable metaphor for the bureaucratic mentality behind authority.

DIR: The committee recurs in *Crimes in Hot Countries*, where the soldiers try to abolish authority but still need a committee, and Hacker —

PF: And they *don't* need Toplis, an anarchic revolutionary who has no truck with bureaucracy at all. It's significant that the furore over Alan Bleasdale's version of Percy Toplis in *The Monocled Mutineer* has centred on the supposed non-observance of historical detail!

DIR: And that Bleasdale has a sexual relationship point up, and possibly cause, his downfall. How decisive do you think Toplis's liaison with Erica in *Crimes*?

PF: Certainly, his inability to cope with what he's created, the revolution, is funnelled into Erica. His energy's gone into the promotion of anarchic moments for much of the play. Faced with the last revolution, which he realises is going to be the more powerful one, he would rather destroy himself in a great affair with her, and so would she — but she would carry it through, and he wouldn't. He finds even that finally unsatisfactory. It's like the end of *Downchild*, asking 'What are you going to live for?' After Toplis telling people they will have a better life after the revolution, it will take more account of their demands and reactions, they demand Hacker and he tries giving himself over to the love of a woman —

DIR: Is there a parallel with Krak here? In *The Castle*, Krak has a sense of poise and purpose, remembering the slaughter of his family, but no longer finds himself secure in his mission —

PF: Toplis goes further than Krak. Krak thinks he has his passion under control, but he has explored this relationship with Ann and still finds it wanting: so much so that he won't stop her killing herself. He makes no attempt —

DIR: You're right, it's Stucley who asks for the knife —

PF: Krak's retreated into his own mind to deal with 'the problem of cunt'. Only after Ann's dead, he realises what he's destroyed. Only after he's experienced her death does he find out that the affair, the woman, was really important. There's a journey there from the time of *Crimes* and the rejection of women —

DIR: Including the doll, the 'mother' —?

PF: And in *Downchild*, Scadding tells Heyday 'I would have given it all up for you'. He asks 'Was it because I gave up the leadership you don't want me any more?' — she doesn't answer, but I think it's true, to some extent, although she sees it in terms of her personal redemption — she'd come to a point in her life where she had to follow her heart and soul regardless of Scadding. Krak is the artist, as well as the scientist, figure, with a special strength but also a special danger — where will he go from here, how can he maintain his output in the face of so much hostility? It's interesting to ask why does he appear in the first place — if he were prone to suicide, the time for it would have been when his family were slaughtered. He's a survivor.

DIR: Like Skinner, who at the end briefly wishes she had died, 'The best thing is to perish in the struggle —'

PF: So they have to carry the burden, but they have a future, they each have a self . . .

DIR: Is that something inherent in them, do you think?

PF: Oh yes, it's no accident that *those two* survive. They're not dependent; Stucley and Ann depend on other people. Skinner was obviously very independent before the female revolution, and then when she's let down by Ann her strength and independence begin again. It clearly defines her so she actually enjoys it. She and Krak become reverse sides of the same coin — the outcasts who are the only people left. Perhaps this suggests possibilities of survival for the artist. The playing of the ending of *The Castle* has to leave room for ambiguities.

DIR: The play has shown there are hazards associated with working with Krak, and with Skinner, and the audience has to imagine future possibilities —

PF: Yes, the Pit production suggested too much resolution.

DIR: Is rehearsing Barker about working out an entirely logical way in which your character would react given a certain set of circumstances?

PF: A character reacts how he reacts in the play. For me, what carries you through is the political element: you have to know the politics of each moment: *why* Howard has written what he has, *what* he wants to say at *that* moment. You ask what do the events of this scene mean for this society, and make that as clear as you can. You can subvert the play if you indulge in characterisation too much. These ideas are part of my theatrical upbringing with Joint Stock, and they work well with Howard's work. With *No End of Blame*, we worked out what were the political points we had to make: when you do that, all else falls into place. When Joint Stock did David Hare's *Fanshen*, one actor did a lot of very good detailed character work on a Chinese peasant, involving a lot of coughing and spitting — well researched, apparently this is what they did. The scene was intended to depict 100 000 years of Chinese suffering: what came about was a scene in which one actor was coughing and spitting! Larger significance was lost to a good piece of character acting. You must stay faithful to the point of the scene

and thereby the point of the play — which is why, when playing in *No End of Blame* and finding myself at that time resistant to
the existence of magic suggested in the last scene, I just made a
leap of faith in the play. I doubt whether I would have been able
to have played the last scene of *Women Beware Women*, however,
if I were in that position. I understood intellectually but didn't
have much personal sympathy for Krak, the way he has his head
turned by 'The Book of Cunt' and partially loses his mind is fair
enough, but the change when he regains it because Ann's killed
herself I found a strain —

DIR: Presumably when he allows her to kill herself, his mind is still
full of the abstract, his drawings of cunt, not the actual woman — to
his credit, he points out, like Bela, that there's no such thing as
the 'Woods Option' —

PF: This cold implacable revenger engineers the Castle *and* its
downfall; but you never see his love for Ann. You see the beginning of it when he slaps her, then the next time they come on, you
see the end of it.

DIR: Whether his revelation that there is 'No such thing' as the rock
pushes her over the edge is another matter —

PF: Because he returns to his ivory tower and his drawings afterwards — the result of the sexual experience is not life-enhancing,
on the contrary, it pushes him back further into himself to examine the thing that has happened to him, as if it has nothing to
do with Ann's fear. If he'd said 'There is no way out, but we are
together', that would have salvaged something — like the end of
Bond's *Saved*, at least we can mend a chair. Instead he cuts her
off, has nothing more to do with her, retreats into his mind; she
kills herself because of it, and then he goes completely the other
way and realises what he's lost. I'm not saying I don't believe it, I
believe it completely and it's terrifying, just very difficult.

DIR: So he's stuck with the fact that he's a survivor — and he comes
back and offers his services?

PF: Well, there's nothing else for him to do — by that time, he has lost
everything for the second time, and he is still alive. *Crimes in Hot
Countries* was my favourite play of the Pit season and I thought it
sadly underrated. Its anarchic nature appealed to me enormously.

DIR: I've drawn a comparison with *Antony and Cleopatra* —

PF: Yes, two middle-aged people find a sort of sexual salvation but
Toplis can't accept it. He's trying to abscond again rather than face
the possibility of what life with Erica might actually be like. The

question is what love means, what redemption through a woman means — and he prefers to be shot, rather than confront it! Scadding was also very satisfying to play — his speech about the Real World is very sympathetic within a play which has been very concerned to be pro-Downchild. By that point, my sense is that the audience are slightly fed up with Downchild; the weight of the trial scene is such that Downchild has too much to say, whereas Scadding is silent but comes in with that one speech that undermines so much of Downchild's theatricals. It's an unexpected and effective movement in the scene, where Downchild loses control and sympathy. It's a flawed play which contains great speeches — one of the flaws is that Heyday disappears during that scene too. You lose her as a character and her importance in the play. Downchild tries to make a political point by dropping the baby, asking 'What is there to live for?', but there's a sense that the *play* finished with the trial in the previous scene, the cliffs scene provides a coda.

Gary Oldman
Sordido in *Women Beware Women* (Royal Court)
January 1987, Manchester

GO: When I received the script I didn't fully understand it but instinct said 'there's a jewel in there, in rehearsal you'll dig for it and hopefully a bolt of inspiration will fall'. I had to find the anger, frustration and despair of this 30-year-old virgin, in whom purity and obscenity are running side by side. I saw him as a rat: I shaved my hair back to suggest an intelligent high forehead, sprayed myself from a gun filled with glycerine and water so I was perpetually wet, apparently oozing oil and sweat, with yellowed teeth; then amongst the men, he behaved like a manic bird, nervously fluttering its wings when its feathers are ruffled.

Sordido is always a beat ahead of everyone else, he floats amongst them like a ghost; like Iago, he gives other characters cues to act on or not, as when he advances his plan to Leantio, then dismisses it as a vision that comes of 'poverty and weird alcohols'. There's a wonderful sense of truth that runs through Sordido; when he sees Bianca in the street he's obsessed with his own virginity and hers too, in the sense that he insists there's something in her untouched as yet; he *knows* the truth that society's rotten, he's like a jester, but a thin angry one next to the Ward's fat-boy clown. There's a purity and logic beneath his rotten exterior; when he tells the Ward 'Nice place you got', the Ward himself knows he shouldn't be in that position, but he's yet to follow up its implications, whereas Sordido believes people can actually manufacture or engineer their own destiny; he leaves the Ward alone to give him time to do what is demanded of him, then turns up again in his life.

Having found the anger, I had to bottle it behind the eyes; it's a force he contains and only shows twice, when he voices his plans and when he executes them. You have to tease the audience with the obsession, excite the imaginations, show glimpses to them and Leantio, then slam the lid and sit on it while they think about what they've seen; then it comes out for the rape, where he becomes a thing possessed, foaming at the mouth, with the strength of a moment of emergency, homing into Bianca like a missile. I thought of a poor person looking at a fur coat in a shop window; he wants something badly but has been told it's unattainable, out of his sphere, so he breaks the window — whatever the penalty, he'll take his chances, because he knows the state *stinks* and that change will result. There's a collision between two worlds, that has to be played out as realistically and disgustingly as possible so that the audience can't just sit back from it cosily. Barker's characters go to extremes to exorcise their obsessions, which they're happy to die for; Sordido's death almost has that Elizabethan sense of sexual climax, he's prepared to be destroyed.

You don't have to manufacture emotions or work for Barker's text, the relationships are there and play themselves; you invest it with your own intelligence, energy and sex, which are also there in the text to guide you and encourage you. Good male acting comes from the soul and from the cock — which is what Barker's writing gives opportunities for.

Maggie Steed
Erica in *Crimes in Hot Countries* (RSC), Livia in *Women Beware Women* (Royal Court), *The Breath of the Crowd* (1986 Cheltenham Festival)
April 1987, Leicester
DIR: How did you react to the role of Erica on your first reading of *Crimes?*
MS: I hadn't seen any of Howard's work before *Victory* and in fact when I first read *Crimes* I was a little disappointed, I thought it fell too much in love with English eccentricity. But that was my

short-sightedness. It wasn't until we started working on it I realised how much space he gives actors. His words are so precisely
chosen, there's no slack, and you can really *plumb*. This is unbe-
lievably liberating to an actor.

DIR: In terms of using more of yourself than is usually called on?

MS: Yes, his control of language is so precise, it's invigorating —
you have to try to plumb it with corresponding precision and
depth. On my first reading, I simply thought here's another victim prepared to die for love — it wasn't until we started rehearsing I felt how conscious she is of her predicament, and how
much she needed any sort of life. Howard's work gives wonderful opportunities for creating characters rather than being simply mouthpieces for opinions. In *Victory*, Devonshire speaks of
a woman's life being a 'shambles', and he has found the woman
who would speak those lines.

DIR: The way the characters aren't restricted to a single definable
point of view argues against a Stanislavskian approach —

MS: I don't think it does. I think Howard's scripts provide the actor
with tools for an actor to work with in a Stanislavskian mode:
different sorts of clues. He writes characters who speak their
thoughts, though they might not act in accordance with them,
and we have to find the people who have those thoughts, and
they exist.

DIR: So in Barker's work we find more totality of characterisation,
through self-awareness, than is the norm? Characters and actors
are called upon the expose more of themselves than is conventionally required —

MS: So it's more shocking, and more releasing. They may be expos-
ing one aspect of their selves, and still acting in a different way.
People do this in life, but usually in restricted, limited ways. In
Howard's work, they explode, and expose chasms of life.

DIR: The first scene of *Crimes* where Erica meets Toplis and commands him naked at gunpoint sets the tone of intermingled play
and danger —

MS: But you can't play a character who can come out and do that
unless you've sounded the rest of the play to know the circumstances she's living with to make that act possible. The more
extreme the acts, the more you have to establish the surrounding
pressure that provokes them, otherwise the acts are merely garish. Actors love Howard's work because it asks such big questions of them, personally.

DIR: When Trellis attempts to reconcile Erica to 'New England', Erica's rejection of it is crucial —

MS: Yes, Erica is a real woman. You might expect Trellis to be 'The Voice Of The Play' there; but then again her experiences are limited, she's in the midst of educating herself, and Erica tells her she might be right, but she's boring. The limitations of Trellis's opinions prevent them from being a source of enlightenment to Erica. There are, in fact, so many characters in the play that each carry a different part of its voice. That's what confuses people — delightfully. It's another of Barker's great strengths: in terms of audience perceptions of events, there's no way they can go away with something 'packaged'. They may be very upset and at the same time seduced: they'll be hearing things they agree with, and things they disagree with, seeing people they like and people they don't like, hearing the words they agree with come out of people they don't like, hearing the words they disagree with come out of people they like.

DIR: Trellis really is 'burdened' with 'borrowed, chanted, coagulated opinion' there, in the words of *The Breath of the Crowd*.

MS: From the same section — the woman 'Whose eye was wilder with the/Deterioration of the state' recalls Livia, who had previously been 'burdened with opinion'. Livia has effectively had the top of her head taken off! But there's a sense that she knows she isn't much longer for this world —

DIR: Like Erica . . .

MS: Yes. There is a sense that Livia might have burdened people with her opinions having Discovered The Truth — but she goes straight for action —

DIR: Through Sordido —

MS: Yes, before Leantio met Sordido, she didn' know how to act on the basis of what she'd discovered. She recognises that his plan is the quickest, cleanest, cruellest and kindest thing to do. It shocked a lot of women —

DIR: How did you feel about it?

MS: It was terrifying and I was very frightened by it — whilst recognising that it was the quickest, cleanest, cruellest and kindest thing to do. I was frightened, not by people's opinions of it, but by having to find the personal revolution to enable a character to proceed to those actions. As actors, we are almost never asked to look for such things. More often, we're asked to be messengers of single viewpoints. If you're asking questions of the audience, as in a Barker play, you also have to ask them of yourself. Otherwise you might as well be in a play saying 'Pass the cigarettes' or 'Have another gin and tonic'. It's rare for actors to find writing they can ride on, and for the audience to find writing where they have to move through confusion to realisation.

DIR: The fulcrum of *Women Beware Women* is Livia's assertion that 'a thing is vile, not in itself, but only in relation to its usage'.

MS: And 'Realism I hate the word'. It's difficult for people to countenance, the inevitability of having to do this. Correspondingly, Howard's work depends on complete conviction from the actors in carrying it out, otherwise it won't work.

DIR: As Livia says, 'Don't call me hyprocrite, what I have dealt in I attend right to the finish'. Leantio's on the backslide at that point —

MS: I don't think I could have done *Women Beware Women* without doing another Barker play, *Crimes*, beforehand, and possibly without seeing *The Castle*, which I think is the best play of the last ten years at least. I don't think *Women Beware Women* goes so far, though we had letters at the Royal Court from people saying they saw their lives there onstage, came to see it five times.

DIR: When the Duke suggests Livia and Leantio rule, I can see her strength but I think Leantio should be taken outside and dispatched like Stucley —

MS: He's a completely lost man! And from this point, you're into semi-permanent revolution. They'd only be there for about six months, if that! The tumbling effect has started. Livia still carries all of her class prejudices with her: when out amongst the people in the street, she is still disgusted by them, whilst understanding them. She loves and hates. She's not long for the world —

DIR: Will she mind?

MS: No, she won't.

DIR: Skinner is so focused on Ann, restrictive in her concentration, but Livia finds her engagement with Leantio inspires her to new action —

MS: In that sense, Livia's a progression, I suppose, but in a way more difficult to believe. Skinner I found such a character to identify with because she spoke all the doubts and fears as well as the beliefs, but then they come from a different class background. Just as, in *The Castle*, Skinner is not of Ann's class background, and lacks her sense of assurance and choice.

DIR: On the point of identification, I know some women who saw *The Castle* and really wanted Skinner to be a superheroine and were disappointed that she was not —

MS: But it's wonderful that she's not, isn't it? That's asking for it to be too easy.

DIR: I think so. Livia might be closer to being a superheroine, with all the problems that involves.

MS: I thought it was wonderful how *The Castle* took recognisable things, like elements of the women's camp at Greenham Common, to the ultimate, the dropping bodies. Audiences look for everything to come true in one character. It can't; otherwise we'd always look for leaders.

DIR: *Women Beware Women* suggests to me, why look to others to be your heroes, when you can be your own heroes? The sewn-up circuit of worship from afar keeps so many people 'in their place' and defines that place to the reassurance of many, but to the ultimate ends of a minority, who flatter through association. But individual revolution could be the spark to recognition by others *on their own terms*, so that realigned choices of affirmation and denial run riot and spread like wildfire. What are your abiding memories of playing Livia?

MS: Knowing it was on an absolute knife-edge — you had to hold it like iron. You have to learn to let the words in, which you have to learn over and over again, because of the screaming defences you have to discard to let yourself follow the power of language. And the marriage of emotions and ideas, usually hinted at obliquely or which you hope to make the audience pick up.

DIR: You encounter cerebral or institutionalised politics in plays, or romantic sentiment, but rarely the convergence of power and desire —

MS: Or hope and loss, which are political, they're all the world insofar as you can define them — which Barker finds and dramatises. Some people will be upset, some people will feel they've seen their lives onstage — that tells you that you exist, as very few other things tell you.

DIR: Confirmation through challenge. Or, rather, affirmation through challenge.

MS: Yes, people want that, there's a hunger for it. Though I don't think there's a hunger for his work in the institutions, they find him perilous.

DIR: What about working on *The Breath of the Crowd?*

MS: I asked a few little questions then just read it over and over again and let it seep in.

DIR: I found doing *Don't Exaggerate* was a matter of getting the words into my bloodstream, but I evolved quite a definite sense of persona, the Exaggerater —

MS: Yes, that's a real acting piece, *The Breath of the Crowd* isn't, in the same sense.

DIR: There isn't a sense of persona in *The Breath of the Crowd* — it's contrary to that in a way. In *Don't Exaggerate*, I was conscious I was a character who wanted to get through to people and take them and shake them and say 'listen, damn you' but I couldn't get through to them because I was a ghost; sometimes the anger turned into sadness, others it just stuck at anger; as if a transparent screen divided us and however much I shouted or lamented they couldn't hear, which in turn gave me the right to be evil, not defined by the community because I was separated from the community — I'd been forcibly separated from the community because of the community, fighting a war on their behalf! And I was forgotten. Ever the misfit, now terminally the misfit. The only person in whom I could find an ignition of sympathy was the suicide in Leicester Square, who is also silhouetted against the crowd and can't get through to them: there could be no contact between him and anyone else which could change the way things were for him, his possibilities were so diminished — which leads to the point where you say, right, fuck this for a game of soldiers, at least have the dignity to shut it down and turn it off. In *The Breath of the Crowd* there's always that sense of potential —

MS: Because it's *The BREATH of the Crowd* — the sense of potential for and in everybody. It's a series of poems on different people in different situations, with tremendous pleas for compassion running alongside disgust —

DIR: There's a testimony to variety and a *hope* in variety —

MS: It's mature in the fullest sense. Howard is truly a revolutionary in the way other playwrights aren't, and he has honed his skill with extraordinary concentration and persistence.

DIR: How did the park bench setting for *The Breath* come about?

MS: It was Ian McDiarmid's idea — the idea of being alone amongst people.

DIR: Also the sense of accident in your picking up the unknown book, and exploring it with curiosity — like a chance meeting you were drawn into —

MS: It occurred — very appropriately! As the days go by we all change, and the poem will hit me differently each time I do it.

DIR: How does it feel? Like being a conductor for voices, a radio receiver?

MS: I suppose so — it's difficult to talk about. Another feature of his language is the long sentences you have to sail on to the end — it actually physically makes you extend yourself in a way other work doesn't —

DIR: The presence and absence of the comma, the shift in gear —

MS: You continually jump up to top your previous height, the layering up, it releases in you the energy to do it. Barker's texts are by far the best I've done, the way he marries politics and passion in his subject matter parallels the way that the impetus of the writing physically stretches the actor to surprise themselves into realisation.

DIR: Going beyond what you've been taught, beyond the norm, beyond the point where you're surprising yourself, and then past that, and chase it wherever it goes.

MS: In an interview, Anthony Hopkins speaks of how you have to 'Give up and win!' You can't try to carve it — you have to identify, and face, and have a delight in contradictions, and I'm sure there are people who wouldn't want to be in Howard's work. You find yourself doing things you never thought you could. And when you end a run, there's a terrible sense of loss. We become worse actors on a diet of more mundane material. Howard has lacked the institutional support, and professional status within the institutions, enjoyed by some of his peers. He's really had to live the writing, but has become the better writer through this: the attraction of the group or crowd, but the insistence on individuality and singularity, is a tension at the heart of his work.

Robert Wilcher
Lecturer in English at Birmingham University
April 1987, Birmingham: a discussion of *Women Beware Women*

DIR: You have a closer knowledge of Middleton's play than I — what struck you about Barker's changes?

RW: He seems to find the ending a betrayal of the first three acts, with the introduction of the character of the Cardinal, who imposes a set of religious and moral perceptions on what we've been watching so far, constituting a retreat from the discoveries that have been made up to that point. I think Middleton's aware of the structure and allows us the first three acts to follow the sheer fascination of the sexual psychology of these people, many of whom are aware of moral restraints and are rationalising how far they're prepared to go. One of the things I think Barker loses from Middleton's play is the resolution of the Isabella theme, which is more interesting in its end than its beginning. She is quite happy to accept clandestine meetings with the man everyone thinks is her uncle but she thinks is not. Even though habituated to that relationship in a quite cynical way, when she finally learns the truth that he really is her uncle, she is horrified and withdraws. Barker drops that revelation, which I think is part of Middleton's exploration — the moral retreat from actions which go beyond some privately drawn limit of sexual transgression.

DIR: I think that happens with Leantio in Barker's version.

RW: Yes, he is completely caught up in the processes and enjoyment of his sexual liberation at the start of Barker's Part Two, but as he thinks about it, so retreats. Perhaps Barker has transferred, from Isabella to Leantio, that psychological process. Barker's other radical change is the function of the Cardinal: by transferring into the first half of the revised version some of his late speeches, Barker introduces much earlier a conventional Christian moral perspective on the behaviour of these people. I think one of the exciting things about Middleton's play is that he doesn't do that until the fourth act, that he allows us to follow his exploration and never invites us to apply moral criteria to our perceptions in the first three and a half acts. Then it's a marvellous *coup de theatre* to bring in the Cardinal *'with lights'*, with his new way of seeing events, from the traditional perspective: at that point, an audience may be horrified at what they've been enjoying —

DIR: A similar effect occurred at the Royal Court production when Livia identified audience members in Part Two, Scene One, asking the audience how far will you go, or do you usually go, towards *'Transformation'* . . .

RW: That's interesting, because it seems to be another point at which Barker has taken over technique from Middleton but used it in the service of his own vision. The shock of the beginning of Part Two is partly linguistic, reinforcing the cultural shift to there being 'buses' outside, as in Churchill's *Cloud Nine*: a move from one historical plane to another. We're moved into a different idiom, which is what happens with the appearance of the Cardinal in Middleton's play; not only his viewpoint but his language is different — a shock technique to make us readjust our view of things. In Middleton's play, the characters have not broken away from the rules entirely, it's not total liberation: Isabella will countenance adultery but not incest —

DIR: Whereas in Barker's version, some can break from rules altogether — and the Cardinal can express doubts, sense things are not completely sewn up by the Duke, for all his self-confidence.

RW: Middleton uses the Cardinal to remind the audience of moral values most of them would have said they lived by, though they are happy to forget them, in the theatre, for the play's first three acts. Whereas Barker's Cardinal begins Part Two by making Middletonian moral comments, but subsequently proves an insightful commentator, sensing the 'birth of an idea' and even in Scene Two sensing 'another sex' — politics. While everyone else in the play is living through their experience, he is the one character who can observe, outside it all, and set limits to their confidence, asking 'But have you thought of this . . .?' He certainly doesn't embody the authorial viewpoint, but he's an external commentator in a different way to that in Middleton's play —

DIR: Livia is a dramatist/stage-manager figure, like the Duke in *Measure for Measure*, engineering collisions as an organisational force: 'I must, who makes dreams come to life, witness the occurrence'. Like Prospero, she can't personally enforce change but can bring people together that they might change, Isabella and the Ward, Sordido and Bianca —

RW: Yes, though she's also inside the sexual action of the play; she's the main spokeswoman for personal liberation. Sordido is the crucial figure for Barker, whereas in Middleton he just disappears like Lear's Fool, and the Ward dies in the final holocaust. Barker makes Sordido the central consciousness of the play, the mean between the Cardinal outside the action and Livia inside it; Sordido says he's been celibate, but now, unlike the Cardinal resolves to intervene for political ends, and brings Livia towards a recognition of the political. It seems to me that Livia, in the opening of Part Two, looks out at the people in the street and sees chiefly their 'Repetition of the mundane life'; but what Sordido brings to her is the recognition of something of which the

Cardinal is also aware: that those people are not just people whose self-fulfilment is to be contrasted to her self-fulfilment through sexuality — they are restrained by sexual conventions as she is not — but that in those people resides political power, and that sexual aspects of the State Wedding can be used as a means to affect the people. The Cardinal sees the danger of the 'birth of an idea', but then that idea does not remain at the level of ideas — Sordido's significance is that he takes the idea through into action, performs it, and that's what brings about the collapse and final revolutionary situation, where anything can emerge.

DIR: There's a circuit of voyeurism in the play, where the Duke is vicariously admired for his indiscretions, Bianca advanced as the subject of fantasy, then it's developed to the point where Bianca, about to be raped by Sordido, appeals to the Mother, but she says 'I won't go, dear. I think they'll throttle me. And I've never seen this done . . . '. She who has profited from voyeurism is undone by it.

RW: Perhaps the seed of the Barker version — three acts of Middleton are voyeurism! Middleton says, watch these people breaking all the rules, wouldn't you like to be able to do the same? Then the Cardinal comes in and asks, What are you doing? And the Ward is much more astute and in control of his situation in Barker's version. The prying scene is eliminated and his self-assertion against the old men is delightful.

DIR: Like Skinner, he's offered power but draws back. He and Isabella are moving towards a consummation of their marriage, but when Sordido bursts in, 'This is my entrance', Isabella expresses consternation, not knowing the extent of the plan's development, and finally seems appalled by it. She finally goes to stand by Bianca in a gesture of sisterhood, but conscious of Livia's crucial involvement — Bianca slaps but thanks Livia; Isabella, more than Bianca, may be moving towards a radical feminism —

RW: Barker completely redirects her as a character. At the end of Part Two, she's making up to the Ward and her relationship with her uncle has been displaced.

DIR: Hope resides in the unexpected.

RW: Barker leaves the audience feeling that what the characters discover — even the Cardinal — leads to open possibilities. Middleton finally reimposes a set of conventional values, although I'm not sure how steady they are; the subversive elements of the first three acts cannot be cancelled out. The play

creates a sense of tension between refreshed or even new understanding of the sheer power in human beings to go their own
way, and their ability to use human reason to justify the way in
which they want to go, although they can't break totally free of
the ways they've been taught to judge behaviour, so that when
Middleton lets the voice of the Cardinal emerge, reiterating convention, it has a powerful presence but is nevertheless shaken.
I assume Middleton is saying that the material of the first three
Acts is fascinating but nonetheless dangerous, and some form
of order is necessary; whereas Barker is suggesting the only way
forward is through breaking down conventions and order — we
don't know where we're going, but we'll never go anywhere
unless we do break these down. Barker has moved beyond the
mixed passion and impotence of the satirist. He's not preaching
from a moral viewpoint or imposing rules.

DIR: Plays based in sexuality have particular reverberation and
ability to lodge in people, in a way beyond imparting ideological
ideas, from which people can recoil. Everyone at some point has
to face sexual engagement, the facts, lack, or form of it.

RW: Yes, some of the recent plays in this field strike me as being
much more powerful and effective agents for change, at least on
an individual level. Whereas audiences can dissociate themselves
from purely political ideas by saying 'I don't agree' or 'My politics are different', the sexual core of the individual affords less
opportunities for insulation. 1970s British plays for the intelli-
gentsia have tended to offer ideas for people who deal in ideas,
for them to deal with in their own way; plays like *The Castle* and
Women Beware Women strike more vulnerable areas where audiences can't think their way out of their responses or intellectual-
ise levels of experience: you either stay the way you are, or you
change.

Harriet Walter
Skinner in *The Castle* (RSC)
April 1987, Manchester.
(DIR here accompanied by Suzan Holding, who played Skinner in
the Lurking Truth/Gwir Sy'n Llechu production)

DIR: What surprised you the most in playing Skinner?

HW: That I managed it! And I was grateful for the challenge it posed
and the opportunity to engage with the challenge of a role with
which I wouldn't previously been associated by casting directors.

SH: In performance, it could rarely be a planned thing. Having reached a certain point, I had to leap up to the moment —

HW: As in Shakespeare, the language is so multi-layered you have to opt for one of many ways of reading a line, that is itself the sum total of many lines said in a certain way which indicate a choice. Barker's characters seem to spring from, and are driven by, instincts — not just ideas — which the actor has to tap into. After initially sympathising with Ann, I surprised myself how much I began relating to Skinner's clarity of vision and sense of purpose. It actually made me as a person develop into other areas — that's the ideal, when a character actually makes you develop.

SH: Though hard, Skinner is caring, and isolated. In the second scene, when she appears draped in flowers, she tries to communicate with Holiday and Krak, with no support from the other women.

HW: The fabric of their unity is giving way from the beginning; after she fails to kill Krak, there's a sense that the web has been burst and the catastrophe unleashed. Other dramatists often determine what single point of view each character will represent, then they interact in a controlled debate, and we have a synthesis of these ideas at the end. Here there's a genius for creating living dilemmas — where inconsistencies abound in each individual as in life —

SH: Yes, the politics are present *inside* the characters' emotions —

HW: And they're eaten up with their own contradictions —

DIR: It's the pain of their positions which engages an audience. Skinner says 'It is the pain of witches to see to the very end of things'; Stucley correspondingly realises 'Everything I fear, it comes to pass. Everything I imagine is vindicated. Awful talent I possess'. Every transformation Skinner fears, even the way Ann plaits her hair, is vindicated.

HW: Skinner's burden is enormous. She can't let go like Stucley and drift into madness. She appears to be going mad in the trial scene but cannot. The hardest scene to play is when she first appears with Holiday's corpse strapped to her: she is trying to let go of her love for Ann, divest herself of temporality and break all the bonds that bind her into life and make it hurt; her love has been betrayed so she wants to kill it. Then faced with Ann trying to be considerate, saying 'Go where you might find peace and rub the thing off you', she's torn apart. She loves torturing Ann, doesn't want her to be indifferent; yet she's trying to rid herself of desire to become the clean polished instrument, but there are feelings she still can't control because she still feels pain and wants to stir pain in others. After all her terrible experiences, there is an area she cannot control. She has the burden of knowing what's happening and not having a release into insanity —

DIR: As she says in the trial, 'I do my best to be contained' —

HW: And 'the children say the castle has been here a thousand years'. But she can't run off into escape, she is tied in, 'I am the castle also', she knows she can't relinquish involvement. She has a purity of vision from the beginning, and it may come from the fact that she does not need or want what the men's world has rotated around. You're in some ways superior to a society if you don't need what it runs on, money or whatever. Ann is caught up in the former ethic, she wants elements of the male society and nevertheless wants to change the world. Skinner has an unwavering sureness of the superiority of women to men and never feels inferior for a minute. Pain occurs when, very quickly, her support disappears; and the only time she wins back support is when she is considered a figure who is emptied, who has conquered pain and is above and beyond desire and therefore a political totem, the perfect leader. She attracts the villagers with their thought of that personal vacuum, but she knows she still has embers burning inside which, in the final scene, she does not want to have stirred up again. Right at her core is a connection between power and love; if love is killed, what use is power — why give me power, she asks Nailer and Batter, what's the vision behind the world I want anyway? Her agony is that she can't be a martyr, she persists messily and lives with the numbness of survival rather than being granted a beautiful death. If there's any hope for Skinner and the audience it is that she's plugged into some kind of history, even though she wishes she weren't, and has tried to un-plug it, because it would make life, or death, easier.

DIR: She is 'in the grip of the eccentric view that sworn love is binding', and Krak says 'Why not? If sworn hatred is' —

HW: Yes, she's driven by love and he's driven by hate —

DIR: But it turns out that neither sworn love nor sworn hate *are* binding. Every bond is broken by the end.

HW: They're mirror-images of each other in a way, their clarity of purpose as well as pain attracts Ann. But the main question is what is the drive for power? Do people who want power and control start with an image of what they want the world to be, then persist beyond its failure out of hunger or habit? Did Skinner love women and love the world, and want to distribute crops and abolish God because it made everyone happier, and consequently need power to make that happen? Or does she want power out of a self-serving ideal? She happens to be a lesbian so the construction of a female-based and female-centred society will serve her personal wants. But at the same time, if you don't have a personal connection and love and desire behind what you do, you're not human —

DIR: And you probably won't do it very well —

SH: She's offered power, not love, at the end, when for her they've been the same thing. It's a question also as to whether her actions spring from her nature or her situation —

HW: That's right — they've *made* her the bitch with her hackles up by treating her as subhuman. By outlawing your enemy, you make them resort to that definition of themselves in order to fight back, 'I am the castle also', I am another side of this coin and they have made me that; and I hate myself in that, although I preach love, I have killed, but I am at least facing the violence in myself. She always takes on responsibility though she hates what's done to her — she's made herself what she is, not Ann, who asks 'What have I done to you?'

DIR: Skinner insists on her own definitions, 'I call it death, they call it murder, they call it battle, I call it slaughter' —

HW: There's a purity of logic in her saying she does not regret killing Holiday, deducing 'The castle went backwards' as a result; and on the other hand Stucley says 'This changes nothing'. The two truths of their respective visions exist side by side. Skinner has no allies but carries on. In that, she has an easier life than Ann, who sees the logic and says 'Yes to all you say and *yet* — I think I must talk with my husband'. Ann experiences the battle of ambivalence of where she belongs, but Skinner has the benefit of 'knowing', that's why she's considered a witch — she rejects all their gods. It's the opposite side of the coin to the Crusaders: if you believe your scheme of things to be true, you want and need everyone else to believe it too, and become a bully, because unless everybody believes it the whole ideology collapses. She becomes prescriptive, telling Cant that Cant's weakness makes Skinner cruel — the Crusaders believe in their God so find Arabs and Jews a threat — ideologies need total belief in order to confirm themselves, so you have clashes, where if people are unconvertible brick walls, you smash them.

DIR: That core of the will and also the pain is I think a kernel line in the play, 'I am obsessive, why aren't you?'

HW: It's the problem of accepting someone is separate. When lovers part, there's pain of no longer having control over someone you've been so bonded with. On a larger political level, it's the extremist horror, not simply of physical torture, but forbidding subversive *thought* —

DIR: So you have shame, as self-regulation —

HW: Though in her defence, Skinner always takes the blame and never passes it on. She castigates Cant, but tells her you don't lie down and accept things, you change yourself — you have the responsibility, I can't change you — though she bullies her, she always lets go and realises she can't make someone else in her own image, whereas Stucley will go to any lengths, and organises everyone around him to enforce his world. Skinner has a sense of humour about herself in this area, 'There I go again', 'I am like that', that's the sympathetic angle in this initially apparently myopic character with a clean dagger of thought. It's not a matter of simply animating the text, you have to anchor it in someone or something you believe in. You never see her being soft, but she has compassion; Barker suspects the easy, kind word, and quite rightly at this point in history. Skinner knows softness and kindness are a luxury, it's a position she's had to harden into at her working-class level, she's never had the courtly marriage, civilised companionship or romance of Ann and Stucley. At the end she can pitch right down, almost into a race memory, and see she hasn't cut off anything though she tried; she can recall 'There was no government'. Her contradiction is that she can see furthest, forwards and backwards, but is also completely personally bonded to one person in the moment, 'one randomly encountered individual' . The characters in the play around her think she's their only hope because she's survived — whereas the audience can only feel she's their hope if she's still got memory and vision. Of course vision is frightening, Thatcher has a vision —

SH: But Skinner is saying social hierarchy is unnecessary, and has been proved unnecessary —

HW: And even if we don't know what that community was, and even if we can't readily relate to it, we have to have the vision that *there could be no government* as we understand it and that human life would go on, whereas governments think these structures are central, have always been maintained and never will be broken down. When she senses 'this cruel floor will become the site of giggling picnics', 'not one will think a woman writhed here once, the problem is to divest yourself of temporality': I played it two different ways: a horror that the history of personal lives will mean so little, be blown out like matches; then I thought, it's her charging herself up to not care about where she's immediately at, her history is the most important thing to communicate, not the immediate moment. It's comparatively easy for Cant, who initially doesn't have the perception and therefore doesn't sense the responsibility which is 'the pain of witches'. When, under a given ideology, one set of people subjugate another, the subjugated divide themselves into those who internalise that society's picture of themselves, and those who have the agony of knowing their worth, knowing those in power are wrong and not being able to see a way out of it. It takes vision of an alternative possibility to point the finger.

DIR: The redefinition of self and others — to use your phrase in Susan Todd's book *Women and Theatre*, the ability to 'burst through your own outline' which is so crucial in Barker's work —

HW: Skinner moves through so much, to be finally offered power when everything she cares about has been destroyed; there's a capacity for self-criticism when she refuses, sensing her inclination to cruelty and revenge. Then the last-minute realisation, like a penny dropping down a well, that all the transitions and experiences she's been through are still there, she still has all the layers in her memory somewhere because of how she's connected with her memory and the future. Skinner's strength lies in the fact that there is nothing anyone can buy her off with; there's no reason for her to make a deal, or compromise —

DIR: In many respects, she's beyond the temptations of hope —

HW: And that's why she's called a witch. Unlike Ann, she's forced to confront the Two Horrors — 'there is nothing you can't get used to' and 'you can live without others', even though everything she believes in has collapsed. She's jealous of Ann, finally; the arrogance of her killing herself when it was Skinner who wanted to die, and Ann had more effect on others, indirectly instigating the chain of pregnant women suicides, than Skinner ever had: Ann's gesture has actually ended up being more important than Skinner's gesture. *The Castle* isn't a perfect political theory and treatise embedded in a play: change becomes muddy, messy, difficult, hard to digest, and unsentimental: and that's why I love it, because anything easier than that here and now would be a cop-out.

Ian McDiarmid
Clive in *Bang* (Open Space), Billy McPhee in *That Good Between Us* (RSC), Ronald Hacker in *The Love of a Good Man* (Oxford Playhouse), Murgatroyd in *Pity in History* (BBCTV), *Don't Exaggerate* (RSC & Not The RSC), Alfred Hacker in *Crimes in Hot Countries*, Tom Downchild in *Downchild*, Stucley in *The Castle*
July 1987, London, just off Leicester Square

DIR: In approaching many dramatic roles, I think we are fettered with spurious notions of sham Stanislavski, which are of little use for anything but particularly inadequate for approaching Barker's work —

IMcD: Few actors I know feel allegiance to any theoretical system; their loyalty is to their instincts.

DIR: In your *Gambit* article, you talk about catching the rhythm of the words and then infusing them with your own sensibilities, drawing on your own experiences of particular emotional extremity, though not in a 'Method Acting' way —

IMcD: My approach is impressionistic. Acting, for me, is not about building a character. I try to let the play 'act' on me, to open myself to its echoes, its possibilities. Howard Barker writes what I need to act; not deliberately, he just does it, and I seize on it — ravenously.

DIR: Where do you think that need's located?

IMcD: I'm not sure. We agree about many things, we share certain political ideas, but it's more than that. We don't *proceed from* a shared political view. I suppose there are links in certain areas of the imagination and the emotional subconscious. We seem to inhabit the same world, though we don't talk about it much . . .

DIR: Barker trusts intuitions and instincts —

IMcD: And celebrates them — we have that in common. He sees the power of the imagination as the supreme liberating force. It makes him unpopular with many political and critical schools of thought.

DIR: The axes of his work are politics and desire, or power and the body. But I think demolition is also important, that explosive force is vital and characteristic.

IMcD: And *a feeling* for such words, banishing generalisation, trying to be particular about seemingly abstract and over-romanticised (and therefore denigrated) concepts, like love. *Women Beware Women* struggles with that word in an attempt to restore its potency. It seeks like all Barker's recent work to reclaim language in order to restore us to ourselves. I emerged from that play fortified; not suffused with a sense of catharsis, nor equipped with a programme for radical change, but with more courage than I had when I came in. It didn't confirm things I felt, it articulated them in a way I hadn't been able to articulate to myself. I find Barker's attitude to sex, or, as he would insist on calling it, *desire* ('sex being part of the happiness racket' — *Don't Exaggerate*), particularly liberating. Actors seize on his scripts because they're rich and succulent yet formal and elegant — not distantly cerebral or distantly poetic but *immediately* poetic.

DIR: Have you found improvisation helpful approaching Barker's work?

IMcD: Improvisation doesn't help you act, although it can get you out of a rut. The play's the thing. Once the language of the play is allowed to resonate in actors, things take off, be it Barker, Shakespeare or Christopher Marlowe. The particular fascination for me with Stucley in *The Castle* was in exploring his childish and childlike behaviour ('Not me, though!') — he makes naive assumptions about the nature of desire; like Marlowe's Edward II, who thinks he can unite power and the body, publicly enjoying Gaveston once he is king, celebrate his sexuality openly and give Gaveston public status. Isabel's sub-plot is a parallel to Ann's in *The Castle:* Isabel is liberated as a result of Edward's rejection. She finds a man who awakens her sexually and as a result becomes stronger, for a time.

DIR: Billy McPhee also demonstrates an essential naivety —

IMcD: Billy is almost too naive to survive, but his spirit is irrepressible. He himself is astonished to find himself still alive.

DIR: The audience has to work through everything that is put in their way to find that affection for Billy — his complicity in the gang rape, his abuse of the stripper in the disco, his naivety about Godber. *Don't Exaggerate* shares some chords, for me, with Murgatroyd, the self-conscious corpse imparting facts in *Pity in History*, and Downchild presiding over his court as Great Judge Crab, compelling his audience to listen to him nail his targets, with a great amount of self-referentiality and self-characterisation, given the dubious 'vantage point' from which to perform this —

IMcD: It's the expression of the need to avenge, which once unleashed takes a terrible toll. *Downchild* was written for me and it was a great relief to play it in the 1985 RSC Barker season after trying to get it performed for eight years. Tom Downchild is a wonderfully complex, Wildean, Rabelaisian character, hijacking the play with a shocking diatribe against the scabrous nature of so-called social democracy, but pathetic in his 'weakness' for his 'criminal'. Downchild loves Stoat as truly as Ronald Hacker loves Sylvia Toynbee. Alfred Hacker in *Crimes in Hot Countries* and *Credentials of a Sympathiser* is Ronald's brother, who shares the same obsession with capitalism and his dignity within it but is not 'sidetracked' by desire.

DIR: Alfred is more vulnerable — like Falstaff in *2 Henry IV*, he's the butt, rather than the maker, of the jokes. Rhythm is vital in speaking Barker's words, the lack of the full stop, the comma and ride-on, often with a gear shift from the capitalised to the lower-case with deflationary effect. Some people are initially thrown by this, not being used to so many changes in any given speech. But surfing on the rhythms is the key, it becomes literally sensual —

IMcD: It prevents you from generalising, overlaying and taking refuge in a spurious naturalism. Words throb, like beats of the heart: they contain energy and they pulsate, you have to find them in, and let them pulsate through you, embody them and colour them. All the characters have their own dignity and are very recognisably human.

DIR: Acting Barker involves what Leopold in *The Europeans* terms acting 'the insecurity of all order'.

IMcD: Actors have the power to make people collude with banality or to encourage them to oppose it.

DIR: And directors —

IMcD: And writers too. It is a choice; to subscribe to 'prevalent situations' and tendencies or to try to break down the barriers and extend the limits. Like the idea of the laugh — it can be a source of integration or disruption. Barker is suspicious of people's readiness to capitulate to it, to make a loud noise collectively in an auditorium.

DIR: Theatre practitioners are constantly beset with prescriptions towards achieving 'ORDER'. Acting its instability is profoundly threatening to all institutions and institutionalised modes of thought, instruction and evaluation, the dominant notions of 'artistic criteria', which are often forms of enforced myopia.

IMcD: Yes. Articulateness is of limited help if you're striving to make a leap of the imagination. That can't be predicted and so quantified, and budgeted for and so deemed cost-effective.

DIR: You've spoken before about creating something multifaceted and contradictory and therefore likely to move and engage an audience, whereby actors do not contain or avoid a part but open themselves to all its contradictions and problems.

IMcD: Over the years, you are also confronted with some notional concept of development, or progress of movement. I don't believe in linear progression. Theatre is too often geared to providing a confirmation of what you already know, as the First Prologue to *The Bite of the Night* proclaims, and the experience becomes impoverishingly intellectual.

DIR: Barker's work refuses and attacks linear concepts, the narratives of *The Bite* and *The Europeans* particularly so, they are liberationist texts.

IMcD: Yes. His work liberates within people what they want, perhaps need expressed and is regarded with fear in an atmosphere of prescription. This can also be true of acting which aspires to put an audience in touch with its own pain.

DIR: Theatre practitioners and academics operate like intellectual high priests or 'grown-ups', suggesting 'I have the answers and when are you going to find them out' —

IMcD: One director talks about 'letting the play breathe' — but you can't 'let a play breathe' — actors, audiences breathe and the play will only come alive when they enliven it.

DIR: As Savage would say, 'these obstacles we ourselves erect'.

IMcD: Savage realises he has to leave behind his luggage in order to go forward, or, in a Faustian sense, 'beyond'. His son and his father constitute his luggage. He gives away his son and encourages his father to kill himself. These are not the anarchist wonderings of a misanthropic writer. Barker is rather suggesting that in this extraordinary situation is the possibility of further knowledge and exploration for truth. He's not recommending it. He is simply opening up the impossibilities, allowing the imagination to speculate; a proper function of art. And if you think that's pompous, Hrkaly in *The Europeans* appears to be emerging as an authorial mouthpiece in the discussion of art.

Then Barker suddenly undermines him and our vanity at having identified his authority. We are left reeling.

DIR: Yes, we are *not* given a complete and exhaustive definition, that would be wrong, he would be imposing shapes and forms on us, and we would rightly resist their sinking in.

IMcD: Theatre should not alienate people or 'remind them they're in a theatre' in some debased neo-Brechtian way — why should they think they're anywhere else *but* in a theatre? The point is to remind them there are human beings on that stage able to take on and to express both the actors' and the audience's pain and anger, and through that find renewal and regeneration. People aren't moved by Oedipus because he's put his eyes out, but by recognising what has gone into the action of self-blinding, they have at some stage experienced that impulse, and here find it expressed so they can take it on, and the truth of that situation is recognised, and people are moved by the recognition of truth, not by someone stabbing their eyes out.

DIR: They understand and sense certain circumstances under which *they* might stab their eyes out. The audience are not consumers presented with a shrink-wrapped finished product, like a box of chocolates for them to dip into, then go away; there's a sense of *something happening*, that is *not* completed, they are part of a process of mutual and self-discovery. The English are so frightened of excitement in theatre, and of sex. To take a line from *Gary Upright*, 'I choose the public place to be unpublic in': true of many Barker characters who explicitly reveal their layers of philosophical, sexual, instinctive reality, which conventionally and naturalistically are consigned to subtext. Spurious notions of discretion abound.

IMcD: One actor told me, 'You should only act 60 per cent, so that the audience can fill in the other 40 per cent themselves', but that's not my idea of theatre.

DIR: Yes, as you said in *City Limits*, 'an audience concentrates best when it shares the emotional predicaments of the characters. Empathy has been underrated for too long. I always want to engage with an audience. If I come off and feel that I haven't then I've failed . . .'

IMcD: The actor's potential relationship with an audience is highly tensile. Barker writes with this in mind. He appeals directly to actors and audiences. The difficulties lie with those in between.

DIR: Because of insecurity, they want things reinforced, habitually. Institutions prefer theatre that smooths and digests pain in a spirit of wisdom and maturity — there are parallels with state attitudes to Skinner and Katrin, who nevertheless expose and perform their pain.

IMcD: Starhemberg is a departure for Howard in that he's a watcher. He works through silence, but not through abnegation; he's always there, being part of things but not engaging. He's a presence, who then does nothing of what is expected of him, which is fascinating.

DIR: Why do you want to direct *The Possibilities*?

IMcD: *The Possibilities* is a series of tragic fragments, each complete in itself, but in some way colliding with one another. I want to find a way of their colliding with an audience.

DIR: Gary Oldman's animal images provide useful initial imaginative constructions, I've since used them in approaching roles — it's good scaffolding from which to jump, but you finally have to jump: like Starhemberg, you can imagine yourself in a given shape and jump into it, but the biggest jump is into that which you can't imagine, which Barker's work finally demands. Sometimes I've failed and played my imagination of myself playing that role, but occasionally my self-consciousness as performer has completely vanished to rare and liberating effect, and afterwards you feel completely alive: again, there's a sexual parallel, risk and hyperactivity in brain and blood with a terrible relief at the end, you feel vague around the edges of your own definition of your self. The keynote to Barker's work, for performer and audience, is that risk and danger, exposing and creating and re-creating the self compulsively through encountering characters who do these very things, showing themselves in all their terrible beauty, shameless -

IMcD: I believe like Barker that Tragedy is the dramatic form for our times and subscribe to Nietzsche's aphorism: 'the tragic artist is not a pessimist. He says Yes to every thing questionable and terrible'. Strength and weakness, good and evil, are forever bumping into each other. There's a joy and release in finding out what you are, for all the pain involved in being forced to consider the totality of the body and the self.

Notes

1. LUBRICATING PROGRESS THROUGH THE FORBIDDEN

1. Howard Barker, conversation with David Ian Rabey, 14 March 1987.
2. Antonin Artaud, *The Theatre and its Double* (London: Calder & Boyars, 1970) p. 66.
3. Bettina L. Knapp, in Kenneth Steele White (ed.), *Savage Comedy: Structures of Humour* (Amsterdam: Rodopi, 1978) pp. 18, 23.
4. Kenneth Steele White, *Savage Comedy Since King Ubu* (Washington: University Press of America, 1980) pp. 8, 64. Thanks to Ian Lucas for bringing these two books to my attention.
5. Roger Howard, in Leslie Bell (ed.), *Contradictory Theatres* (Essex University Press, 1984) p. 214.
6. Maro Germanou, ibid., pp. 20–1.
7. Howard Barker, Notes to *The Bite of the Night*, Royal Court Playreading Programme, April 1987.

2. INNOCENCE AND AUTHORITY

1. John Berger and others, *Ways of Seeing* (London: Penguin, 1972) p. 154.
2. Barker: 'The avoidance of the work experience is very basic to the working class. It annoys me when socialists glorify work, when all the work available is of a soul-destroying nature, and always likely to be'; in Catherine Itzin, *Stages in the Revolution* (London: Methuen, 1980) p. 251.

3. INDEPENDENCE AND THE FAMILY

1. Leo Lowenthal, 'Henryk Ibsen: Motifs in the Realistic Plays', in Rolf Fjelde (ed.), *Ibsen: A Collection of Critical Essays* (New Jersey: Englewood Cliffs, 1965) pp. 142–3.

2.   Simon Trussler (ed.), *New Theatre Voices of the Seventies* (London: Methuen, 1981) p. 186.

3.   For a subsequent view of aristocracy fascinated by illegitimate criminal power and seeking fetishistic association with it, see Caryl Churchill, *Softcops* (written 1978, staged 1983).

4.   Tony Dunn, 'Howard Barker: Socialist Playwright for our Times', in *Gambit* XI no. 41 (London: John Calder, 1984) p. 60.

5.   Ibid., p. 61.

6.   John Berger and others, *Ways of Seeing* (London: Penguin, 1972) p. 133.

7.   Dunn, op. cit., p. 61.

8.   Ruth Shade, 'All Passion is a Risk', in *Gambit* XI no. 41, p. 103.

4. BETWEEN TWO WORLDS

1.   Simon Trussler (ed.), *New Theatre Voices of the Seventies* (London: Methuen, 1981) p. 193.

2.   Eric Mottram, 'The Vital Language of Impotence', in *Gambit* XI no. 41, p. 56.

3.   By way of illustration: 'The word Wales is derived from the Anglo-Saxon "welisc" or "wealh" meaning "foreigner". Despite attempts to anglicize them, the Welsh have always remained "foreigners" to their English neighbours . . . In their own language Wales is called Cymru — the land of comrades', P. Beresford Ellis, *Wales — A Nation Again: The Nationalist Struggle for Freedom* (London: Tandem, 1968) p. 15. Thanks to George Jones for bringing this to my attention.

4.   Rosalind Reedman, 'Howard Barker's Treatment of Women, unpublished essay (University College of Wales, Aberystwyth, Drama Department, 1986).

5.   Howard Barker, *On 'The Loud Boy's Life'* (RSC Warehouse Writers no. 9), p. 1.

6.   A parallel heightened in the 1985 RSC production (directed by Bill Alexander and Nick Hamm) by Downchild's (Ian McDiarmid's) donning a Claw-like silver suit at one point.

7.   Tony Dunn, 'Howard Barker: Socialist Playwright for our Times', in *Gambit* XI no. 41 (London: John Calder, 1984) p. 89.

5. NEW MANNER FOR NEW SITUATION

1. Thanks to Martin Seymour for this observation.
2. Rape is later described in terms of theft in *Women Beware Women*.
3. Rosalind Reedman, 'Howard Barker's Treatment of Women, unpublished essay (University College of Wales, Aberystwyth, Drama Department, 1986).
4. Tony Dunn, 'Howard Barker: Socialist Playwright for our Times', in *Gambit* XI no. 41 (1984) p. 71.
5. Ibid.
6. Jean-Paul Sartre, *What is Literature?* (London: Methuen, 1950) p. 60.

6. LANDSCAPES OF SHAME, ERUPTIONS OF DESIRE

1. Ian Lucas, 'The question of comedy and humour in the plays of Howard Barker' unpublished essay (University College of Wales, Aberystwyth, Drama Department, 1987).
2. Tony Dunn, 'Howard Barker: Socialist Playwright for our Times', in *Gambit* XI no. 41 (London: John Calder, 1984) p. 73.
3. Charles Lamb points out, 'The fact that Pain's first words here echo Scott of the Antarctic's suggests the anguish of attempting to sustain an ideology in conditions totally inimical to it' — 'Directing *Crimes in Hot Countries*', in *Contradictory Theatres*, p. 124.
4. Howard Barker, interview with Tony Dunn, in *Gambit* XI no. 41, p. 39.
5. Demands for celebration and solidarity tend to be the hallmarks of community plays. However, contrast this extract from Brith Gof Theatre Company's manifesto: 'A theatre company should be a unit of cultural regeneration. Theatre is *witnessing*, not celebration'. Thanks to Charmian Savill for bringing this to my attention.
6. Howard Barker, *Gambit* interview (see note 4) p. 43.

7. SPLINTERED FAITH AND SCAR TISSUE

1. Howard Barker, conversation with David Ian Rabey, 2 January 1987.

2.   Eric Mottram, 'The Vital Language of Impotence', in *Gambit* XI no. 41 (London: John Calder, 1984) p. 52.

3.   Ruth Shade, 'All Passion is a Risk', in *Gambit* XI no. 41, p. 107.

4.   Friedrich Nietzsche, from *Human, All Too Human*; selected and translated by R. J. Hollingdale, *A Nietzsche Reader* (London: Penguin, 1977) pp. 43–4.

5.   Ian Cooper, 'Edgar's *Maydays* v. Barker's *A Passion in Six Days*', unpublished essay (University College of Wales, Aberystwyth, Drama Department, 1986).

6.   Angela Carter, *The Sadeian Woman* (London: Virago, 1979) pp. 144–6.

7.   Howard Barker, 'Oppression, Resistance and the Writer's Testament', interview with Finlay Donesky, in *New Theatre Quarterly* II no. 8 (November 1986) p. 338.

8. POWER AND THE BODY

1.   Batter's 'HEY!' can be an exultation in Stucley's action, or his first dissociation from his master, provoked by a sense of excess.

2.   Thanks to Gwyn Thomas for this observation.

3.   Compare also the dead child in *Birth on a Hard Shoulder* and *Downchild's* threatened baby as fundamental questionings of the terms of existence.

4.   See David Ian Rabey, 'Play, Satire, Self-Definition and Individuation in *Hamlet*', in *Hamlet Studies* V, nos. 1 and 2 (Summer/Winter 1983), pp. 6–26.

5.   Stephen Booth, *'King Lear', 'Macbeth', Indefinition and Tragedy* (Yale, 1983).

6.   Ibid., p. 11.

7.   Ibid., p. 6.

8.   Howard Barker, conversation with David Ian Rabey, 2 January 1987.

9.   Howard Barker, *Women Beware Women*, Royal Court programme note (1986).

10.   Howard Barker and Thomas Middleton, 'The Redemptive Power of Desire' in *The Times*, 6 February 1986.

9. EVERY MAN'S EVIL EXPRESSES ME

1.   Howard Barker, conversation with D. I. Rabey, 14 April 1987.

2. Howard Barker, conversation with David Ian Rabey, 2 January 1987.
3. Ibid.
4. Tony Tanner, *City of Words* (London: Cape, 1971) pp. 82–4.
5. Howard Barker, '49 Asides for a Tragic Theatre', in *Guardian*, 10 February 1986, p. 11 (see Bibliography).
6. 'The Redemptive Power of Desire', in *The Times*, 6 February 1986.

10. PAIN AND BREAKTHROUGH

1. William Burroughs, *The Place of Dead Roads* (London: Paladin Overseas edition, 1986) p. 195.
2. Ibid.
3. Ibid., p. 23.
4. Compare Frank Miller's and Bill Sienkiewicz's comic book series *Elektra: Assassin* (New York: Epic/Marvel, 1986–87) I–VIII, where a Protean sense of voracious destruction is matched only by the atrocious reconstruction of the human form, extending experience, but also insistence on imaginative resistance, to new Promethean extremes.
5. R. D. Laing has attempted to identify the archetypal associations of the maimed figure of Ippolita in D'Annunzio's *The Triumph of Death* in terms relevant to both Lavinia in Shakespeare's *Titus Andronicus* and Helen in *The Bite of the Night*: 'Once more we have the umbilical pattern — two wrists side by side, bare arms held out, two red fountains gushing from the severed veins of her wrists, the placental woman destined to die, the cervical door, the two wrists chopped through with one stroke, the cut cord' (Laing, *The Voice of Experience* (London: Pelican, 1983) p. 139). This line of imagery would reverberate into the associations of stillborn death present in Shakespeare's description of Lavinia's forcibly estranged prospective partner, Bassianus, couched in the 'ragged entrails' of the pit. Though Barker's Helen is amputated at the shoulders, and not at the wrists, the grotesque inversions of conventional natal conditions continue, for instance, in Helen's killing of her child, Hogbin's 'genetic crime' in fathering Charity, and the baby discovered by Yorakim in the Second Interlude.

11. CATASTROPHE IS ALSO BIRTH: INCONCLUSION

1. Other examples of Catastrophist drama, beyond Barker's, are rare, but I would nominate Shakespeare's *Titus Andronicus* and *King Lear*; other possible candidates might be David Rudkin's *The Sons of Light* and *The Saxon Shore*, and Timberlake Wertenbaker's *The Grace of Mary Traverse*. Burroughs claims: 'Happiness is a by-product of function. Those who seek happiness for itself seek victory without war. This is the flaw in all utopias. A society, like the individuals who compose it, is an artifact designed for a purpose. As to what life may be worth when the purpose is gone . . .' (*The Place of Dead Roads* (London: Paladin Overseas edition, 1986) p. 210). Catastrophism attempts to answer this question, examining the aftermath of social disintegration and attempted restitutions of moral order.
2. Thanks to Charmian Savill for this observation.
3. R. D. Laing, *The Voice of Experience* (London: Pelican, 1983) pp. 76–7.
4. For example, Michelene Wandor's *Look Back in Gender: Sexuality and the Family in Post-War British Drama* (London: Methuen, 1987) avoids any mention of Barker's work and thereby undermines its authority.

APPENDIX: CONVERSATIONS

1. This conversation predates the performances of the Lurking Truth Company/Cwmni'r Gwir Sy'n Llechu production of *The Castle*, which took place in October 1986, and informs my future comments in many ways; indeed, Suzan Holding appears as a participant in the conversation with Harriet Walter.
2. Based on an original idea by our lighting designer/technical director George Jones. Memo to all directors: listen to the suggestions of your lighting designer.

Bibliography

Part One: Works by Barker referred to in this study
(1) Plays and Poems by Barker
One Afternoon on the 63rd Level of the North Face of the Pyramid of Cheops the Great (BBC Broadcasting House Play Library, 1970; copy made available for reference through the kind intercession of Roger Gregory)
Henry V in Two Parts (as above, 1971)
Herman, with Millie and Mick (as above, 1972)
Cheek, in *New Short Plays: 3* (London: Eyre Methuen Playscripts, 1972, volume credited to Barker, Grillo, Haworth, Simmons)
*No One Was Saved**
*Edward — The Final Days**
Alpha Alpha†
Stripwell and *Claw* (London: John Calder, 1977)
*Skipper**
*My Sister and I**
*Wax**
Heroes of Labour, in *Gambit* 29 (London: John Calder, 1976)
Fair Slaughter (London: John Calder, 1978)
That Good Between Us and *Credentials of a Sympathiser* (London: John Calder, 1980)
The Love of a Good Man and *All Bleeding* (London: John Calder, 1980)
The Hang of the Gaol and *Heaven* (London: John Calder, 1982)
Two Plays for the Right (The Loud Boy's Life and *Birth on a Hard Shoulder)* (London: John Calder, 1982)
No End of Blame (London: John Calder, 1981)
*The Poor Man's Friend**
Victory (London: John Calder, 1983)
Pity in History, in *Gambit* 41 (London: John Calder, 1984)
Crimes in Hot Countries and *Fair Slaughter* (London: John Calder, 1984)

---

*Indicates script made available on request to Judy Daish Associates Ltd;
†Indicates script made available by Howard Barker; in both cases, these scripts unpublished at the time of writing.

A Passion in Six Days and *Downchild* (London: John Calder, 1985)
The Power of the Dog (London: John Calder, 1985)
Don't Exaggerate (desire and abuse) (London: John Calder, 1985)
The Castle and *Scenes from an Execution* (London: John Calder, 1985)
The Blow†
Women Beware Women (with Thomas Middleton) (London: John Calder, 1986)
The Breath of the Crowd (London: John Calder, 1986)
The Bite of the Night††
The Possibilities (London: John Calder, 1988)
The Europeans†
Gary the Thief/Gary Upright (London: John Calder, 1987)

(2) Essays and Articles by Barker
On *'The Love of a Good Man'* (RSC Publication, undated, probably 1978)
On *'The Hang of the Gaol'* (RSC Warehouse Writers 1, undated, probably 1978)
On *'The Loud Boy's Life'* (RSC Warehouse Writers 9, undated, probably 1980)
'Barker + McDiarmid', joint interview in *City Limits*, 18–24 October 1985, pp. 78–9.
'The Redemptive Power of Desire', in *The Times*, 6 February 1986.
'49 Asides for a Tragic Theatre', in *Guardian*, 10 February 1986, p. 11; reprinted in *Englisch Amerikanische Studien* 3, 4/86, pp. 474–5.

Part Two: Selective Bibliography of Published Material Centring on or Referring to Barker
The most important single item up to the time of writing is *Gambit* 41 (London: John Calder, 1984), containing the text of *Pity in History*, interview with Barker by Tony Dunn, and articles by Eric Mottram, Tony Dunn, Ian McDiarmid and Ruth Shade, all cited at some stage of this study. The television documentaries *A Play for Bridport* (BBC Arena, 1982?) and *Refuse to Dance: The Theatre of Howard Barker* (Channel 4, 1986) are also noteworthy, particularly the latter.
See also:

Bell, Leslie (ed.), *Contradictory Theatres* (Essex University Press, 1984).

Craig, Sandy (ed.), *Dreams and Deconstructions* (London: Amber Lane Press, 1980).

Donesky, Finlay, 'Oppression, Resistance and the Writer's Testament' (unauthorised interview), in *New Theatre Quarterly* 2, no. 8 (November 1986) pp. 336–44.

Grant, Steve, 'Barker's Bite' (article/interview), in *Plays and Players* 23, no. 3 (December 1975) pp. 36–9.

Itzin, Catherine, *Stages in the Revolution* (London: Methuen, 1980).

Jellicoe, Ann, *Community Plays* (London: Methuen, 1987).

Kerensky, Oleg, *The New British Drama* (London: Hamish Hamilton, 1977).

Rabey, David Ian, *British and Irish Political Drama in the Twentieth Century* (London: Macmillan, 1986).

Trussler, Simon, 'The Small Rediscovery of Dignity' (interview), in S. Trussler (ed.), *New Theatre Voices of the Seventies* (London: Methuen, 1980).

A Selection of Further Critical Reading on Barker

IN ENGLISH

Full-length Studies

Gambit 41 (London: John Calder, 1984) (contains text of *Pity in History*, interview with Barker by Tony Dunn, and articles by Eric Mottram, Tony Dunn, Ian McDiarmid and Ruth Shade, all cited at some point of this study)

Gritzner, Karoline and Rabey, David Ian (eds.): *Theatre of Catastrophe: New Essays on Howard Barker* (London: Oberon Books, 2006)

— *The Theatre of Howard Barker* (Oxford: Routledge, 2005)

Lamb, Charles: *Howard Barker's Theatre of Seduction* (London: Harwood Academic Press/Routledge, 1997)

Rabey, David Ian : *Howard Barker: Politics and Desire: An Expository Study of his Drama and Poetry, 1969–1987* (London: Macmillan, 1989)

Articles and Essays Centring on Barker

Barker, Howard: 'On *The Love of a Good Man*' (RSC Publication, undated, probably 1978)

Barker, Howard: 'On *The Hang of the Gaol*' (Warehouse Writers 1, RSC Publication, undated, probably 1978)

Barker, Howard: 'On *The Loud Boy's Life*' (Warehouse Writers 9, RSC Publication, undated, probably 1980)

Barker, Howard and Mc Diarmid, Ian: 'Barker + McDiarmid', joint interview in *City Limits*, 18–24 October 1985, pp. 78–9

Barker, Howard: 'On Naturalism and its Pretensions', in *Studies in Theatre and Performance* 27: 3 (2007), pp. 289–93, doi: 10.1386/stap.27.3.289/3

Barnett, David: 'Howard Barker: Polemic Theatre and Dramatic Practice, Nietzsche, Metatheatre and the Play *The Europeans*', *Modern Drama* 44.4 (Winter 2001), pp. 458–75

Bas, Georges: 'The Cunts, the Knobs and the Corpse: Obscenity and Horror in Howard Barker's *Victory*', in *Contemporary Theatre Review* 5 (1996), pp. 33–50

Cornforth, Andy and Rabey, David Ian: 'Kissing Holes for the Bullets: Consciousness in Directing and Playing Barker's *(Uncle) Vanya*', *Performance and Consciousness* 1.4 (1999), pp. 25–45

Gallant, Desmond: 'Brechtian Sexual Politics in the Plays of Howard Barker', *Modern Drama*, 40 (1997), pp. 403–13

Gritzner, Karoline: 'Catastrophic Sexualities in Howard Barker's Theatre of Transgression', in M. Sönser Breen and F. Peters (eds), *Genealogies of Identity: Interdisciplinary Readings on Sex and Sexuality* (Amsterdam and New York: Rodopi, 2006)

— 'Adorno on Tragedy: Reading Catastrophe in Late Capitalist Culture', *Critical Engagements* 1.2 (Autumn/Winter 2007), pp. 25–52

Hammond, Brean: 'Is Everything History? Churchill, Barker and the Modern History Play', *Comparative Drama* 41.1 (Winter 2007), pp. 1–23

Kilpatrick, David: 'The Myth's the Thing: Barker's Revision of Elsinore in *Gertrude – The Cry*', *Text and Presentation* 24 (New York: McFarland, 2003)

Klotz, Günther: 'Howard Barker: Paradigm of Postmodernism', *New Theatre Quarterly* 7.25 (February 1991), pp. 20–6

Megson, Chris: 'Howard Barker and the Theatre of Catastrophe' in Mary Luckhurst (ed.), *A Companion to Modern British and Irish Drama* (Oxford: Blackwell, 2006)

Neubert, Isolde: 'The Doorman of the Century is a Transient Phenomenon: the Symbolism of Dancer in Howard Barker's *Hated Nightfall*', in Bernhard Reitz (ed.), *Drama and Reality. Contemporary Drama in English 3* (Trier: Wissenschaftlicher Verlag Trier, 1996), pp. 145–53.

Rabey, David Ian: 'For the Absent Truth Erect: Impotence and Potency in Howard Barker's Recent Drama', *Essays in Theatre/ Études théâtrales* 10 (1991), pp. 31–7

— 'What Do You See?': Howard Barker's *The Europeans*', in *Studies in Theatre Production* 6 (December 1992), pp. 23–34

— 'Howard Barker', in W. W. Demastes (ed.), *British Playwrights, 1956–1995: A Research and Production Sourcebook* (London: Greenwood Press, 1996), pp. 28–38

— 'Two Against Nature: Rehearsing and Performing Howard Barker's Production of His Play *The Twelfth Battle of Isonzo*', in *Theatre Research International* 30.2 (July 2005), pp. 175–89

Sakellaridou, Elizabeth: 'A Lover's Discourse – But Whose? Inversions of the Fascist Aesthetic in Howard Barker's *Und* and Other Recent English Plays', *European Journal of English Studies*, 7.1 (April 2003), pp. 87–108

Saunders, Graham: 'Missing Mothers and Absent Fathers': Howard Barker's *Seven Lears* and Elaine Feinstein's *Lear's Daughters'*, *Modern Drama* 42 (1999), pp. 401–10

Tomlin, Liz: 'The Politics of Catastrophe', *Modern Drama* 43, no 1 (2000), pp. 66–77

— 'Howard Barker', in John Bull (ed.), *Dictionary of Literary Biography, Volume 233: British and Irish Dramatists Since World War II, Second Series* (New York: Buccoli Clark, 2001), pp. 9–21

Wilcher, Robert: 'Honoring the Audience: the Theatre of Howard Barker', in James Acheson (ed.), *British and Irish Drama Since 1960* (Basingstoke: Macmillan, 1993), pp. 176–89

Zimmermann, Heiner: 'Howard Barker's Appropriation of Classical Tragedy', Savas Patsalidis and Elizabeth Sakellaridou (eds.) in *(Dis)Placing Classical Tragedy* (Thessaloniki: University Studio Press, 1999), pp. 359–73

— 'Howard Barker's Brecht or Brecht as Whipping Boy', in Bernhard Reitz and Heiko Stahl (eds.), *What Revels Are in Hand (Essays in Honour of Wolfgang Lippke)* (CDE-Studies 8. Trier: Wissenschaftlicher Verlag Trier, 2001. 221–6

— 'Howard Barker in the Nineties', 'British Drama of the 1990s': *Anglistik & Englischunterricht* 64 (2002), pp. 181–201

Selective bibliography of other material containing references to Barker

Bell, Leslie (ed.), *Contradictory Theatres* (Colchester: Essex University Press, 1984)

Craig, Sandy (ed.), *Dreams and Deconstructions* (London: Amber Lane Press, 1980)

Itzin, Catherine, *Stages in the Revolution* (London: Methuen, 1980)

Keresnsky, Oleg, *The New British Drama* (London: Hamish Hamilton, 1977)

Rabey, David Ian, *British and Irish Political Drama in the Twentieth Century* (London: Macmillan, 1986)

— 'Barker: Appalling Enhancements', in *English Drama Since 1940* (London: Longman Literature in English series, Pearson Education, 2003) pp. 182–190

Trussler, Simon (ed.), 'The Small Rediscovery of Dignity' (interview) in *New Theatre Voices of the Seventies* (London: Methuen, 1980)

Television documentaries

A Play for Bridport (BBC Arena, 1982?)
Refuse to Dance: The Theatre of Howard Barker (Channel Four, 1986)

IN FRENCH

Alternatives Théâtrales 57 (mai 1998). Numéro spécial Howard Barker, coordonné par Mike Sens
Angel-Perez, E. (ed.) *Howard Barker et le Théâatre de la Catastrophe*; éd. (Paris: Editions Théâatrales, 2006)
— 'L'espace de la catastrophe', éd. Geneviève Chevallier, *Cycnos* 12 (1–1995)
— 'Pour un théâtre de la barbarie : Peter Barnes et Howard Barker', éd. É. Angel-Perez et Nicole Boireau, *Études anglaises* 52, n° 2 (avril–juin 1999),' 198-210. Rééd. in *Le Théâeatre anglais contemporain (1985–2005)* (Paris: Klincksieck, 2006)
— Préfaces aux volumes 1–5 des *Howard Barker: Œuvres choisies*. (Paris: éditions Théâtrales)
— Notice sur Howard Barker de l'*Encyclopédie Universalis* (Paris: Encyclopaedia Universalis, 2003)
— 'Howard Barker: de la catastrophe à l'épiphanie', in E. Angel-Perez, *Voyages au bout du possible. Les théâtres du traumatisme* (Paris: Klincksieck, 2006)
Boireau, Nicole, 'Le paysage dramatique en Angleterre: consensus et transgression', *Alternatives Théâtrales* 61 (1999), 8–10
— 'Dystopies', in N. Boireau, *Théâtre et société en Angleterre des années 1950 à nos jours* (Paris: PUPS, 2000)
Hirchmuller, Sarah, 'Howard Barker ou la déconsécration du sens. À propos de *Maudit crépuscule*', Éd. Jean-Marc Lantéri, *Écritures contemporaines* 5 (2002), 25–42
Morel, Michel, 'La "catastrophe" selon Barker', Éd. Geneviève Chevallier, *Cycnos* 18, n°1 (2001), 65–76

My thanks to Elisabeth Angel-Perez for assistance in compiling the French section of this bibliography.

Index